PLA
CRICKE

1979

32nd edition

EDITED BY GORDON ROSS

Statistics by Michael Fordham and Geoffrey Saulez

GILLETTE PICK-A-TEAM COMPETITION	2
EDITORIAL PREFACE	5
AUSTRALIA v ENGLAND, 1978–79	8
ENGLAND v PAKISTAN 1978	14
ENGLAND v NEW ZEALAND 1978	19
PAKISTAN v INDIA 1978–79	24
NEW ZEALAND v ENGLAND 1977–78	27
WEST INDIES v AUSTRALIA 1977–78	30
ENGLAND v INDIA 1932 TO 1976–77	35
GILLETTE CUP	39
BENSON & HEDGES CUP	47
JOHN PLAYER LEAGUE	51
SCHWEPPES COUNTY CHAMPIONSHIP	53
THE COUNTIES AND THEIR PLAYERS	57
FIRST-CLASS UMPIRES 1979	154
FIRST-CLASS AVERAGES 1978	158
CAREER FIGURES FOR LEADING PLAYERS	174
CAREER RECORDS	175
FIRST-CLASS CRICKET RECORDS	192
TEST CRICKET RECORDS	201
I.C.C. ASSOCIATE MEMBERS' WORLD CUP	208
TEST CAREER RECORDS	209
PRINCIPAL FIXTURES 1979	218

Front cover: Ian Botham. Photo: Colorsport

GILLETTE 'PICK A TEAM' COMPETITION
£500 TO BE WON

Prizes **1st: £200 2nd: £100 3rd: £50 4th: £25**
Twenty-five runners-up: £5 each.

Plus A selection of Gillette products from the range advertised in this Annual.

How to enter: **Pick the Best Gillette Cup Team from the 40 cricketers shown below** who have appeared in a winning Gillette Cup final team in England, assuming them all to be at the top of their form. Then write in 20 words which year produced the best Gillette Cup final and why.

Write the names on the entry form on the opposite page with your name and address and post to the address shown.

Your Choice
Dennis Amiss, Geoff Arnold, Bob Barber, Bishen Bedi, Geoff Boycott, Mike Brearley, David Brown, Tom Cartwright, Colin Cowdrey, Brian Close, Wayne Daniel, Mike Denness, Ted Dexter, Phil Edmonds, Farokh Engineer, Lance Gibbs, John Hampshire, Frank Hayes, Ray Illingworth, Imran Khan, Rohan Kanhai, Alan Knott, Peter Lever, Clive Lloyd, David Lloyd, Brian Luckhurst, Mushtaq Mohammad, Javed Miandad, Chris Old, Jim Parks, Mike Procter, Clive Radley, Sadiq Mohammad, Mike Smith (Warwickshire), John Snow, Fred Trueman, Bob Woolmer, Barry Wood, Derek Underwood, Zaheer Abbas.

Rules
Judging: Each entry will be considered by a panel of cricket experts and the entry which, in the opinion of the judges, constitutes the best Gillette Cup team will be adjudged the winner. The decision of the judges is final and binding; no correspondence will be entered into. Employees of Gillette and Macdonald and Jane's and their families are not eligible to compete.
Proof of Entry: All entries must be on the entry form provided. Proof of posting is not proof of entry.

ISBN 0354 09066 6
© 1979 Queen Anne Press
Division of Macdonald and Jane's
(Publishers) Ltd, Paulton House,
8 Shepherdess Walk, London N1.
Printed by C. Nicholls & Company Ltd
The Philips Park Press, Manchester

ENGLAND'S ASHES
by Gordon Ross

England retained the Ashes when Mike Brearley's team won the fourth Test match in Sydney to make it 3–1 with two games to go. At best, Australia could then only draw the series, but an astonishing collapse in the fifth Test robbed Australia of even that chance. Instead it was a decisive beating in the series. For England, this team looks good for some time to come. Australia, deprived of their Packer players, began the series as if they were no match for this England side, losing the first Test by seven wickets, and the second by 166 runs. Then, just when everybody expected them to lose the third, Australia staged a stirring rally to win, deservedly, at Melbourne, by 103 runs, Wood scoring a century, but Hogg was the real hero taking 5–30 and 5 for 36. In fact Hogg was the man of the series, bowling so superbly that in the fifth Test (Australia had lost the vital fourth one) he surpassed Arthur Mailey's long-standing record of 36 England wickets in a series which Mailey established 59 years previously. Here, indeed, was an exciting discovery. Few Test sides in history could have experienced a more disastrous start to a match than England's 27–5 in the fifth Test at Adelaide, but from this perilous situation, England contrived a magnificent victory due to Botham's first innings 74 and then the superb Derbyshire partnership in the second innings of Miller and Taylor, the latter failing by only three runs to record his first century. On the last day England's bowlers had one devastating spell and Australia collapsed to total defeat. The last Test thus became merely academic.

Since the 1977 'Summer of Discontent', almost totally overshadowed by the Packer explosion, established cricket has suffered little change, although there have been a number of developments on the Packer front. Having lost the Court case, the ICC and the TCCB decided not to appeal against the ruling, and left individual countries to go their own way, it being appreciated that circumstances vary considerably from country to country. The dismal showing of the depleted Pakistan side in England last summer became a matter of national pride and Pakistan were soon including their Packer

5

players again. West Indies, too, with finance always a crucial matter with them, included their Packer players, although there was a rumpus in the series against Australia, when just before the third Test, three Packer players were dropped and replaced by non-Packer players. Clive Lloyd resigned in protest, at which the whole Packer set withdrew from the series.

The eyes of the world, therefore, were upon the members of the International Cricket Conference when they met at Lord's towards the end of July, on the eve of which Mr D. G. Clark, President of MCC and Chairman of the ICC, resigned from the Kent committee as soon as that committee offered new contracts to their three Packer players. As Chairman of the ICC, Kent's action placed him between the devil and the deep, and he had little option but to dissociate himself from Kent's decision. The conference produced nothing in the way of a compromise. Packer had put up proposals which even he must have known had precious little chance of being accepted. The Conference turned them down, as was inevitable. At least the doors were to be kept open, although that statement meant very little. Trouble rumbled on. Amiss was in dispute with Warwickshire over the decision not to re-engage him. That was left on ice; meanwhile Thomson, in Australia, did another turn-about and signed for Packer despite his contract with the Australian Board who had expected him to be the main spearhead against England. The Board sued and won, with the result that Thomson played no cricket in the winter. The battle goes on with not the slightest indication of an armistice at the moment of writing – the two sides are as far apart as ever.

Happily, the wrangling had little effect on the domestic season in England. In the two series of Test matches, first against a depleted Pakistan team, and then a comparatively weak New Zealand party, England were never fully stretched, and the main topic, after two very poor series with the bat, was whether or not Mike Brearley would captain the side in Australia. In the end he was chosen purely because of his qualities of leadership. Hot on the heels of this was Boycott's troubles with Yorkshire when he was relieved of the captaincy and replaced by Hampshire. Boycott's future is now settled and he stays with Yorkshire.

Helmets were creeping more and more into the game, raising the question whether or not close fielders should be allowed to wear helmets. After all, how close a fielder stands to the bat in a highly dangerous position depends largely on his courage; that has always been the case. If he is to be given assisted courage then he is surely being able to take unfair advantage. I cannot imagine Stuart Surridge ever wearing a helmet, and I have seen very few players stand closer to the bat than he did. If short-pitched bowling is to be allowed to go unchecked (although ICC have limited its use) then you can hardly blame the batsman for wanting to avoid a broken skull, although I still believe that a blow over the heart could be more lethal.

Highlight of the domestic cricket was the Gillette Cup win by Sussex – against all expectations, and after fourteen lean years. Sussex were all but eliminated from the competition by a Minor County – Staffordshire – finally scrambling home by two runs; and having beaten Suffolk, another Minor County, in the first round. This was followed by a ten-over slog against Yorkshire – so having beaten two Minor Counties and Yorkshire in a slogging match, many were entitled to think that Sussex's advancement so far was no true reflection of their ability. But Sussex were to prove the whole world wrong, by completely outclassing Lancashire in the semi-final at Hove, and then doing precisely the same thing to much-fancied Somerset in the final. There was no doubting that they had fully earned their success in the end. Kent took the Schweppes County Championship, narrowly defeating Essex, who have never won any sort of honour in the game and who had a great deal of impartial support. Many would have liked Essex to have won particularly in view of the amount of honours Kent have won over the years including, of course, the Benson and Hedges Cup earlier last season. Essex had shown themselves gallant fighters, especially in the Gillette game to cap all Gillette games when they were set to make 288 to win or 287 with less than six wickets down, and they actually scored 287, but with more wickets down than Somerset – a herculean effort which deserved a better fate.

Somerset, having failed in the Gillette Cup final, could have compensated themselves the very next day when they needed only to beat Essex at Taunton to win the John Player League. This time Essex did thwart them, so the Somerset cupboard was bare; like Essex, they have yet to win any competition.

FIRST TEST MATCH

PLAYED AT BRISBANE, 1, 2, 3, 5, 6 DECEMBER
ENGLAND WON BY 7 WICKETS

AUSTRALIA

G. M. Wood c Taylor b Old	7	lbw b Old	19
G. J. Cosier run out	1	b Willis	0
P. M. Toohey b Willis	1	lbw b Botham	1
†G. N. Yallop c Gooch b Willis	7	c & b Willis	102
K. J. Hughes c Taylor b Botham	4	c Edmonds b Willis	129
T. J. Laughlin c sub (Lever) b Willis	2	lbw b Old	5
‡J. A. Maclean not out	33	lbw b Miller	15
B. Yardley c Taylor b Hogg	17	c Brearley b Miller	16
R. M. Hogg c Taylor b Botham	36	b Botham	16
A. G. Hurst c Taylor b Botham	0	b Botham	0
J. D. Higgs b Old	1	not out	0
Extras (LB1, NB6)	7	(B9, LB5, NB22)	36
Total	**116**		**339**

ENGLAND

G. Boycott c Hughes b Hogg	13	run out	16
G. A. Gooch c Laughlin b Hogg	2	c Yardley b Hogg	2
D. W. Randall c Laughlin b Hurst	75	not out	74
‡R. W. Taylor lbw b Hurst	20		
†J. M. Brearley c Maclean b Hogg	6	c Maclean b Yardley	13
D. I. Gower c Maclean b Hurst	44	not out	48
I. T. Botham c Maclean b Hogg	49		
G. Miller lbw b Hogg	27		
P. H. Edmonds c Maclean b Hogg	1		
C. M. Old not out	29		
R. G. D. Willis c Maclean b Hurst	8		
Extras (B7, LB4, NB1)	12	(B12, LB3, NB2)	17
Total	**286**	(3 wkts)	**170**

BOWLING

ENGLAND	O	M	R	W		O	M	R	W
Willis	14	2	44	4	—	27.6	3	69	3
Old	9.7	1	24	2	—	17	1	60	2
Botham	12	1	40	3	—	26	5	95	3
Gooch	1	0	1	0					
Edmonds	1	1	0	0	—	12	1	27	0
Miller						34	12	52	2
AUSTRALIA									
Hurst	27.4	6	93	4	—	10	4	17	0
Hogg	28	8	74	6	—	12.5	2	35	1
Laughlin	22	6	54	0	—	3	0	6	0
Yardley	7	1	34	0	—	13	1	41	1
Cosier	5	1	10	0	—	3	0	11	0
Higgs	6	2	9	0	—	12	1	43	0

FALL OF WICKETS

	A	E	A	E
	1st	1st	2nd	2nd
1st	2	2	0	16
2nd	5	38	2	37
3rd	14	111	49	74
4th	22	120	219	
5th	24	120	229	
6th	26	215	261	
7th	53	219	310	
8th	113	226	339	
9th	113	266	339	
10th	116	286	339	

SECOND TEST MATCH

PLAYED AT PERTH, 15, 16, 17, 19, 20 DECEMBER

ENGLAND WON BY 166 RUNS

ENGLAND

G. Boycott lbw b Hurst	77	lbw b Hogg	23
G. A. Gooch c Maclean b Hogg	1	lbw b Hogg	43
D. W. Randall c Wood b Hogg	0	c Cosier b Yardley	45
†J. M. Brearley c Maclean b Dymock	17	c Maclean b Hogg	0
D. I. Gower b Hogg	102	c Maclean b Hogg	12
I. T. Botham lbw b Hurst	11	c Wood b Yardley	30
G. Miller b Hogg	40	c Toohey b Yardley	25
‡R. W. Taylor c Hurst b Yardley	12	c Maclean b Hogg	2
J. K. Lever c Cosier b Hurst	14	c Maclean b Hurst	10
R. G. D. Willis c Yallop b Hogg	2	not out	3
M. Hendrick not out	7	b Dymock	1
Extras (B6, LB9, W3, NB8)	26	(LB6, NB8)	14
Total	**309**		**208**

AUSTRALIA

G. M. Wood lbw b Lever	5	c Taylor b Lever	64
W. M. Darling run out	25	c Boycott b Lever	5
K. J. Hughes b Willis	16	c Gooch b Willis	12
†G. N. Yallop b Willis	3	c Taylor b Hendrick	3
P. M. Toohey not out	81	c Taylor b Hendrick	0
G. J. Cosier c Gooch b Willis	4	lbw b Miller	47
‡J. A. Maclean c Gooch b Miller	0	c Brearley b Miller	1
B. Yardley c Taylor b Hendrick	12	c Botham b Lever	7
R. M. Hogg c Taylor b Willis	18	b Miller	0
G. Dymock b Hendrick	11	not out	6
A. G. Hurst c Taylor b Willis	5	b Lever	5
Extras (LB7, W1, NB2)	10	(LB3, W4, NB4)	11
Total	**190**		**161**

BOWLING

AUSTRALIA	O	M	R	W	O	M	R	W
Hogg	30.5	9	65	5	17	2	57	5
Dymock	34	4	72	1	16.3	2	53	1
Hurst	26	7	70	3	17	—	43	1
Yardley	23	1	62	1	16	1	41	3
Cosier	4	2	14	0				

ENGLAND	O	M	R	W	O	M	R	W
Lever	7	0	20	1	8.1	2	28	4
Botham	11	2	46	0	11	1	54	0
Willis	18.5	5	44	5	12	1	36	1
Hendrick	14	1	39	2	8	3	11	2
Miller	16	6	31	1	7	4	21	3

FALL OF WICKETS

	E 1st	A 1st	E 2nd	A 2nd
1st	3	8	58	8
2nd	3	34	93	36
3rd	41	38	93	58
4th	199	60	135	58
5th	219	78	151	141
6th	224	79	176	143
7th	253	100	201	143
8th	295	128	201	147
9th	300	185	206	151
10th	309	190	208	161

THIRD TEST MATCH

PLAYED AT MELBOURNE, 29, 30, 31 DECEMBER 2, 3, JANUARY

AUSTRALIA WON BY 103 RUNS

AUSTRALIA

Batsman	1st innings		2nd innings	
G. M. Wood c Emburey b Miller	100	b Botham	34
W. M. Darling run out	33	c Randall b Miller	21
K. J. Hughes c Taylor b Botham	0	c Gower b Botham	48
*G. N. Yallop c Hendrick b Botham	41	c Taylor b Miller	16
P. M. Toohey c Randall b Miller	32	c Botham b Emburey	20
A. R. Border c Brearley b Hendrick	29	run out	0
†J. A. Maclean b Botham	8	c Hendrick b Emburey	10
R. M. Hogg c Randall b Miller	0	b Botham	1
G. Dymock b Hendrick	0	c Brearley b Hendrick	6
J. D. Higgs not out	1	st Taylor b Emburey	0
A. G. Hurst b Hendrick	0	not out	0
Extras (LB8, NB6)	14	(B4, LB6, NB1)	11
Total	**258**		**167**

ENGLAND

Batsman	1st innings		2nd innings	
G. Boycott b Hogg	1	lbw b Hurst	38
*J. M. Brearley lbw b Hogg	1	c Maclean b Dymock	0
D. W. Randall lbw b Hurst	13	lbw b Hogg	2
G. A. Gooch c Border b Dymock	25	lbw b Hogg	40
D. I. Gower lbw b Dymock	29	lbw b Dymock	49
I. T. Botham c Darling b Higgs	22	c Maclean b Higgs	10
G. Miller b Hogg	7	c Hughes b Higgs	1
†R. W. Taylor b Hogg	1	c Maclean b Hogg	5
J. E. Emburey b Hogg	0	not out	7
R. G. D. Willis c Darling b Dymock	19	c Yallop b Hogg	3
M. Hendrick not out	6	b Hogg	0
Extras (B6, LB4, NB9)	19	(B10, LB7, NB6, W1)	24
Extras	**143**		**179**

BOWLING

ENGLAND	O	M	R	W		O	M	R	W
Willis	13	2	47	0	—	7	0	21	0
Botham	20.1	4	68	3	—	15	2	41	3
Hendrick	23	3	50	3	—	14	4	25	1
Emburey	14	1	44	0	—	21.2	12	30	3
Miller	19	6	35	3	—	14	5	39	2
AUSTRALIA									
Hogg	17	7	30	5	—	17	5	36	5
Hurst	12	2	24	1	—	11	1	39	1
Dymock	15.6	4	38	3	—	18	4	37	2
Higgs	19	9	32	1	—	16	2	29	2
Border					—	5	0	14	0

FALL OF WICKETS

	A	E	A	E
1st	65	2	55	1
2nd	65	3	81	6
3rd	126	40	101	71
4th	189	52	136	122
5th	247	81	136	163
6th	250	100	152	163
7th	250	101	157	167
8th	251	101	167	171
9th	252	120	167	179
10th	258	143	167	179

FOURTH TEST MATCH

PLAYED AT SYDNEY, 6, 7, 8, 10, 11 JANUARY

ENGLAND WON BY 93 RUNS

ENGLAND

G. Boycott c Border b Hurst	8	lbw b Hogg	0
*J. M. Brearley b Hogg	17	b Border	53
D. W. Randall c Wood b Hurst	0	lbw b Hogg	150
G. A. Gooch c Toohey b Higgs	18	c Wood b Higgs	22
D. I. Gower c Maclean b Hurst	7	c Maclean b Hogg	34
I. T. Botham c Yallop b Hogg	59	c Wood b Higgs	6
G. Miller c Maclean b Hurst	4	lbw b Hogg	17
†R. W. Taylor c Border b Higgs	10	not out	21
J. E. Emburey c Wood b Higgs	0	c Darling b Higgs	14
R. G. D. Willis not out	7	c Toohey b Higgs	0
M. Hendrick b Hurst	10	c Toohey b Higgs	7
Extras (B1, LB1, W2, NB8)	12	(B5, LB3, NB14)	22
	152		346

AUSTRALIA

G. M. Wood b Willis	0	run out	27
W. M. Darling c Botham b Miller	91	c Gooch b Hendrick	13
K. J. Hughes c Emburey b Willis	48	c Emburey b Miller	15
*G. N. Yallop c Botham b Hendrick	44	c & b Hendrick	1
P. M. Toohey c Gooch b Botham	1	b Miller	5
A. R. Border not out	60	not out	45
†J. A. Maclean lbw b Emburey	12	c Botham b Miller	0
R. M. Hogg run out	6	c Botham b Emburey	0
G. Dymock b Botham	5	b Emburey	0
J. D. Higgs c Botham b Hendrick	11	lbw b Emburey	3
A. G. Hurst run out	0	b Emburey	0
Extras (B2, LB3, NB11)	16	(LB1, NB1)	2
Total	294		111

BOWLING									FALL OF WICKETS				
AUSTRALIA	O	M	R	W	O	M	R	W		A	E	A	E
Hogg	11	3	36	2	28	10	67	4	1st	18	1	0	38
Dymock	13	1	34	0	17	4	35	0	2nd	18	126	111	44
Hurst	10.6	2	28	5	19	3	43	0	3rd	35	178	169	45
Higgs	18	4	42	3	59.6	15	148	5	4th	51	179	237	59
Border					23	11	31	1	5th	66	210	267	74
ENGLAND									6th	70	235	292	76
Willis	9	2	33	2	2	0	8	0	7th	94	245	307	85
Botham	28	3	87	2					8th	98	276	334	85
Hendrick	24	4	50	2	10	3	17	2	9th	141	290	346	105
Miller	13	2	37	1	20	7	38	3	10th	152	294	346	111
Emburey	29	10	57	1	17.2	2	46	4					
Gooch	5	1	14	0									

FIFTH TEST MATCH

PLAYED AT ADELAIDE, 27, 28, 29, 31 JANUARY, 1 FEBRUARY
ENGLAND WON BY 205 RUNS

ENGLAND

G. Boycott c Wright b Hurst	6	c Hughes b Hurst	49
*J. M. Brearley c Wright b Hogg	2	lbw b Carlson	9
D. W. Randall c Carlson b Hurst	4	c Yardley b Hurst	15
G. A. Gooch c Hughes b Hogg	1	b Carlson	18
D. I. Gower lbw b Hurst	9	lbw b Higgs	21
I. T. Botham c Wright b Higgs	74	c Yardley b Hurst	7
G. Miller lbw b Hogg	31	c Wright b Hurst	64
†R. W. Taylor run out	4	c Wright b Hogg	97
J. E. Emburey b Higgs	4	b Hogg	42
R. G. D. Willis c Darling b Hogg	24	c Wright b Hogg	12
M. Hendrick not out	0	not out	3
Extras (B1, LB4, W3, NB2)	10	Extras (B1, LB16, NB4, W2)	23
Total	**169**		**360**

AUSTRALIA

W. M. Darling c Willis b Botham	15	b Botham	18
G. M. Wood c Randall b Emburey	35	run out	9
K. J. Hughes c Emburey b Hendrick	4	c Gower b Hendrick	46
*G. N. Yallop b Hendrick	0	b Hendrick	36
A. R. Border c Taylor b Botham	11	b Willis	1
P. H. Carlson c Taylor b Botham	0	c Gower b Hendrick	21
B. Yardley b Botham	28	c Brearley b Willis	0
†K. J. Wright lbw b Emburey	29	c Emburey b Miller	0
R. M. Hogg b Willis	0	b Miller	2
J. D. Higgs run out	16	not out	3
A. R. Hurst not out	17	b Willis	13
Extras (B1, LB3, NB5)	9	Extras (LB1, NB10)	11
Total	**164**		**160**

BOWLING

AUSTRALIA	O	M	R	W	O	M	R	W
Hogg	10.4	1	26	4	27.6	7	59	5
Hurst	14	1	65	3	37	9	97	4
Carlson	9	1	34	0	27	8	41	2
Yardley	4	0	25	0	20	6	60	0
Higgs	3	1	9	2	28	4	75	1
Border					3	2	5	0
ENGLAND								
Willis	11	1	55	1	12	3	41	3
Hendrick	19	1	45	2	14	6	19	3
Botham	11.4	0	42	4	14	4	37	1
Emburey	12	7	13	2	9	5	16	0
Miller					18	3	36	2

FALL OF WICKETS

	E	A	E	A
1st	10	5	31	31
2nd	12	10	57	36
3rd	16	22	97	115
4th	18	24	106	120
5th	27	72	130	121
6th	80	94	132	121
7th	113	114	267	124
8th	136	116	336	130
9th	147	133	347	147
10th	169	164	360	160

SIXTH TEST MATCH

PLAYED AT SYDNEY 10, 11, 12, 14 FEBRUARY

ENGLAND WON BY 9 WICKETS

AUSTRALIA

G. M. Wood c Botham b Hendrick	15	c Willis b Miller			29
A. M. Hilditch run out	3	c Taylor b Hendrick			1
K. J. Hughes c Botham b Willis	16	c Gooch b Emburey			7
*G. N. Yallop c Gower b Botham	121	c Taylor b Miller			17
P. M. Toohey c Taylor b Botham	8	c Gooch b Emburey			0
P. H. Carlson c Gooch b Botham	8	c Botham b Emburey			0
B. Yardley b Emburey	7	not out			61
†K. J. Wright st Taylor b Emburey	3	c Boycott b Miller			5
R. M. Hogg c Emburey b Miller	9	b Miller			7
J. D. Higgs not out	9	c Botham b Emburey			2
A. G. Hurst b Botham	0	c & b Miller			4
Extras (LB3, NB2)	5	Extras (B3, LB6, NB1)			10
	—				—
Total	**198**				**143**

ENGLAND

G. Boycott c Hilditch b Hurst	19	c Hughes b Higgs			13
*J. M. Brearley c Toohey b Higgs	46	not out			20
D. W. Randall lbw b Hogg	7	not out			0
G. A. Gooch st Wright b Higgs	74				
D. I. Gower c Wright b Higgs	65				
I. T. Botham c Carlson b Yardley	23				
G. Miller lbw b Hurst	18				
†R. W. Taylor not out	36				
J. E. Emburey c Hilditch b Hurst	0				
R. G. D. Willis b Higgs	10				
M Hendrick c & b Yardley	0	Extras (NB2)			2
Extras (B3, LB5, NB2)	10	(1 wkt)			
	—				—
	308				**35**

BOWLING

ENGLAND	O	M	R	W		O	M	R	W
Willis	11	4	48	1	—	3	0	15	0
Hendrick	12	2	21	1	—	7	3	22	1
Botham	9.7	1	57	4	—				
Emburey	18	3	48	2	—	24	4	52	4
Miller	9	3	13	1	—	27.1	6	44	5
Boycott	10	0	6	0	—				
AUSTRALIA									
Hogg	18	6	42	1	—				
Hurst	20	4	58	3	—				
Yardley	25	2	105	2	—	5.2	0	21	0
Carlson	10	1	24	0	—				
Higgs	30	8	69	4	—	5	1	12	1

FALL OF WICKETS

	A	E	A	E
1st	18	37	8	31
2nd	19	46	28	
3rd	67	115	48	
4th	101	182	48	
5th	109	233	48	
6th	116	247	82	
7th	124	270	114	
8th	159	280	130	
9th	198	306	136	
10th	198	308	143	

England v Pakistan, 1978

FIRST TEST MATCH

PLAYED AT EDGBASTON, 1 2, 3, 5 JUNE
ENGLAND WON BY AN INNINGS AND 57 RUNS

PAKISTAN

Mudassar Nazar c & b Botham	14	b Edmonds	30
Sadiq Mohammad c Radley b Old	23	lbw b Old	79
Mohsin Khan b Willis	35	c Old b Miller	38
Javed Miandad c Taylor b Old	15	c Brearley b Edmonds	39
Haroon Rashid c Roope b Willis	3	b Willis	4
Wasim Raja c Taylor b Old	17	b Edmonds	9
Sarfraz Nawaz not out	32	not out	6
†‡Wasim Bari b Old	0	c Miller b Edmonds	3
Iqbal Qasim c Taylor b Old	0	retired hurt	5
Sikander Bakht c Roope b Old	0	c Roope b Miller	2
Liaqat Ali c Brearley b Old	9	b Willis	3
Extras (LB3, NB13)	16	(B4, LB4, W1, NB4)	13
Total	164		231

ENGLAND

†J. M. Brearley run out	38
B. Wood lbw b Sikander	14
C. T. Radley lbw b Sikander	106
D. I. Gower c Javed b Sikander	58
G. R. J. Roope b Sikander	32
G. Miller c Bari b Mudassar	48
I. T. Botham c Qasim b Liaqat	100
C. M. Old c Mudassar b Qasim	5
P. H. Edmonds not out	4
‡R. W. Taylor } did not bat	
R. G. D. Willis	
Extras (LB26, W5, NB16)	47
Total (8 wkts dec)	452

BOWLING

ENGLAND	O	M	R	W		O	M	M	R	W
Willis	16	2	42	2	..	23.4	3	70	2	
Old	22.4	6	50	7	..	25	12	38	1	
Botham	15	4	52	1	..	17	3	47	0	
Wood	3	2	2	0	..					
Edmonds	4	2	2	0	..	26	10	44	4	
Miller						12	4	19	2	

PAKISTAN	O	M	R	W	
Sarfraz	6	1	12	0	..
Liaqat	42	9	114	1	..
Sikander	45	13	132	4	..
Mudassar	27	7	59	1	..
Qasim	14	2	56	1	..
Raja	10	1	32	0	..

FALL OF WICKETS

	P	E	P
	1st	1st	2nd
1st	20	36	94
2nd	56	101	123
3rd	91	190	176
4th	94	275	193
5th	103	276	214
6th	125	399	220
7th	125	448	224
8th	126	452	227
9th	126	—	231
10th	164	—	—

In Pakistan's 2nd innings, Iqbal Qasim retired hurt at 123–1.
Man of the Match: C. M. Old. Adjudicator: M. J. K. Smith.

SECOND TEST MATCH

ENGLAND

†J. M. Brearley lbw b Liaqat	2
G. A. Gooch lbw b Raja	54
C. T. Radley c Mohsin b Liaqat	8
D. I. Gower b Qasim	56
G. R. J. Roope c Mohsin b Qasim	69
G. Miller c Javed b Qasim	0
I. T. Botham b Liaqat	108
‡R. W. Taylor c Mudassar b Sikander	10
C. M. Old c Mohsin b Sikander	0
P. H. Edmunds not out	36
R. G. D. Willis b Mudassar	18
Extras (LB2, NB1)	3
Total	**364**

PAKISTAN

Mudassar Nazar c Edmonds b Willis	1	c Taylor b Botham	10
Sadiq Mohammad c Botham b Willis	11	c Taylor b Willis	0
Mohsin Khan c Willis b Edmonds	31	c Roope b Willis	46
Haroon Rashid b Old	15	b Botham	4
Javed Miandad c Taylor b Willis	0	c Gooch b Botham	22
Wasim Raja b Edmonds	28	c & b Botham	1
Talat Ali c Radley b Edmonds	2	c Roope b Botham	40
††Wasim Bari c Brearley b Willis	0	c Taylor b Botham	2
Iqbal Qasim b Willis	0	b Botham	0
Sikander Bakht c Brearley b Edmonds	4	c Roope b Botham	1
Liaqat Ali not out	4	not out	0
Extras (NB9)	9	(B1, LB3, W5, NB4)	13
Total	**105**		**139**

BOWLING

PAKISTAN	O	M	R	W		O	R	M	W
Sikander	27	3	115	2	..				
Liaqat	18	1	80	3	..				
Mudassar	4.2	0	16	1	..				
Qasim	30	5	101	3	..				
Raja	12	3	49	1	..				

ENGLAND	O	M	R	W		O	R	M	W
Willis	13	1	47	5	..	10	2	26	2
Old	10	3	26	1	..	15	4	36	0
Botham	5	2	17	0	..	20.5	6	34	8
Edmonds	8	6	4	..		12	4	21	0
Miller					..	9	3	9	0

FALL OF WICKETS

	E	P	P
	1st	1st	2nd
1st	5	11	1
2nd	19	22	45
3rd	120	40	100
4th	120	41	108
5th	134	84	114
6th	252	96	119
7th	290	97	121
8th	290	97	130
9th	324	97	130
10th	364	105	139

Man of the Match: I. T. Botham. Adjudicator: T. G. Evans.

THIRD TEST MATCH

PAKISTAN

Sadiq Mohammad c Brearley b Botham	97
Mudassar Nazar c Botham b Old	31
Mohsin Khan lbw b Willis	41
Talat Ali c Gooch b Willis	0
Haroon Rashid c Brearley b Botham	7
Javed Miandad b Old	1
Wasim Raja lbw b Botham	0
Sarfraz Nawaz c Taylor b Botham	4
Sikander Bakht b Old	4
†‡Wasim Bari not out	7
Iqbal Qasim lbw b Old	0
Extras (LB8, NB1)	9
Total	**201**

ENGLAND

†J. M. Brearley c Bari b Sarfraz	0
G. A. Gooch lbw b Sarfraz	20
C. T. Radley b Sikander	7
D. I. Gower lbw b Sarfraz	39
G. R. J. Roope c Sadiq b Javed	11
G. Miller not out	18
‡R. W. Taylor c Bari b Sarfraz	2
I. T. Botham lbw b Sarfraz	4
P. H. Edmonds not out	1
C. M. Old	} did not bat
R. G. D. Willis	
Extras (B1, LB5, W1, NB10)	17
Total (7 wkts)	**119**

BOWLING

ENGLAND	O	M	R	W
Willis	26	8	48	2
Old	41.4	22	41	4
Botham	18	2	59	4
Edmonds	11	2	22	0
Miller	9	3	22	0
PAKISTAN				
Sarfraz	20	6	39	5
Sikander	15	4	26	1
Mudassar	5	2	12	0
Qasim	11	8	11	0
Javed	3	0	14	1

FALL OF WICKETS

	P	E
	1st	1st
1st	75	0
2nd	147	24
3rd	147	51
4th	169	77
5th	182	102
6th	183	110
7th	189	116
8th	190	—
9th	201	—
10th	201	—

Man of the Match: Sadiq Mohammad. **Adjudicator:** N. W. D. Yardley.

TEST MATCH AVERAGES

ENGLAND—BATTING AND FIELDING

	M	I	NO	Runs	HS	Avge	100	50	Ct	St
I. T. Botham	3	3	0	212	108	70.66	2	—	4	—
D. I. Gower	3	3	0	153	58	51.00	—	2	—	—
C. T. Radley	3	3	0	121	106	40.33	1	—	2	—
G. R. J. Roope	3	3	0	112	69	37.33	—	1	6	—
G. A. Gooch	2	2	0	74	54	37.00	—	1	2	—
G. Miller	3	3	1	66	48	33.00	—	—	1	—
J. M. Brearley	3	3	0	40	38	13.33	—	—	6	—
R. W. Taylor	3	3	0	12	10	6.00	—	—	8	—
C. M. Old	3	2	0	5	5	2.50	—	—	1	—

Also batted: (3 Tests) P. H. Edmonds 4*, 36*, 1* (1ct); R. G. D. Willis 18 (1ct); (1 Test) B. Wood 14.

ENGLAND—BOWLING

	Overs	Mdns	Runs	Wkts	Avge	Best	5 wI	10 wM
P. H. Edmonds	61	24	95	8	11.87	4-6	—	—
C. M. Old	114.2	47	191	13	14.69	7-50	1	—
I. T. Botham	75.5	19	209	13	16.07	8-34	1	—
R. G. D. Willis	88.4	16	233	13	17.92	5-47	1	—

Also bowled: G. Miller 30–10–50–2; B. Wood 3–2–2–0.

PAKISTAN—BATTING AND FIELDING

	M	I	NO	Runs	HS	Avge	100	50	Ct	St
Sadiq Mohammad	3	5	0	210	97	42.00	—	2	1	—
Sarfraz Nawaz	2	3	2	42	32*	42.00	—	—	—	—
Mohsin Khan	3	5	0	191	46	38.20	—	—	3	—
Mudassar Nazar	3	5	0	86	31	17.20	—	—	2	—
Javed Miadad	3	5	0	77	39	15.40	—	—	2	—
Talat Ali	2	3	0	42	40	14.00	—	—	—	—
Wasim Raja	3	5	0	55	28	11.00	—	—	—	—
Liaquat Ali	2	4	2	16	9	8.00	+	—	—	—
Haroon Rashid	3	5	0	33	15	6.60	—	—	—	—
Wasim Bari	3	5	1	12	7*	3.00	—	—	3	—
Sikander Bakht	3	5	0	11	4	2.20	—	—	—	—
Iqbal Qasim	3	5	1	5	5*	1.25	—	—	1	—

PAKISTAN—BOWLING

	Overs	Mdns	Runs	Wkts	Avge	Best	5 wI	10 wM
Sarfraz Nawaz	26	7	51	5	10.20	5-39	1	—
Sikander Bakht	87	20	273	7	39.00	4-132	—	—
Iqbal Qasim	55	15	168	4	42.00	3-101	—	—
Liaquat Ali	60	10	194	4	48.50	3-80	—	—

Also bowled: Javed Miandad 3–0–14–1; Mudassar Nazar 36.2–9–87–2; Wasim Raja 22–4–81–1.

TOUR AVERAGES

BATTING AND FIELDING

	M	I	NO	Runs	HS	Avge	100	50	Ct	S
Sadiq Mohammad	13	20	2	675	161	37.50	1	3	5	—
Mudassar Nazar	13	21	1	677	107	33.85	1	3	5	—
Wasim Raja	12	17	5	324	56*	27.00	—	2	3	—
Talat Ali	8	14	3	278	60	25.27	—	1	1	—
Javed Miandad	13	20	4	397	59	24.81	—	2	5	—
Mohsin Khan	11	16	0	386	79	24.12	—	1	4	—
Sarfraz Nawaz	8	8	4	90	32*	22.50	—	—	3	—
Haroon Rashid	10	15	0	268	78	17.86	—	1	2	—
Wasim Bari	12	11	2	123	38*	13.66	—	—	13	—
Aamer Hameed	6	3	1	26	13	13.00	—	—	—	—
Arshad Pervez	3	5	0	59	30	11.80	—	—	1	—
Liaquat Ali	8	7	5	18	9	9.00	—	—	—	—
Abdul Qadir	7	6	0	16	9	2.66	—	—	4	—
Iqbal Qasim	9	9	2	16	8*	2.28	—	—	4	—
Sikander Bakht	6	6	1	11	4	2.20	—	—	—	—

Also batted: Masood Iqbal 8 (3ct); Naeem Ahmed 2; Jamal Hassan 7,2*.

BOWLING

	Overs	Mdns	Runs	Wkts	Avge	Best	5 wI	10 wM
Sarfraz Nawaz	147.3	35	330	18	18.33	5–39	1	—
Liaquat Ali	188	45	510	18	28.33	3–26	—	—
Mudassar Nazar	100.1	23	253	8	31.62	2–28	—	—
Wasim Raja	89.2	15	258	8	32.25	2–15	—	—
Sikander Baht	149	31	450	12	37.50	4–132	—	—
Aamer Quasim	95	28	237	6	39.50	3–71	—	—
Iqbal Qasim	115.4	3	310	7	44.28	3–101	—	—
Abdul Qadir	123	22	396	6	66.00	2–29	—	—

Also bowled: Hassan 24–3–77–2; Miandad 43–4–137–2; Naeem 47–7–136–2 ;Sadiq 12–4–25–1.

PRUDENTIAL TROPHY

ONE-DAY MATCHES

ENGLAND v PAKISTAN

Old Trafford: England won by 132 runs
England 217–7 (Radley 79)
Pakistan 85 (Willis 4–15)
Man of the Match: R. G. D. Willis
Adjudicator: K. V. Andrew.

The Oval: England won by 94 runs
England 248–6 (Gower 114*)
Pakistan 154
Man of the Match: D. I. Gower
Adjudicator: A. J. McIntyre

England v New Zealand, 1978

FIRST TEST MATCH

PLAYED AT THE OVAL, 27, 28, 29, 31 JULY, 1 AUGUST
ENGLAND WON BY 7 WICKETS

NEW ZEALAND

J. G. Wright c Radley b Willis		62	lbw b Botham	25
R. W. Anderson b Old		4	c Taylor b Botham	2
G. P. Howarth c Edmonds b Botham		94	b Willis	38
B. A. Edgar c & b Miller		0	b Edmonds	7
†M. G. Burgess lbw b Willis		34	l bw b Botham	36
B. E. Congdon run out		2	b Edmonds	11
‡G. N. Edwards b Miller		6	c Brearley b Edmonds	7
R. J. Hadlee c Brearley b Willis		5	b Edmonds	27
B. L. Cairns lbw b Willis		5	b Miller	0
B. P. Bracewell c Taylor b Willis		0	b Miller	0
S. L. Boock not out		3	not out	0
Extras (B1, LB7, NB11)		19	(B8, LB10, NB11)	29
Total		234		182

ENGLAND

†J. M. Brearley c Edwards b Bracewell		2	lbw b Boock	11
G. A. Gooch lbw b Bracewell		0	not out	91
C. T. Radley run out		49	lbw b Bracewell	2
D. I. Gower run out		111	c Howarth b Cairns	11
G. R. J. Roope b Boock		14	not out	10
G. Miller lbw b Cairns		0		
I. T. Botham c Bracewell b Boock		22		
‡R. W. Taylor c Edwards b Hadlee		8		
P. H. Edmonds lbw b Hadlee		28		
C. M. Old c Edwards b Cairns		16		
R. G. D. Willis not out		3		
Extras (B15, LB8, NB3)		26	(B2, LB3, N8)	13
Total		279	(3 wkts)	138

BOWLING

ENGLAND	O	M	R	W		O	M	R	W
Willis	20.2	9	42	5	..	13	2	39	1
Old	20	7	43	1	..	5	2	13	0
Botham	22	7	58	1	..	19	2	46	3
Miller	25	10	31	2	..	34	19	35	2
Edmonds	17	2	41	0	..	34.1	23	20	4

NEW ZEALAND	O	M	R	W		O	M	R	W
Hadlee	21.5	6	43	2	..	11.3	3	18	0
Bracewell	17	8	46	2	..	13	3	26	1
Cairns	40	16	65	2	..	7	0	21	1
Boock	35	18	61	2	..	20	5	55	1
Congdon	21	6	38	0	..	1	0	5	0

FALL OF WICKETS

	NZ	E	NZ	E
	1st	1st	2nd	2nd
1st	7	2	15	26
2nd	130	7	19	51
3rd	131	123	30	82
4th	191	165	70	—
5th	197	166	86	—
6th	207	208	105	—
7th	224	212	113	—
8th	230	232	182	—
9th	231	257	182	—
10th	234	279	182	—

Man of the Match : D. I. Gower. Adjudicator : T. E. Bailey.

SECOND TEST MATCH

PLAYED AT TRENT BRIDGE, 10, 11, 12, 14 AUGUST
ENGLAND WON BY AN INNINGS AND 119 RUNS

ENGLAND

G. A. Gooch c Burgess b Bracewell	55
G. Boycott c & b Hadlee	131
C. T. Radley lbw b Hadlee	59
D. I. Gower c Cairns b Boock	46
†J. M. Brearley c Parker b Bracewell	50
I. T. Botham c Hadlee b Boock	8
G. Miller c Howarth b Hadlee	4
P. H. Edmonds b Cairns	6
‡R. W. Taylor b Hadlee	22
M. Hendrick c Edwards b Bracewell	7
R. G. D. Willis not out	1
Extras (B16, LB12, W1, NB11)	40
Total	**429**

NEW ZEALAND

R. W. Anderson lbw b Botham	19	run out	0
B. A. Edgar c Taylor b Botham	6	c Botham b Edmonds	60
G. P. Howarth not out	31	c Botham b Hendrick	34
S. L. Boock c Taylor b Willis	8	b Edmonds	2
J. M. Parker c Taylor b Hendrick	0	run out	38
†M. G. Burgess c Taylor b Botham	5	c Brearley b Edmonds	7
B. E. Congdon c Hendrick b Botham	27	c Brearley b Botham	4
‡G. N. Edwards c Taylor b Botham	0	c & b Edmonds	18
B. L. Cairns b Edmonds	9	lbw b Botham	0
R. J. Hadlee c Gooch b Botham	4	c Taylor b Botham	1
B. P. Bracewell b Edmonds	0	not out	0
Extras (LB1, W1, NB9)	11	(LB6, W1, NB9)	16
Total	**120**		**190**

BOWLING

NEW ZEALAND

	O	M	R	W		O	M	R	W
Hadlee	42	11	94	4	..				
Bracewell	33.5	2	110	3	..				
Cairns	38	7	85	1	..				
Congdon	39	15	71	0	..				
Boock	28	18	29	2	..				

ENGLAND

	O	M	R	W		O	M	R	W
Willis	12	5	22	1	..	9	0	31	0
Hendrick	15	9	18	1	..	20	7	30	1
Botham	21	9	34	6	..	24	7	59	3
Edmonds	15.4	5	21	2	..	33.1	15	44	4
Miller	6	1	14	0	..	6	3	10	0

FALL OF WICKETS

	E	NZ	NZ
	1st	1st	2nd
1st	111	12	5
2nd	240	27	63
3rd	301	35	127
4th	342	47	148
5th	350	49	152
6th	364	99	164
7th	374	99	168
8th	419	110	180
9th	427	115	190
10th	429	120	190

In New Zealand's 1st innings Howarth retired hurt at 34–2 and resumed at 49–5.

Man of the Match: I. T. Botham. Adjudicator: R. T. Simpson.

THIRD TEST MATCH

PLAYED AT LORD'S, 24, 25, 26, 28 AUGUST

ENGLAND WON BY 7 WICKETS

NEW ZEALAND

J. G. Wright c Edmonds b Botham	17	b Botham	12
‡B. A. Edgar c Edmonds b Emburey	39	b Botham	4
G. P. Howarth c Taylor b Botham	123	not out	14
J. M. Parker lbw b Hendrick	14	c Taylor b Botham	3
†M. G. Burgess lbw b Botham	68	c Hendrick b Botham	14
B. E. Congdon c Emburey b Botham	2	c Taylor b Willis	3
R. W. Anderson b Botham	16	c Taylor b Willis	1
R. J. Hadlee c Brearley b Botham	0	run out	5
R. O. Collinge c Emburey b Willis	19	b Botham	0
S. L. Boock not out	4	c Radley b Willis	0
B. P. Bracewell st Taylor b Emburey	4	c Hendrick b Willis	0
Extras (B4, LB18, W4, NB7)	33	(LB3, NB8)	11
Total	337		67

ENGLAND

G. A. Gooch c Boock b Hadlee	2	not out	42
G. Boycott c Hadlee b Bracewell	24	b Hadlee	4
C. T. Radley c Congdon b Hadlee	77	b Hadlee	0
D. I. Gower c Wright b Hadlee	71	c Congdon b Bracewell	46
†J. M. Brearley c Edgar b Hadlee	33	not out	8
I. T. Botham c Edgar b Collinge	21		
‡R. W. Taylor lbw b Hadlee	1		
P. H. Edmonds c Edgar b Hadlee	5		
J. E. Emburey c Collinge	2		
M. Hendrick b Bracewell	12		
R. G. D. Willis not out	7		
Extras (B7, LB5, NB22)	34	(LB3, W4, NB11)	18
Total	289	(3 wkts)	118

BOWLING

ENGLAND	O	M	R	W		O	M	R	W		FALL OF WICKETS			
											NZ	E	NZ	E
											1st	1st	2nd	2nd
Willis	29	9	79	1	..	16	8	16	4	1st	65	2	10	14
Hendrick	28	14	39	1	..					2nd	70	66	14	14
Botham	38	13	101	6	..	18.1	4	39	3	3rd	117	180	20	84
Edmonds	12	3	19	0	..					4th	247	211	29	—
Emburey	26.1	12	39	2	..	3	2	1	0	5th	253	249	33	—
Gooch	10	0	29	0	..					6th	290	255	37	—
NEW ZEALAND										7th	290	258	37	—
Hadlee	32	9	84	5	..	13.5	2	31	2	8th	321	263	43	—
Collinge	38	9	58	2	..	6	1	26	0	9th	333	274	57	—
Bracewell	19.3	1	68	2	..	6	0	32	1	10th	339	289	67	—
Boock	25	10	33	1	..	5	1	11	0					
Congdon	5	1	12	0	..									

Man of the Match: G. P. Howarth. Adjudicator: J. C. Laker.

TEST MATCH AVERAGES

ENGLAND—BATTING AND FIELDING

	M	I	NO	Runs	HS	Avge	100	50	Ct	St
G. A. Gooch	3	5	2	190	91*	63.33	—	2	1	—
D. I. Gower	3	5	0	285	111	57.00	1	1	—	—
G. Boycott	2	3	0	159	131	53.00	1	—	—	—
C. T. Radley	3	5	0	187	77	37.40	—	2	2	—
J. M. Brearley	3	5	1	104	50	26.00	—	1	5	—
I. T. Botham	3	3	0	51	22	17.00	—	—	2	—
P. H. Edmonds	3	3	0	39	28	13.00	—	—	4	—
R. W. Taylor	3	3	0	31	22	10.33	—	—	12	1
M. Hendrick	2	2	0	19	12	9.50	—	—	3	—
G. Miller	2	2	0	4	4	2.00	—	—	1	—

Also batted: (3 Tests) R. G. D. Willis 3*, 1*, 7*; (1 Test) J. E. Emburey 2 (2ct); C. M. Old 16; G. R. J. Roope 14, 10*.

ENGLAND—BOWLING

	Overs	Mdns	Runs	Wkts	Avge	Best	5 wI	10 wM
I. T. Botham	142.1	42	337	24	14.04	6-34	3	1
P. H. Edmonds	112	48	145	10	14.50	4-20	—	—
R. G. D. Willis	99.2	33	229	12	19.08	5-42	1	—
G. Miller	71	33	90	4	22.50	2-31	—	—

Also bowled: J. E. Emburey 29.1–14–40–2; G. A. Gooch 10–0–29–0; M. Hendrick 63–30–87–3; C. M. Old 25–9–56–1.

NEW ZEALAND—BATTING AND FIELDING

	M	I	NO	Runs	HS	Avge	100	50	Ct	St
G. P. Howarth	3	6	2	296	123	74.00	1	1	2	—
J. G. Wright	3	6	0	116	62	29.00	—	1	1	—
B. A. Edgar	3	6	0	147	60	24.50	—	1	3	—
M. G. Burgess	3	6	0	135	68	22.50	—	1	1	—
J. M. Parker	2	4	0	55	38	13.75	—	—	1	—
B. E. Congdon	3	6	0	74	41	12.33	—	—	2	—
B. L. Cairns	2	4	0	41	27	10.25	—	—	1	—
G. N. Edwards	2	4	0	35	18	8.75	—	—	4	—
R. W. Anderson	3	6	0	42	19	7.00	—	—	1	—
S. L. Boock	3	6	3	17	8	5.66	—	—	1	—
R. J. Hadlee	3	6	0	32	11	5.33	—	—	3	—
B. P. Bracewell	3	6	1	4	4	0.80	—	—	1	—

Also batted: (1 Test) R. O. Collinge 19, 0.

NEW ZEALAND—BOWLING

	Overs	Mdns	Runs	Wkts	Avge	Best	5 wI	10 wM
R. J. Hadlee	121.1	31	270	13	20.76	5-84	1	—
B. P. Bracewell	89.2	14	282	9	31.33	3-110	—	—
S. L. Boock	113	53	189	6	31.50	2-29	—	—
B. L. Cairns	85	23	171	4	42.75	2-65	—	—

Also bowled: R. O. Collinge 36–10–84–2; B. E. Congdon 67–22–126–0.

TOUR AVERAGES

BATTING AND FIELDING

	M	I	NO	Runs	HS	Avge	100	50	Ct	St
G. P. Howarth	12	20	2	816	123	45.33	1	5	11	—
B. A. Edgar	15	24	2	883	113	37.40	1	8	19	—
J. M. Parker	12	17	2	549	104*	36.60	2	1	7	1
R. W. Anderson	14	24	3	739	155	35.19	2	2	6	—
B. E. Congdon	13	21	5	556	110*	34.75	1	1	10	—
J. G. Wright	14	24	3	675	111	32.14	1	4	7	—
M. G. Burgess	15	24	1	552	68	24.00	—	5	8	—
R. O. Collinge	6	5	1	91	63*	22.75	—	1	—	—
G. N. Edwards	14	21	3	401	83	22.27	—	3	22	1
B. L. Cairns	11	16	2	239	41	17.07	—	—	7	—
J. M. McIntyre	9	9	4	85	24*	17.00	—	—	3	—
S. L. Boock	9	9	4	85	14*	14.25	—	—	5	—
G. B. Thomson	13	14	10	57		13.00	—	—	2	—
R. J. Hadlee	7	3	2	13	9		—	—		—
B. P. Bracewell	10	13	0	149	40	11.46	—	—	9	—
	9	10	3	18	10*	2.57	—	—	4	—

Also batted: D. R. Hadlee 8; G. B. Troup 19 (1ct).

BOWLING

	Overs	Mdns	Runs	Wkts	Avge	Best	5 wI	10 wM
R. J. Hadlee	280.4	72	714	41	17.41	7-77	3	1
S. L. Boock	386.3	156	865	39	22.17	5-9	2	1
B. L. Cairns	370	101	882	35	25.20	5-51	2	1
B. E. Congdon	288.2	85	650	23	28.26	5-40	1	—
B. P. Bracewell	221.2	38	694	24	28.91	3-38	—	—
G. B. Thomson	188	50	521	15	34.73	4-42	—	—
R. O. Collinge	158	35	455	13	35.00	3-43	—	—
J. M. McIntyre	204.4	71	546	14	39.00	3-40	—	—

Also bowled: D. R. Hadlee 16-0-70-1; G. P. Howarth 12-2-47-3;
J. M. Parker 5-1-30-1; G. B. Troup 37-6-108-2.

PRUDENTIAL TROPHY

ONE DAY MATCHES

ENGLAND v NEW ZEALAND

Scarborough: England won by 19 runs
England 206— (Gooch 94, Cairns 5—28)
New Zealand 87—8 (Congdon 52*)
Man of the Match: G. A. Gooch
Adjudicator: Sir Leonard Hutton

Old Trafford: England won by 126 runs
England 278— (Radley 117*, Gower 50)
New Zealand 152 (Cairns 60)
Man of the Match: C. T. Radley
Adjudicator: P. Lever

Pakistan v India, 1978-79

FIRST TEST MATCH

PLAYED AT FAISALABAD, 16, 17, 18, 20, 21 OCTOBER

MATCH DRAWN

PAKISTAN

Majid Khan b Bedi	47	c Chauhan b Prasanna	34
Sadiq Mohammad c & b Bedi	41	c Gavaskar b Dev	16
Zaheer Abbas lbw b Prasanna	176	c Chauhan b Gavaskar	96
†Mushtaq Mohammad c Gavaskar b Chandrasekhar	5		
Javed Miandad not out	154	not out	6
Asif Iqbal c Chauhan b Bedi	0	b S. Amarnath	104
Imran Khan c Vengsarkar b Chandrasekhar	32		
‡Wasim Bari b Chandrasekhar	3		
Sarfraz Nawaz lbw b Chandrasekhar	18		
Sikander Bakht not out	16		
Iqbal Qasim did not bat			
Extras (LB5 NB6)	11	(B2, LB3, NB3)	8
Total (8 wkts. dec.)	503	(4 wkts. dec.)	264

INDIA

S. M. Gavaskar b Qasim	89	not out	8
C. P. S. Chauhan c Wasim b Sarfraz	46	not out	30
S. Amarnath c Javed b Mushtaq	35		
G. R. Viswanath b Mushtaq	145		
D. B. Vengsarkar c Wasim b Imran	83		
M. Amarnath c Wasim b Sarfraz	4		
‡S. M. H. Kirmani c Qasim b Mushtaq	1		
Kapil Dev c sub (Haroon Rashid) b Mushtaq	8		
E. A. S. Prasanna not out	10		
†B. S. Bedi run out	1		
B. S. Chandrasekhar did not bat			
Extras (B3, LB3, NB34)	40	(B1, LB1, NB3)	5
Total (9 wkts. dec.)	462	(0 wkts.)	43

BOWLING

INDIA	O	M	R	W	O	M	R	W
Dev	16	2	71	0	12	3	25	1
M. Amarnath	7	0	44	0	10	1	43	0
Prasanna	42	11	123	1	14	4	34	1
Bedi	49	9	124	3	12	4	40	0
Chandrasekhar	38	6	130	4	12	1	49	0
Chauhan					5	0	26	0
Gavaskar					5	0	34	1
S. Amarnath					1.5	0	5	1
PAKISTAN								
Imran	34.5	7	111	1	6	2	15	0
Sarfraz	37	6	105	2	2	1	3	0
Sikander	24	1	86	0				
Mushtaq	27	10	55	4				
Qasim	20	3	65	1	4	0	0	
Javed					3	1	4	0
Sadiq					4	0	16	0

FALL OF WICKETS

	P	I	P	I
	1st	1st	2nd	2nd
1st	84	97	54	—
2nd	99	147	60	—
3rd	110	248	226	—
4th	365	414	264	—
5th	378	421	—	—
6th	445	425	—	—
7th	452	445	—	—
8th	476	447	—	—
9th	—	462	—	—
10th				—

SECOND TEST MATCH

PLAYED AT LAHORE, 27, 28, 29, 31 OCTOBER, 1 NOVEMBER
PAKISTAN WON BY 8 WICKETS

INDIA

S. M. Gavaskar c Majid b Salim	5	c Sarfraz b Mushtaq	97
C. P. S. Chauhan b Imran	10	c Wasim b Javed	93
S. Amarnath c Asif b Imran	8	c Mudassar b Mushtaq	60
G. R. Viswanath b Sarfraz	20	b Mudassar	83
D. B. Vengsarkar c Wasim b Imran	76	c Wasim b Mudassar	17
M. Amarnath hit wkt b Sarfraz	20	c Qasim b Sarfraz	7
‡S. M. H. Kirmani lbw b Mudassar	12	not out	39
Kapil Dev lbw b Sarfraz	15	c Majid b Imran	43
E. A. S. Prasanna not out	1	c Mushtaq b Imran	4
†B. S. Bedi lbw b Sarfraz	4	b Sarfraz	1
B. S. Chandrasekhar b Imran	0	b Imran	4
Extras (B17, LB4, NB7)	28	(B8, LB4, NB5)	17
Total	**199**		**465**

PAKISTAN

Majid Khan c Kirmani b Bedi	45	c & b M. Amarnath	38
Mudassar Nazar c Gavaskar b Dev	12	b Dev	29
‡Wasim Bari c Kirmani b Bedi	85		
Zaheer Abbas not out	235	not out	34
Asif Iqbal b Chandrasekhar	29	not out	21
Javed Miandad b M. Amarnath	35		
†Mushtaq Mohammad run out	67		
Imran Khan not out	9		
Sarfraz Nawaz did not bat			
Iqbal Qasim did not bat			
Salim Altaf did not bat			
Extras (B12, LB8, W1, NB1)	22	(LB6)	6
Total (6 wkts. dec.)	**539**	**(2 wkts.)**	**128**

BOWLING

PAKISTAN	O	M	R	W	O	M	R	W
Imran	18.5	2	54	4	42.3	12	110	3
Salim	13	3	34	1	16	6	36	0
Sarfraz	16	4	46	4	38	7	112	2
Mushtaq	6	0	32	0	30	6	106	2
Mudassar	3	2	5	1	4	1	4	2
Qasim					33	12	68	0
Javed					5	1	7	1
Majid					2	0	5	0
INDIA								
Dev	28	1	98	1	10	1	53	1
Gavaskar	4	1	10	0				
Bedi	34	6	130	2	4	0	23	0
Chandrasekhar	21	2	109	1				
M. Amarnath	21	4	76	1	6	0	39	1
Prasanna	25	2	94	0				

FALL OF WICKETS

	I	P	I	P
	1st	1st	2nd	2nd
1st	15	19	192	57
2nd	19	144	202	89
3rd	48	161	301	—
4th	49	216	371	—
5th	151	356	406	—
6th	186	525	407	—
7th	192	—	415	—
8th	194	—	437	—
9th	194	—	438	—
10th	199	—	465	—

In India's first innings M. Amarnath retired hurt at 106–4 and resumed his innings later

PLAYED AT KARACHI, 14, 15, 17, 18, 19 NOVEMBER
PAKISTAN WON BY 8 WICKETS

INDIA

S. M. Gavaskar c Sarfraz b Imran	111	c Wasim b Sarfraz	137
C. P. S. Chauhan c Qasim b Sarfraz	33	c Wasim b Sarfraz	0
S. Amarnath c Mushtaq b Qasim	30	run out	14
G. R. Viswanath b Imran	0	c Wasim b Sarfraz	1
D. B. Vengsarkar c Majid b Sikander	11	c Wasim b Sikander	1
M. Amarnath lbw b Sarfraz	14	b Imran	53
‡S. M. H. Kirmani c Mushtaq b Sikander	14	c Qasim b Imran	4
K. D. Ghavri c Majid b Sarfraz	42	c Mudassar b Imran	35
Kapil Dev lbw b Sarfraz	59	c Mushtaq b Sarfraz	34
†B. S. Bedi c Majid b Imran	4	not out	0
B. S. Chandrasekhar not out	0	b Sarfraz	0
Extras (B10, LB6, W1, NB9)	26	(B9, LB4, W1, NB7)	21
Total	344		300

PAKISTAN

Majid Khan b Dev	44	c Chauhan b Dev	14
Mudassar Nazar c Chauhan b Chandrasekhar	57		
‡Wasim Bari c Kirmani b Ghavri	3		
Zaheer Abbas c Viswanath b Bedi	42		
Asif Iqbal lbw b Chandrasekhar	1	c Kirmani b M. Amarnath	44
Javed Miandad c Kirmani b Dev	100	not out	62
†Mushtaq Mohammad c sub b Ghavri	78		
Imran Khan b Chandrasekhar	32	not out	31
Sarfraz Nawaz c sub b Dev	28		
Iqbal Qasim not out	29		
Sikander Bakht not out	22		
Extras (B5, LB20, W1, NB19)	45	(B3, LB9, NB1)	13
Total (9 wkts dec)	481	(2 wkts)	164

BOWLING

PAKISTAN	O	M	R	W		O	M	R	W
Imran	32	12	75	3	—	28	7	76	3
Sarfraz	31.2	4	89	4	—	24	5	70	5
Sikander	22	6	76	2	—	10	2	42	1
Qasim	23	6	67	1	—	7	1	27	0
Mudassar	4	2	5	0	—	2	0	13	0
Mushtaq	3	0	6	0	—	3	0	36	0
Javed					—	2	0	15	0
INDIA									
Dev	42	4	132	3	—	9	0	47	1
Ghavri	24	5	66	2	—	6	0	36	0
M. Amarnath	14	2	39	0	—	5.5	0	35	1
Chandrasekhar	25	4	97	3					
Bedi	35	5	99	1	—	4	0	33	0
Chauhan	1	0	3	0					

FALL OF WICKETS

	I	P	I	P
	1st	2nd	1st	2nd
1st	58	84	5	21
2nd	131	104	122	118
3rd	132	153	143	
4th	179	155	147	
5th	217	187	170	
6th	219	341	173	
7th	253	374	246	
8th	337	408	297	
9th	344	447	299	
10th	344		300	

New Zealand v England 1977-78

FIRST TEST MATCH

PLAYED AT WELLINGTON, 10, 11, 12, 14, 15 FEBRUARY
NEW ZEALAND WON BY 72 RUNS

NEW ZEALAND

J. G. Wright lbw b Botham	55	c Roope b Willis	19
R. W. Anderson c Taylor b Old	28	lbw b Old	26
G. P. Howarth c Botham b Old	13	c Edmonds b Willis	21
†M. G. Burgess b Willis	9	c Boycott b Botham	6
B. E. Congdon c Taylor b Old	44	c Roope b Willis	0
J. M. Parker c Rose b Willis	16	c Edmonds b Willis	4
‡W. K. Lees c Taylor b Old	1	lbw b Hendrick	11
R. J. Hadlee not out	27	c Boycott b Willis	2
D. R. Hadlee c Taylor b Old	1	c Roope b Botham	2
R. O. Collinge b Old	1	c Edmonds b Hendrick	6
S. L. Boock b Botham	4	not out	0
Extras (B12, LB3, W1, NB13)	29	(B2, LB9, W2, NB13)	26
Total	228		123

ENGLAND

B. C. Rose c Lees b Collinge	21	not out	5
†G. Boycott c Congdon b Collinge	77	b Collinge	1
G. Miller b Boock	24	c Anderson b Collinge	4
‡R. W. Taylor c & b Collinge	8	run out	0
D. W. Randall c Burgess b R. Hadlee	4	lbw b Collinge	9
G. R. J. Roope c Lees b R. Hadlee	37	c Lees b R. Hadlee	0
I. T. Botham c Burgess b R. Hadlee	7	c Boock b R. Hadlee	19
C. M. Old b R. Hadlee	10	lbw b R. Hadlee	9
P. H. Edmonds lbw b Congdon	4	c Parker b R. Hadlee	11
M. Hendrick lbw b Congdon	0	c Parker b R. Hadlee	0
R. G. D. Willis not out	6	c Howarth b R. Hadlee	3
Extras (LB4, NB13)	17	(NB3)	3
Total	215		64

BOWLING

ENGLAND	O	M	R	W		O	M	R	W
Willis	25	7	65	2	..	15	2	32	5
Hendrick	17	2	46	0	..	10	2	16	2
Old	30	11	54	6	..	9	2	32	1
Edmonds	3	1	7	0	..	1	0	4	0
Botham	12.6	2	27	2	..	9.3	3	13	2
NEW ZEALAND									
R. Hadlee	28	5	74	4	..	13.3	4	26	6
Collinge	18	5	42	3	..	13	5	35	3
D. Hadlee	21	5	47	0	..	1	1	0	0
Boock	10	5	21	1	..				
Congdon	17.4	11	14	2	..				

FALL OF WICKETS

	NZ	E	NZ	E
	1st	1st	2nd	2nd
1st	42	39	54	2
2nd	96	89	82	8
3rd	114	108	93	18
4th	152	126	93	18
5th	191	183	98	38
6th	193	188	99	38
7th	194	203	104	53
8th	196	205	116	53
9th	208	206	123	63
10th	228	215	123	64

Note: In England's second innings Rose retired hurt at 14–2 and resumed at 63–9.

SECOND TEST MATCH

PLAYED AT CHRISTCHURCH, 24, 25, 26, 28 FEBRUARY, 1 MARCH

ENGLAND WON BY 174 RUNS

ENGLAND

B. C. Rose c Howarth b Chatfield	11	c Lees b Collinge	**7**
†G. Boycott lbw b Collinge	8	run out	26
D. W. Randall c Burgess b Hadlee	0	run out	13
G. R. J. Roope c Burgess b Hadlee	50	not out	9
G. Miller c Congdon b Collinge	89		
C. T. Radley c Lees b Hadlee	15		
I. T. Botham c Lees b Boock	103	not out	30
‡R. W. Taylor run out	45		
C. M. Old b Hadlee	8	b Collinge	1
P. H. Edmonds c Lees b Collinge	50		
R. G. D. Willis not out	6		
Extras (B14, LB9, NB10)	33	(B4, LB3, NB3)	10
Total	418	(4 wkts dec)	96

NEW ZEALAND

J. G. Wright c & b Edmonds	4	c Roope b Willis	0
R. W. Anderson b Edmonds	62	b Willis	15
G. P. Howarth c Edmonds b Willis	5	c Edmonds b Old	1
†M. G. Burgess c Roope b Botham	29	not out	6
B. E. Congdon lbw b Botham	20	c Botham b Willis	0
J. M. Parker not out	53	c Botham b Edmonds	16
‡W. K. Lees c Miller b Botham	0	b Willis	0
R. J. Hadlee b Edmonds	1	c Botham b Edmonds	39
R. O. Collinge c Edmonds b Botham	32	c Miller b Botham	0
S. L. Boock c Taylor b Edmonds	2	c Taylor b Botham	0
E. J. Chatfield c Edmonds b Botham	3	lbw b Botham	6
Extras (B4, LB1, NB19)	24	(LB6, NB16)	22
Total	235		105

BOWLING

NEW ZEALAND

	O	M	R	W	..	O	M	R	W
Hadlee	43	10	147	4	..	6	1	17	0
Collinge	26.5	6	89	3	..	9	2	29	2
Chatfield	37	8	94	1	..	5	0	22	0
Congdon	18	11	14	0	..	2	0	18	0
Boock	21	11	41	1	..				

ENGLAND

	O	M	R	W	..	O	M	R	W
Willis	20	5	45	1	..	7	2	14	4
Old	14	4	55	0	..	7	4	9	1
Botham	24.7	6	73	5	..	7	1	38	3
Edmonds	34	11	38	4	..	6	2	22	2

FALL OF WICKETS

	E	NZ	E	NZ
	1st	1st	2nd	2nd
1st	15	37	25	2
2nd	18	52	47	14
3rd	26	82	67	19
4th	127	119	74	25
5th	128	148	—	25
6th	288	151	—	59
7th	294	153	—	81
8th	305	211	—	90
9th	375	216	—	95
10th	418	235	—	105

Notes: In England's first innings, Miller retired hurt at 103–3 and resumed at 288–6. In New Zealand's second innings, Burgess retired hurt at 18–2 and resumed at 95–9.

THIRD TEST MATCH

MATCH DRAWN

NEW ZEALAND

J. G. Wright c Taylor b Lever	4	c Taylor b Edmonds	25
R. W. Anderson c Gatting b Botham	17	c Botham b Miller	55
G. P. Howarth c Roope b Willis	122	b Miller	102
†M. G. Burgess c Randall b Botham	50	c Taylor b Edmonds	17
B. E. Congdon c Miller b Botham	5	c Roope b Lever	20
J. M. Parker lbw b Botham	14	not out	47
‡G. N. Edwards lbw b Lever	55	c Randall b Lever	54
R. J. Hadlee c Roope b Botham	1	b Miller	10
B. L. Cairns b Lever	11	lbw b Edmonds	20
R. O. Collinge not out	5	not out	12
S. L. Boock c Edmonds b Willis	1		
Extras (B5, LB10, NB15)	30	(B6, LB4, NB10)	20
Total	**315**	**(8 wkts)**	**382**

ENGLAND

†G. Boycott c Burgess b Collinge	54
D. W. Randall lbw b Hadlee	30
C. T. Radley c Wright b Collinge	158
G. R. J. Roope c Burgess b Boock	68
M. W. Gatting b Boock	0
I. T. Botham c Edwards b Collinge	53
‡R. W. Taylor b Boock	16
G. Miller lbw b Collinge	15
P. H. Edmonds b Boock	8
J. K. Lever c sub b Boock	1
R. G. D. Willis not out	0
Extras (B6, LB6, W4, NB10)	26
Total	**429**

BOWLING

ENGLAND	O	M	R	W		O	M	R	W
Willis	26	8	57	2	..	10	3	42	0
Lever	34	5	96	3	..	17	4	59	2
Botham	34	4	90	5	..	13	1	51	0
Edmonds	10	2	23	0	..	45	15	107	3
Miller	1	1	0	0	..	30	10	99	3
Gatting					..	1	0	1	0
Roope					..	1	0	2	0
Randall					..	1	0	1	0
NEW ZEALAND									
Hadlee	31	6	107	1	..				
Collinge	38	9	98	4	..				
Cairns	35	9	63	0	..				
Congdon	26	8	68	0	..				
Boock	28.3	4	67	5	..				

FALL OF WICKETS

	NZ	E	NZ
	1st	1st	2nd
1st	12	52	69
2nd	32	115	98
3rd	113	254	125
4th	129	258	185
5th	182	355	272
6th	278	396	287
7th	285	418	305
8th	302	427	350
9th	314	428	—
10th	315	429	—

West Indies v Australia 1977-78

FIRST TEST MATCH

PLAYED AT PORT-OF-SPAIN, 3, 4, 5 MARCH

WEST INDIES WON BY AN INNINGS AND 106 RUNS

AUSTRALIA

G. M. Wood	c Haynes b Croft	2	lbw b Roberts		32
C. S. Serjeant	c Murray b Croft	3	lbw b Garner		40
G. N. Yallop	c Richards b Croft	2	b Roberts		81
P. M. Toohey	b Garner	20	absent hurt		
†R. B. Simpson	lbw b Garner	0	b Parry		14
G. J. Cosier	c Greenidge b Croft	46	lbw b Garner		19
‡S. J. Rixon	run out	1	c Parry b Roberts		0
B. Yardley	c Murray b Roberts	2	not out		7
J. R. Thomson	c Austin b Roberts	0	b Parry		4
W. M. Clark	b Garner	0	b Roberts		0
J. D. Higgs	not out	0	b Roberts		2
Extras	(B4, LB6, NB4)	14	(B5, LB2, W1, NB2)		10
		90			**209**

WEST INDIES

C. G. Greenidge	b Yardley	43
D. L. Haynes	c Rixon b Higgs	61
I. V. A. Richards	lbw b Thomson	39
A. I. Kallicharran	b Yardley	127
†C. H. Lloyd	b Thomson	86
R. A. Austin	c sub (Laughlin) b Thomson	2
‡D. L. Murray	c Rixon b Higgs	21
D. R. Parry	b Yardley	0
A. M. E. Roberts	st Rixon b Higgs	7
J. Garner	c Cosier b Higgs	0
C. E. H. Croft	not out	4
Extras	(LB9, NB6)	15
Total		**405**

BOWLING

WEST INDIES

	O	M	R	W	O	M	R	W
Roberts	12	4	26	2	16.2	3	56	5
Croft	9.1	5	15	4	13	1	55	0
Garner	14	6	35	3	17	5	39	2
Parry					17	1	49	2

AUSTRALIA

	O	M	R	W
Thomson	21	6	84	3
Clark	16	3	41	0
Higgs	24.5	3	91	4
Simpson	16	2	65	0
Yardley	19	1	64	3
Cosier	13	2	45	0

FALL OF WICKETS

	A	WI	A
	1st	1st	2nd
1st	7	87	59
2nd	10	143	90
3rd	16	143	149
4th	23	313	194
5th	45	324	194
6th	75	385	196
7th	75	385	200
8th	84	391	201
9th	90	391	209
10th	90	405	—

SECOND TEST MATCH

PLAYED AT BRIDGETOWN, 17, 18 19 MARCH

WEST INDIES WON BY 9 WICKETS

AUSTRALIA

Batsman		1st		2nd
W. M. Darling	c Richards b Croft	4	c Murray b Croft	8
G. M. Wood	lbw b Croft	69	run out	56
G. N. Yallop	c Austin b Croft	47	c Lloyd b Garner	14
C. S. Serjeant	c Murray b Parry	4	c Murray b Roberts	2
†R. B. Simpson	c Murray b Croft	9	c Murray b Roberts	17
G. J. Cosier	c Murray b Roberts	1	c Croft b Roberts	8
‡S. J. Rixon	lbw b Garner	16	c Lloyd b Roberts	0
B. Yardley	b Garner	74	b Garner	43
J. R. Thomson	b Garner	12	c Richards b Garner	11
W. M. Clark	b Garner	0	lbw b Garner	0
J. D. Higgs	not out	4	not out	0
Extras	(B3, LB4, NB3)	10	(B1, LB8, NB10)	19
Total		**250**		**178**

WEST INDIES

Batsman		1st		2nd
C. G. Greenidge	c Cosier b Thomson	8	not out	80
D. L. Haynes	c Rixon b Higgs	66	c Yardley b Higgs	55
I. V. A. Richards	c Clark b Thomson	23		
A. I. Kallicharran	c Yardley b Thomson	8		
†C. H. Lloyd	c Serjeant b Clark	42		
R. A. Austin	c Serjeant b Clark	20		
‡D. L. Murray	c Darling b Thomson	60		
D. R. Parry	c Serjeant b Simpson	27	not out	3
A. M. E. Roberts	lbw b Thomson	4		
J. Garner	not out	5		
C. E. H. Croft	lbw b Thomson	3		
Extras	(LB3, NB19)	22	(LB2, W1)	3
Total		**288**	**(1 wkt)**	**141**

BOWLING

WEST INDIES

	O	M	R	W		O	M	R	W
Roberts	18	2	79	1	..	18	5	50	4
Croft	18	3	47	4	..	15	4	53	1
Garner	16.	2	65	4	..	15	3	56	4
Parry	12	4	44	1	..				
Austin	1	0	5	0	..				

AUSTRALIA

	O	M	R	W		O	M	R	W
Thomson	13	1	77	6	..	6	1	22	0
Clark	24	3	77	2	..	6	0	27	0
Cosier	9	4	24	0	..				
Higgs	16	4	46	1	..	13	3	34	1
Simpson	7	1	30	1	..				
Yardley	2	0	12	0	..	10.5	2	55	0

FALL OF WICKETS

	A	WI	A	WI
	1st	1st	2nd	2nd
1st	13	16	21	131
2nd	105	56	62	—
3rd	116	71	69	—
4th	134	154	80	—
5th	135	172	95	—
6th	149	198	99	—
7th	161	263	154	—
8th	216	269	167	—
9th	216	282	173	—
10th	250	288	178	—

THIRD TEST MATCH

PLAYED AT GEORGETOWN, 31 MARCH, 1, 2, 4, 5 APRIL

AUSTRALIA WON BY 3 WICKETS

WEST INDIES

A. T. Greenidge	lbw b Thomson	56	b Clark	11
A. B. Williams	lbw b Clark	10	c Serjeant b Clark	100
H. A. Gomes	b Clark	4	c Simpson b Yardley	101
†A. I. Kallicharran	b Thomson	0	b Yardley	22
I. T. Shillingford	c Clark b Laughlin	3	c & b Thomson	16
‡D. A. Murray	c Ogilvie b Clark	21	lbw b Simpson	16
S. Shivnarine	c Rixon b Thomson	53	b Cosier	63
N. Phillip	c Yardley b Simpson	15	st Rixon b Yardley	4
V. A. Holder	c Laughlin b Clark	1	lbw b Clark	31
D. R. Parry	not out	21	lbw b Clark	51
S. Clarke	b Thomson	6	not out	5
Extras	(LB2, NB13)	15	(B4, LB5, NB10)	19
Total		205		439

AUSTRALIA

W. M. Darling	c Greenidge b Phillip	15	c Williams b Clarke	0
G. M. Wood	lbw b Holder	50	run out	126
A. D. Ogilvie	c & b Philip	4	lbw b Clarke	0
G. J. Cosier	lbw b Clarke	9	b Phillip	0
C. S. Serjeant	b Clarke	0	c sub (Bacchus) b Phillip	124
†R. B. Simpson	run out	67	c Murray b Clarke	4
T. J. Laughlin	c Greenidge b Parry	21	c & b Parry	24
‡S. J. Rixon	c Holder b Phillip	54	not out	39
B. Yardley	b Clarke	33	not out	15
J. R. Thomson	c & b Phillip	3		
W. M. Clark	not out	2		
Extras	(LB12, W1, NB15)	28	(B8, LB4, W2, NB16)	30
Total		286	(7 wkts)	362

BOWLING

AUSTRALIA

	O	M	R	W		O	M	R	W
Thomson	16.2	1	57	4	..	20	2	83	1
Clark	24	6	64	4	..	34.4	4	124	4
Laughlin	10	4	34	1	..	7	1	33	0
Cosier	2	1	1	0	..	6	1	14	1
Simpson	8	1	34	1	..	19	4	70	1
Yardley					..	30	6	96	3

WEST INDIES

	O	M	R	W		O	M	R	W
Phillip	18	0	75	4	..	19	2	65	2
Clarke	22	3	58	3	..	27	5	83	3
Holder	17	1	40	1	..	20	3	55	0
Gomes	3	0	8	0					
Parry	15	2	39	1	..	16.5	1	61	1
Shivnarine	8	0	38	0	..	18	2	68	0

FALL OF WICKETS

	WI	A	WI	A
	1st	1st	2nd	2nd
1st	31	28	36	11
2nd	36	36	95	13
3rd	48	77	172	22
4th	77	.85	199	273
5th	84	90	249	279
6th	130	142	285	290
7th	165	237	355	338
8th	166	256	369	—
9th	193	268	431	—
10th	205	286	439	—

FOURTH TEST MATCH

PLAYED AT PORT-OF-SPAIN 15, 16, 17, 18 APRIL

WEST INDIES WON BY 198 RUNS

WEST INDIES

A. T. Greenidge c Wood b Clark	6	c Thomson b Yardley	69
A. B. Williams c Yallop b Higgs	87	c Yallop b Simpson	24
‡D. A. Murray c Wood b Yardley	4	lbw b Clark	4
H. A. Gomes c Simpson b Clark	30	c Simpson b Higgs	14
†A. I. Kallicharran c Yallop b Clark	92	c & b Clark	27
S. F. A. Bacchus b Higgs	9	c Wood b Yardley	4
S. Shivnarine c Simpson b Thomson	10	c Serjeant b Simpson	11
D. R. Parry st Rixon b Higgs	22	c Serjeant b Yardley	65
N. Phillip c Rixon b Thomson	3	c Wood b Yardley	46
V. A. Holder b Thomson	7	b Simpson	0
R. R. Jumadeen not out	0	not out	2
Extras (B7, LB1, W2, NB12)	22	(B1, LB13, NB7)	21
Total	292		290

AUSTRALIA

G. M. Wood c Murray b Phillip	16	lbw b Holder	17
W. M. Darling c Jumadeen b Holder	10	b Phillip	6
P. M. Toohey c Williams b Parry	40	c Bacchus b Jumadeen	17
G. N. Yallop c Murray b Jumadeen	75	c Kallicharran b Parry	18
C. S. Serjeant st Murray b Jumadeen	49	c Bacchus b Jumadeen	4
†R. B. Simpson lbw b Holder	36	lbw b Jumadeen	6
‡S. J. Rixon c Murray b Holder	21	not out	13
B. Yardley c Williams b Holder	22	b Parry	3
J. R. Thomson b Holder	0	b Parry	1
W. M. Clark b Holder	4	b Parry	0
J. D. Higgs not out	0	b Parry	4
Extras (B4, LB2, NB11)	17	(LB2, NB3)	5
Total	290		94

BOWLING

AUSTRALIA	O	M	R	W	O	M	R	W	FALL OF WICKETS			
									WI	A	WI	A
									1st	1st	2nd	2nd
Thomson	23	8	64	3	..	15	1	76	0			
Clark	24	6	65	3	..	21	4	62	2			
Yardley	18	5	48	1	..	30.2	15	40	5	1st	7	23	36	9
Higgs	16.5	3	53	3	..	21	7	46	1	2nd	16	43	51	42
Simpson	15	4	40	0	..	14	2	45	3	3rd	111	92	79	44
WEST INDIES										4th	166	193	134	60
Phillip	17	1	73	1	..	7	0	24	1	5th	185	204	151	72
Holder	12.5	4	28	6	..	11	3	16	1	6th	242	254	151	76
Jumadeen	24	4	83	2	..	15	3	34	3	7th	258	275	204	80
Parry	30	5	77	1	..	10.4	3	15	5	8th	262	275	273	86
Shivnarine	6	1	12	0	..					9th	291	289	280	86
										10th	292	290	290	94

33

FIFTH TEST MATCH

PLAYED AT KINGSTON, 28, 29, 30 APRIL, 2, 3 MAY
MATCH DRAWN

AUSTRALIA

G. M. Wood c Parry b Phillip	16	c Bacchus b Jumadeen	90
A. D. Ogilvie c Shivnarine b Holder	0	st Murray b Parry	43
P. M. Toohey c Williams b Holder	122	st Murray b Jumadeen	97
G. N. Yallop c sub (H. Gordon) b Shivnarine	57	not out	23
C. S. Serjeant b Holder	26	not out	32
†R. B. Simpson c Murray b Foster	46		
T. J. Laughlin c sub (H. Gordon) b Jumadeen	35		
‡S. J. Rixon not out	13		
B. Yardley b Jumadeen	7		
J. R. Thomson c Murray b Jumadeen	4		
J. D. Higgs c Foster b Jumadeen	0		
Extras (LB5, W1, NB11)	17	(B5, LB8, NB7)	20
Total	343	(3 wkts dec)	305

WEST INDIES

A. B. Williams c Serjeant b Laughlin	17	c Wood b Yardley	19
S. F. A. Bacchus c Yardley b Thomson	5	c Simpson b Thomson	21
‡D. A. Murray c Wood b Laughlin	12	b Yardley	10
H. A. Gomes b Thomson	115	c Rixon b Higgs	1
†A. I. Kallicharran c Ogilvie b Laughlin	6	lbw b Higgs	126
S. Shivnarine st Rixon b Higgs	53	c Yallop b Yardley	27
M. L. C. Foster c Rixon b Laughlin	8	run out	5
D. R. Parry lbw b Higgs	4	c Serjeant b Yardley	0
N. Phillip c Rixon b Simpson	26	not out	26
V. A. Holder lbw b Laughlin	24	c Rixon b Higgs	6
R. R. Jumadeen not out	4	not out	0
Extras (LB1, NB5)	6	(B14, LB1, NB2)	17
Total	280	(9 wkts)	258

BOWLING

WEST INDIES	O	M	R	W		O	M	R	W
Phillip	32	5	90	1	..	17	1	64	0
Holder	31	9	68	3	..	18	2	41	0
Parry	5	0	15	0	..	18	3	60	1
Jumadeen	38.4	6	72	4	..	23	2	90	2
Foster	32	11	68	1	..	7	1	22	0
Shivnarine	9	2	13	1	..	3	1	8	0
AUSTRALIA									
Thomson	22	4	61	2	..	15	1	53	1
Laughlin	25.4	4	101	5	..	10	1	34	0
Yardley	14	4	27	0	..	29	18	35	4
Simpson	10	0	38	1	..	11	4	44	0
Higgs	19	3	47	2	..	28.4	10	67	3
Yallop					..	2	1	8	0

FALL OF WICKETS

	A	WI	A	WI
	1st	1st	2nd	2nd
1st	0	13	65	42
2nd	38	28	245	43
3rd	171	41	246	43
4th	217	47	—	59
5th	266	63	—	88
6th	308	159	—	179
7th	324	173	—	181
8th	335	219	—	242
9th	343	276	—	258
10th	343	280	—	—

ENGLAND v INDIA
1932 TO 1976-77

SERIES BY SERIES

Season		Touring Team Captain	P	E W	I W	D
1932	In England	C. K. Nayudu (I)	1	1	0	0
1933–34	In India	D. R. Jardine (E)	3	2	0	1
1936	In England	Maharaj of Vizianagram (I)	3	2	0	1
1946	In England	Nawab of Pataudi, Senior (I)	3	1	0	2
1951–52	In India	N. D. Howard (E)	5	1	1	3
1952	In England	V. S. Hazare (I)	4	3	0	1
1959	In England	D. K. Gaekwad (I)	5	5	0	0
1961–62	In India	E. R. Dexter (E)	5	0	2	3
1963–64	In India	M. J. K. Smith (E)	5	0	0	5
1967	In England	Nawab of Pataudi, Junior (I)	3	3	0	0
1971	In England	A. L. Wadekar (I)	3	0	1	2
1972–73	In India	A. R. Lewis (E)	5	1	2	2
1974	In England	A. L. Wadekar (I)	3	3	0	0
1976–77	In India	A. W. Greig (E)	5	3	1	1
		At Lord's	8	7	0	1
		At The Oval	5	2	1	2
		At Leeds	3	3	0	0
		At Manchester	6	3	0	3
		At Nottingham	1	1	0	0
		At Birmingham	2	2	0	0
		At Bombay	6	1	0	5
		At Calcutta	6	1	2	3
		At Madras	6	2	3	1
		At Delhi	5	2	0	3
		At Kanpur	4	1	0	3
		At Bangalore	1	0	1	0
		In England	25	18	1	6
		In India	28	7	6	15
		Total	53	25	7	21

35

HIGHEST INNINGS TOTALS			LOWEST INNINGS TOTALS		
	England			England	
629	at Lord's	1974	101 at The Oval		1971
571–8d	at Manchester	1936	134 at Lord's		1936
559–8d	at Kanpur	1963–64	159 at Madras		1972–73
550–4d	at Leeds	1963	163 at Calcutta		
537	at Lord's	1952	(2nd inns.)		1972–73
500–8d	at Bombay	1961–62	174 at Calcutta		
497–5	at Kanpur	1961–62	(1st inns.)		1972–73
490	at Manchester	1959	177 at Bangalore		1976–77
483–8d	at Leeds	1959	183 at Madras		1951–52
480	at Bombay	1972–73	191 at Lord's		1971

HIGHEST INNINGS TOTALS			LOWEST INNINGS TOTAL		
	India			India	
510	at Leeds	1967	42 at Lord's		1974
485–9d	at Bombay	1951–52	58 at Manchester		1952
467–8d	at Kanpur	1961–62	82 at Manchester		1957
466	at Delhi	1961–62	83 at Madras		1976–77
463–4	at Delhi	1963–64	92 at Birmingham		1967
457–9d	at Madras	1951–52	93 at Lord's		1936
457–7d	at Madras	1963–64	98 at The Oval		1952

HIGHEST INDIVIDUAL INNINGS FOR ENGLAND

246*	G. Boycott	at Leeds	1967
217	W. R. Hammond	at The Oval	1936
214*	D. Lloyd	at Birmingham	1974
205*	J. Hardstaff	at Lord's	1946
188	D. L. Amiss	at Lord's	1974
179	D. L. Amiss	at Delhi	1976–77
175	T. W. Graveney	at Bombay	1951–52

A total of 42 centuries have been scored for England.

HIGHEST INDIVIDUAL INNINGS FOR INDIA

203*	Nawab of Pataudi, Junior	at Delhi	1963–64
192	B. K. Kunderan	at Madras	1963–64
189*	V. L. Manjrekar	at Delhi	1961–62
184	V. M. H. Mankad	at Lord's	1952
164*	V. S. Hazare	at Delhi	1951–52
155	V. S. Hazare	at Bombay	1951–52
154	V. M. Merchant	at Delhi	1951–52

A total of 31 centuries have been scored for India.

A CENTURY IN EACH INNINGS OF A MATCH
No instance for either side.

A CENTURY ON DEBUT IN ENGLAND v INDIA TESTS
FOR ENGLAND

246*	G. Boycott	at Leeds	1967
109	B. L. D'Oliveira	at Leeds	1967
175	T. W. Graveney	at Bombay	1951–52
100	M. J. K. Smith	at Manchester	1959
136	B.H.Valentine (on Test debut)	at Bombay	1933–34
138*	A. J. Watkins	at Delhi	1951–52

FOR INDIA

118	L. Amarnath (on Test debut)	at Bombay	1933–34
112	A. A. Baig (on Test debut)	at Manchester	1959
105	Hanumant Singh (on Test debut)	at Delhi	1963–64

RECORD WICKET PARTNERSHIPS FOR ENGLAND

1st	159	P. E. Richardson & G. Pullar at Bombay	1961–62
2nd	221	D. L. Amiss & J. H. Edrich at Lord's	1974
3rd	169	R. Subba Row & M. J. K. Smith at The Oval	1959
4th	266	W. R. Hammond & T. S. Worthington at The Oval	1936
5th	254	K. W. R. Fletcher & A. W. Greig at Bombay	1972–73
6th	159	T. W. Graveney & T. G. Evans at Lord's	1952
7th	103	A. P. E. Knott & R. A. Hutton at The Oval	1971
8th	168	R. Illingworth & P. Lever at Manchester	1971
9th	83	K. W. R. Fletcher & N. Gifford at Madras	1972–73
10th	57	J. T. Murray & R. N. S. Hobbs at Birmingham	1967

RECORD WICKET PARTNERSHIPS FOR INDIA

1st	203	V. M. Merchant & Mushtaq Ali at Manchester	1936
2nd	192	F. M. Engineer & A. L. Wadekar at Bombay	1972–73
3rd {	211	V. M. Merchant & V. S. Hazare at Delhi	1951–52
	211	V. M. H. Mankad & V. S. Hazare at Lord's	1952
4th	222	V. S. Hazare & V. L. Manjrekar at Leeds	1952
5th	190*	Nawab of Pataudi, Jnr. & C. G. Borde at Delhi	1963–64
6th	105	V. S. Hazare & D. G. Phadkar at Leeds	1952
7th	153	C. G. Borde & S. A. Durani at Bombay	1963–64
8th	101	R. G. Nadkarni & F. M. Engineer at Madras	1961–62
9th	54	G. S. Ramchand & S. G. Shinde at Lord's	1952
10th	51	R. G. Nadkarni & B. S. Chandrasekhar at Calcutta	1963–64

HIGHEST RUN AGGREGATE IN A TEST RUBBER FOR

England in England	399 (Av. 79.80)	L. Hutton	1952
England in India	594 (Av. 99.00)	K. F. Barrington	1961–62
India in England	333 (Av. 55.50)	V. S. Hazare	1952
India in India	586 (Av. 83.71)	V. L. Manjrekar	1961–62

BEST INNINGS BOWLING FIGURES FOR

England in England	8–31 F. S. Trueman at Manchester	1952
England in India	7–46 J. K. Lever at Delhi	1976–77
India in England	6–35 Amar Singh at Lord's	1936
India in India	8–55 V. M. H. Mankad at Madras	1951–52

TEN WICKETS OR MORE IN A MATCH FOR ENGLAND

11–93 A. V. Bedser at Manchester	1946
11–145 A. V. Bedser at Lord's	1946
11–153 H. Verity at Madras	1933–34
10–70 J. K. Lever at Delhi (test debut)	1976–77
10–78 G. O. Allen at Lord's	1936

TEN WICKETS OR MORE IN A MATCH FOR INDIA

12–108 V. M. H. Mankad at Madras	1951–52
10–177 S. A. Durani at Madras	1961–62

HIGHEST WICKET AGGREGATE IN A TEST RUBBER FOR

England in England	F. S. Trueman	29 (Av. 13.31)	1952
England in India	D. L. Underwood	29 (Av. 17.55)	1976–77
India in England	S. P. Gupte	17 (Av. 34.64)	1959
India in India	B. S. Chandrasekhar	35 (Av. 18.91)	1972–73

HIGHEST MATCH AGGREGATE: 1,350–28 wkts at Leeds, 1963

LOWEST MATCH AGGREGATE: 482–31 wkts at Lord's, 1936

The highest innings total ever made in a Test match was the
903–7, declared, by England against Australia at The Oval in
1938. Len Hutton scored 364, Maurice Leyland 187, and Joe
Hardstaff 169 not out. Of the Australian bowlers, Fleetwood-
Smith suffered most. He took 1 for 298. When Australia
batted to face this mammoth total they lost their first wicket
without a run on the board, and were all out for 201, and
123, to lose by an innings and 579 runs.

SUSSEX

Their Third Gillette Cup

Sussex, after a long gap – they last won the Gillette Cup in the first two years of the competition, 1963 and 1964 – became the second county to win the Cup three times, when they beat Somerset by five wickets in the final at Lord's. Lancashire, of course, achieved their three in succession in 1970, 1971 and 1972, and added a fourth in 1975. But there is one common denominator; each has appeared in six finals. Warwickshire come next with four, and Kent with three, both these counties having won twice, as have Yorkshire. This means that five counties have won the Gillette Cup 13 times out of 16, the three individual winners being Gloucestershire, Northants and Middlesex. Nine have yet to win, and four of those nine – Essex, Hampshire, Leicestershire and Nottinghamshire – have yet to appear in the final.

At the beginning of the 1978 season, Sussex would have been regarded as being most unlikely to carry off one of cricket's major prizes, although there seemed little doubt that they would easily jump the first two hurdles against two minor counties. The game at Hove against Suffolk went pretty much according to plan, but at Stone Staffordshire came within an inch of creating the big surprise of the round; in the end Sussex scrambled home by two runs. Next, Sussex went to Headingley where appalling weather caused the original match to be abandoned, and replaced by a ten-over slog. Boycott chose to bat at number nine, and Sussex won by nine runs. Surely, had Boycott opened, he could have made the dozen which would have turned the scales, but he didn't, and Sussex were through. Lucky Sussex, the cricketing world said; what a passage to the quarter-finals. It was here that Sussex surprised the critics. They thoroughly outplayed Lancashire at Hove, never looked in any doubt of losing, and won comfortably by 136 runs. They played some fine cricket in every department of the game – batting, bowling and especially fielding, so that whatever had happened in the early rounds they came to Lord's for the final strictly on merit after the semi-final.

Even so, Somerset were firm favourites. They had scored 297 for 4 to win against Warwickshire; then 330 for 4 against

Glamorgan; 122 for 5 in a low-scoring game in poor weather at Canterbury, and 287 for 6 in the semi-final against Essex at Taunton, a game which will go down in history as one of the greatest games of cricket of all time. It was a tie, but Somerset won by virtue of having lost fewer wickets. Even if Somerset were favourites to win at Lord's, it had not escaped the notice of the connoisseurs that whilst Somerset had scored a packet of runs in the Gillette Cup (two centuries by Viv Richards and one by Peter Denning), a fair amount had been scored against them – 292 by Warwickshire, 260 by Glamorgan, 287 by Essex, so that on balance, Imran Khan and Arnold, on form, could possibly pose a greater threat than Somerset's attack. In the event, Imran took two wickets and Arnold none, Miandad and Imran Khan failed with the bat, and Sussex were carried high by the off-spin bowling and batting of John Barclay, by Gehan Mendis, and some superb batting by Paul Parker. Botham's 80 was all in vain, and having been 110 for 4 in search of 208 to win, Sussex rode home after Parker and Paul Phillipson had added 97 for the fifth wicket.

Ken Barrington, judging the Man of the Match award had a difficult decision – Botham had scored 80, Barclay in a superb piece of off-spin bowling had taken 2 for 21 in 12 overs and then put on 93 for the first wicket with Gehan Mendis, and then Parker had scored 62 not out. It was obviously touch and go between Barclay and Parker, and Parker got it in the end because Barrington felt that had he got out when Somerset were on top with Sussex 110 for 4, the match could have turned decisively Somerset's way. But all that mattered to both Barclay and Parker was that Sussex had won; after all, cricket is a team game overall, although individual performances are obviously of crucial importance.

The great fascination of Cup sport is borne out by the fact that Middlesex were well fancied to win; they were put out by Lancashire who were then fancied, certainly to beat Sussex in the semi-final. Kent were strongest contenders; they were put out by Somerset who, in turn, were beaten by Sussex, at one time rank outsiders. The unluckiest team of this Gillette year – Essex without a doubt. What a magnificent fight they put up at Taunton in a breathtaking day. It was all superb cup cricket. Gillette certainly started something when they came into the field in 1963.

THE GILLETTE CUP 1979
FIRST ROUND

Matches to be played on 27 June
Leicestershire v Devon at Leicester
Gloucestershire v Hampshire at Bristol
Durham v Berkshire at Durham City
Buckinghamshire v Suffolk at High Wycombe
Glamorgan v Kent at Swansea
Lancashire v Essex at Old Trafford

SECOND ROUND

Matches to be played on 18 July
Durham or Berkshire v Yorkshire
Warwickshire v Nottinghamshire at Edgbaston
Glamorgan or Kent v Lancashire or Essex
Northamptonshire v Surrey at Northampton
Sussex v Buckinghamshire or Suffolk at Hove
Middlesex v Gloucestershire or Hampshire at Lord's
Leicester or Devon v Worcestershire
Somerset v Derbyshire at Taunton
Quarter-finals 8 August; semi-finals 22 August;
final at Lord's 8 September.

Previous Man of the Match Awards are given in brackets where relevant.

1978 RESULTS
FIRST ROUND—5 JULY
Devon v Staffordshire at Torquay
Devon 205–8 in 60 overs (Matthews 66, Tolchard 40)
Staffordshire 208–6 in 58 overs (Gill 52, Moore 49*)
Result: Staffordshire won by 4 wickets
Man of the Match: J. D. Moore
Adjudicator: C. J. Barnett
Somerset v Warwickshire at Taunton
Warwickshire 292–5 in 60 overs (Whitehouse 94, Amiss 70)
Somerset 297–4 in 57.1 overs (Richards 139*, Denning 60)
Result: Somerset won by 6 wickets
Man of the Match: I. V. A. Richards
Adjudicator: W. J. Edrich
Sussex v Suffolk at Hove
Suffolk 101 in 39.1 overs
Sussex 102–4 in 33.1 overs (Parker 53)
Result: Sussex won by 6 wickets
Man of the Match: P. W. G. Parker
Adjudicator: K. F. Barrington
6 JULY
Shropshire v Surrey at Wellington
Shropshire 148–9 in 60 overs (Slade 54)
Surrey 149–6 in 53.4 overs (Edrich 72*)
Result: Surrey won by 4 wickets
Man of the Match: J. H. Edrich (3)
Adjudicators: A. E. G. Rhodes and T. G. Wilson

41

Worcestershire v Derbyshire at Worcester
Derbyshire 158–9 in 60 overs (Miller 59*)
Worcestershire 153 in 59.4 overs
Result: Derbyshire won by 5 runs
Man of the Match: E. J. Barlow (3)
Adjudicators: R. Julian and F. R. Goodall

7 JULY
Yorkshire v Durham at Middlesbrough
Yorkshire 249–6 in 45 overs (Hampshire 110)
Durham 136–7 in 45 overs (Riddell 52, Old 4–9)
Result: Yorkshire won by 113 runs
Man of the Match: J. H. Hampshire (4)
Adjudicator: C. Washbrook

SECOND ROUND—19 JULY
Northamptonshire v Kent at Northampton
Northamptonshire 248–9 in 60 overs (Willey 77, Shepherd 4–38)
Kent 249–5 in 59.5 overs (Johnson 76, Tavare 54)
Result: Kent won by 5 wickets
Man of the Match: P. Willey (3)
Adjudicator: J. T. Murray

Derbyshire v Middlesex at Derby
Middlesex 199 in 59.2 overs (Gould 58, Radley 52)
Derbyshire 166 in 54 overs (Hill 72)
Result: Middlesex won by 33 runs
Man of the Match: A. Hill
Adjudicator: R. T. Simpson

Essex v Surrey at Colchester
Essex 268–9 in 60 overs (Denness 71, McEwan 52)
Surrey 196 in 58.1 overs (Lever 4–25)
Result: Essex won by 72 runs
Man of the Match: M. H. Denness (2–1 for Kent)
Adjudicators: R. Aspinall and C. G. Pepper

Glamorgan v Somerset at Cardiff
Somerset 330–4 in 60 overs (Denning 145, Richards 52)
Glamorgan 260 in 60 overs (Ontong 64)
Result: Somerset won by 70 runs
Man of the Match: P. W. Denning (3)
Adjudicator: C. Washbrook

Lancashire v Gloucestershire at Old Trafford
Gloucestershire 266–5 in 60 overs (Zaheer 73)
Lancashire 267–3 in 57.3 overs (D. Lloyd 121*, C. H. Lloyd 119*)
Result: Lancashire won by 7 wickets
Man of the Match: D. Lloyd (3)
Adjudicator: W. J. Edrich

Leicestershire v Hampshire at Leicester
Leicestershire 214–8 in 60 overs (Balderstone 73)
Hampshire 140 in 51.2 overs
Result: Leicesershire won by 74 runs
Man of the Match: J. C. Balderstone (2)
Adjudicators: K. F. Barrington

Yorkshire v Nottinghamshire at Bradford
Nottinghamshire 225–7 in 60 overs (Rice 71, Tunnicliffe 53*)
Yorkshire 226–9 in 59.3 overs (Boycott 62)
Result: Yorkshire won by 1 wicket
Man of the Match: C. E. B. Rice
Adjudicator: J. D. Robertson

Staffordshire v Sussex at Stone
Sussex 221–6 in 60 overs (Parker 61)
Staffordshire 219–9 in 60 overs (Nasim-ul-Ghani 85, Hancock 68)
Result: Sussex won by 2 runs
Man of the Match: G. G. Arnold (3–2 for Surrey)
Adjudicator: C. J. Barnett

QUARTER FINALS—AUGUST 2, 3 and 4
Lancashire v Middlesex at Old Trafford
Lancashire 279–6 in 60 overs (Kennedy 131, Lloyd 68)
Middlesex 258 in 57.5 overs (Gatting 62, Radley 58)
Result: Lancashire won by 21 runs
Man of the Match: A. Kennedy
Adjudicator: K. F. Barrington

Kent v Somerset at Canterbury
Kent 120 in 53.5 overs (Dredge 4–23)
Somerset 122–5 in 47 overs
Result: Somerset won by 5 wickets
Man of the Match: C. H. Dredge
Adjudicator: J. D. Robertson

Yorkshire v Sussex at Headingly
Sussex 68–6 in 10 overs (Miandad 27)
Yorkshire 59–8 in 10 overs (Imran Khan 3–22)
Result: Sussex won by 9 runs
Man of the Match: Imran Khan (2–1 for Worcestershire)
Adjudicator: W. J. Edrich

Leicestershire v Essex at Leicester
Essex 73–2 in 10 overs (Phillip 24*)
Leicestershire 70–8 in 10 overs (Lever 4–27)
Result: Essex won by 3 runs
Man of the Match: J. K. Lever (3)
Adjudicators: W. E. Alley and K. E. Palmer

SEMI-FINALS—AUGUST 16
Sussex v Lancashire at Hove
Sussex 277–8 in 60 overs (Miandad 75, Parker 69)
Lancashire 141 in 60 overs
Result: Sussex won by 136 runs
Man of the Match: Javed Miandad
Adjudicator: K. F. Barrington

Somerset v Essex at Taunton
Somerset 287–6 in 60 overs (Richards 116)
Essex 287 in 60 overs (Fletcher 67, Gooch 61)
Result: Somerset won on least wickets lost in tied match
Man of the Match: I. V. A. Richards (2)
Adjudicator: J. C. Laker

THE GILLETTE CUP FINAL
SOMERSET V SUSSEX
Played at Lord's 2 September. Sussex won by 5 wickets

SOMERSET

†B. C. Rose	c Long b Cheatle	30
P. W. Denning	b Imran	0
I. V. A. Richards	c Arnold b Barclay	44
P. M. Roebuck	c Mendis b Cheatle	9
I. T. Botham	b Imran	80
V. J. Marks	c Arnold b Barclay	4
G. I. Burgess	run out	3
‡D. J. S. Taylor	not out	13
J. Garner	not out	8
C. H. Dredge	} did not bat	
K. F. Jennings		
Extras	(LB10 NB6)	16
Total (60 overs) (7 wkts.)		**207**

SUSSEX

J. R. T. Barclay	c Roebuck b Botham	44
G. D. Mendis	c Marks b Burgess	44
P. W. G. Parker	not out	62
Javed Miandad	c Taylor b Garner	3
Imran Khan	c & b Botham	3
C. P. Phillipson	c Taylor b Dredge	3^2
S. J. Storey	not out	0
††A. Long	} did not bat	
G. G. Arnold		
J. Spencer		
R. G. L. Cheatle		
Extras	(B1, LB9, W7, NB9)	26
Total (53.1 overs) (5 wkts.)		**211**

Man of the Match: P. W. G. Parker (2).
Adjudicator: K. F. Barrington.

BOWLING

SUSSEX	O	M	R	W		FALL OF WICKETS	
						Som	Sx
Imran	12	1	50	2		1st	1st
Arnold	12	2	43	0			
Spencer	12	3	27	0	1st	22	93
Cheatle	12	3	50	2	2nd	53	106
Barclay	12	3	21	2	3rd	73	106
					4th	115	110
SOMERSET					5th	151	207
Garner	12	3	34	1	6th	157	—
Dredge	10	2	26	1	7th	194	—
Botham	12	1	65	2	8th	—	—
Jennings	9	1	29	0	9th	—	—
Burgess	10	2	27	1	10th	—	—
Denning	0.1	0	4	0			

GILLETTE CUP
PRINCIPAL RECORDS

Highest innings total: 371–4 off 60 overs, Hampshire v Glamorgan (Southampton) 1975.

Highest innings total by a Minor County: 224–7 off 60 overs, Buckinghamshire v Cambridgeshire (Cambridge) 1972.

Highest innings total by a side batting second: 297–4 off 57.1 overs, Somerset v Warwickshire (Taunton) 1978.

Highest innings total by a side batting first and losing: 292–5 off 60 overs, Warwickshire v Somerset (Taunton) 1978.

Lowest innings total: 41 off 20 overs, Cambridgeshire v Buckinghamshire (Cambridge) 1972; 41 off 19.4 overs, Middlesex v Essex (Westcliff) 1972; 41 off 36.1 overs, Shropshire v Essex (Wellington) 1974.

Lowest innings total by a side batting first and winning: 98 off 56.2 overs, Worcestershire v Durham (Chester-le-Street) 1968.

Highest individual innings: 177 C. G. Greenidge, Hampshire v Glamorgan (Southampton) 1975.

Highest individual innings by a Minor County player: 132 G. Robinson, Lincolnshire v Northumberland (Jesmond) 1971.

Record Wicket Partnerships

1st	227	R. E. Marshall & B. L. Reed, Hampshire v Bedfordshire (Goldington)	1968
2nd	223	M. J. Smith & C. T. Radley, Middlesex v Hampshire (Lord's)	1977
3rd	160	B. Wood & F. C. Hayes, Lancashire v Warwickshire (Birmingham)	1976
4th	234*	D. Lloyd & C. H. Lloyd, Lancashire v Gloucestershire (Manchester)	1978
5th	135	J. F. Harvey & I. R. Buxton, Derbyshire v Worcester (Derby)	1972
6th	105	G. S. Sobers & R. A. White, Nottinghamshire v Worcestershire (Worcester)	1974
7th	107	D. R. Shepherd & D. A. Graveney, Gloucestershire v Surrey (Bristol)	1973
8th	69	S. J. Rouse & D. J. Brown, Warwickshire v Middlesex (Lord's)	1977
9th	87	M. A. Nash & A. E. Cordle, Glamorgan v Lincolnshire (Swansea)	1974
10th	45	A. T. Castell & D. W. White, Hampshire v Lancashire (Manchester)	1970

Hat-tricks:	J. D. F. Larter, Northamptonshire v Sussex (Northampton) 1963
	D. A. D. Sydenham, Surrey v Cheshire (Hoylake) 1964
	R. N. S. Hobbs, Essex v Middlesex (Lord's) 1968
	N. M. McVicker, Warwickshire v Lincolnshire (Birmingham) 1971

Seven wickets in an innings: 7–15 A. L. Dixon, Kent v Surrey (The Oval) 1967 P. J. Sainsbury (Hampshire) 7–30 in 1965 and R. D. Jackman (Surrey) 7–33 in 1970 have also achieved this feat.

Most 'Man of the Match' awards: 6 B. L. D'Oliveira (Worcestershire), C. H. Lloyd (Lancashire) and B. Wood (Lancashire); 5 M. C. Cowdrey (Kent), A. W. Greig (Sussex).

80 centuries have been scored in the competition.

1963 Sussex	1971 Lancashire
1964 Sussex	1972 Lancashire
1965 Yorkshire	1973 Gloucestershire
1966 Warwickshire	1974 Kent
1967 Kent	1975 Lancashire
1968 Warwickshire	1976 Northamptonshire
1969 Yorkshire	1977 Middlesex
1970 Lancashire	1978 Sussex

WINNERS OF THE 1978 GILLETTE
'PICK A TEAM' COMPETITION

Readers were asked to pick the best Gillette Cup team from a list of 40 English cricketers who have played in the competition, assuming them all to be at the top of their form. The team picked by the panel of judges was, Geoff Boycott (1), John Edrich (2), Ted Dexter (3), Tom Graveney (4): M. J. K. Smith (Warwickshire) (5), Basil D'Oliveira (6), Jim Parks (7), Ray Illingworth (Captain) (8), Fred Trueman (9), Derek Underwood (10), Bob Willis (11). The batting order is in brackets.

First Prize: £200 J. Gradden, Ledanor, London Road, Hythe, Kent; Second Prize: £100 E. L. Roberts, 72 Minster Road, London NW2; Third Prize: £50 E. Burge, 8 The Verneys, Cheltenham, Gloucestershire GL53 7DB; Fourth Prize: £25 G. P. Wallis, Dept of Genetics, NSBW University College of Swansea; 25 Runners-up: £5 each E. Baker, 68 Mill Street, Farington, Leyland, Preston PR5 2GJ, Lancashire; P. Crompton, 110 Chester Road, Warrington, Cheshire; C. Gilbert, 1 Launcestone Close, Earley, Reading, Berkshire; H. J. Webber, 39 Victoria Road, Bridgwater, Somerset; C. Short, 16 Manor Road, Solihull, West Midlands; F. E. Roberts, 51 Hill Mead, Horsham, Sussex; P. F. Taylor, 63 Stanborough Road, Plymstock, Plymouth, Devon PL9 8TN; D. S. Gall, 18 West Grove, Montpelier, Bristol 6; J. Croft, 62 Waterbeach Road, Dagenham, Essex; A. E. Couper, Cleeveland, St. Pauls Cray Road, Chislehurst, Kent; M. Vere, 56 Manor Park Avenue, Princes Risborough, Aylesbury, Bucks. HP17 9AR; J. D. Woodhead, 6 Edale Rise, Dodworth, Near Barnsley, S. Yorkshire; R. Opala, 10 Violet Road, Carlton, Nottingham; R. D. Allen, 16 Barrie House, 29 St. Edmunds Terrace, St. John's Wood, London NW8; P. A. Jones, 4 Glantane Road, Ystradgynlais, Nr. Swansea SA9 1ES; P. J. Warwick, 107 Brookfield Road, Pollard Park, Bradford 3, Yorkshire; M. Clayton, 45 Wolsey Croft, Sherburn-in-Elmet, Leeds, Yorkshire; D. Gray, 46 Turner Road, Edgware, Middlesex; J. Duffill, 1a Highfield Road, Bromsgrove, Worcestershire BG1 7BD; R. M. Barlow, 73 Enfield Road, Acton, London W3; I. Wilkins, 6 Myatt Road, Offenham, Nr. Evesham, Worcester WR11 5SD; Miss G. E. Pearse, 6 Bramble Close, Kettering, Northants; C. Farmer, Masbury Cottage, High Street, Wrington, Bristol BS18 7QA; V. G. Capsey, Wickhurst Farm, Lamberhurst, Tunbridge Wells, Kent TH3 8BH; K. James, 9 South End, High Pittington, Co. Durham DH6 1AQ.

Each prize carries with it a selection of Gillette products.

KENT'S THIRD
BENSON AND HEDGES CUP

Kent won the Benson and Hedges Cup for the third time
in only seven years of the competition by a comprehensive
victory over Derbyshire who could not match the great
experience of Kent in the one-day game. Derbyshire, at one
time going quite well at 121 for 4, collapsed totally, to be all
out for 147 – no target at all for a side with the batting
talents of Kent, who won for the loss of four wickets.
Woolmer, with 79, dominated Kent's batting and was made
Man of the Match by the chairman of the England selectors,
Alec Bedser. Woolmer had had a couple of slices of luck off
successive balls from the unfortunate Hendrick, being dropped first by Barlow and then Taylor, when he had scored 52,
but the job in hand had been virtually accomplished by then.
John Shepherd had a particularly good match taking four
for 25 in eleven overs, scoring 19 not out, and catching out
Kirsten, top-scorer in the Derbyshire side. In fact, Kirsten
and Miller between them scored 79 of Derbyshire's 147 and
there were 15 extras, leaving the other nine players only 53
runs between them.

When the final Group tables were complete, Middlesex,
Sussex and Leicestershire were all on nine points in Group C,
Sussex getting through to the quarter-finals on striking rate,
and Notts and Surrey were both on seven in Group D, Notts
going through, much to the chagrin of Surrey. No one could
understand Boycott's tactics against Notts, which included
bowling himself as first-change, giving his wicket-keeper,
Bairstow three overs – apparently because Bairstow had clean
bowled Boycott in the nets – and then dropping himself to
number six in the batting order. Not altogether surprisingly,
Notts won, and nosed out Surrey in the bargain, who in a
dismal season all round, could have done with a little bit of
luck.

Notts were swiftly disposed of by Kent in the quarter-
finals by seven wickets and two other sides had comparatively
easy games, Somerset beating Sussex by 102 runs, and
Warwickshire beating Glamorgan by 46, but Derbyshire had
to struggle a little harder to beat Middlesex by 29 runs.
Ironically, both semi-finals were won by 41 runs.

THE BENSON & HEDGES CUP FINAL

DERBYSHIRE v KENT

PLAYED AT LORD'S 22 JULY
KENT WON BY SIX WICKETS

DERBYSHIRE

A. Hill	c Tavare b Jarvis	17
A. J. Borrington	c Downton b Shepherd	0
P. N. Kirsten	c Shepherd b Asif	41
†E. J. Barlow	b Underwood	1
G. Miller	b Shepherd	38
H. Cartwright	c Ealham b Woolmer	12
A. J. Harvey-Walker	b Shepherd	6
‡R. W. Taylor	c Downton b Shepherd	0
P. E. Russell	c Downton b Jarvis	4
R. C. Wincer	not out	6
M. Hendrick	run out	7
Extras (LB10, W4, NB1)		15
Total (54.4 overs)		147

KENT

R. A. Woolmer	c Hendrick b Barlow	79
G. W. Johnson	c Barlow b Russell	16
C. J. Tavare	b Russell	0
Asif Iqbal	c Taylor b Russell	9
†A. G. E. Ealham	not out	23
J. N. Shepherd	not out	19
C. J. C. Rowe		
C. S. Cowdrey		
D. L. Underwood	did not bat	
‡P. R. Downton		
K. B. S. Jarvis		
Extras (LB3, W1, NB1)		
Total (41.4 overs) (4 wkts)		151

Gold Award: R. A. Woolmer (3).
Adjudicator: A. V. Bedser.

BOWLING

KENT	O	M	R	W
Jarvis	9.4	3	19	2
Shepherd	11	2	25	4
Underwood	11	3	22	1
Woolmer	10	2	15	1
Asif	8	1	26	1
Johnson	5	0	25	0
DERBYSHIRE				
Hendrick	11	2	23	0
Wincer	7	0	29	0
Russell	11	2	28	0
Barlow	8.4	0	44	1
Miller	2	0	8	0
Kirsten	2	0	14	0

FALL OF WICKETS

	D 1st	K 1st
1st	11	32
2nd	32	34
3rd	33	70
4th	88	117
5th	121	—
6th	127	—
7th	127	—
8th	132	—
9th	134	—
10th	147	—

BENSON & HEDGES CUP
PRINCIPAL RECORDS

Highest innings total: 327–4 off 55 overs, Leicestershire v Warwickshire (Coventry) 1972.

Highest innings total by a side batting second: 282 off 50.5 overs, Gloucestershire v Hampshire (Bristol) 1974.

Highest innings total by a side batting first and losing: 268–5 off 55 overs, Leicestershire v Worcestershire (Worcester) 1976.

Lowest completed innings total: 61 off 26 overs, Sussex v Middlesex (Hove) 1978.

Highest individual innings: 173* C. G. Greenidge, Hampshire v Minor Counties (South) (Amersham) 1973.

54 centuries have been scored in the competition.

Record Wicket Partnerships

1st	199	M. J. Harris & B. Hassan, Nottinghamshire v Yorkshire (Hull) 1973.
2nd	285*	C. G. Greenidge & D. R. Turner, Hampshire v Minor Counties (South) (Amersham) 1973.
3rd	227	M. E. J. C. Norman & B. F. Davison, Leicestershire v Warwickshire (Coventry) 1972.
	227	D. Lloyd & F. C. Hayes, Lancashire v Minor Counties (North) (Manchester) 1973.
4th	165*	Mushtaq Mohammad & W. Larkins, Northamptonshire v Essex (Chelmsford) 1977.
5th	134	M. Maslin & D. N. F. Slade, Minor Counties (East) v Nottinghamshire (Nottingham) 1976.
6th	114	M. J. Khan & G. P. Ellis, Glamorgan v Gloucestershire (Bristol) 1975.
7th	102	E. W. Jones & M. A. Nash, Glamorgan v Hampshire (Swansea) 1976.
8th	109	R. E. East & N. Smith, Essex v Northamptonshire (Chelmsford) 1977.
9th	81	J. N. Shepherd & D. L. Underwood, Kent v Middlesex (Lord's) 1975.
10th	61	J. M. Rice & A. M. E. Roberts, Hampshire v Gloucestershire (Bristol) 1975.

Note: A higher 1st wicket partnership of 224 occurred between Sadiq Mohammad, A. W. Stovold and Zaheer Abbas for Gloucestershire v Worcestershire (Worcester) 1975, Sadiq retiring hurt after 67 runs had been scored.

Hat-tricks: G. D. McKenzie, Leicestershire v Worcestershire (Worcester) 1972. K. Higgs, Leicestershire v Surrey (Lord's) 1974. A. A. Jones Middlesex v Essex (Lord's) 1977, M. J. Procter, Gloucestershire v Hampshire (Southampton) 1977.

Seven wickets in an innings: 7–12 W. W. Daniel, Middlesex v Minor Counties (East) (Ipswich) 1978.

Most 'Gold' awards: 9 J. H. Edrich (Surrey), 8 B. Wood (Lancashire).

BENSON & HEDGES CUP WINNERS

1972 Leicestershire	1976 Kent
1973 Kent	1977 Gloucestershire
1974 Surrey	1978 Kent
1975 Leicestershire	

Why not a Gillette Techmatic Bat?

HAMPSHIRE WIN THE
JOHN PLAYER LEAGUE

Once again the John Player League produced a dramatic finish to the season when Somerset, having only to beat Essex at Taunton to win the John Player League for the first time failed to do so and so let in Hampshire. Even then there was a third contender breathing down both their necks – Leicestershire – and in the end, all three finished with 48 points, Hampshire winning by the technical yard-sticks which pertain in this competition.

The whole table produced a remarkable turn-around from the previous season. Hampshire in 1977 were fourth and Somerset ninth, whilst at the bottom of the table in 1978 were Middlesex (third in 1977), Warwickshire (ninth in 1977) and Gloucestershire (sixth in 1977). Weather plays an important part in this competition especially in a consistently bad summer like 1978, but few would begrudge Hampshire their success.

JOHN PLAYER LEAGUE
PRINCIPAL RECORDS

Highest innings total: 307–4 off 38 overs, Worcestershire v Derbyshire (Worcester) 1975.

Highest innings total by side batting second: 261–8 off 39.1 overs, Warwickshire v Nottinghamshire (Birmingham) 1976.

Highest innings total by side batting first and losing: 260–5 off 40 overs, Nottinghamshire v Warwickshire (Birmingham) 1976.

Lowest completed innings total: 23 off 19.4 overs, Middlesex v Yorkshire (Leeds) 1974.

Highest individual innings: 155* B. A. Richards, Hampshire v Yorkshire (Hull), 1970.

124 centuries have been scored in the League.

Record Wicket Partnerships

1st	218	A. R. Butcher & G. P. Howarth, Surrey v Gloucestershire (Oval) 1976.
2nd	179	B. W. Luckhurst & M. H. Denness, Kent v Somerset (Canterbury) 1973.
3rd	182	H. Pilling & C. H. Lloyd, Lancashire v Somerset (Manchester) 1970.
4th	175*	M. J. K. Smith & D. L. Amiss, Warwickshire v Yorkshire (Birmingham) 1970.
5th	163	A. G. E. Ealham & B. D. Julien, Kent v Leicestershire (Leicester) 1977.

6th	121	C. P. Wilkins & A. J. Borrington, Derbyshire v Warwickshire (Chesterfield) 1972.				
7th	96*	R. Illingworth & J. Birkenshaw, Leicestershire v Somerset (Leicester) 1971.				
8th	95*	D. Breakwell & K. F. Jennings, Somerset v Nottinghamshire (Nottingham) 1976.				
9th	86	D. P. Hughes & P. Lever, Lancashire v Essex (Leyton) 1973.				
10th	57	D. A. Graveney & J. B. Mortimore, Gloucestershire v Lancashire (Tewkesbury) 1973.				

Four wickets in four balls: A. Ward, Derbyshire v Sussex (Derby) 1970.

Hat-tricks (excluding above): R. Palmer, Somerset v Gloucestershire (Bristol) 1970, K. D. Boyce, Essex v Somerset (Westcliff) 1971, G. D. McKenzie, Leicestershire v Essex (Leicester) 1972, R. G. D. Willis, Warwickshire v Yorkshire (Birmingham) 1973, W. Blenkiron, Warwickshire v Derbyshire (Buxton), 1974, A. Buss, Sussex v Worcestershire (Hastings) 1974, J. M. Rice, Hampshire v Northamptonshire (Southampton) 1975, M. A. Nash, Glamorgan v Worcestershire (Worcester) 1975, A. Hodgson, Northamptonshire v Sussex (Northampton) 1976.

Eight wickets in an innings: 8–26 K. D. Boyce, Essex v Lancashire (Manchester) 1971.

JOHN PLAYER LEAGUE CHAMPIONS

1969	Lancashire	1974	Leicestershire
1970	Lancashire	1975	Hampshire
1971	Worcestershire	1976	Kent
1972	Kent	1977	Leicestershire
1973	Kent	1978	Hampshire

JOHN PLAYER LEAGUE FINAL TABLE

	P	W	L	NR	Pts	Run Rate	Sixes
1 Hampshire (4)	16	11	3	2	48	5.355	42
2 Somerset (9)	16	11	3	2	48	4.580	24
3 Leicestershire (1)	16	11	3	2	48	4.265	17
4 Worcestershire (13)	16	10	5	1	42		22
5 Lancashire (16)	16	9	6	1	38		27
6 Essex (2)	16	7	6	3	34		16
7 Yorkshire (13)	16	7	7	2	32		19
8 Derbyshire (9)	16	6	7	3	30		20
Sussex (4)	16	6	7	3	30		12
10 Glamorgan (8)	16	6	8	2	28		16
Kent (6)	16	6	8	2	28		13
Surrey (13)	16	6	8	2	28		19
13 Northamptonshire (17)	16	5	8	3	16		25
Nottinghamshire (12)	16	4	7	5	16		19
15 Middlesex (3)	16	5	9	2	24		13
16 Warwickshire (9)	16	4	11	1	18		15
17 Gloucestershire (6)	16	3	11	2	16		24

1977 positions in brackets

KENT WIN SCHWEPPES
OUTRIGHT IN 1978

Kent pressed home their superiority in the summer of 1978, having had to share the County Championship with Middlesex in 1977. It had been suggested that with their Packer players available all season Kent ought to finish on top; but it might be mentioned that Kent have not done too badly in previous seasons when they have lost three or four players to Test matches. Their success reflects great credit on Alan Ealham who was suddenly thrust into the limelight to captain Kent in place of the dismissed Asif. Young players were given their chances, especially Downton who kept wicket regularly, and Tavare, Rowe and Cowdrey. Tavare had an extremely good season finishing with an average of 43.06 and Rowe had an average of 33.79. Many feel that Tavare is being groomed for a place in the England side and there were whispers that he might have gone to Australia. Underwood had a marvellous season for Kent, taking 110 wickets at a cost of 14.49 and proving again – though no proof was necessary – that he is one of the world's great bowlers, ranking with the greats of all-time.

Essex hoisted themselves from sixth in 1977 to second place in 1978 and, Kent excepted, proved to be the best balanced team in the country. The signing of Phillip in an effort to plug the gap left by the departure of Keith Boyce proved to be a master-stroke, and his bowling and attractive batting were invaluable assets. The brunt of the attack however was borne by Lever and East, Lever finishing close on the heels of Underwood with 97 wickets for Essex. McEwan and Fletcher headed the batting averages with Gooch close behind; Gooch's promotion to opener serving Essex and England well.

Third in the table were Middlesex, who in 1977 had shared the spoils with Kent. Middlesex did, of course, make major contributions to Test cricket – Brearley, Edmonds, Radley, Emburey – and it is to their great credit that despite this, they were still able to offer a serious challenge for the Championship. Theirs was largely an all-round performance; someone always got runs when they were needed, and six of their players scored centuries. Selvey was only six short of

100 wickets for Middlesex though Daniel came out with the best bowling average – 75 wickets at 14.50.

Despite their many problems, Yorkshire finished in fourth place behind Middlesex having only made twelfth position the previous season. It was not Boycott however but Hampshire who headed the batting averages with a remarkable 54.18, Boycott following closely behind with 50.94. Old's injury and a lack of penetration in the bowling hampered Yorkshire's efforts to bring back the feats of days gone by and win the Championship.

Somerset – nearly Gillette Cup-winners, nearly John Player League Champions, fancied at one time for the Championship as well – finished fifth: an exceptionally good season if somewhat disappointing for their supporters. Richards, Slocombe and Rose all scored 1,000 runs, but there was no one decisive bowler like an Underwood or a Lever to make sure of ultimate success.

One of the success stories of the summer was the rise of Nottinghamshire from bottom place in 1977 to seventh in 1978, almost entirely due to the superb performance of Clive Rice.

SCHWEPPES COUNTY CHAMPIONSHIP
FINAL TABLE

		P	W	D	L	NR	Bt	Bw	Pts
1	Kent (1)	22	13	6	3	0	56	80	292
2	Essex (6)	22	12	9	1	0	55	74	273
3	Middlesex (1)	22	11	5	5	1	48	75	255
4	Yorkshire (12)	22	10	9	3	0	58	55	233
5	Somerset (4)	22	9	9	4	0	44	76	228
6	Leicestershire (5)	22	4	13	5	0	57	68	173
7	Nottinghamshire (17)	22	3	12	7	0	63	67	166
8	Hampshire (11)	22	4	11	6	1	53	60	161
9	Sussex* (8)	22	4	11	7	0	39	64	151
10	Gloucestershire (3)	22	4	9	8	1	42	55	145
11	Warwickshire (10)	22	4	13	5	0	39	56	143
12	Lancashire* (16)	22	4	9	8	1	28	59	135
13	Glamorgan (14)	22	3	11	8	0	43	54	133
14	Derbyshire (7)	22	3	12	7	0	33	63	132
15	Worcestershire (13)	22	2	15	5	0	56	51	131
16	Surrey (14)	22	3	12	7	0	36	58	130
17	Northamptonshire (9)	22	2	12	6	2	41	56	121

1977 positions in brackets.
*Six points deducted for breach of regulations.

COUNTY CHAMPIONS

1864	Surrey	1895	Surrey	1939	Yorkshire
1865	Nottinghamshire	1896	Yorkshire	1946	Yorkshire
1866	Middlesex	1897	Lancashire	1947	Middlesex
1867	Yorkshire	1898	Yorkshire	1948	Glamorgan
1868	Nottinghamshire	1899	Surrey	1949 {	Middlesex
1869 {	Nottinghamshire	1900	Yorkshire		Yorkshire
	Yorkshire	1901	Yorkshire	1950 {	Lancashire
1870	Yorkshire	1902	Yorkshire		Surrey
1871	Nottinghamshire	1903	Middlesex	1951	Warwickshire
1872	Nottinghamshire	1904	Lancashire	1952	Surrey
1873 {	Gloucestershire	1905	Yorkshire	1953	Surrey
	Nottinghamshire	1906	Kent	1954	Surrey
1874	Gloucestershire	1907	Nottinghamshire	1955	Surrey
1875	Nottinghamshire	1908	Yorkshire	1956	Surrey
1876	Gloucestershire	1909	Kent	1957	Surrey
1877	Gloucestershire	1910	Kent	1958	Surrey
1878	Undecided	1911	Warwickshire	1959	Yorkshire
1879 {	Lancashire	1912	Yorkshire	1960	Yorkshire
	Nottinghamshire	1913	Kent	1961	Hampshire
1880	Nottinghamshire	1914	Surrey	1962	Yorkshire
1881	Lancashire	1919	Yorkshire	1963	Yorkshire
1882 {	Lancashire	1920	Middlesex	1964	Worcestershire
	Nottinghamshire	1921	Middlesex	1965	Worcestershire
1883	Nottinghamshire	1922	Yorkshire	1966	Yorkshire
1884	Nottinghamshire	1923	Yorkshire	1967	Yorkshire
1885	Nottinghamshire	1924	Yorkshire	1968	Yorkshire
1886	Nottinghamshire	1925	Yorkshire	1969	Glamorgan
1887	Surrey	1926	Lancashire	1970	Kent
1888	Surrey	1927	Lancashire	1971	Surrey
1889 {	Lancashire	1928	Lancashire	1972	Warwickshire
	Nottinghamshire	1929	Nottinghamshire	1973	Hampshire
	Surrey	1930	Lancashire	1974	Worcestershire
1890	Surrey	1931	Yorkshire	1975	Leicestershire
1891	Surrey	1932	Yorkshire	1976	Middlesex
1892	Surrey	1933	Yorkshire	1977 {	Kent
1893	Yorkshire	1934	Lancashire		Middlesex
1894	Surrey	1935	Yorkshire	1978	Kent
		1936	Derbyshire		
		1937	Yorkshire		
		1938	Yorkshire		

Fifteen Test matches have been completed in two days, the most recent being in the winter of 1945–46 when Australia bowled New Zealand out for 42 and 54. Australia used five bowlers in the second innings and all five took wickets.

Who changed the face of English bowling?

Some say Gillette, others the BBC. Really they're both right. Gone are the days when a bowler trudged back to his mark, alone in a batsman-hating reverie. Today, the camera follows every frown and fumble: for twenty camera-hogging yards he impresses his personality upon an expectant cricket-watching audience.

Some bowlers thrive on it, some take drama classes, others crack under the strain. All pay for more attention to their shaves—which means Gillette blades—either Platinum or Super Silver. Both give a shave that stays beyond criticism until stumps.

Gillette BLADES
As keen as cup cricket

THE COUNTIES AND
THEIR PLAYERS
Compiled by Michael Fordham

Abbreviations

B	Born	HSC	Highest score for County if different from highest first-class score
RHB	Right-hand bat		
LHB	Left-hand bat		
RF	Right-arm fast	HSGC	Highest score Gillette Cup
RFM	Right-arm fast medium	HSJPL	Highest score John Player League
RM	Right-arm medium		
LF	Left-arm fast	HSBH	Highest score Benson & Hedges Cup
LFM	Left-arm fast medium		
LM	Left-arm medium	BB	Best bowling figures
OB	Off-break	BBUK	Best bowling figures in this country
LB	Leg-break		
LBG	Leg-break and googly	BBTC	Best bowling figures in Test cricket if different from above
SLA	Slow left-arm orthodox		
SLC	Slow left-arm 'chinaman'		
WK	Wicket-keeper	BBC	Best bowling figures for County if different from above
*	Not out or unfinished stand		
HS	Highest score	BBGC	Best bowling figures Gillette Cup
HSUK	Highest score in this country		
		BBJPL	Best bowling figures John Player League
HSTC	Highest score in Test cricket if different from above	BBBH	Best bowling figures Benson & Hedges Cup

When a player is known by a name other than his first name, the name in question has been underlined.

All Test match appearances are complete to 30 September 1978.

'Debut' denotes 'first-class debut' and 'Cap' means '1st XI county cap'.

Wisden 1978' indicates that a player was selected as one of *Wisden's* Five Cricketers of the Year for his achievements in 1978.

Owing to the increasing number of privately arranged overseas tours of short duration, only those which may be regarded as major tours have been included.

DERBYSHIRE

Formation of present club: 1870.
Colours: Chocolate, amber, and pale blue.
Badge: Rose and crown.
County Champions (1): 1936.
Gillette Cup finalists: 1969.
Best final position in John Player League: 3rd in 1970.
Benson & Hedges Cup Finalists: 1978.
Gillette Man of the Match Awards: 15.
Benson & Hedges Gold Awards: 20.
Secretary: D. A. Harrison, County Cricket
Ground: Nottingham Road, Derby, DE2 6DA
Captain: D. S. Steele

DERBYSHIRE

Iain Stuart ANDERSON (Dovecliff GS and Wulfric School, Burton-on-Trent) B Derby 24/4/1960. RHB, OB. Debut 1978. Is studying at University and will not be available for first half of season. HS: 75 v Worcs (Worcester) 1978.

Anthony John (Tony) BORRINGTON (Spondon Park GS) B Derby 8/12/1948. RHB, LB. Played for MCC Schools at Lord's in 1967. Played in one John Player League match in 1970. Debut 1971. Cap 1977. Benson & Hedges Gold awards: 3. HS: 137 v Yorks (Sheffield) 1978. HSGC: 28 v Hants (Southampton) 1976. HSJPL: 101 v Somerset (Taunton) 1977. HSBH: 81 v Notts (Nottingham) 1974. Trained as a teacher at Loughborough College of Education.

Harold CARTWRIGHT B Halfway (Derbyshire) 12/5/1951. RHB. Played in John Player and Gillette Cup matches in 1971 and 1972. Debut 1973. Cap 1978. Benson & Hedges Gold Awards: 1. HS: 141* v Warwickshire (Chesterfield) 1977. HSGC: 36 v Somerset (Ilkeston) 1977. HSJPL: 76* v Middlesex (Chesterfield) 1973. HSBH: 56* v Minor Counties (West) (Derby) 1978.

Michael (Mike) HENDRICK B Darley Dale (Derbyshire) 22/10/1948. RHB, RFM. Debut 1969. Cap 1972. Elected Best Young Cricketer of the Year in 1973 by the Cricket Writers Club. *Wisden* 1977. Tests: 16 between 1974 and 1978. Tours: West Indies 1973–74, Australia and New Zealand 1974–75, Pakistan and New Zealand 1977–78, Australia 1978–79. Gillette Man of the Match awards: 1. Benson & Hedges Gold awards: 3. HS: 46 v Essex (Chelmsford) 1973. HSTC: 15 v Australia (Oval) 1977. HSGC: 17 v Middlesex (Derby) 1978. HSJPL: 21 v Warwickshire (Buxton) 1974. HSBH: 32 v Notts (Chesterfield) 1973. BB: 8–45 v Warwickshire (Chesterfield) 1973. BBTC: 4–28 v India (Birmingham) 1974. BBGC: 4–16 v Middlesex (Chesterfield) 1975. BBJPL: 6–7 v Notts (Nottingham) 1972. BBBH: 5–30 v Notts (Chesterfield) 1975 and 5–30 v Lancs (Southport) 1976.

Alan HILL (New Mills GS) B Buxworth (Derbyshire) 29/6/1950. RHB, OB. Joined staff 1970. Debut 1972. Cap 1976. Played for Orange Free State in 1976–77 Currie Cup competition. Gillette Man of the Match awards: 1. Benson & Hedges Gold awards: 1. 1,000 runs (2) – 1,303 runs (av. 34.28) in 1976 best. HS: 160* v Warwickshire (Coventry) 1976. HSGC: 72 v Middlesex (Derby) 1978. HSJPL: 120 v Northants (Buxton) 1976. HSBH: 102* v Warwickshire (Ilkeston) 1978. BB: 3–5 Orange Free State v Northern Transvaal (Pretoria) 1976–77.

Peter Noel KIRSTEN (South African College School, Cape Town). B Pietermaritzburg, Natal, South Africa 14/5/1955. RHB, OB. Debut for Western Province in Currie Cup 1973–74. Played for Sussex v Australians 1975 as well as playing for county 2nd XI. Played for Derbyshire 2nd XI in 1977 and made debut for county in 1978. Scored 4 centuries in 4 consecutive innings and 6 in 7 innings including two in match – 173* and 103 Western Province v Eastern Province 1976–77. Scored 1,133 runs (av. 36.54) in 1978. Also scored 1,074 runs (av. 76.71) in 1976–77. HS: 206* v Glamorgan (Chesterfield) 1978. HSJPL: 88 v Glos (Derby) 1978. HSBH: 41 v Kent (Lord's) 1978. BB: 4–51 v Notts (Derby) 1978. BBJPL: 4–13 v Hants (Bournemouth) 1978.

John Wilton LISTER B Darlington 1/4/1959. RHB, RM. Debut 1978. HS: 48 v Warwickshire (Birmingham) 1978.

58

Alan James McLELLAN (Williamstown HS, Melbourne, Australia and Hartshead Secondary School, Ashton-under-Lyne). B Ashton-under-Lyne (Lancashire) 2/9/1958. RHB, WK. Played for both Derbyshire and Lancs 2nd XIs in 1977. Debut 1978. HS: 11* v Surrey (Ilkeston) 1978.

Alan John MELLOR (Dovecliff GS). B Burton-on-Trent 4/7/1959. RHB, SLA. Played for 2nd XI since 1976. Debut 1978. HS: 10* v Essex (Southend) 1978. BB: 5–52 v Kent (Maidstone) 1978 (in debut match).

Geoffrey (Geoff) MILLER (Chesterfield GS) B Chesterfield 8/9/1952. RHB, OB. Toured India 1970–71 and West Indies 1972 with England Young Cricketers. Won Sir Frank Worrell Trophy as Outstanding Boy Cricketer of 1972. Debut 1973. Cap 1976. Elected Best Young Cricketer of the Year in 1976 by the Cricket Writers Club. Tests: 14 between 1976 and 1978. Tours: India, Sri Lanka and Australia 1976–77, Pakistan and New Zealand 1977–78, Australia 1978–79. Benson & Hedges Gold awards: 1. HS: 98* England v Pakistan (Lahore) 1977–78. HSUK: 95 v Lancs (Manchester) 1978. HSGC: 59* v Worcs (Worcester) 1978. HSJPL: 44 v Kent (Chesterfield) 1973. HSBH: 75 v Warwickshire (Derby) 1977. BB: 7–54 v Sussex (Hove) 1977. BBTC: 3–99 v New Zealand (Auckland) 1977–78. BBJPL: 4–22 v Yorks (Huddersfield) 1978.

Philip Edgar (Phil) RUSSELL (Ilkeston GS) B Ilkeston 9/5/1944. RHB, RM/OB. Debut 1965. Not re-engaged after 1972 season, but rejoined staff in 1974 and is now county coach. Cap 1975. HS: 72 v Glamorgan (Swansea) 1970. HSGC: 27* v Middlesex (Derby) 1978. HSJPL: 47* v Glamorgan (Buxton) 1975. HSBH: 22* v Lancs (Southport) 1976. BB: 7–46 v Yorks (Sheffield) 1976. BBGC: 3–44 v Somerset (Taunton) 1975. BBJPL: 6–10 v Northants (Buxton) 1976. BBBH: 3–28 v Kent (Lord's) 1978.

David Stanley STEELE B Stoke-on-Trent 29/9/41. Elder brother of J. F. Steele of Leics and cousin of B. S. Crump, former Northants player. Wears glasses. RHB, SLA. Played for Staffordshire from 1958 to 1962. Debut for Northants 1963. Cap. 1965. Benefit (£25,500) in 1975. *Wisden* 1975. Has joined Derbyshire for 1979 as County Captain. Tests: 8 in 1975 and 1976. 1,000 runs (9) – 1,756 runs (av. 48.77) 1975 best. Had match double of 100 runs and 10 wkts. (130, 6–36 and 5–39) v Derbyshire (Northampton) 1978. Gillette Man of Match Awards: 1 (for Northants). HS: 140* Northants v Worcs. (Worcester) 1971. HTSC: 106 v West Indies (Nottingham) 1976. HSGC: 109 Northants v Cambs. (March) 1975. HSJPL: 76 Northants (Hove) 1974. HSBH: 69 Northants v Warwickshire (Northampton) 1974. HSBH: 69 Northants v Warwickshire (Northampton) 1974. BB: 8–29 Northants v. Lancs (Northampton) 1966.

Frederick William (Fred) SWARBROOK B Derby 17/12/1950. LHB, SLA. Debut 1967 aged 16 years 6 months, youngest player ever to appear for county. Cap 1975. Played for Griqualand West between 1972–73 and 1976–77 in Currie Cup competition. Gillette Man of the Match awards: 2. HS: 90 v Essex (Leyton) 1970. HSGC: 58* v Surrey (Ilkeston) 1976. HSJPL: 42*v Glamorgan (Ilkeston) 1977 and 42* v Notts (Ilkeston) 1977. HSBH: 20* v Hants (Southampton) 1976. BB: 9–20 (13–62 match) v Sussex (Hove) 1975. BBGC: 3–53 v Middlesex (Chesterfield) 1975. BBJPL: 4–15 v Glos (Bristol) 1976. BBBH: 4–33 v Warwickshire (Ilkeston) 1978. Soccer for Derby County Juniors.

DERBYSHIRE

Robert William (Bob) TAYLOR B Stoke 17/7/1941. RHB, WK, RM. Played for Bignall End (N. Staffs and S. Cheshire League) when only 15 and for Staffordshire from 1958 to 1960. Debut 1960 for Minor Counties v South Africans (Stoke-on-Trent). Debut for county 1961. Cap 1962. Testimonial (£6,672) in 1973. Appointed county captain during 1975 season. Relinquished post during 1976 season. *Wisden* 1976. Tests: 13 between 1970–71 and 1978. Tours: Australia and New Zealand 1970–71, 1974–75, Australia with Rest of the World team 1971–72, West Indies 1973–74, Pakistan and New Zealand 1977–78, Australia 1978–79. Withdrew from India, Sri Lanka, and Pakistan tour 1972–73. Dismissed 80 batsmen (77 ct 3 st) in 1962. 83 batsmen (81 ct 2 st) in 1963, and 86 batsmen (79 ct 7 st) in 1965. Dismissed 10 batsmen in match, all caught v Hants (Chesterfield) 1963 and 7 in innings, all caught v Glamorgan (Derby) 1966. Gillette Man of Match awards: 1. Benson & Hedges Gold awards: 1. HS: 97 International Wanderers v South African Invitation XI (Johannesburg) 1975–76. HSUK: 74* v Glamorgan (Derby) 1971. HSTC: 45 v New Zealand (Christchurch) 1977–78. HSGC: 53* v Middlesex (Lord's) 1965. HSJPL: 43* v Glos (Burton-on-Trent) 1969. HSBH: 31* v Hants (Southampton) 1976.

Colin John TUNNICLIFFE B Derby 11/8/1951. RHB, LFM. Debut 1973. Left staff after 1974 season. Re-appeared in 1976. Cap 1977. HS: 82* v Middlesex (Ilkeston) 1977. HSGC: 13 v Somerset (Ilkeston) 1977. HSJPL: 42 v Yorks (Huddersfield) 1978. HSBH: 25* v Minor Counties (North) (Derby) 1974. BB: 4–22 v Middlesex (Ilkeston) 1977. BBJPL: 3–12 v Essex (Chesterfield) 1974. BBBH: 3–16 v Lancs (Manchester) 1978.

John WALTERS B Brampton (Yorks) 7/8/1949. LHB, RFM. Has played in Huddersfield League. Debut 1977. HS: 90 v Yorks (Chesterfield) 1978. HSJPL: 55* v Worcs (Worcester) 1978. BB: 3–70 v Hants (Derby) 1978.

Robert Colin (Bob) WINCER (Hemsworth GS, Yorkshire) B Portsmouth 2/4/1952. LHB, RFM. Debut 1978. HS: 16* v Yorks (Chesterfield) 1978. BB: 4–42 v Leics (Derby) 1978.

John Geoffrey WRIGHT (Christ's College, Christchurch and Otago University) B Darfield, New Zealand 5/7/1954. LHB, RM. Debut for Northern Districts in Shell Cup in 1975–76. Debut for county 1977. Cap 1977. Tests: 5 for New Zealand in 1977–78 and 1978 tour: New Zealand to England 1978. Scored 1,080 runs (av 32.72) in 1977. Benson & Hedges Gold awards: 1. HS: 164 v Pakistanis (Chesterfield) 1978. HSTC: 62 New Zealand v England (Oval) 1978. HSGC: 87* v Sussex (Hove) 1977. HSJPL: 75 v Glos (Heanor) 1977. HSBH: 102 v Worcs (Chesterfield) 1977.

NB: The following players whose particulars appeared in the 1978 Annual have been omitted: E. J. Barlow (left staff), J. M. H. Graham-Brown (not re-engaged), A. J. Harvey-Walker (not re-engaged), A. Morris (not re-engaged) and R. S. Swindell.

The career records of Barlow, Graham-Brown, Harvey-Walker and Morris will be found elsewhere in this Annual.

COUNTY AVERAGES

Schweppes Championship: Played 22, won 3, drawn 12, lost 7
All first-class matches: Played 24, won 3, drawn 14, lost 7

BATTING AND FIELDING

Cap		M	I	NO	Runs	HS	Avge	100	50	Ct	St
1976	G. Miller	12	20	4	604	95	37.75	—	5	13	—
1978	P. N. Kirsten	20	35	4	1133	206*	36.54	1	7	11	—
1976	E. J. Barlow	16	25	4	765	127	36.42	1	3	25	—
1977	J. G. Wright	4	7	0	226	164	32.28	1	—	1	—
1977	A. J. Borrington	17	27	3	669	137	27.87	1	2	3	—
—	J. Walters	14	22	4	482	90	26.77	—	2	2	—
1975	F. W. Swarbrook	12	16	6	240	60*	24.00	—	1	5	—
1976	A. Hill	24	41	1	928	153*	23.20	1	2	12	—
—	J. W. Lister	3	6	0	137	48	22.83	—	—	1	—
—	A. J. Harvey-Walker	9	13	2	230	80	20.90	—	2	4	—
1978	H. Cartwright	24	37	4	644	77*	19.51	—	2	8	—
—	A. Morris	5	7	0	116	55	16.57	—	1	4	—
—	I. S. Anderson	6	10	1	140	75	15.55	—	1	3	—
1972	M. Hendrick	14	13	6	108	33	15.42	—	—	6	—
—	J. M. H. Graham-Brown	11	17	2	209	43	13.93	—	—	1	—
1962	R. W. Taylor	10	12	1	136	32	12.36	—	—	24	2
1975	P. E. Russell	15	12	2	90	22	9.00	—	—	15	—
1977	C. J. Tunnicliffe	19	23	4	146	45	7.68	—	—	7	—
—	R. C. Wincer	10	10	4	43	16*	7.16	—	—	5	—
—	A. J. Mellor	5	7	2	19	10*	3.80	—	—	1	—
—	A. J. McLellan	14	14	5	27	11*	3.00	—	—	17	—

BOWLING

	Type	O	M	R	W	Avge	Best	5 wI	10 wM
M. Hendrick	RFM	393.5	129	781	56	13.94	5-32	2	—
P. E. Russell	RM/OB	235.4	88	423	21	20.14	4-23	—	—
E. J. Barlow	RM	214.5	58	528	24	22.00	4-34	—	—
A. J. Harvey-Walker	OB	145	42	408	17	24.00	7-35	1	1
C. J. Tunnicliffe	LFM	456.4	127	1241	44	28.20	4-30	—	—
F. W. Swarbrook	SLA	134	43	344	12	28.66	4-22	—	—
G. Miller	OB	371.2	121	869	30	28.96	5-43	2	—
J. Walters	RFM	166	31	497	16	31.06	3-70	—	—
P. N. Kirsten	OB	207.4	55	581	18	32.27	4-51	—	—
A. J. Mellor	SLA	106	33	305	9	33.88	5-52	1	—
R. C. Wincer	RFM	203.2	40	680	19	35.78	4-42	—	—
J. M. H. Graham-Brown	RM	114.2	28	338	7	48.28	2-23	—	—

Also bowled I. S. Anderson 43–10–150–2; H. Cartwright 1–0–1–0;
A. Hill 2–0–14–0; A. Morris 16–2–58–0.

County Records

First-class cricket

Highest innings	For....645 v Hampshire (Derby)		1898
totals:	Agst....662 by Yorkshire (Chesterfield)		1898
Lowest innings	For....16 v Nottinghamshire (Nottingham)		1879
totals:	Agst.... 23 by Hampshire (Burton-on-Trent)		1958
Highest indi-	For....274 G. Davidson v Lancashire (Manchester)		1896
vidual innings:	Agst....343* P. A. Perrin for Essex (Chesterfield)		1904
Best bowling	For....10–40 W. Bestwick v Glamorgan (Cardiff)		1921
in an innings:	Agst....10–47 T. F. Smailes for Yorkshire (Sheffield)		1939
Best bowling	For....16–84 C. Gladwin v Worcs (Stourbridge)		1952
in a match:	Agst....16–101 G. Giffen for Australians (Derby)		1886
Most runs in a season:	2165 (av. 48.1) D. B. Carr		1959
runs in a career:	20516 (av 31.41) D. Smith	1927–1952	
100s in a season:	6 by L. F. Townsend		1933
100s in a career:	30 by D. Smith	1927–1952	
wickets in a season:	168 (av 19.55) T. B. Mitchell		1935
wickets in a career:	1670 (av 17.11) H. L. Jackson	1947–1963	

RECORD WICKET STANDS

1st	322	H. Storer & J. Bowden v Essex (Derby)	1929
2nd	349	C. S. Elliott & J. D. Eggar v Notts (Nottingham)	1947
3rd	246	J. Kelly & D. B. Carr v Leicestershire (Chesterfield)	1957
4th	328	P. Vaulkhard & D. Smith v Notts (Nottingham)	1946
5th	203	C. P. Wilkins & I. R. Buxton v Lancashire (Manchester)	1971
6th	212	G. M. Lee & T. S. Worthington v Essex (Chesterfield)	1932
7th	241*	G. H. Pope & A. E. G. Rhodes v Hampshire (Portsmouth)	1948
8th	182	A. H. M. Jackson & W. Carter v Leicestershire (Leicester)	1922
9th	283	A. R. Warren & J. Chapman v Warwickshire (Blackwell)	1910
0th	93	J. Humphries & J. Horsley v Lancashire (Derby)	1914

One-day cricket

Highest innings	Gillette Cup	250–9 v Hants (Bournemouth)	1963
totals:	John Player League	260–6 v Glos (Derby)	1972
	Benson & Hedges Cup	225–6 v Notts (Nottingham)	1974
Lowest innings	Gillette Cup	79 v Surrey (Oval)	1967
totals:	John Player League	70 v Surrey (Derby)	1972
	Benson & Hedges Cup	102 v Yorks (Bradford)	1975
Highest indi-	Gillette Cup	87* J. G. Wright v Sussex (Hove)	1977
vidual innings:	John Player League	120 A. Hill v Northants (Buxton)	1976
	Benson & Hedges Cup	111* P. J. Sharpe v Glamorgan (Chesterfield)	1976
Best bowling	Gillette Cup	6–18 T. J. P. Eyre v Sussex (Chesterfield)	1969
figures:	John Player League	6–7 M. Hendrick v Notts (Nottingham)	1972
	Benson & Hedges Cup	6–33 E. J. Barlow v Gloucestershire (Bristol)	1978

ESSEX

Formation of present club: 1876.
Colours: Blue, gold and, red.
Badge: Three seaxes with word 'Essex' underneath.
County Championship runners-up: 1978.
Gillette Cup semi-finalists: 1978
John Player League runners-up: (3): 1971, 1976
and 1977.
Benson & Hedges Cup semi-finalists: 1973.
Gillette Man of the Match awards: 13.
Benson & Hedges Gold awards: 16.

Secretary: S. R. Cox, The County Ground, New Writtle Street.
Chelmsford CM2 0RW.
Captain: K. W. R. Fletcher.
Prospects of Play telephone no.: Chelmsford matches only. Chelmsford
(0245) 66794.

David Laurence ACFIELD (Brentwood School & Cambridge) B
Chelmsford 24/7/1947. RHB, OB. Debut 1966. Blue 1967–68. Cap 1970.
HS: 42 Cambridge U v Leics (Leicester) 1967. BB: 7–36 v Sussex (Ilford)
1973. BBJPL: 5–14 v Northants (Northampton) 1970. Also obtained
Blue for fencing (sabre). Has appeared in internationals in this sport and
represented Great Britain in Olympic Games at Mexico City and Munich.

Michael Henry (Mike) DENNESS (Ayr Academy) B Bellshill (Lanark-
shire) 1/12/1940. RHB, RM/OB. Debut for Scotland 1959. Debut for
Kent 1962. Cap 1964. County captain from 1972 to 1976. Benefit (£19,219)
in 1974. *Wisden* 1974. Left county after 1976 season and made debut for
Essex in 1977. Cap 1977. Tests: 28 between 1969 and 1975, captaining
England in 19 Tests between 1973–74 and 1975. Played in one match
against Rest of the World in 1970. Tours: India, Sri Lanka, and Pakistan
1972–73 (vice-captain), West Indies 1973–74 (captain), Australia and New
Zealand 1974–75 (captain). Gillette Man of Match awards: 2 (1 for Kent).
Benson & Hedges Gold awards: 1 (for Kent). 1,000 runs (13)—1,606 runs
(av 31.49) in 1966 best. Scored 1,136 runs (av 54.09) in Australia and New
Zealand 1974–75. HS: 195 v Leics (Leicester) 1977. HSTC: 188 England v
Australia (Melbourne) 1974–75. HSGC: 85 Kent v Leics (Leicester) 1971.
HSJPL: 118* Kent v Yorks (Scarborough) 1976. HSBH: 112* Kent v
Surrey (Oval) 1973.

Raymond Eric (Ray) EAST B Manningtree (Essex) 20/6/1947. RHB,
SLA. Debut 1965. Cap 1967. Benefit in 1978. Hat-trick: The Rest v MCC
Tour XI (Hove) 1973. Benson & Hedges Gold awards: 3. HS: 113 v
Hants (Chelmsford) 1976. HSGC: 38* v Glos (Chelmsford) 1973. HSJPL:
25* v Glamorgan (Colchester) 1976. HSBH: 54 v Northants (Chelmsford)
1977. BB: 8–30 v Notts (Ilford) 1977. HSGC: 4–28 v Herts (Hitchin) 1976.
BBJPL: 6–18 v Yorks (Hull) 1969. BBBH: 5–33 v Kent (Chelmsford) 1975.

ESSEX

Keith William Robert FLETCHER B Worcester 20/5/1944. RHB, LB. Debut 1962. Cap 1963. Appointed county vice-captain in 1971 and county captain in 1974. Benefit (£13,000) in 1973. *Wisden* 1973. Tests: 52 between 1968 and 1976–77. Also played in 4 matches v Rest of the World in 1970. Tours: Pakistan 1966–67, Ceylon and Pakistan 1968–69, Australia and New Zealand, 1970–71, 1974–75, India, Sri Lanka and Pakistan 1972–73, West Indies 1973–74, India, Sri Lanka and Australia 1976–77. 1,000 runs (14)—1,890 runs (av 41.08) in 1968 best. Scored two centuries in match (111 and 102*) v Notts (Nottingham) 1976. Gillette Man of Match awards: 1. Benson & Hedges Gold awards: 1. HS: 228* v Sussex (Hastings) 1968. HSTC: 216 v New Zealand (Auckland) 1974–75. HSGC: 74 v Notts (Nottingham) 1969. HSJPL: 99* v Notts (Ilford) 1974. HSBH: 90 v Surrey (Oval) 1974. BB: 4–50 MCC under-25 v North Zone (Peshawar) 1966–67.

Graham Alan GOOCH (Norlington Junior HS, Leyton) B Leytonstone 23/7/1953. Cousin of G. J. Saville, former Essex player and assistant secretary of club. RHB, RM. Toured West Indies with England Young Cricketers 1972. Debut 1973. Cap 1975. Tests: 7 in 1975 and 1978. Tour: Australia 1978-79. 1,000 runs (3)—1,273 runs (av 42.43) in 1976 best. Shared in 2nd wicket partnership record for county, 321 with K. S. McEwan v Northants (Ilford) 1978. Benson & Hedges Gold awards: 1. HS: 136 v Worcs (Westcliff) 1976. HSTC: 91* v New Zealand (Oval) 1978. HSGC: 61 v Somerset (Taunton) 1978. HSJPL: 90* v Middlesex (Lord's) 1978. HSBH: 89 v Surrey (Oval) 1976. BB: 5–40 v West Indians (Chelmsford) 1976. BBJPL: 3–14 v Derbyshire (Derby) 1978.

Brian Ross HARDIE (Larbert HS) B Stenhousemuir 14/1/1950. RHB, RM. Has played for Stenhousemuir in East of Scotland League. Debut for Scotland 1970. His father and elder brother K. M. Hardie have also played for Scotland. Debut for Essex by special registration in 1973. Cap 1974. 1,000 runs (3)—1,522 runs (av 43.48) in 1975 best. Scored two centuries in match for Scotland v MCC, Aberdeen 1971, a match not regarded as first-class. HS: 162 v Warwickshire (Birmingham) 1975. HSGC: 83 v Staffs (Stone) 1976. HSJPL: 94 v Northants (Northampton) 1973. HSBH: 42* v Cambridge U (Cambridge) 1974.

Reuben HERBERT (Barstaple Comprehensive School, Basildon) B Cape Town 1/12/1957. RHB, OB. Debut 1976. Did not play in 1978. HS: 12 v Cambridge U (Cambridge) 1977.

John Kenneth LEVER B Ilford 24/2/1949. RHB, LFM. Debut 1967. Cap 1970. *Wisden* 1978. Tests: 13 between 1976–77 and 1977–78. Tours: India, Sri Lanka and Australia 1976–77. Pakistan and New Zealand 1977–78. Australia 1978–79. Took 106 wickets (av 15.18) in 1978. Gillette Man of Match awards: 3. Benson & Hedges Gold awards: 1. HS: 91 v Glamorgan (Cardiff) 1970. HSTC: 53 v India (Delhi) 1976–77 (on debut). HSJPL: 23 v Worcs (Worcester) 1974. HSBH: 12* v Warwickshire (Birmingham) 1975. BB: 8–127 v Glos (Cheltenham) 1976. BBTC: 7–46 v India (Delhi) 1976–77 (on debut). BBGC: 5–8 v Middlesex (Westcliff) 1972. BBJPL: 5–13 v Glamorgan (Ebbw Vale) 1975. BBBH: 5–16 v Middlesex (Chelmsford) 1976.

Alan William LILLEY (Caterham Secondary High School, Ilford) B Ilford 8/5/1959. RHB, WK. Debut 1978. One match v Notts (Nottingham) scoring century in second innings. Also played in last two John Player League matches of season. HS: 100* v Notts (Nottingham) 1978. HJPL: 54 v Surrey (Southend) 1978.

Michael Stephen Anthony McEVOY (Colchester RGS) B Jorhat Assam, India 25/1/1956. RHB, RM. Debut 1976. HS: 67* v Yorks (Middlesbrough) 1977. Trained as a teacher at Borough Road College of Education.

Kenneth Scott (Ken) McEWAN (Queen's College, Queenstown) B Bedford, Cape Province, South Africa 16/7/1952. RHB, OB. Debut for Eastern Province in 1972–73 Currie Cup competition. Played for T. N. Pearce's XI v West Indians (Scarborough) 1973. Debut for county and cap 1974. *Wisden* 1977. 1,000 runs (5)—1,821 runs (av 49.21) in 1976 best. Scored 4 consecutive centuries in 1977 including two centuries in match (102 and 116) v Warwickshire (Birmingham). Shared in 2nd wicket partnership record for county, 321 with G. A. Gooch v Northants (Ilford) 1978. Benson & Hedges Gold awards: 4. HS: 218 v Sussex (Chelmsford) 1977. HSGC: 63 v Somerset (Westcliff) 1974. HSJPL: 123 v Warwickshire (Ilford) 1976. HSBH: 133 v Notts (Chelmsford) 1978.

Steven John MALONE (King's School, Ely) B Chelmsford 19/10/1953. RHB, RM. Debut 1975 playing in one match v Cambridge U (Cambridge). Re-appeared in corresponding match in 1978.

Norbert PHILLIP (Dominica G S, Roseau) B Bioche, Dominica 12/6/1948. RHB, RFM. Debut 1969–70 for Windward Islands v Glamorgan and has played subsequently for Combined Islands in Shell Shield competition. Debut for county and cap 1978. Tests: 3 for West Indies 1977–78. Tour: West Indies to India and Sri Lanka 1978–79. Had match double of 100 runs and 10 wickets (160 and 10–130), Combined Islands v Guyana (Georgetown) 1977–78. HS: 134 v Glos (Gloucester) 1978. HSGC: 24* v Leics (Leicester) 1978. HSJPL: 17* v Warwickshire (Colchester) 1978. BB: 6–33 v Pakistan (Chelmsford) 1978. BBJPL: 3–28 v Glos (Gloucester) 1978.

Keith Rupert PONT B Wanstead 16/1/1953. RHB., RM. Debut 1970. Cap 1976. Benson & Hedges Gold awards: 1. HS: 113 v Warwickshire (Birmingham) 1973. HSGC: 39 v Somerset (Taunton) 1978. HSJPL: 50* v Leics (Westcliff) 1976. HSBH: 60* v Notts (Ilford) 1976. BB: 4–100 v Middlesex (Southend) 1977.

Derek Raymond PRINGLE (Felsted School). B Nairobi, Kenya 18/9/1958. 6 ft 4½ ins. tall. Son of late Donald Pringle who played for East Africa in 1975 Prudential Cup. RHB, RM. Toured India with England Schools C.A. 1977–78. Debut 1978. HS: 50* v Cambridge U (Cambridge) 1978. Is now studying at Cambridge University.

Neil SMITH (Ossett GS) B Dewsbury 1/4/1949. RHB, WK. Debut for Yorks 1970. Debut for county by special registration in 1973. Cap 1975. HS: 126 v Somerset (Leyton) 1976. HSGC: 12 v Leics (Southend) 1977. HSJPL: 26* v Kent (Canterbury) 1978. HSBH: 61 v Northampton (Chelmsford) 1977.

ESSEX

Stuart TURNER B Chester 18/7/1943. RHB, RFM. Debut 1965. Cap 1970. Played for Natal in 1976–77 and 1977–78 Currie Cup competition. Benefit in 1979. Hat-trick: v Surrey (Oval) 1971. HS: 121 v Somerset (Taunton) 1970. HSGC: 50 v Lancs (Chelmsford) 1971. HSJPL: 87 v Worcs (Chelmsford) 1975. HSBH: 41* v Minor Counties (East) (Chelmsford) 1977. BB: 6–26 v Northants (Northampton) 1977. BBGC: 3–16 v Glamorgan (Ilford) 1971. BBJPL: 5–35 v Hants (Chelmsford) 1978. BBBH: 4–22 v Minor Counties (South) (Bedford) 1975.

NB The following players whose particulars appeared in the 1978 annual have been omitted: M. K. Fosh and P. A. Hector (not re-engaged). The career record of Fosh will be found elsewhere in this annual.

COUNTY AVERAGES

Schweppes Championship: Played 22, won 12, drawn 9, lost 1
All first-class matches: Played 24, won 12, drawn 11, lost 1

BATTING AND FIELDING

Cap		M	I	NO	Runs	HS	Avge	100	50	Ct	St
1974	K. S. McEwan	24	37	3	1682	186	49.47	5	8	21	—
1963	K. W. R. Fletcher	24	35	8	1127	89	41.74	—	10	27	—
1974	B. R. Hardie	23	33	7	1044	109	40.15	1	6	28	—
1975	G. A. Gooch	15	25	1	933	129	38.87	2	5	16	—
1970	S. Turner	23	29	8	636	89*	30.28	—	3	13	—
1978	N. Phillip	20	28	4	645	134	26.87	1	3	4	—
1977	M. H. Denness	22	37	2	870	126	24.85	1	4	10	—
1976	K. R. Pont	12	18	2	366	101	22.87	1	2	8	—
1967	R. E. East	23	26	5	391	57	18.61	—	1	14	—
1975	N. Smith	24	24	6	323	59*	17.94	—	1	51	8
—	D. R. Pringle	3	5	1	60	50*	15.00	—	1	1	—
—	M. S. A. McEvoy	4	6	0	87	51	14.50	—	1	2	—
1970	J. K. Lever	21	14	7	55	8	7.85	—	—	8	—
1970	D. L. Acfield	22	15	9	44	12*	7.33	—	—	8	—

Played in two matches: M. K. Fosh 10, 32, 3, 0 (1 ct.)
Played in one match: A. W. Lilley 22, 100*. S. J. Malone did not bat.

BOWLING

	Type	O	M	R	W	Avge	Best	5 wI	10 wM
J. K. Lever	LFM	645.5	149	1555	102	15.24	7–32	9	1
R. E. East	SLA	700.2	226	1506	92	16.36	8–41	6	1
N. Phillip	RFM	583.1	114	1591	71	22.40	6–33	4	—
S. Turner	RFM	532	149	1183	48	24.64	4–9	—	—
D. L. Acfield	OB	456.5	136	1013	36	28.13	3–33	—	—

Also bowled: G. A. Gooch 16–3–37–2; S. J. Malone 15–6–28–1, K. R. Pont 65–17–193–3; D. R. Pringle 23–8–50–1.

County Records

First-class cricket

Highest innings totals:	For	692 v Somerset (Taunton)	1895
	Agst.	803–4 by Kent (Brentwood)	1934
Lowest innings totals:	For	30 v Yorkshire (Leyton)	1901
	Agst.	31 by Derbyshire (Derby) and by Yorkshire (Huddersfield)	1914 & 1935
Highest individual innings:	For	343* P. A. Perrin v Derbyshire (Chesterfield)	1904
	Agst.	332 W. H. Ashdown for Kent (Brentwood)	1934
Best bowling in an innings:	For	10–32 H. Pickett v Leicestershire (Leyton)	1895
	Agst.	10–40 G. Dennett for Gloucestershire (Bristol)	1906
Best bowling in a match:	For	17–119 W. Mead v Hampshire (Southampton)	1895
	Agst.	17–56 C. W. L. Parker for Gloucestershire (Gloucester)	1925

Most runs in a season:	2308 (av 56.29) J. O'Connor	1934
runs in a career:	29162 (av 36.18) P. A. Perrin	1896–1928
100s in a season:	9 by J. O'Connor and D. J. Insole	1934 & 1955
100s in a career:	71 by J. O'Connor	1921–1939
wickets in a season:	172 (av 27.13) T. P. B. Smith	1947
wickets in a career:	1611 (av 26.26) T. P. B. Smith	1929–1951

RECORD WICKET STANDS

1st	270	A. V. Avery & T. C. Dodds v Surrey (The Oval)	1946
2nd	321	G. A. Gooch & K. S. McEwan v Northamptonshire (Ilford)	1978
3rd	343	P. A. Gibb & R. Horsfall v Kent (Blackheath)	1951
4th	298	A. V. Avery & R. Horsfall v Worcestershire (Clacton)	1948
5th	287	C. T. Ashton & J. O'Connor v Surrey (Brentwood)	1934
6th	206	J. W. H. T. Douglas & J. O'Connor v Gloucestershire (Cheltenham)	1923
		B. R. Knight & R. A. G. Luckin v Middlesex (Brentwood)	1962
7th	261	J. W. H. T. Douglas & J. Freeman v Lancashire (Leyton)	1914
8th	263	D. R. Wilcox & R. M. Taylor v Warwickshire (Southend)	1946
9th	251	J. W. H. T. Douglas & S. N. Hare v Derbyshire (Leyton)	1921
10th	218	F. H. Vigar & T. P. B. Smith v Derbyshire (Chesterfield)	1947

GLAMORGAN

One-day cricket

Highest innings totals:	Gillette Cup	316–6 v Staffordshire (Stone)	1976
	John Player League	283–6 v Gloucestershire (Cheltenham)	1975
	Benson & Hedges Cup	294–4 v Minor Counties (East) (Norwich)	1976
Lowest innings totals:	Gillette Cup	100 v Derbyshire (Brentwood)	1965
	John Player League	69 v Derbyshire (Chesterfield)	1974
	Benson & Hedges Cup	123 v Kent (Canterbury)	1973
Highest individual innings:	Gillette Cup	101 B. Ward v Bedfordshire (Chelmsford)	1971
	John Player League	123 K. S. McEwan v Warwickshire (Ilford)	1976
	Benson & Hedges Cup	133 K. S. McEwan v Nottinghamshire (Chelmsford)	1978
Best bowling figures:	Gillette Cup	5–8 J. K. Lever v Middlesex (Westcliff)	1972
	John Player League	8–26 K. D. Boyce v Lancs (Manchester)	1971
	Benson & Hedges Cup	5–16 J. K. Lever v Middlesex (Chelmsford)	1976

GLAMORGAN

Formation of present club: 1888.
Colours: Blue and gold.
Badge: Gold daffodil.
County Champions (2): 1948 and 1969.
Gillette Cup finalists: 1977.
Best final position in John Player League: 8th in 1977.
Benson & Hedges Cup quarter-finalists (4): 1972, 1973, 1977 and 1978.
Gillette Man of the Match awards: 13.
Benson & Hedges Gold awards: 16.

Secretary: P. B. Clift, 6 High Street, Cardiff CF1 2PW
Captain: R. N. S. Hobbs
Prospects of Play telephone nos.:   Cardiff (0222) 29956 or 38736
                                    Swansea (0792) 59351

Anthony Elton (Tony) CORDLE B St Michael, Barbados 21/9/1940. RHB, RFM. Debut 1963. Cap 1967. Benefit (£8,000) in 1977. HS: 81 v Cambridge U (Swansea) 1972. HSGC: 36 v Lincs (Swansea) 1974. HSJPL: 87 v Notts (Nottingham) 1971. HSBH: 27* v Hants (Swansea) 1976. BB: 9–49 (13–100 match) v Leics (Colwyn Bay) 1969. BBGC: 4–42 v Worcs (Worcester) 1977. BBJPL: 4–16 v Somerset (Swansea) 1974. BBBH: 4–14 v Hants (Swansea) 1973.

68

David Arthur FRANCIS (Cwmtawe Comprehensive School, Pontardawe) B Clydach (Glamorgan) 29/11/1953. RHB, OB. Debut 1973 after playing for 2nd XI in 1971 and 1972. HS: 110 v Warwickshire (Nuneaton) 1977. HSGC: 62* v Worcs (Worcester) 1977. HSJPL: 50 v Surrey (Byfleet) 1976. HSBH: 59 v Warwickshire (Birmingham) 1977.

Robin Nicholas Stuart HOBBS (Raine's Foundation School, Stepney), B Chippenham (Wilts.) 8/5/1942. RHB, LBG. Debut for Essex 1961. Cap 1964. Benefit (£13,500) in 1974. Retired at end of 1975 season. Played for Suffolk from 1976 to 1978. Has joined Glamorgan as County Captain for 1979. Tests: 7 between 1967 and 1971. Tours: South Africa 1964–65, Pakistan 1966–67, West Indies 1967–68, Ceylon and Pakistan 1968–69. 100 wkts. (2) – 102 wkts. (av. 21.40) in 1970 best. Hat-trick Essex v. Middlesex (Lord's) 1968 in Gillette Cup. Benson & Hedges Gold Awards: 1 (for Essex). HS: 100 Essex v. Glamorgan (Ilford) 1968 and 100 Essex v. Austalians (Chelmsford) 1975 in 44 minutes. HSTC: 15* v India (Birmingham) 1967. HSGC: 34 Essex v. Lancs (Chelmsford) 1971. HSJPL: 54* Essex v Yorks (Colchester) 1970. HSBH: 40 Essex v Middlesex (Lord's) 1972. BB: 8/63 (13–164 match) Essex v. Glamorgan (Swansea) 1966. BBTC: 3–25 v India (Birmingham) 1967. BBGC: 4–55 Essex v Wilts (Chelmsford) 1969. BBJPL: 6–22 Essex v Hants (Harlow) 1973.

Geoffrey Clark HOLMES (West Denton HS, Newcastle-upon-Tyne) B Newcastle-upon-Tyne 16/9/1958. RHB, RM. Debut 1978 (Two matches) HS: 17* v Warwickshire (Cardiff) 1978.

John Anthony HOPKINS B Maesteg 16/6/1953. Younger brother of J. D. Hopkins, formerly on staff and who appeared for Middlesex. RHB, WK. Debut 1970. Cap 1977. 1000, runs (2)–1,371 runs (av 33.43)). in 1978 best. Gillette Man of the Match awards: 1. Benson & Hedges Gold awards: 2. HS: 230 v Worcs (Worcester) 1977 – the fourth highest score for the county. HSGC: 63 v Leics (Swansea) 1977. HSJPL: 50 v Northants (Northampton) 1977. HSBH: 81 v Worcs (Swansea) 1977. Trained as a teacher at Trinity College of Education, Carmarthen.

Alan JONES B Swansea 4/11/1938. LHB, OB. Joined staff in 1955. Debut 1957. Cap 1962. Played for Western Australia in 1963–64, for Northern Transvaal in 1975–76 and for Natal in 1976–77. Benefit (£10,000) in 1972. County captain from 1976 to 1978. *Wisden* 1977. Played one match v Rest of World 1970. 1,000 runs (18)–1,865 runs (av 34.53) in 1966 and 1,862 runs (av 38,00) in 1968 best. Scored two centuries in match (187* and 105*) v Somerset (Glastonbury) 1963, (132 and 156*) v Yorks (Middlesbrough) 1976 and (147 and 100) v Hants (Swansea) 1978. Shared in record partnership for any wicket for county, 330 for 1st wkt with R. C. Fredericks v Northants (Swansea) 1972. Shared in 2nd wkt partnership record for county, 238 with A. R. Lewis v Sussex (Hastings) 1962. Has scored more runs and centuries for county than any other player. Gillette Man of the Match awards: 1. Benson & Hedges Gold awards: 1. HS: 187* v Somerset (Glastonbury) 1963. HSGC: 124* v Warwickshire (Birmingham) 1976. HSJPL: 110* v Glos (Cardiff) 1978. HSBH: 67 v Derbyshire (Cardiff) 1977.

Alan Lewis JONES (Ystalyfera GS and Cwmtawe Comprehensive School) B Alltwen (Glamorgan) 1/6/1957. No relation to A. and E. W. Jones. LHB. Played for 2nd XI in 1972. Debut 1973 at age of 16 years 3 months. Toured West Indies with England Young Cricketers 1976. HS:

57 v Oxford U (Oxford) 1976. HSGC: 11 v Hants (Southampton) 1975. HSJPL: 62 v Hants (Cardiff) 1975. HSBH: 30 v Glos (Bristol) 1975.

Eifion Wyn JONES B Velindre (Glamorgan) 25/6/1942. Brother of A. Jones. RHB, WK. Debut 1961. Cap 1967. Benefit (£17,000) in 1975. Dismissed 94 batsmen (85 ct 9 st) in 1970. Dismissed 7 batsmen (6 ct 1 st) in innings v Cambridge U (Cambridge) 1970. Benson & Hedges Gold awards: 1. HS: 146* v Sussex (Hove) 1968. HSGC: 67* v Herts (Swansea) 1969. HSJPL: 48 v Hants (Cardiff) 1971. HSBH: 39* v Minor Counties (West) (Amersham) 1977.

Michael John (Mike) LLEWELLYN B Clydach (Glamorgan) 27/11/1953. LHB, OB. Debut 1970. Cap 1977. Gillette Man of the Match awards: 1. Benson & Hedges Gold awards: 2. HS: 129* v Oxford U (Oxford) 1977. HSGC: 62 v Middlesex (Lord's) 1977. HSJPL: 79* v Glos (Bristol) 1977. HSBH: 63 v Hants (Swansea) 1973. BB: 4–35 v Oxford U (Oxford) 1970.

Barry John LLOYD B Neath 6/9/1953. RHB, OB. Formerly on MCC groundstaff. Debut 1972. HS: 45* v Hants (Portsmouth) 1973. HSJPL: 13 v Derbyshire (Swansea) 1976. BB: 4–49 v Hants (Portsmouth) 1973. Trained as a teacher at Bangor Normal College.

Andrew James (Andy) MACK B Aylsham (Norfolk) 14/1/1956. 6ft 5in tall. LHB, LM. Joined Surrey staff 1973. Played in five John Player League matches in 1975. Debut for Surrey 1976. Left County after 1977 season and made debut for Glamorgan in 1978. HS: 16 Surrey v Somerset (Weston-super-Mare) 1977. HSJPL: 16 Surrey v Hants (Southampton) 1977. BB: 4–28 v Worcs (Worcester) 1978. BBJPL: 3–48 Surrey v Hants (Southampton) 1977. BBBH: 3–34 Surrey v Combined Universities (Oval) 1976.

Malcolm Andrew NASH (Wells Cathedral School) B Abergavenny (Monmouthshire) 9/5/1945. LHB, LM. Debut 1966. Cap 1969. Benefit in 1978. Benson & Hedges Gold awards: 3. Hat-trick in John Player League v Worcs (Worcester) 1975. HS: 130 v Surrey (Oval) 1976. HSGC: 51 v Lincs (Swansea) 1974. HSJPL: 68 v Essex (Purfleet) 1972. HSBH: 103* v Hants (Swansea) 1976. BB: 9–56 (14–137 match) v Hants (Basingstoke) 1975. BBGC: 3–14 v Staffs (Stoke) 1971. BBJPL: 6–29 v Worcs (Worcester) 1975. BBBH: 4–12 v Surrey (Cardiff) 1975.

Rodney Craig ONTONG (Selborne College, East London) B Johannesburg, South Africa 9/9/1955. RHB, RFM. Debut 1972–73 for Border in Currie Cup competition. Debut for county 1975 after being on MCC staff. Transferred to Transvaal for 1976–77 season. HS: 116* v Essex (Cardiff) and 116 v Surrey (Oval) 1978. HSGC: 64 v Somerset (Cardiff) 1978. HSJPL: 47 v Surrey (Ebbw Vale) 1977, 47* v Somerset (Cardiff) 1978 and 47 v Kent (Maidstone) 1978. HSBH: 35* v Warwickshire (Birmingham) 1977. BB: 7–60 Border v Northern Transvaal (Pretoria) 1975–76. BBUK: 5–71 v Hants (Cardiff) 1977. BBJPL: 3–17 v Surrey (Ebbw Vale) 1977. BBBH: 3–12 v Minor Counties (West) (Amersham) 1977.

Gwyn RICHARDS B Maesteg 29/11/1951. RHB, OB. Formerly on MCC staff. Debut 1971. Cap 1976. Benson & Hedges Gold awards: 1. HS: 102* v Yorks (Middlesbrough) 1976. HSGC: 18 v Surrey (Cardiff) 1977. HSJPL: 73 v Glos (Cardiff) 1978. HSBH: 52 v Hants (Swansea) 1975. BB: 5–55 v Somerset (Taunton) 1978. BBJPL: 5–29 v Lancs (Swansea) 1977.

Peter Douglas SWART (Jameson HS, Gatooma, Rhodesia) B Bulawayo, Rhodesia 27/4/1946. RHB, RM. Debut 1965–66 for Rhodesia in Currie Cup Competition. Subsequently played for Western Province from 1967–68. Played for International Cavaliers v Barbados (Scarborough) 1969 and for D. H. Robins' XI v Pakistanis (Eastbourne) 1974. Professional for Accrington in 1969 and for Haslingden from 1974 to 1977 in Lancashire League. Debut for County 1978. Scored 1,078 runs (av 31.70) in 1978. Benson & Hedges Gold awards: 1. HS: 115 v Oxford U. (Oxford) 1978 HSGC: 44 v Somerset (Cardiff) 1978. HSJPL: 85* v Surrey (Oval) 1978 HSBH: 83* v Combined Universities (Oxford) U. 1978.JBB: 6–85 Western Province v Natal (Pietermaritzburg) 1971–72. BBUK: 4–74 International Cavaliers v Barbados (Scarborough) 1969. BBC: 4–95 v Hants (Southampton) 1978.

Alan Haydn WILKINS (Whitchurch HS, Cardiff) B Cardiff 22/8/1953. RHB, LM. Played in two John Player League matches in 1975. Debut 1976. HS: 70 v Notts (Worksop) 1977. HSGC: 18* v Somerset (Cardiff) 1978. BB: 5–58 v Hants (Portsmouth) 1977. BBJPL: 5–23 v Warwickshire (Birmingham) 1978. BBBH: 5–17 v Worcs (Worcester) 1978. Trained as a teacher at Loughborough College of Education.

NB The following players whose particulars appeared in the 1978 Annual have been omitted: T. W. Cartwright, P. G. Crowther, S. C. Harrison, K. J. Lyons and D. L. Williams.
The career record of Crowther will be found elsewhere in this annual.

COUNTY AVERAGES

Schweppes Championship: Played 22, won 3, drawn 11, lost 8
All first-class matches: Played 24, won 4, drawn 12, lost 8

BATTING AND FIELDING

Cap		M	I	NO	Runs	HS	Avge	100	50	Ct	St
1977	J. A. Hopkins	24	42	3	1358	116	34.82	3	7	18	—
1977	M. J. Llewellyn	21	31	6	849	82	33.96	—	7	9	—
—	R. C. Ontong	21	34	4	969	116*	32.30	2	5	7	—
—	P. D. Swart	23	37	3	1078	115	31.70	3	5	19	—
1962	A. Jones	24	39	1	1133	147	29.81	3	4	—	—
1976	G. Richards	22	36	10	768	74	29.53	—	5	6	—
1969	M. A. Nash	23	34	5	794	124*	27.37	1	5	9	—
—	D. A. Francis	7	10	1	154	56	17.11	—	2	5	—
—	A. L. Jones	9	16	2	213	54	15.21	—	1	7	—
1967	A. E. Cordle	15	15	3	161	33*	13.41	—	—	7	—
—	B. J. Lloyd	24	28	8	245	27	12.25	—	—	11	—
1967	E. W. Jones	22	25	5	232	58	11.60	—	1	39	1
—	P. G. Crowther	4	7	0	47	27	6.71	—	—	1	—
—	A. H. Wilkins	18	21	10	61	17	5.54	—	—	10	—
—	A. J. Mack	5	4	2	8	8*	4.00	—	—	2	—

Played in two matches G. C. Holmes 17*, 1*, 8, 11 (1 ct).

GLAMORGAN

BOWLING

	Type	O	M	R	W	Avge	Best	5 wI	10 wM
A. J. Mack	LM	77.3	26	195	16	12.18	4–28	—	—
L. D. Swart	RM	358	73	1112	43	25.86	4–24	—	—
A. H. Wilkins	LM	370.3	74	1267	37	34.24	5–96	1	—
E. A. Nash	LM	519.2	135	1631	42	38.83	6–74	2	—
E. C. Ontong	RFM	262.5	58	856	22	38.90	4–95	—	—
C. Richards	OB	218.3	45	750	19	39.47	5–55	1	—
E. J. Lloyd	OB	561.3	155	1590	40	39.75	4–82	—	—
A. E. Cordle	RFM	307.5	73	864	21	41.14	5–33	1	—

Also bowled: G. C. Holmes 4–0–41–0; J. A. Hopkins 2–0–10–0; A. Jones 2½–0–10–0; A. L. Jones 0.2–0–4–0.

County Records

First-class cricket

Highest innings	For	587–8d v Derbyshire (Cardiff)	1951
totals:	Agst	653–6d by Gloucestershire (Bristol)	1928
Lowest innings	For	22 v Lancashire (Liverpool)	1924
totals:	Agst	33 by Leicestershire (Ebbw Vale)	1965
Highest indi-	For	287* E. Davies v Gloucestershire (Newport)	1939
vidual innings:	Agst	302* W. R. Hammond for Glos (Bristol)	1934
		302 W. R. Hammond for Glos (Newport)	1939
Best bowling	For	10–51 J. Mercer v Worcs (Worcester)	1936
in an innings:	Agst	10–18 G. Geary for Leics (Pontypridd)	1929
Best bowling	For	17–212 J. C. Clay v Worcs (Swansea)	1937
in match:	Agst	16–96 G. Geary for Leics (Pontypridd)	1929
Most runs in a season:		2071 (av 49.30) W. G. A. Parkhouse	1959
runs in a career:		27,723 (av 32.61) A. Jones	1957–1978
100s in a season:		7 by W. G. A. Parkhouse	1950
100s in a career:		42 by A. Jones	1957–1978
wickets in a season:		176 (av 17.34) J. C. Clay	1937
wickets in a career:		2174 (av 20.95) D. J. Shepherd	1950–1972

RECORD WICKET STANDS

1st	330	A. Jones & R. C. Fredericks v Northamptonshire (Swansea)	1972
2nd	238	A. Jones & A. R. Lewis v Sussex (Hastings)	1962
3rd	313	E. Davies & W. E. Jones v Essex (Brentwood)	1948
4th	263	G. Lavis & C. Smart v Worcestershire (Cardiff)	1934
5th	264	M. Robinson & S. W. Montgomery v Hampshire (Bournemouth)	1949
6th	230	W. E. Jones & B. L. Muncer v Worcestershire (Worcester)	1953
7th	195*	W. Wooller & W. E. Jones v Lancashire (Liverpool)	1947
8th	202	D. Davies & J. J. Hills v Sussex (Eastbourne)	1928
9th	203*	J. J. Hills & J. C. Clay v Worcestershire (Swansea)	1929
10th	131*	C. Smart & W. D. Hughes v South Africans (Cardiff)	1935

72

One-day cricket			
Highest innings totals:	Gillette Cup	283–3 v Warwickshire (Birmingham)	1976
	John Player League	266–6 v Northants (Wellingborough)	1975
	Benson & Hedges Cup	245–7 v Hampshire (Swansea)	1976
Lowest innings totals:	Gillette Cup	76 v Northants (Northampton)	1968
	John Player League	65 v Surrey (Oval)	1969
	Benson & Hedges Cup	68 v Lancs (Manchester)	1973
Highest individual innings:	Gillette Cup	124* A. Jones v Warwickshire (Birmingham)	1976
	John Player League:	110* A. Jones v Glos. (Cardiff)	1978
	Benson & Hedges Cup	103* M. A. Nash v Hants (Swansea)	1976
Best bowling figures:	Gillette Cup	5–21 P. M. Walker v Cornwall (Truro)	1970
	John Player League	6–29 M. A. Nash v Worcs (Worcester)	1975
	Benson & Hedges Cup	5–17 A. H. Wilkins v Worcestershire (Worcester)	1978

GLOUCESTERSHIRE

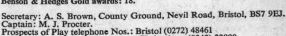

Formation of present club: 1871.
Colours: Blue, gold, brown, sky-blue, green, and red.
Badge: Coat of Arms of the City and County of Bristol.
County Champions: (3) 1874, 1876 and 1877.
Joint Champions: 1873.
Gillette Cup Winners: 1973.
Best Position in John Player League: 6th in 1969, 1973 and 1977.
Benson & Hedges Cup Winners: 1977.
Gillette Man of the Match awards: 17.
Benson & Hedges Gold awards: 18.

Secretary: A. S. Brown, County Ground, Nevil Road, Bristol, BS7 9EJ.
Captain: M. J. Procter.
Prospects of Play telephone Nos.: Bristol (0272) 48461
Cheltenham (0242) 22000.

Philip BAINBRIDGE (Hanley HS and Stoke-on-Trent Sixth Form College) B Stoke-on-Trent 16/4/1958. RHB, RM. Played for four 2nd XI's in 1976 – Derbyshire, Glos, Northants and Warwickshire. Debut 1977. HS: 76* v Worcs (Worcester) 1978. HSJPL: 20 v Warwickshire (Birmingham) 1978. Trained as a teacher at Borough Road College of Education.

GLOUCESTER

Brian Maurice BRAIN (King's School, Worcester), B Worcester 13/9/1940). RHB, RFM. Debut for Worcs 1959. Left staff in 1960. Rejoined staff in 1963 and reappeared in 1964. Cap 1966. Left staff in 1971, but rejoined in 1973. Not re-engaged after 1975 season and joined Glos in 1976. Cap 1977. Gillette Man of the Match awards: 1 (for Worcs). HS: 57 v Essex (Cheltenham) 1976. HSGC: 21* Worcs v Sussex (Worcester) 1967. HSJPL: 33 v Kent (Canterbury) 1978. HSBH: 16 v Warwickshire (Bristol) 1978. BB: 8–55 Worcs v Essex (Worcester) 1975. BBC: 7–51 v Australians (Bristol) 1977. BBGC: 4–13 Worcs v Durham (Chester-le-Street) 1968. BBJPL: 4–27 Worcs v Somerset (Taunton) 1970. BBBH: 4–30 v Somerset (Bristol) 1977.

Andrew James (Andy) BRASSINGTON B Bagnall (Staffordshire) 9/8/1954. RHB, WK. Debut 1974. Cap 1978. HS: 28 v Glamorgan (Cardiff) 1975. Plays soccer as a goalkeeper.

John Henry CHILDS B Plymouth 15/8/1951. LHB, SLA. Played for Devon 1973–74. Debut 1975. Cap 1977. HS: 12 v Derbyshire (Ilkeston) 1977. HSJPL: 11* v Essex (Cheltenham) 1975. BB: 8–34 v Hants (Basingstoke) 1978. BBJPL: 4–15 v Northants (Northampton) 1976.

Jack DAVEY (Tavistock GS) B Tavistock (Devon) 4/9/1944. LHB LFM. Played for Devonshire in 1964 and 1965. Debut 1966. Cap 1971. Joint benefit in 1978 with D. R. Shepherd. Hat-trick v Oxford U (Oxford) 1976. HS: 53* v Glamorgan (Bristol) 1977. HSBH: 16 v Somerset (Street) 1975. BB: 6–95 v Notts (Gloucester) 1967. BBGC: 4–35 v Essex (Chelmsford) 1973. BBJPL: 4–11 v Glamorgan (Lydney) 1975. BBBH: 3–26 v Somerset (Taunton) 1972.

Nicholas Hugh (Nick) FINAN (St Brendan's College, Bristol) B Knowle, Bristol 3/7/1954. 6ft 3in tall. RHB, RM. Debut 1975. Plays mostly in one-day matches. HS: 18 v Worcs (Worcester) 1977. HSJPL: 11 v Essex (Cheltenham) 1975.

James Clive (Jim) FOAT (Millfield School) B Salford Priors (Warwickshire) 21/11/1952. RHB, RM. Debut 1972. Benson & Hedges Gold awards: 1. HS: 116 v Glamorgan (Bristol) 1975. HSGC: 49* v Northants (Bristol) 1977. HSJPL: 60 v Glamorgan (Bristol) 1973. HSBH: 73* v Somerset (Street) 1975.

Michael Anthony (Mike) GARNHAM (Camberwell GS, Melbourne, Scotch College, Perth, Australia, Park School, Barnstaple) B Johannesburg 20/8/1960. RHB, WK. Played for Devon and county 2nd XI since 1976. Toured India with English Schools Cricket Association in 1977. Played in last John Player League match of 1978 v Warwickshire (Birmingham). Has yet to appear in first-class cricket. Is studying at East Anglia University.

David Anthony GRAVENEY (Millfield School) B Bristol 2/1/1953. Son of J. K. R. Graveney, RHB, SLA. Debut 1972. Cap 1976. HS: 92 v Warwickshire (Birmingham) 1978. HSGC: 44 v Surrey (Bristol) 1973. HSJPL: 44 v Essex (Cheltenham) 1975. HSBH: 21 v Somerset (Street) 1975. BB: 8–85 v Notts (Cheltenham) 1974. BBGC: 3–67 v Leics (Leicester) 1975. BBJPL: 4–22 v Hants (Lydney) 1974. BBBH: 3–32 v Middlesex (Bristol) 1977.

74

Thomas Michael Geoffrey (Tom) HANSELL (Millfield School) B Sutton Coldfield (Warwickshire) 24/8/1954. LHB, SLA. Joined Surrey staff 1974. Debut for Surrey 1975. Did not play in 1978 and joined Glos for 1979. HS: 54 Surrey v Notts (Oval) 1976. HSJPL: 26 Surrey v Northants (Guildford) 1977.

Alastair James HIGNELL (Denstone College and Cambridge) B Cambridge 4/9/1955. RHB, LB. Scored 117* and 78* for England Schools v All India Schools (Birmingham) 1973 and 133 for England Young Cricketers v West Indies Young Cricketers (Arundel) 1974. Debut 1974. Cap 1977. Blue 1975–76–77–78. Captain in last two years. 1,000 runs (2)— 1,140 runs (av 30.81) in 1976 best. Scored two centuries in match (108 and 145) for Cambridge U v Surrey (Cambridge) 1978. Benson & Hedges Gold awards: 1 (for Combined Universities). HS: 149 Cambridge U v Glamorgan (Cambridge) 1977. HSC: 119 v West Indians (Bristol) 1976. HSGC: 85* v Northants (Bristol) 1977. HSJPL: 51 v Northants (Northampton) 1976. HSBH: 63 Combined Universities v Worcs (Worcester) 1978. Blue for rugby 1974–75 (captain)–76–77 (captain). Plays for Bristol. Toured Australia with England Rugby team 1975. 10 caps for England between 1975 and 1977–78.

Martin David PARTRIDGE (Marling School, Stroud) B Birdlip (Glos) 25/10/1954. LHB, RM. Debut 1976. HS: 50 v Worcs (Bristol) 1978. HSJPL: 20 v Kent (Canterbury) and 20* v Somerset (Bristol) 1978. HSBH: 27 v Warwickshire (Bristol) 1978. BBJPL: 5–47 v Kent (Cheltenham) 1977. Studied civil engineering at Bradford University.

Michael John (Mike) PROCTER (Hilton College, Natal) B Durban 15/9/1946. RHB, RF/OB. Vice-captain of South African Schools team to England 1963. Debut for county 1965 in one match v South Africans. Returned home to make debut for Natal in 1965–66 Currie Cup competition. Joined staff in 1968. Cap 1968. *Wisden* 1969. Transferred to Western Province for 1969–70 Currie Cup competition, Rhodesia in 1970–71 and Natal 1976–77. Appointed county captain in 1977. Benefit (£15,500) in 1976. Tests: 7 for South Africa v Australia 1966–67 and 1969–70. Played in 5 matches for Rest of World v England in 1970. 1,000 runs (7)—1,786 runs (av 45.79) in 1971 best. 100 wkts (2)—109 wkts (av 18.04) in 1977 best. Scored 6 centuries in 6 consecutive innings for Rhodesia 1970–71 to equal world record. Scored two centuries in match (114 and 131) for Rhodesia v International Wanderers (Salisbury) 1972–73. Hat-tricks (2): v Essex (Westcliff) 1972—all lbw—and also scored a century in the match, and v Essex (Southend) 1977. Also v Hants (Southampton) in Benson & Hedges Cup, 1977. Had match double of 100 runs and 10 wkts (108 and 13–73) v Worcs (Cheltenham) 1977. Gillette Man of the Match awards: 2. Benson & Hedges Gold awards: 5. HS: 254 Rhodesia v Western Province (Salisbury) 1970–71. HSUK: 203 v Essex (Gloucester) 1978. HSTC: 48 South Africa v Australia (Cape Town) 1969–70. HSGC: 107 v Sussex (Hove) 1971. HSJPL: 109 v Warwickshire (Cheltenham) 1972. HSBH: 154* v Somerset (Taunton) 1972. BB: 9–71 Rhodesia v Transvaal (Bulawayo) 1972–73. BBUK: 7–35 v Worcs (Cheltenham) 1977. BBTC: 6–73 South Africa v Australia (Port Elizabeth) 1969–70. BBGC: 4–21 v Yorks (Leeds) 1976. BBJPL: 5–8 v Middlesex (Gloucester) 1977. BBBH: 6–13 v Hants (Southampton) 1977.

75

SADIQ MOHAMMAD B Junagadh (India) 3/5/1945. LHB, LBG. Youngest of family of five cricket-playing brothers which includes Hanif and Mushtaq Mohammad. Debut in Pakistan 1959–60 at age of 14 years 9 months and has played subsequently for various Karachi sides, Pakistan International Airways and United Bank. Played for Northants 2nd XI in 1967 and 1968, for Nelson in Lancs League in 1968, and subsequently for Poloc, Glasgow in Scottish Western Union. Played for D. H. Robins' XI v Oxford U 1969 and for Essex v Jamaica XI in 1970. Debut for county 1972. Cap 1973. Played for Tasmania against MCC in 1974–75. Tests: 34 for Pakistan between 1969–70 and 1978. Tours: Pakistan to England 1971, 1974 and 1978. Australia and New Zealand 1972–73, Australia and West Indies 1976–77. 1,000 runs (5)—1,759 runs (av 47.54) in 1976 best. Scored 1,169 runs (av 41.75) in Australia and New Zealand 1972–73. Scored 4 centuries in 4 consecutive innings in 1976 including two centuries in match (163* and 150) v Derbyshire (Bristol). Gillette Man of Match awards: 1. Benson & Hedges Gold awards: 3. HS: 184* v New Zealanders (Bristol) 1973. HSTC: 166 Pakistan v New Zealand (Wellington) 1972–73. HSGC: 122 v Lancs (Manchester) 1975. HSJPL: 131 v Somerset (Imperial Ground, Bristol) 1975. HSBH: 128 v Minor Counties (South) (Bristol) 1974. BB: 5–29 Pakistan International Airways v Dacca (Dacca) 1964–65 and 5–29 Karachi Blues v Lahore Greens (Karachi) 1970–71. BBUK: 5–37 v Kent (Bristol) 1973. BBGC: 3–19 v Oxfordshire (Bristol) 1975. BBJPL: 3–27 v Hants (Bristol) 1972. BBBH: 3–20 v Minor Counties (South) (Bristol) 1972.

Brian Keith SHANTRY (Whitefield Fishponds Comprehensive School) B Bristol 26/5/1955. 6ft 3 ins. tall. LHB, LFM. Played for county 2nd XI in 1976 and Warwickshire 2nd XI in 1977. Debut 1978 (two matches). Also played in two John Player League matches.

David Robert SHEPHERD (Barnstaple GS) B Bideford (Devon) 27/12/1940. RHB, RM. Played for Devonshire from 1959 to 1964. Played for Minor Counties v Australians 1964. Debut 1965 scoring 108 in first match v Oxford U. Cap 1969. Joint benefit in 1978 with J. Davey. 1,000 runs (2)—1,079 runs (av 26.97) in 1970 best. Gillette Man of Match awards: 1. Benson & Hedges Gold awards: 1. HS: 153 v Middlesex (Bristol) 1968. HSGC: 72* v Surrey (Bristol) 1973. HSJPL: 100 v Glamorgan (Cardiff) 1978. HSBH: 81 v Hants (Bristol) 1974. Has played rugby for Bideford.

Andrew Willis STOVOLD (Filton HS) B Bristol 19/3/1953. RHB, WK. Toured West Indies with England Young Cricketers 1972. Played for 2nd XI since 1971. Debut 1973. Cap 1976. Played for Orange Free State in 1974–75 and 1975–76. Currie Cup competition. 1,000 runs (2)— 1,223 runs (av 34.94) in 1977 best. Benson & Hedges Gold awards: 4. HS: 196 v Notts (Nottingham) 1977. HSGC: 45 v Lancs (Manchester) 1978. HSJPL: 98* v Kent (Cheltenham) 1977. HSBH: 104 v Leics (Leicester) 1977.

Martin Willis STOVOLD (Thornbury GS) B Bristol 28/12/1955. Younger brother of A. W. Stovold. LHB. Played in one John Player League match v Essex (Gloucester) 1978. Has yet to appear in first-class cricket. Trained as a teacher at Loughborough College.

Stephen (Steve) WILLIAMS (Hreod Burna Senior High School, Swindon) B Swindon 11/3/1954. RHB, LB. Played for Wiltshire since 1975. Debut 1978. One match v New Zealanders (Bristol).

Syed **ZAHEER ABBAS** B Sialkot (Pakistan) 24/7/1947. RHB, OB. Wears glasses. Debut for Karachi Whites 1965–66. subsequently playing for Pakistan International Airways. *Wisden* 1971. Debut for county 1972. Cap 1975. Tests: 26 for Pakistan between 1969–70 and 1976–77. Played in 5 matches for Rest of the World v Australia 1971–72. Tours: Pakistan to England 1971 and 1974, Australia and New Zealand 1972–73, Australia and West Indies 1976–77, Rest of World to Australia 1971–72. 1,000 runs (7)—2,554 runs (av 75.11) in 1976 best. Scored 1,597 runs (av 84.05) in Pakistan 1973–74—the record aggregate for a Pakistan season. Scored 4 centuries in 4 consecutive innings in 1970–71. Scored two centuries in a match twice in 1976–216* and 156* v Surrey (Oval) and 230* and 104* v Kent (Canterbury) and once in 1977—205* and 108* v Sussex (Cheltenham) to create record of being only player ever to score a double-century and a century in a match on three occasions. Was dismissed, hit the ball twice, for Pakistan International Airways v Karachi Blues (Karachi) 1969–70. Gillette Man of Match awards: 4. HS: 274 Pakistan v England (Birmingham) 1971, sharing in record 2nd wkt partnership for Pakistan first-class cricket 291 with Mushtaq Mohammad. HSC: 230* v Kent (Canterbury) 1977. HSGC: 131* v Leics (Leicester) 1975. HSJPL: 114* v Hants (Bristol) 1976. HSBH: 98 v Surrey (Oval) 1977. BB: 5–15 Dawood Club v Railways (Lahore) 1975–76.

NB. The following players whose particulars appeared in the 1978 annual have been omitted: A. R. Border, N. H. C. Cooper (not re-engaged), I. C. Crawford (not re-engaged). J. H. Shackleton (not re-engaged), and M. J. Vernon (not re-engaged).

In addition, A. Tait the former Northamptonshire player who appeared during the first half of the season has not been re-engaged and has therefore not been included.

The career records of Cooper, Crawford, Shackleton and Tait will be found elsewhere in this annual.

COUNTY AVERAGES

Schweppes Championship: Played 21, won 4, drawn 9, lost 8, abandoned 1
All first-class matches: Played 24, won 5, drawn 11, lost 8, abandoned 1
BATTING AND FIELDING

Cap		M	I	NO	Runs	HS	Avge	100	50	Ct	St
—	P. Bainbridge	3	5	2	233	76*	77.66	—	3	1	—
1968	M. J. Procter	21	36	3	1655	203	50.15	3	7	11	—
1975	Zaheer Abbas	22	35	1	1535	213	45.14	6	4	15	—
1973	Sadiq Mohammad	13	22	2	774	176	38.70	1	3	4	—
1976	A. W. Stovold	21	35	2	962	139	29.15	1	5	9	3
—	J. C. Foat	19	29	4	722	102*	28.88	2	3	7	—
1976	D. A. Graveney	24	35	8	740	92	27.40	—	4	16	—
1969	D. R. Shepherd	16	24	1	446	72	19.39	—	3	4	—
—	A. Tait	11	19	1	348	53	19.33	—	2	2	—
—	M. D. Partridge	7	10	3	133	50	19.00	—	1	4	—
—	N. H. C. Cooper	6	12	0	219	94	18.25	—	1	3	—
1977	B. M. Brain	23	27	7	268	35	13.40	—	—	3	—
1971	J. Davey	15	19	6	135	20*	10.38	—	—	5	—
—	J. H. Shackleton	7	9	4	49	22	9.80	—	—	1	—
1977	A. J. Hignell	11	19	0	182	44	9.57	—	—	10	—
1978	A. J. Brassington	21	30	3	192	22	7.11	—	—	42	3
1977	J. H. Childs	11	11	1	28	4*	5.60	—	—	8	—

Played in two matches: I. C. Crawford 73, 2, 14. B. K. Shantry did not bat. *Played in one match:* S. Williams 0.

GLOUCESTER
BOWLING

	Type	O	M	R	W	Avge	Best	5 wI	10 wM
B. M. Brain	RFM	573.2	138	1589	76	20.90	5-48	2	—
M. J. Procter	RF/OB	665.2	185	1649	69	23.89	7-45	2	—
J. H. Childs	SLA	520.2	154	1440	59	24.40	8-34	5	2
J. Davey	LFM	309.3	65	900	30	30.00	4-52	—	—
D. A. Graveney	SLA	517	156	1425	31	45.96	4-47	—	—

Also bowled: P Bainbridge 25–8–59–0; N. H. C. Cooper 3–0–26–0; I. C. Crawford 17–8–37–0; J. C. Foat 1–0–7–0; M. D. Partridge 85–15–312–3; Sadiq Mohammad 4.3–3–8–0; J. H. Shackleton 96–22–275–4; B. K. Shantry 39–6–167–3; D. R. Shepherd 4.5–0–26–0; A. Tait 0.1–0–0–0; Zaheer Abbas 8–1–26–0.

County Records
First-class cricket

Highest innings totals:	For	......653–6d v Glamorgan (Bristol)	1928
	Agst.	774–7d by Australians (Bristol)	1948
Lowest innings totals:	For	......17 v Australians (Cheltenham)	1896
	Agst.	12 by Northamptonshire (Gloucester)	1907
Highest individual innings:	For	......318*W.G.Grace v Yorkshire (Cheltenham)	1876
	Agst.	296 A. O. Jones for Notts (Nottingham)	1903
Best bowling in an innings:	For	......10–40 G. Dennett v Essex (Bristol)	1906
	Agst.	10–66 A. A. Mailey for Aust (Cheltenham)	1921
		and K. Smales for Notts (Stroud)	1956
Best bowling in a match:	For	......17–56 C. W. L. Parker v Essex (Gloucester)	1925
	Agst.	15–87 A. J. Conway for Worcestershire (Moreton-in-Marsh)	1914
Most runs in a season:		2860 (av 69.75) W. R. Hammond	1933
runs in a career:		33664 (av 57.05) W.R.Hammond 1920–1951	
100s in a season:		13 by W. R. Hammond	1938
100s in a career:		113 by W. R. Hammond 1920–1951	
wickets in a season:		222 (av 16.80 & 16.37) T. W. Goddard 1937 & 1947	
wickets in a career:		3171 (av 19.43) C.W.L. Parker 1903–1935	

RECORD WICKET STANDS

1st	395	D. M. Young & R. B. Nicholls v Oxford U (Oxford)	1962
2nd	256	C. T. M. Pugh & T. W. Graveney v Derbyshire (Chesterfield)	1960
3rd	336	W. R. Hammond & B. H. Lyon v Leicestershire (Leicester)	1933
4th	321	W. R. Hammond & W. L. Neale v Leicestershire (Gloucester)	1937
5th	261	W. G. Grace & W. O. Moberley v Yorkshire (Cheltenham)	1876
6th	320	G. L. Jessop & J. H. Board v Sussex (Hove)	1902
7th	248	W. G. Grace & E. L. Thomas v Sussex (Hove)	1896
8th	239	W. R. Hammond & A. E. Wilson v Lancashire (Bristol)	1938
9th	193	W. G. Grace & S. A. Kitcat v Sussex (Bristol)	1896
10th	131	W. R.Gouldsworthy & J.G. Bessant v Somerset (Bristol)	1923

One-day cricket

Highest innings totals:	Gillette Cup	327–7 v Berkshire (Reading)	1966
	John Player League	255 v Somerset (Imperial Ground, Bristol)	1975
	Benson & Hedges Cup	282 v Hants (Bristol)	1974
Lowest innings totals:	Gillette Cup	86 v Sussex (Hove)	1969
	John Player League	49 v Middlesex (Bristol)	1978
	Benson & Hedges Cup	62 v Hants (Bristol)	1975
Highest individual innings:	Gillette Cup	131* Zaheer Abbas v Leics (Leicester)	1975
	John Player League	131 Sadiq Mohammad v Somerset (Imperial Ground, Bristol)	1975
	Benson & Hedges Cup	154* M. J. Procter v Somerset (Taunton)	1972
Best bowling figures:	Gillette Cup	5–39 R. D. V. Knight v Surrey (Bristol)	1971
	John Player League	5–8 M. J. Procter v Middlesex (Gloucester)	1977
	Benson & Hedges Cup	6–13 M. J. Procter v Hampshire (Southampton)	1977

HAMPSHIRE

ormation of present club: 1863.
Colours: Blue, gold, and white.
Badge: Tudor rose and crown.
County Champions (2): 1961 and 1973.
Gillette Cup semi-finalists (2): 1966 and 1976.
John Player League Champions (2): 1975 and 1978.
Benson & Hedges Cup semi-finalists (2): 1975 and 1977.
Fenner Trophy Winners (3): 1975, 1976 and 1977.
Gillette Man of the Match awards: 22.
Benson & Hedges Gold awards: 22.

Secretary: A. K. James, County Cricket
  Ground, Northlands Road, Southampton, SO9 2TY.
Captain: G. R. Stephenson.

  Nigel Geoffrey COWLEY B Shaftesbury (Dorset) 1/3/1953. RHB. OB, Debut 1974. Cap 1978. HS: 109* v Somerset (Taunton) 1977. HSGC: 32 v Middlesex (Lord's) 1977. HSJPL: 47 v Notts (Nottingham) 1978. HSBH: 59 v Glos (Southampton) 1977. BB: 5–93 v Warwickshire (Bournemouth) 1978. BBJPL: 3–19 v Glos (Cheltenham) 1978.

HAMPSHIRE

Cuthbert Gordon GREENIDGE B St Peter, Barbados 1/5/1951. RHB, RM. Debut 1970. Cap 1972. Has subsequently played for Barbados. *Wisden* 1976. Tests: 19 for West Indies between 1974—75 and 1977—78. Tours: West Indies to India. Sri Lanka and Pakistan 1974—75, Australia 1975—76, England 1976. 1,000 runs (8)—1,952 runs (av 55.77) in 1976 best. Scored two centuries in match (134 and 101) West Indies v England (Manchester) 1976, and (136 and 120) v Kent (Bournemouth) 1978. Gillette Man of Match awards: 2. Benson & Hedges Gold awards: 4. HS: 273* D. H. Robins' XI v Pakistan (Eastbourne) 1974. HSC: 259 v Sussex (Southampton) 1975. HSTC: 134 West Indies v England (Manchester) 1976. HSGC: 177 v Glamorgan (Southampton) 1975—record for all one day competitions. HSJPL: 122 v Middlesex (Bournemouth) 1978. HSBH: 173* v Minor Counties (South) (Amersham) 1973—record for competition —and shared in partnership of 285* for second wicket with D. R. Turner — the record partnership for all one-day competitions. BB: 5—49 v Surrey (Southampton) 1971.

Trevor Edward JESTY B Gosport 2/6/1948. RHB, RM. Debut 1966. Cap 1971. Played for Border in 1973—74 and Griqualand West in 1974—75 and 1975—76 Currie Cup competitions. 1,000 runs (3)—1,288 runs (av 35.77) in 1976 best. Gillette Man of Match awards: 1. Benson & Hedges Gold awards: 5. Took 3 wkts in 4 balls v Somerset (Portsmouth) 1969. HS: 159* v Somerset (Bournemouth) 1976. HSGC: 69 v Yorks (Bournemouth) 1977. HSJPL: 107 v Surrey (Southampton) 1977. HSBH: 105 v Glamorgan (Swansea) 1977. BB: 7—75 v Worcs (Southampton) 1976. BBGC: 4—32 v Notts (Nottingham) 1972. BBJPL: 6—20 v Glamorgan (Cardiff) 1975. BBBH: 4—28 v Somerset (Taunton) 1974.

Malcolm Denzil MARSHALL B Barbados 18/4/1958. RHB, RFM. Debut for Barbados 1977—78 in last match of Shell Shield competition. Has joined county for 1979. Tour: West Indies to India and Sri Lanka 1978—79 BB: 6—77 Barbados v Jamaica (Bridgetown) 1977—78.

Andrew Joseph (Andy) MURTAGH (St Joseph's College, Beulah Hill, London) B Dublin 6/5/1949. RHB, RM. Played for Surrey 2nd XI 1967—68 and for county 2nd XI since 1969. Debut 1973. Played for Eastern Province in 1973—74 Currie Cup competition. Did not play in 1978 and not re-engaged after end of season. May play occasionally in one-day matches in 1979. HS: 65 v Glos (Bournemouth) 1975. HSGC: 32 v Derbyshire (Southampton) 1976. HSJPL: 65* v Derbyshire (Bournemouth) 1976. HSBH: 17 v Derbyshire (Southampton) 1976. BBJPL: 5—33 v Yorks (Huddersfield) 1977.

Mark Charles Jefford NICHOLAS (Bradfield College) B London 29/9/1957. RHB, RFM. Debut 1978 (three matches). HS: 40* v Oxford U. (Oxford) 1978.

Nicholas Edward Julian POCOCK (Shrewsbury School) B Maracaibo, Venezuela 15/12/1951. RHB, LM. Debut 1976. HS: 68 v Leics (Bournemouth) 1976. HSJPL: 53* v Northants (Northampton) 1978.

John Michael RICE (Brockley CGS, London) B Chandler's Ford (Hants) 23/10/1949. RHB, RM. On Surrey staff 1970, but not re-engaged. Debut 1971. Cap 1975. Hat-trick in John Player League v Northants (Southampton) 1975. Gillette Man of the Match awards: 1. Benson & Hedges Gold awards: 1. HS: 96* v Somerset (Weston-super-Mare) 1975. HSGC: 38 v Leics (Leicester) 1976. HSJPL: 54* v Somerset (Street) 1977. HSBH: 43 v Lancs (Southampton) 1977. BB: 7–48 v Worcs (Worcester) 1977. BBGC: 5–35 v Yorks (Bournemouth) 1977. BBJPL: 5–14 v Northants (Southampton) 1975. BBBH: 3–20 v Somerset (Bournemouth) 1975.

David John ROCK (Portsmouth GS) B Southsea 20/4/1957. RHB, RM. Debut 1976. HS: 114 v Leics (Leicester) 1977. HSGC: 50 v Middlesex (Lord's) 1977. HSJPL: 68 v Glos (Portsmouth) 1977.

John William SOUTHERN (The William Ellis School, Highgate) B King's Cross, London 2/9/1952. 6ft 3½in tall. RHB, SLA. Debut 1975. Cap 1978. HS: 51 v Glos (Basingstoke) 1978. BB: 6–46 v Glos (Bournemouth) 1975. Obtained BSc degree in Chemistry at Southampton University.

George Robert (Bob) STEPHENSON (Derby School) B Derby 19/11/1942. RHB, WK. Debut for Derbyshire 1967 following injury to R. W. Taylor. Joined Hants by special registration in 1969 following resignation of B. S. V. Timms. Cap 1969. Benefit in 1979. Benson & Hedges Gold awards: 1. Dismissed 80 batsmen (73st and 7ct) in 1970. HS: 100* v Somerset (Taunton) 1976. HSGC: 29 v Notts (Nottingham) 1972. HSJPL: 24* v Notts (Nottingham) 1976. HSBH: 29* v Somerset (Taunton) 1974. Soccer for Derby County, Shrewsbury Town. and Rochdale. Appointed county captain for 1979

Keith STEVENSON (Bemrose GS, Derby) B Derby 6/10/1950. RHB, RFM. Debut for Derbyshire 1974. Left county after 1977 season and made debut for Hants in 1978. HS: 33 Derbyshire v Northants (Chesterfield) 1974. HSC: 18 v Glamorgan (Swansea) 1978. HSGC: 14 Derbyshire v Surrey (Ilkeston) 1976. BB: 7–68 Warwickshire v Warwickshire (Chesterfield) 1977. BBC: 6–73 v Sussex (Hove) 1978. BBGC: 4–21 Derbyshire v Surrey (Ilkeston) 1976. BBJPL: 3–29 Derbyshire v Surrey (Chesterfield) 1975.

Michael Norman Somerset TAYLOR (Amersham College) B Amersham (Bucks) 12/11/1942. Twin brother of D. J. S. Taylor of Somerset. RHB, RM. Played for Buckinghamshire in 1961–62. Debut for Notts 1964, Cap 1967. Not re-engaged after 1972 season and made debut for Hants 1973. Cap 1973. Took 99 wkts (av 21.00) in 1968. Hat-trick Notts v Kent (Dover) 1965. Gillette Man of Match awards: 1. Benson & Hedges Gold awards: 1 (for Notts). HS: 105 Notts v Lancs (Nottingham) 1967. HSC: 103* v Glamorgan (Southampton) 1978. HSGC: 58 Notts v Hants (Nottingham) 1972. HSJPL: 57* v Notts (Nottingham) 1978. HSBH: 41 v Minor Counties (South) (Portsmouth) 1974. BB: 7–23 v Notts (Basingstoke) 1977. BBGC: 4–31 Notts v Lancs (Nottingham) 1968. BBJPL: 4–20 Notts v Surrey (Nottingham) 1969. BBBH: 3–15 v Somerset (Taunton) 1974.

Vivian Paul TERRY (Millfield School) B Osnabruck, West Germany 14/1/1959. RHB, RM. Played for 2nd XI since 1976. Debut 1978. Played in two matches and one John Player League match. HS: 8 v Leics (Southampton) 1978.

HAMPSHIRE

Timothy Maurice (Tim) TREMLETT (Richard Taunton College, Southampton) B Wellington (Somerset) 26/7/1956. Son of M. F. Tremlett, former Somerset player. RHB, RM. Debut 1976. HS: 50 v Glos (Basingstoke) 978. BBBH: 3–21 v Combined Universities (Cambridge) 1978.

David Roy TURNER B Chippenham (Wilts) 5/2/1949. LHB, RM. Played for Wiltshire in 1965. Debut 1966. Cap 1970. Played for Western Province in 1977–78 Currie Cup competition. 1,000 runs (6)—1,269 runs (av 36.25) in 1976 best. Gillette Man of Match awards: 1. Benson & Hedge. Gold awards: 3. HS: 181* v Surrey (Oval) 1969. HSGC: 86 v Northants (Southampton) 1976. HSJPL: 99* v Glos (Bristol) 1972. HSBH: 123* v Minor Counties (South) (Amersham) 1973.

NB The following players whose particulars appeared in the 1978 annual have been omitted: R. B. Elms (not re-engaged), R. M. C. Gilliat (retired), T. J. Mottram, B. A. Richards (left staff) and A. M. E. Roberts (left staff). The career records of Elms, Gilliat, Richards and Roberts will be found elsewhere in this annual.

COUNTY AVERAGES

Schweppes Championship: Played 21, won 4, drawn 11, lost 6, abandoned 1
All first-class matches: Played 23, won 5, drawn 12, lost 6, abandoned 1
BATTING AND FIELDING

Cap		M	I	NO	Runs	HS	Avge	100	50	Ct	St
1972	C. G. Greenidge	19	34	1	1771	211	53.66	5	9	34	—
1973	M. N. S. Taylor	22	29	9	770	103*	38.50	1	6	8	—
1970	D. R. Turner	23	42	3	1255	148*	32.17	3	2	9	—
1971	T. E. Jesty	23	42	5	1174	125*	31.72	5	2	10	—
1968	B. A. Richards	6	11	0	337	73	30.63	—	2	8	—
—	M. C. J. Nicholas	3	5	2	77	40*	25.66	—	—	2	—
1969	R. M. C. Gilliat	16	27	9	453	54	25.16	—	1	13	—
—	R. B. Elms	3	2	0	48	48	24.00	—	—	1	—
1974	A. M. E. Roberts	9	14	5	209	37*	23.22	—	—	—	—
—	T. M. Tremlett	6	10	2	183	50	22.87	—	1	1	—
1975	J. M. Rice	19	31	2	630	63	21.72	—	3	15	—
1978	N. G. Cowley	23	38	5	650	64	19.69	—	2	16	—
—	D. J. Rock	7	13	0	231	54	17.76	—	2	6	—
1969	G. R. Stephenson	23	30	5	350	66	14.00	—	1	46	9
1978	J. W. Southern	23	22	8	148	51	10.57	—	1	7	—
—	N. E. J. Pocock	5	8	1	71	18	10.14	—	—	8	—
—	K. Stevenson	21	21	4	111	19	6.52	—	—	8	—

Played in two matches: V. P. Terry 5, 8, 3.
BOWLING

	Type	O	M	R	W	Avge	Best	5 wI	10 wM
A. M. E. Roberts	RF	254.1	74	617	27	22.85	5–20	1	—
J. W. Southern	SLA	762.3	247	1833	76	24.11	5–32	4	—
J. M. Rice	RM	267.1	70	709	29	24.44	4–49	—	—
N. G. Cowley	OB	672.3	192	1700	56	30.35	5–93	1	—
K. Stevenson	RFM	515.5	101	1706	56	30.46	6–73	2	—
T. M. Tremlett	RM	95	27	219	7	31.28	2–25	—	—
M. N. S. Taylor	RM	346.1	104	900	27	33.33	5–67	1	—
T. E. Jesty	RM	257.5	71	660	19	34.73	6–50	1	—

Also bowled: R. B. Elms 27–6–89–1; C. G. Greenidge 4–2–8–1; N. E. J. Pocock 3–0–5–0; B. A. Richards 1–0–1–0; G. R. Stephenson 0.1–0–1–0.

County Records
First-class cricket

Highest innings totals:	For ....672–7d v Somerset (Taunton)	1899
	Agst....742 by Surrey (The Oval)	1909
Lowest innings totals:	For ....15 v Warwickshire (Birmingham)	1922
	Agst....23 by Yorkshire (Middlesbrough)	1965
Highest individual innings:	For ....316 R. H. Moore v Warwickshire (Bournemouth)	1937
	Agst....302* P. Holmes for Yorkshire (Portsmouth)	1920
Best bowling in an innings:	For ....9–25 R.M.H. Cottam v Lancs (Manchester)	1965
	Agst....9–21L.B. Richmond for Notts (Nottingham)	1921
Best bowling in a match:	For ....16–88 J. A. Newman v Somerset (Weston-super-Mare)	1927
	Agst....17–119 W. Mead for Essex (Southampton)	1895

Most runs in a season:	2854 (av 79.27) C. P. Mead	1928
runs in a career:	48892 (av 48.84) C. P. Mead	1905–1936
100s in a season:	12 by C. P. Mead	1928
100s in a career:	138 by C. P. Mead	1905–1936
wickets in a season:	190 (av 15.61) A. S. Kennedy	1922
wickets in a career:	2669 (av 18.22) D. Shackleton	1948–1969

RECORD WICKET STANDS

1st	249	R. E. Marshall & J. R. Gray v Middlesex (Portsmouth)	1960
2nd	321	G. Brown & E. I. M. Barrett v Gloucestershire (Southampton)	1920
3rd	344	C. P. Mead & G. Brown v Yorkshire (Portsmouth)	1927
4th	263	R. E. Marshall & D. A. Livingstone v Middlesex (Lord's)	1970
5th	235	G. Hill & D. F. Walker v Sussex (Portsmouth)	1937
6th	411	R. M. Poore & E. G. Wynyard v Somerset (Taunton)	1899
7th	325	G. Brown & C. H. Abercrombie v Essex (Leyton)	1913
8th	178	C. P. Mead & C. P. Brutton v Worcestershire (Bournemouth)	1925
9th	230	D. A. Livingstone & A. T. Castell v Surrey (Southampton)	1962
10th	192	A. Bowell & W. H. Livsey v Worcestershire (Bournemouth)	1921

NB   A partnership of 334 for the first wicket by B. A. Richards, C. G. Greenidge and D. R. Turner occurred against Kent at Southampton in 1973. Richards retired hurt after 241 runs had been scored and in the absence of any official ruling on the matter, it is a matter of opinion as to whether it should be regarded as the first-wicket record for the county.

One-day cricket

Highest innings totals:	Gillette Cup	371–4 v Glamorgan (Southampton)	1975
	John Player League	288–5 v Somerset (Weston-super-Mare)	1975
	Benson & Hedges Cup	321–1 v Minor Counties (South) (Amersham)	1973
Lowest innings totals:	Gillette Cup	98 v Lancashire (Manchester)	1975
	John Player League	43 v Essex (Basingstoke)	1972
	Benson & Hedges Cup	94 v Glamorgan (Swansea)	1973
Highest individual innings:	Gillette Cup	177 C. G. Greenidge v Glamorgan (Southampton)	1975
	John Player League	155* B. A Richards v Yorks (Hull)	1970
	Benson & Hedges Cup	173* C. G. Greenidge v Minor Counties (South) (Amersham)	1973
Best bowling figures:	Gillette Cup	7–30 P. J. Sainsbury v Norfolk (Southampton)	1965
	John Player League	6–20 T. E. Jesty v Glamorgan (Cardiff)	1975
	Benson & Hedges Cup	5–24 R. S. Herman v Gloucestershire (Bristol)	1975

KENT

Formation of present club: 1859, re-organised 1870.
Colours: Red and white.
Badge: White horse.
County Champions (6): 1906, 1909, 1910, 1913, 1970 and 1978.
Joint Champions: 1977.
Gillette Cup winners (2): 1967 and 1974.
Gillette Cup finalists: 1971.
John Player League Champions (3): 1972, 1973 and 1976.
Benson & Hedges Cup winners (3): 1973, 1976 and 1978.
Benson & Hedges Cup finalists: 1977.
Fenner Trophy winners (2): 1971 and 1973.
Gillette Man of the Match awards: 21.
Benson & Hedges Gold awards: 28.

Secretary: M. D. Fenner, St Lawrence Ground, Canterbury, CT1 3NZ.
Captain: A. G. E. Ealham.

ASIF IQBAL RAZVI (Osmania University, Hyderabad, India) B Hyderabad 6/6/1943. Nephew of Ghulam Ahmed, former Indian off-break bowler and Test cricketer. RHB, RM. Debut 1959–60 for Hyderabad in Ranji Trophy. Migrated to Pakistan in 1961 and has since appeared for various Karachi teams, Pakistan International Airways and National Bank.Captained Pakistan under-25 v England under-25 in 1966–67. Debut for county and cap 1968. *Wisden* 1967. County captain in 1977. Tests: 45 for Pakistan between 1964–65 and 1976–77. Tours: Pakistan to Australia and New Zealand 1964–65, 1972–73 (vice-captain), England 1967, 1971 (vice-captain) and 1974 (vice-captain) Australia and West Indies 1976–77, Pakistan Eaglets to England 1963, Pakistan 'A' to Ceylon 1964, Pakistan International Airways to East Africa 1964. 1,000 runs (6)—1,379 runs (av 39.40) in 1970 best. Scored 1,029 runs (av 41.16) in Australia and New Zealand 1972–73. Scored 146 v England (Oval) 1967 sharing in 9th wkt partnership of 190 with Intikhab Alam after Pakistan were 65–8—record 9th wkt stand in Test cricket. Gillette Man of Match awards: 2. Benson & Hedges Gold awards: 4. HS: 196 National Bank v Pakistan International Airways (Lahore) 1976–77. HSTC: 175 Pakistan v New Zealand (Dunedin) 1972–73. HSUK: 171 v Glos (Folkestone) 1978. HSGC: 89 v Lancs (Lord's) 1971. HSJPL: 106 v Glos (Maidstone) 1976. HSBH: 75 v Middlesex (Canterbury) 1973. BB: 6–45 Pakistan Eaglets v Cambridge U (Cambridge) 1963. BBTC: 5–48 Pakistan v New Zealand (Wellington) 1964–65. BBC: 4–11 v Lancs (Canterbury) 1968. BBJPL: 3–3 v Northants (Tring) 1977. BBBH: 4–43 v Worcs (Lord's) 1973.

Christopher Stuart COWDREY (Tonbridge School) B Farnborough (Kent) 20/10/1957. Eldest son of M. C. Cowdrey. RHB, RM. Played for 2nd XI at age of 15. Captain of England Young Cricketers team to West Indies 1976. Played in one John Player League match in 1976. Debut 1977. Benson & Hedges Gold awards: 1. HS: 101* v Glamorgan (Swansea) 1977. HSJPL: 74 v Worcs (Worcester) 1978. HSBH: 114 v Sussex (Canterbury) 1977.

Graham Roy DILLEY B Dartford 18/5/1959. 6ft 3ins tall. LHB, RM. Debut 1977. HS: 16 v Cambridge U (Canterbury) 1977. BB: 5–32 v Middlesex (Lord's) 1978. BBJPL: 3–13 v Surrey (Oval) 1978.

Paul Rupert DOWNTON (Sevenoaks School) B Farnborough (Kent) 4/4/1957. Son of G. Downton, former Kent player. RHB, WK. Played for 2nd XI at age of 16. Vice-captain of England Young Cricketers team to West Indies 1976. Debut 1977. Tour: Pakistan and New Zealand 1977–78. HS: 31* v Surrey (Maidstone) 1977 and 31 v Sussex (Hove) 1978. HSJPL: 16* v Glamorgan (Maidstone) 1978. Is studying law at Exeter University and will be unavailable for first half of 1979 season.

Alan George Ernest EALHAM B Ashford (Kent) 30/8/1944. RHB, OB. Debut 1966. Cap 1970. Appointed county captain in 1978. 1,000 runs (3)—1,363 runs (av 34.94) in 1971 best. Held 5 catches in innings v Glos (Folkestone) 1966. all in outfield off D. L. Underwood. Benson & Hedges Gold awards: 4. HS: 134* v Notts (Nottingham) 1976. HSGC: 46 v Leics (Canterbury) 1974. HSJPL: 83 v Leics (Leicester) 1977. HSBH: 94* v Sussex (Canterbury) 1977.

Richard William HILLS B Borough Green (Kent) 8/1/1951. RHB, RM. Debut 1973. Cap 1977. HS: 45 v Hants (Canterbury) 1975. HSJPL: 26 v Somerset (Maidstone) 1978. HSBH: 34 v Surrey (Canterbury) 1977. BB: 6–64 v Glos (Folkestone) 1978. BBJPL: 4–29 v Sussex (Maidstone) 1977. BBBH: 5–28 v Combined Universities (Oxford) 1976.

Kevin Bertram Sidney JARVIS (Springhead School, Northfleet) B Dartford 23/4/1953. 6ft 3in tall. RHB, RFM. Debut 1975. Cap 1977. Benson & Hedges Gold awards: 1. HS: 12* v Cambridge U (Canterbury) 1977 and 12 v Sussex (Hove) 1978. BB: 8–97 v Worcs (Worcester) 1978. BBGC: 3–53 v Sussex (Canterbury) 1976. BBJPL: 4–27 v Surrey (Maidstone) 1977. BBBH: 4–34 v Worcs (Lord's) 1976.

Graham William JOHNSON (Shooters Hill GS) B Beckenham 8/11/1946. RHB, OB. Debut 1965. Cap 1970. 1,000 runs (3)—1,438 runs (av 31.26) in 1973 and 1,438 runs (av 35.95) in 1975 best. Gillette Man of Match awards: 1. Benson & Hedges Gold awards: 3. HS: 168 v Surrey (Oval) 1976. HSGC: 120* v Bucks (Canterbury) 1974. HSJPL: 89 v Sussex (Hove) 1976. HSBH: 85* v Minor Counties (South) (Canterbury) 1975. BB: 6–32 v Surrey (Tunbridge Wells) 1978. BBJPL: 5–26 v Surrey (Oval) 1974. Studied at London School of Economics.

Nicholas John (Nick) KEMP (Tonbridge School) B Bromley 16/12/1956. RHB, RM. Played for 2nd XI since 1974. Toured West Indies with England Young Cricketers 1976. Debut 1977. BB: 3–83 v Pakistan (Canterbury) 1978.

Alan Philip Eric KNOTT B Belvedere 9/4/1946. RHB, WK. Can bowl OB. Debut 1964. Cap 1965. Elected Best Young Cricketer of the Year in 1965 by Cricket Writers Club. *Wisden* 1969. Played for Tasmania 1969–70 whilst coaching there. Benefit (£27,037) in 1976. Did not play in 1978. Tests: 89 between 1967 and 1977. Played in 5 matches against Rest of World in 1970. Tours: Pakistan 1966–67, West Indies, 1967–68 and 1973–74, Ceylon and Pakistan 1968–69, Australia and New Zealand 1970–71, 1974–75, India, Sri Lanka and Pakistan 1972–73, India, Sri Lanka and Australia 1976–77. 1,000 runs (2)—1,209 runs (av 41.68) in 1971 best. Scored two centuries in match (127* and 118*) v Surrey (Maidstone) 1972. Gillette Man of Match awards: 2. Benson & Hedges Gold awards: 1. HS: 156 MCC v South Zone (Bangalore) 1972–73. HSUK: 144 v Sussex (Canterbury) 1976. HSTC: 135 v Australia (Nottingham) 1977. HSGC: 46 v Notts (Nottingham) 1975. HSJPL: 60 v Hants (Canterbury) 1969. ESBH: 65 v Combined Universities (Oxford) 1976. Dismissed 84 batsmen (74 ct 10 st) in 1965. 81 batsmen (73 ct 8 st) in 1966, and 98 batsmen (90 ct 8 st) in 1967. Dismissed 7 batsmen (7 ct) on debut in Test cricket v Pakistan (Nottingham) 1967. Holds record for most dismissals in Test cricket.

David NICHOLLS (Gravesend GS) B East Dereham (Norfolk) 8/12/1943. LHB, reserve WK. LB. Debut 1960. Cap 1969. Scored 1,000 runs (av 32.25) in 1971. Did not play in 1978. Will have benefit in 1980. HS: 211 v Derbyshire (Folkestone) 1963. HSGC: 43 v Warwickshire (Canterbury) 1971. HSJPL: 64 v Glos (Gillingham) 1971. HSBH: 51 v Essex (Chelmsford) 1972.

Charles James Castell ROWE (King's School, Canterbury) B Hong Kong 27/11/1951. RHB, OB. Debut 1974. Cap 1977. Scored 1,065 runs (av 35.50) in 1978. HS: 103 v Sussex (Tunbridge Wells) 1977. HSGC: 18* v Somerset (Canterbury) 1978. HSJPL: 78* v Notts (Canterbury) 1977. HSBH: 40 v Combined Universities (Canterbury) 1977. BB: 6-46 v Derbyshire (Dover) 1976. BBJPL: 5-32 v Worcs (Worcester) 1976.

John Neil SHEPHERD (Alleyn's School, Barbados) B St Andrew, Barbados 9/11/1943. RHB, RM. Debut 1964-65 in one match for Barbados v Cavaliers and has played subsequently for Barbados in Shell Shield competition. Debut for county 1966. Cap 1967. Played for Rhodesia in 1975-76 Currie Cup competition. *Wisden* 1978. Benefit in 1979. Tests: 5 for West Indies in 1969 and 1970-71. Tour: West Indies to England 1969. Scored 1,157 runs (av 29.66) and took 96 wkts (av 18.72) in 1968. Gillette Man of the Match awards: 1. Benson & Hedges Gold awards: 2. HS: 170 v Northants (Folkestone) 1968. HSTC: 32 West Indies v England (Lord's) 1969. HSGC: 101 v Middlesex (Canterbury) 1977. HSJPL: 94 v Hants (Southampton) 1978. HSBH: 96 v Middlesex (Lord's) 1975.BB: 8-40 West Indians v Glos. (Bristol) 1969. BBTC: 5-104 West Indies v England (Manchester) 1969. BBC: 8-83 v Lancs (Tunbridge Wells) 1977. BBGC: 4-23 v Essex (Leyton) 1972. BBJPL: 4-17 v Middlesex (Lord's) 1978. BBBH: 4-25 v Derbyshire (Lord's) 1978.

Guy Dennis SPELMAN (Sevenoaks School) B Westminster 18/10/1958. 6ft 3½ins tall. LHB, RM. Played in three John Player League matches in 1978. Has yet to appear in first-class cricket. BBJPL: 3-39 v Derbyshire (Canterbury) 1978. Is studying at Nottingham University.

Christopher James (Chris) TAVARE (Sevenoaks School and Oxford) B Orpington 27/10/1954. RHB, RM. Scored 124* for England Schools v All-India Schools (Birmingham) 1973. Debut 1974. Blue 1975-76-77. Cap 1978. 1,000 runs (2)—1,534 runs (av 45.11) in 1978 best. Benson & Hedges Gold awards: 3 (2 for Combined Universities). HS: 124* v Notts (Canterbury) 1977. HSGC: 54 v Northants (Northampton) 1978. HSJPL: 136* v Glos (Canterbury) 1978. HSBH: 89 Combined Universities v Surrey (Oval) 1976.

Derek Leslie UNDERWOOD (Beckenham and Penge GS) B Bromley 8/6/1945. RHB, LM. Debut 1963, taking 100 wkts and being the youngest player ever to do so in debut season. Cap 1964 (second youngest Kent player to have received this award). Elected Best Young Cricketer of the Year in 1966 by the Cricket Writers' Club. *Wisden* 1968. Benefit (£24,114) in 1975. Took 1,000th wkt in first-class cricket in New Zealand 1970-71 at age of 25 years 264 days—only W. Rhodes (in 1902) and G. A. Lohmann (in 1890) have achieved the feat at a younger age. Took 200th wkt in Test cricket against Australia in 1975. Tests: 74 between 1966 and 1977. Played in 3 matches against Rest of World in 1970. Tours: Pakistan 1966-67, Ceylon and Pakistan 1968-69, Australia and New Zealand 1970-71, 1974-75, India, Sri Lanka and Pakistan 1972-73. West Indies 1973-74, India, Sri Lanka and Australia 1976-77. 100 wkts (8)—157 wkts (av 13.80) in 1966 best. Hat-trick v Sussex (Hove) 1977. HS: 80 v Lancs (Manchester) 1969. HSTC: 45* v Australia (Leeds) 1968. HSGC: 28 v Sussex (Tunbridge Wells) 1963. HSJPL: 22 v Worcs (Dudley) 1969. HSBH: 17 v Essex (Canterbury) 1973. BB: 9-28 v Sussex (Hastings) 1964 and 9-32 v Surrey (Oval) 1978. BBTC: 8-51 v Pakistan (Lord's) 1974. BBGC: 4-57 v Leics (Canterbury) 1974. BBJPL: 5-19 v Glos (Maidstone) 1972. BBBH: 5-35 v Surrey (Oval) 1976.

Robert Andrew (Bob) WOOLMER (Skinners' School, Tunbridge Wells) B Kanpur (India) 14/5/1948. RHB, RM. Debut 1968. Cap 1970. *Wisden* 1975. Played for Natal between 1973–74 and 1975–76 in Currie Cup competition. Tests: 15 between 1975 and 1977. Tour: India, Sri Lanka and Australia 1976–77. 1,000 runs (4)—1,749 runs (av 47.27) in 1976 best. Hat-trick for MCC v Australians (Lord's) 1975. Gillette Man of Match awards: 2. Benson & Hedges Gold awards: 3. HS: 149 England v Australia (Oval) 1975. HSC: 143 v Notts (Nottingham) 1976. HSGC: 78 v Notts (Nottingham) 1975. HSJPL: 64 v Lancs (Manchester) 1976. HSBH: 79 v Derbyshire (Lord's) 1978. BB: 7–47 v Sussex (Canterbury) 1969. BBGC: 4–37 v Leics (Leicester) 1971. BBJPL: 5–26 v Somerset (Canterbury) 1973. BBBH: 4–14 v Sussex (Tunbridge Wells) 1972.

NB. The following players whose particulars appeared in the 1978 annual have been omitted: J.A. Howgego and B.W. Luckhurst. In addition G. S. Clinton has joined Surrey and his particulars will be found under that county.

COUNTY AVERAGES

Schweppes Championship: Played 22, won 13, drawn 6, lost 3
All first-class matches: Played 24, won 13, drawn 8, lost 3

BATTING AND FIELDING

Cap		M	I	NO	Runs	HS	Avge	100	50	Ct	St
1968	Asif Iqbal	18	25	6	934	171	49.15	3	2	18	—
1978	C. J. Tavare	24	37	5	1432	105	44.75	2	10	48	—
1970	R. A. Woolmer	21	34	3	1245	137	40.16	2	9	25	—
1967	J. N. Shepherd	20	28	6	785	101	35.68	2	3	12	—
1977	C. J. C. Rowe	20	35	5	1065	85	35.50	—	7	7	—
1970	A. G. E. Ealham	23	32	4	856	102*	30.57	1	5	15	—
1970	G. W. Johnson	24	31	6	685	95	27.40	—	3	19	—
—	C. S. Cowdrey	17	17	4	291	69*	22.38	—	1	11	—
—	G. S. Clinton	6	8	2	113	33	18.83	—	—	2	—
1964	D. L. Underwood	22	17	6	145	25	13.18	—	—	7	—
1977	R. W. Hills	14	13	2	122	31*	11.09	—	—	3	—
—	P. R. Downton	24	20	6	147	31	10.50	—	—	53	4
—	N. J. Kemp	3	2	1	8	8*	8.00	—	—	—	—
—	G. R. Dilley	4	4	2	11	8	5.50	—	—	3	—
1977	K. B. S. Jarvis	24	14	7	22	12	3.14	—	—	5	—

BOWLING

	Type	O	M	R	W	Avge	Best	5 wI	10 wM
D. L. Underwood	LM	815.1	359	1594	110	14.49	9–32	8	2
R. A. Woolmer	RM	135.4	46	292	20	14.60	6–27	1	—
G. W. Johnson	OB	510.4	173	1084	56	19.35	6–32	2	—
K. B. S. Jarvis	RFM	579.5	134	1790	80	22.37	8–97	3	1
G. R. Dilley	RM	75	19	197	8	24.62	5–32	1	—
Asif Iqbal	RM	73	15	228	8	28.50	4–47	—	—
R. W. Hills	RM	263.2	63	803	24	33.45	6–64	1	—
J. N. Shepherd	RM	601.2	166	1573	44	35.75	5–70	1	—

Also bowled: G. S. Clinton 1–0–8–2; C. S. Cowdrey 12–5–20–0; A. G. E. Ealham 0.2–0–4–0; N. J. Kemp 28–4–91–3; C. J. C. Rowe 84.3–29–211–3; C. J. Tavare 5–1–20–1.

County Records

First-class cricket

Highest innings totals:	For __803–4d v Essex (Brentwood)		1934
	Agst.__676 by Australians (Canterbury)		1921
Lowest innings totals:	For __18 v Sussex (Gravesend)		1867
	Agst.__16 by Warwickshire (Tonbridge)		1913
Highest individual innings:	For __332 W. H. Ashdown v Essex (Brentwood)		1934
	Agst.__344 W. G. Grace for MCC (Canterbury)		1876
Best bowling in an innings:	For __10–30 C. Blythe v Northamptonshire (Northampton)		1907
	Agst.__10–48 C. H. G. Bland for Sussex (Tonbridge)		1899
Best bowling in a match:	For __17–48 C. Blythe v Northamptonshire (Northampton)		1907
	Agst.__17–106 T. W. Goddard for Gloucestershire (Bristol)		1939
Most runs in a season:	2894 (av 59.06) F. E. Woolley		1928
runs in a career:	48483 (av 42.05) F. E. Woolley	1906–1938	
100s in a season:	10 by F. E. Woolley	1928 & 1934	
100s in a career:	112 by F. E. Woolley	1906–1938	
wickets in a season:	262 (av 14.74) A. P. Freeman		1933
wickets in a career:	3359 (av 14.45) A. P. Freeman	1914–1936	

RECORD WICKET STANDS

1st	283	A. E. Fagg & P. R. Sunnucks v Essex (Colchester)	1938
2nd	352	W. H. Ashdown & F. E. Woolley v Essex (Brentwood)	1934
3rd	321	A. Hearne & J. R. Mason v Nottinghamshire (Nottingham)	1899
4th	297	H. T. W. Hardinge & A. P. F. Chapman v Hampshire (Southampton)	1926
5th	277	F. E. Woolley & L. E. G. Ames v New Zealanders (Canterbury)	1931
6th	284	A.P.F. Chapman & G.B. Legge v Lancashire (Maidstone)	1927
7th	248	A. P. Day & E. Humphreys v Somerset (Taunton)	1908
8th	157	A. L. Hilder & C. Wright v Essex (Gravesend)	1924
9th	161	B. R. Edrich & F. Ridgway v Sussex (Tunbridge Wells)	1949
10th	235	F.E. Woolley & A. Fielder v Worcestershire (Stourbridge)	1909

One-day cricket

Highest innings totals:	Gillette Cup	297–3 v Worcestershire (Canterbury)	1970
	John Player League	278–5 v Gloucestershire (Maidstone)	1976
	Benson & Hedges Cup	280–3 v Surrey (Oval)	1976
Lowest innings totals:	Gillette Cup	110 v Gloucestershire (Bristol)	1968
	John Player League	84 v Gloucestershire (Folkestone)	1969
	Benson & Hedges Cup	118 v Essex (Chelmsford)	1975
Highest individual innings:	Gillette Cup	129 B. W. Luckhurst v Durham (Canterbury)	1974
	John Player League	142 B. W. Luckhurst v Somerset (Weston-super-Mare)	1970
	Benson & Hedges Cup	114 C. S. Cowdrey v Sussex (Canterbury)	1977

89

LANCASHIRE

Formation of present club: 1864.
Colours: Red, green, and blue.
Badge: Red Rose.
County Champions (8): 1881, 1897, 1904, 1926,
  1927, 1928, 1930 and 1934.
Joint Champions (4): 1879, 1882, 1889 and 1950.
Gillette Cup Winners (4): 1970, 1971, 1972 and 1975.
Gillette Cup Finalists (2): 1974 and 1976.
John Player League Champions (2): 1969 and 1970.
Benson & Hedges Cup semi-finalists (2): 1973 and
  1974.
Gillette Man of the Match awards: 34.
Benson & Hedges Gold awards: 18.

Secretary: C. D. Hassell, Old Trafford, Manchester, M16 0PX.
Captain: F. C. Hayes.

John ABRAHAMS (Heywood GS) B Cape Town, South Africa 21/7/
1952. LHB, OB. Son of Cecil J. Abrahams, former professional for
Milnrow and Radcliffe in Central Lancashire League. Has lived in this
country since 1962. Debut 1973. HS: 126 v Cambridge U (Cambridge)
1978. HSGC: 46 v Northants (Lord's) 1976. HSJPL: 58 v Worcs (Worcester) 1976. HSBH: 22 v Hants (Southampton) 1977.

Paul John Walter ALLOTT (Altrincham County Grammar School for
Boys) B Altrincham (Cheshire) 14/9/1956. 6ft 4ins tall. RHB, RFM.
Played for Cheshire in 1976 and for county 2nd XI in 1977. Debut 1978.
BB: 5–98 v Surrey (Oval) 1978. Is studying at Durham University.

Robert (Bob) ARROWSMITH B Denton (Lancs) 21/5/1952. RHB, SLA.
Played in one John Player League match in 1975. Debut 1976. HS: 30* v
Australians (Manchester) 1977. BB: 6–29 v Oxford U (Oxford) 1977.

Graeme FOWLER (Accrington GS) B Accrington 20/4/57. RHB, RM.
played for 2nd XI since 1973. Played in one John Player League match v
Derbyshire (Chesterfield) 1978. Has yet to appear in first-class cricket. Is
studying at Durham University.

Frank Charles HAYES (De La Salle College, Salford) B Preston
6/12/1946. RHB, RM. Debut 1970 scoring 94 and 99 in first two matches
after scoring 203* for 2nd XI v Warwickshire 2nd XI (Birmingham).
Cap 1972. Appointed county captain in 1978. Tests: 9 between 1973 and
1976. Tour: West Indies 1973–74. 1,000 runs (5)—1,311 runs (av 35.43)
in 1974 best. Scored 34 in one over (6 4 6 6 6 6) off M. A. Nash v Glamorgan (Swansea) 1977. Gillette Man of Match awards: 1. Benson & Hedges

Gold awards: 2. HS: 187 v Indians (Manchester) 1974. HSTC: 106* v West Indies (Oval) 1973 in second innings on Test debut. HSGC: 93 v Warwickshire (Birmingham) 1976. HSJPL: 70 v Worcs (Worcester) 1978. HSBH: 102 v Minor Counties (North) (Manchester) 1973. Amateur soccer player. Studied at Sheffield University.

William (Willie) HOGG (Ulverston Comprehensive School) B Ulverston 12/7/1955. RHB, RFM. Debut 1976 after playing as professional for Preston in Northern League. HS: 19 v Middlesex (Lord's) 1978. BB: 7–84 v Warwickshire (Manchester) 1978. BBJPL: 3–41 v Glos (Bristol) 1977.

David Paul HUGHES (Newton-le-Willows GS) B Newton-le-Willows (Lancs) 13/5/1947. RHB, SLA. Debut 1967. Cap 1970. Played for Tasmania in 1975–76 and 1976–77 whilst coaching there. Gillette Man of Match awards: 1. HS: 101 v Cambridge U (Cambridge) 1975. HSGC: 42* v Middlesex (Lord's) 1974. HSJPL: 84 v Essex (Leyton) 1973. HSBH: 42* v Minor Counties (West) (Watford) 1978. BB: 7–24 v Oxford U (Oxford) 1970. BBGC: 4–61 v Somerset (Manchester) 1972. BBJPL: 6–29 v Somerset (Manchester) 1977. BBBH: 5–23 v Minor Counties (West) (Watford) 1978.

Andrew KENNEDY Nelson GS) B Blackburn 4/11/1949. LHB, RM. Debut 1970. Cap 1975. Elected Best Young Cricketer of the Year in 1975 by the Cricket Writers' Club. Scored 1,022 runs (av 42.58) in 1975. Gillette Man of Match awards: 1. HS: 176* v Leics (Leicester) 1976. HSGC: 131 v Middlesex (Manchester) 1978. HSJPL: 89 v Yorks (Manchester) 1978. HSBH: 31 v Leics (Leicester) 1975.

Peter Granville LEE B Arthingworth (Northants) 27/8/1945. RHB, RFM. Debut for Northants 1967. Joined Lancs in 1972. Cap 1972. *Wisden* 1975. Played in only one match in 1978 due to injury. 100 wkts (2)—112 wkts (av 18.45) in 1975 best. HS: 26 Northants v Glos (Northampton) 1969. HSGC: 10* v Middlesex (Lord's) 1974. HSJPL: 27* Northants v Derbyshire (Chesterfield) 1971. BB: 8–53 v Sussex (Hove) 1973. BBGC: 4–7 v Cornwall (Truro) 1977. BBJPL: 4–17 v Derbyshire (Chesterfield) 1972. BBBH: 4–32 v Worcs (Manchester) 1973.

Clive Hubert LLOYD (Chatham HS, Georgetown) B Georgetown, British Guiana 31/8/1944. Cousin of L. R. Gibbs. LHB, RM. Wears glasses. Debut 1963–64 for Guyana (then British Guiana). Played for Haslingden in Lancashire League in 1967 and also for Rest of World XI in 1967 and 1968. Debut for county v Australians 1968. Cap 1969. *Wisden* 1970. Appointed county vice-captain in 1973. Testimonial (£27,199) in 1977, Tests: 65 for West Indies between 1966–67 and 1977–78, captaining West Indies in 30 Tests. Played in 5 matches for Rest of World 1970 and 2 in 1971–72. Scored 118 on debut v England (Port of Spain) 1967–68, 129 on debut v Australia (Brisbane) 1968–69, and 82 and 78* on debut v India (Bombay) 1966–67. Tours: West Indies to India and Ceylon 1966–67, Australia and New Zealand 1968–69, England 1969, 1973 and 1976 (captain). Rest of World to Australia 1971–72 (returning early owing to back injury), India, Sri Lanka and Pakistan 1974–75 (captain), Australia 1975–76 (captain). 1,000 runs (8)—1,603 runs (av 47.14) in 1970 best. Also scored

91

LANCASHIRE

1,000 runs in Australia and New Zealand 1968–69 and in India, Sri Lanka and Pakistan 1974–75. Scored 201* in 120 minutes for West Indians v Glamorgan (Swansea) 1976 to equal record for fastest double century in first class cricket. Gillette Man of Match awards: 6. HS: 242* West Indies v India (Bombay) 1974–75. HSUK: 217* v Warwickshire (Manchester) 1971. HSGC: 126 v Warwickshire (Lord's) 1972. HSJPL: 134* v Somerset (Manchester) 1970. HSBH: 73 v Notts (Manchester) 1974. BB: 4–48 v Leics (Manchester) 1970. BBGC: 3–39 v Somerset (Taunton) 1970. BBJPL: 4–33 v Middlesex (Lord's) 1971. BBBH: 3–23 v Derbyshire (Manchester) 1974.

David LLOYD (Accrington Secondary TS) B Accrington 18/3/1947. LHB. SLA. Debut 1965. Cap 1968. County captain from 1973 to 1977. Testimonial in 1978. Tests: 9 in 1974 and 1974–75. Tour: Australia and New Zealand 1974–75. 1,000 runs (8)—1,510 runs (av 47.18) in 1972 best. Gillette Man of Match awards: 3. HS: 214* England v India (Birmingham) 1974. HSC: 195 v Glos (Manchester) 1973. HSGC: 121* v Glos (Manchester) 1973. HSJPL: 103* v Northants (Bedford) 1971. HSBH: 113 v Minor Counties (North) (Manchester) 1973. BB: 7–38 v Glos (Lydney) 1966.

John LYON (St Helens' Central County Secondary School) B St Helens 17/5/1951. RHB, WK. Played for 2nd XI since 1971. Debut 1973. Cap 1975. HS: 74* v Notts (Manchester) 1978. HSGC: 11 v Sussex (Hove) 1978. HSJPL: 31 v Glos (Gloucester) 1975. HSBH: 19 v Derbyshire (Manchester) 1978.

Harry PILLING (Ashton TS) B Ashton-under-Lyne (Lancs) 23/2/1943. 5 ft 3 ins tall. RHB, OB. Debut 1962. Cap 1965. Testimonial (£9,500) 1974. 1,000 runs (3)—1,606 runs (av 36.50) in 1967 best. Scored two centuries in match (119* and 104*) v Warwickshire (Manchester) 1970. Gillette Man of Match awards: 3. Benson & Hedges Gold awards: 3. HS: 149* v Glamorgan (Liverpool) 1976. HSGC: 90 v Middlesex (Lord's) 1973. HSJPL: 85 v Sussex (Hove) 1970. HSBH: 109* v Glamorgan (Manchester) 1973.

Robert Malcolm (Bob) RATCLIFFE B Accrington 29/11/1951. RHB, RM. Joined staff 1971. Debut 1972. Cap 1976. Gillette Man of Match awards: 1. HS: 48 v Middlesex (Lord's) 1978. HSGC: 17 v Cornwall (Truro) 1977. HSJPL: 28 v Essex (Manchester) 1976. HSBH: 14 v Derbyshire (Southport) 1976. BB: 7–58 v Hants (Bournemouth) 1978. BBGC: 4–25 v Hants (Manchester) 1975. BBJPL: 4–25 v Sussex (Blackpool) 1976. BBBH: 3–33 v Warwickshire (Birmingham) 1976.

Bernard Wilfrid REIDY (St Mary's College, Blackburn) B Bramley Meade, Whalley (Lancs) 18/9/1953. LHB, LM. Toured West Indies with England Young Cricketers 1972. Played for 2nd XI since 1971. Debut 1973. HS: 48 v Worcs (Worcester) 1978. HSGC: 18 v Glos (Manchester) 1975. HSJPL: 58* v Somerset (Manchester) 1975. BBJPL: 3–33 v Surrey (Manchester) 1978.

Paul Andrew ROBINSON B Boksburg, South Africa 16/7/1956. 6ft 8in tall. RHB, RFM. Debut for Northern Transvaal in 1977–78 Currie Cup Competition. Played for Cheshire in 1978. Has joined County for 1979. HS: 25* Northern Transvaal v Griqualand West (Pretoria) 1977–78. BB: 3–33 Northern Transvaal v Border (East London) 1977–78.

Christopher John SCOTT (Ellesmere Port HS) B Swinton, Manchester 16/9/1959. LHB, WK. Played for 2nd XI since 1975. Debut 1977 aged 17 years 8 months. HS: 10 v Oxford U (Oxford) 1977.

Jack SIMMONS (Accrington Secondary TS and Blackburn TS) B Clayton-le-Moors (Lancs) 28/3/1941. RHB, OB. Debut for 2nd XI 1959. Played for Blackpool in Northern League as professional. Debut 1968. Cap 1971. Played for Tasmania from 1972–73 to 1978–79 whilst coaching there. Hat-trick v Notts (Liverpool) 1977. Benson & Hedges Gold awards: 2. HS: 112 v Sussex (Hove) 1970. HSGC: 37* v Cornwall (Truro) 1977. HSJPL: 47* v Warwickshire (Birmingham) 1977. HSBH: 64 v Derbyshire (Manchester) 1978. BB: 7–59 Tasmania v Queensland (Brisbane) 1978–79. BBGC: 5–49 v Worcs. (Worcester) 1974. BBJPL: 5–28 v Northants (Peterborough) 1972. BBBH: 4–31 v Yorks (Manchester) 1975. Has played soccer in Lancs Combination.

Richard John SUTCLIFFE (King Edward VII School, Lytham) B Rochdale 18/9/1954. RHB, RM. Debut 1978. One match v Essex (Southport). HS: 10* v Essex (Southport) 1978.

Geoffrey Edward TRIM B Openshaw Manchester 6/4/1956. RHB, LB. Joined staff 1974. Played in last John Player League match of 1975. season. Debut 1976 (two matches). Did not play in 1977 or 1978. HS: 15 v Notts (Nottingham) 1976.

Barry WOOD B Ossett (Yorks) 26/12/1942. RHB, RM. Brother of R. Wood who played occasionally for Yorkshire some years ago. Debut for Yorks 1964. Joined Lancs by special registration, making debut for county in 1966. Cap 1968. Played for Eastern Province in Currie Cup in 1971–72 and 1973–74. Testimonial in 1979. Tests: 12 between 1972 and 1978. Tours: India, Pakistan, and Sri Lanka 1972–73, New Zealand 1974–75 (flown out as reinforcement). Scored centuries in both 'Roses' matches in 1970 against his native county. 1,000 runs (6)—1,492 runs (av 38.25) in 1971 best. Gillette Man of Match awards: 6. Benson & Hedges Gold awards: 8. HS: 198 v Glamorgan (Liverpool) 1976. HSTC: 90 v Australia (Oval) 1972. HSGC: 105 v Warwickshire (Birmingham) 1976. HSJPL: 90* v Notts (Manchester) 1977. HSBH: 79 v Minor Counties (North) (Longton) 1975. BB: 7–52 v Middlesex (Manchester) 1968. BBGC: 4–17 v Hants (Manchester) 1975. BBJPL: 5–19 v Kent (Manchester) 1971. BBBH: 5–12 v Derbyshire (Southport) 1974.

Alan WORSICK (Accrington GS) B Rawtenstall 13/8/1943. RHB, RM. Played for Worcs 2nd XI and also for county 2nd XI in 1971. Professional for Accrington in Lancashire League. Played in one John Player League match v Essex (Manchester) 1978. Has yet to appear in first-class cricket.

NB The following player whose particulars appeared in the 1978 annual has been omitted: C. E. H. Croft (not re-engaged).
His career record will be found elsewhere in this annual.

COUNTY AVERAGES

Schweppes Championship: Played 21, won 4, drawn 9, lost 8, abandoned 1
All first-class matches: Played 23, won 5, drawn 10, lost 8, abandoned 1

BATTING AND FIELDING

Cap		M	I	NO	Runs	HS	Avge	100	50	Ct	St
1969	C. H. Lloyd	21	36	6	1116	120	37.20	4	6	21	—
1972	F. C. Hayes	20	34	5	1049	136*	36.17	2	4	15	—
1968	D. Lloyd	22	37	2	1113	185	31.80	3	3	18	—
—	B. W. Reidy	10	15	3	360	88	30.00	—	1	2	—
1975	A. Kennedy	19	31	2	859	100	29.62	1	4	8	—
1971	J. Simmons	22	30	7	663	106	28.82	1	2	22	—
—	J. Abrahams	19	30	2	654	126	23.35	1	4	12	—
1968	B. Wood	8	12	1	214	103	19.45	1	—	5	—
1976	R. M. Ratcliffe	20	23	5	318	48	17.66	—	—	8	—
1965	H. Pilling	8	13	1	203	49	16.91	—	2	—	—
1970	D. P. Hughes	13	17	2	243	72	16.20	—	1	13	—
—	R. Arrowsmith	13	10	4	96	24*	16.00	—	—	4	—
1975	J. Lyon	21	25	3	267	74*	12.13	—	1	49	3
—	C. E. H. Croft	18	22	3	124	19*	6.52	—	1	1	—
—	W. Hogg	11	14	5	50	19	5.55	—	—	1	—
—	P. J. W. Allott	4	2	1	1	1*	1.00	—	—	1	—

Played in two matches: C. J. Scott 1*, 8 (3 ct).
Played in one match: P. G. Lee 1 ; R. J. Sutcliffe 10*, 0*.

BOWLING

	Type	O	M	R	W	Avge	Best	5 wI	10 wM
W. Hogg	RFM	256.4	58	775	38	20.39	7–84	1	—
R. M. Ratcliffe	RM	571.3	151	1532	70	21.88	7–58	3	—
C. E. H. Croft	RF	431.3	101	1266	56	22.60	5–58	1	—
D. P. Hughes	SLA	191.1	54	517	22	23.50	5–46	1	—
B. Wood	RM	87	28	240	8	30.00	3–45	—	—
P. J. W. Allott	RFM	129	12	456	14	32.57	5–98	1	—
R. Arrowsmith	SLA	320.1	106	889	27	32.92	4–49	—	—
J. Simmons	OB	501	146	1203	35	34.37	3–33	—	—
B. W. Reidy	LM	163	29	515	6	85.83	2–47	—	—

Also bowled: J. Abrahams 1–1–0–0; A. Kennedy 26–10–59–2; P. G. Lee 8–2–26–2; D. Lloyd 3.5–1–11–0; R. J. Sutcliffe 12–3–37–1.

County Records

First-class cricket

Highest innings totals:	For ―810 v Somerset (Taunton)	1895
	Agst―634 v Surrey (The Oval)	1898
Lowest innings totals:	For ―25 v Derbyshire (Manchester)	1871
	Agst―22 by Glamorgan (Liverpool)	1924
Highest individual innings:	For ―424 A. C. MacLaren v Somerset (Taunton)	1895
	Agst―315* T. Hayward for Surrey (The Oval)	1898
Best bowling in innings:	For ―10–55 J. Briggs v Worcestershire (Manchester)	1900
	Agst―10–40 G. O. Allen for Middlesex (Lord's)	1929
Best bowling in a match:	For ―17–91 H. Dean v Yorkshire (Liverpool)	1913
	Agst―16–65 G. Giffen for Australians (Manchester)	1886

Most runs in a season: 2633 (av 56.02) J. T. Tyldesley   1901
    runs in a career: 34222 (av 45.02) E. Tyldesley   1909–1936
    100s in a season: 11 by C. Hallows   1928
    100s in a career: 90 by E. Tyldesley   1909–1936
    wickets in a season: 198 (av 18.55) E. A. McDonald   1925
    wickets in a career: 1816 (av 15.12) J. B. Statham   1950–1968

RECORD WICKET STANDS

1st	368	A. C. MacLaren & R. H. Spooner v Gloucestershire (Liverpool)	1903
2nd	371	F. Watson & E. Tyldesley v Surrey (Manchester)	1928
3rd	306	E. Paynter & N. Oldfield v Hampshire (Southampton)	1938
4th	324	A. C. MacLaren & J. T. Tyldesley v Nottinghamshire (Nottingham)	1904
5th	249	B. Wood & A. Kennedy v Warwickshire (Birmingham)	1975
6th	278	J. Iddon & H. R. W. Butterworth v Sussex (Manchester)	1932
7th	245	A. H. Hornby & J. Sharp v Leicestershire (Manchester)	1912
8th	150	A. Ward & C. R. Hartley v Leicestershire (Leicester)	1900
9th	142	L. O. S. Poidevin & A. Kermode v Sussex (Eastbourne)	1907
10th	173	J. Briggs & R. Pilling v Surrey (Liverpool)	1885

One-day cricket

Highest innings totals:	Gillette Cup	304–9 v Leicestershire (Manchester)	1963
	John Player League	255–5 v Somerset (Manchester)	1970
	Benson & Hedges Cup	275–5 v Minor Counties (North) (Manchester)	1973
Lowest innings totals:	Gillette Cup	59 v Worcestershire (Worcester)	1963
	John Player League	76 v Somerset (Manchester)	1972
	Benson & Hedges Cup	82 v Yorks (Bradford)	1972
Highest individual innings:	Gillette Cup	131 A Kennedy v Middlesex (Manchester)	1978
	John Player League	134* C. H. Lloyd v Somerset (Manchester)	1970
	Benson & Hedges Cup	113 D. Lloyd v Minor Counties (North) (Manchester)	1973
Best bowling figures:	Gillette Cup	5–28 J. B. Statham v Leics (Manchester)	1963
	John Player League	6–29 D. P. Hughes v Somerset (Manchester)	1977
	Benson & Hedges Cup	5–12 B. Wood v Derbyshire (Southport)	1976

LEICESTERSHIRE

Formation of present club · 1879.
Colours: Scarlet and dark green.
Badge: Running fox (gold) on green background.
County Champions: 1975.
Gillette Cup semi-finalists: 1977.
John Player League Champions (2): 1974 and 1977.
Benson & Hedges Cup Winners (2): 1972 and 1975.
Benson & Hedges Cup finalists: 1974.
Gillette Man of the Match awards: 13.
Benson & Hedges Gold awards: 27.

Secretary: F. M. Turner, County Ground, Grace Road, Leicester,
LE2 8AD.
Captain: K. Higgs.
Prospects of play Telephone No.: Leicester (0533) 832128.

Jonathan Philip AGNEW (Uppingham School) B Macclesfield (Cheshire)
4/4/1960. 6ft. 3½ins tall. RHB, RF. Played for Surrey 2nd XI in 1976 and
1977. Debut 1978. BB: 3–51 v Northants (Leicester) 1978.

John Christopher (Chris) BALDERSTONE B Huddersfield 16/11/1940.
RHB, SLA. Played for Yorks from 1961 to 1970. Specially registered and
made debut for Leics in 1971. Cap 1973. Tests: 2 in 1976. 1,000 runs (4)—
1,409 runs (av 33.54) in 1976 best. Hat-trick v Sussex (Eastbourne) 1976.
Gillette Man of Match awards: 2. Benson & Hedges Gold awards: 5.
HS: 178* v Notts (Nottingham) 1977. HSTC: 35 v West Indies (Leeds)
1976. HSGC: 119* v Somerset (Taunton) 1973. HSJPL: 96 v Northants
(Leicester) 1976. HSBH: 101* v Hants (Leicester) 1975. BB: 6–25 v Hants
(Southampton) 1978. BBGC: 4–33 v Herts (Leicester) 1977. BBJPL: 3–29
v Worcs (Leicester) 1971. Soccer for Huddersfield Town, Carlisle United,
Doncaster Rovers and Queen of the South.

Jack BIRKENSHAW (Rothwell GS) B Rothwell (Yorks) 13/11/1940.
LHB, OB. Played for Yorks 1958 to 1960. Specially registered and made
debut for Leics in 1961. Cap 1965. Benefit (£13,100) in 1974. Tests: 5 in
1972–73 and 1973–74. Tours: India Pakistan and Sri Lanka 1972–73, West
Indies 1973–74. 100 wkts (2)— 111 wkts (av 21.41) in 1967 best. Hat-tricks
(2) v Worcs (Worcester) 1967 and v Cambridge U (Cambridge) 1968.
Shared in 7th wkt partnership record for county, 206 with B Dudleston v
Kent (Canterbury) 1969. Gillette Man of the Match awards: 1. HS: 131 v
Surrey (Guildford) 1969. HSTC: 64 v India (Kanpur) 1972–73. HSGC:
101* v Hants (Leicester) 1976. HSJPL: 79 v Yorks (Leicester) 1978.
HSBH: 35* v Worcs (Worcester) 1972. BB: 8–94 v Somerset (Taunton)
1972. BBGC: 3–19 v Somerset (Leicester) 1968. BBJPL: 5–20 v Essex
(Leicester) 1975.

96

Peter BOOTH (Whitcliffe Mount GS, Cleckheaton) B Shipley (Yorks) 2/11/1952. RHB, RFM. Played for MCC Schools at Lord's 1970 and 1971. Toured West Indies with England Youth Team 1972. Debut 1972. Cap 1976. HS: 58* v Lancs (Leicester) 1976. HSGC: 40* v Glamorgan (Swansea) 1977. HSJPL: 22* v Derbyshire (Leicester) 1976. BB: 6–93 v Glamorgan (Swansea) 1978. BBGC: 5–33 v Northants (Northampton) 1977. BBJPL: 4–20 v Warwickshire (Leicester) 1977. BBBH: 3–27 v Hants (Leicester) 1975. Trained as a teacher at Loughborough College.

Nigel Edwin BRIERS (Lutterworth GS) B Leicester 15/1/1955. RHB, Cousin of N. Briers who played once for county in 1967. Debut 1971 at age of 16 years 104 days. Youngest player ever to appear for county HS: 116* v Cambridge U. (Cambridge) 1978. HSJPL: 81 v Worcs (Worcester) 1978.

Patrick Bernard (Paddy) CLIFT (St George's College, Salisbury) B Salisbury, Rhodesia 14/7/1953. RHB, RM. Debut for Rhodesia 1971–72. Debut for county 1975. Cap 1976. Hat-trick v Yorks (Leicester) 1976. HS: 75* Rhodesia v Eastern Province (Bulawayo) 1972–73. HSUK: 64 v Somerset (Leicester) 1977. HSGC: 33 v Hants (Leicester) 1978. HSJPL: 49* v Sussex (Eastbourne) 1976. HSBH: 58 v Worcs (Worcester) 1976. BB: 8–17 v MCC (Lord's) 1976. BBJPL: 4–14 v Lancs (Leicester) 1978. BBBH: 4–13 v Minor Counties (East) (Amersham) 1978.

Nicholas Grant Billson COOK (Lutterworth GS) B Leicester 17/6/1956. RHB, SLA. Played for 2nd XI since 1974. Debut 1978 (two matches). HS: 31 v Northants (Leicester) 1978.

Brian Fettes DAVISON (Gifford Technical HS, Rhodesia) B Bulawayo, Rhodesia 21/12/1946. RHB, RM. Debut for Rhodesia 1967–68 in Currie Cup competition. Debut for county 1970 after having played for International Cavaliers. Cap 1971. 1,000 runs (8)—1,818 runs (av 56.81) in 1976 best. Gillette Man of Match awards: 1. Benson & Hedges Gold awards: 6. HS: 189 v Australians (Leicester) 1975. HSGC: 99 v Essex (Southend) 1977. HSJPL: 85* v Glamorgan (Cardiff) 1974. HSBH: 158* v Warwickshire (Coventry) 1972. BB: 5–52 Rhodesia v Griqualand West (Bulawayo) 1967–68. BBUK: 4–99 v Northants (Leicester) 1970. BBJPL: 4–29 v Glamorgan (Neath) 1971. Has played hockey for Rhodesia.

Barry DUDLESTON (Stockport School) B Bebington (Cheshire) 16/7/1945. RHB, SLA. Debut 1966. Cap 1969. Played for Rhodesia from 1976–77 to 1978–79 in Currie Cup competitions. 1,000 runs (7)—1,374 runs (av 31.22) in 1970 best. Gillette Man of Match awards: 1. Benson & Hedges Gold awards: 3. Shared in 7th wkt partnership record for county 206 with J. Birkenshaw v Kent (Canterbury) 1969. HS: 172 v Glamorgan (Leicester) 1975. HSGC: 118 v Staffs (Longton) 1975. HSJPL: 152 v Lancs (Manchester) 1975. HSBH: 90 v Warwickshire (Leicester) 1973. BB: 4–6 v Surrey (Leicester) 1972.

David Ivon GOWER (King's School, Canterbury) B Tunbridge Wells 1/4/1957. LHB, OB. Toured South Africa with English Schools XI 1974–75 and West Indies with England Young Cricketers 1976. Debut 1975. Cap 1978. *Wisden* 1978. Elected Best Young Cricketer of the Year in 1978 by Cricket Writers Club. Tests: 6 in 1978. Tour: Australia 1978–79. Scored 1,098 runs (av 37.86) in 1978. Gillette Man of Match awards: 1. HS: 144* v Hants (Leicester) 1977. HSTC: 111 v New Zealand (Oval) 1978. HSGC: 117* v Herts (Leicester) 1977. HSJPL: 135* v Warwickshire (Leicester) 1977. HSBH: 49 v Middlesex (Lord's) 1978. BB: 3–47 v Essex (Leicester) 1977.

Kenneth (Ken) HIGGS B Sandyford (Staffordshire) 14/1/1937. LHB, RFM. Played for Staffordshire 1957. Debut for Lancs 1958. Cap 1959. *Wisden* 1967. Benefit (£8,390) in 1968. Retired after 1969 season. Reappeared for Leics in 1972. Cap 1972. Appointed county vice-captain in 1973 and county captain for 1979. Tests: 15 between 1965 and 1968. Shared in 10th wkt partnership of 128 with J. A. Snow v WI (Oval) 1966—2 runs short of then record 10th wkt partnership in Test cricket. Also shared in 10th wkt partnership record for county, 228 with R. Illingworth v Northants (Leicester) 1977. Tours: Australia and New Zealand 1965–66. West Indies 1967–68. 100 wkts (5)—132 wkts (av 19.42) in 1960 best. Hat-tricks (3): Lancs v Essex (Blackpool) 1960. Lancs v Yorks (Leeds) 1968 and v Hants (Leicester) 1977. Hat-trick also in Benson & Hedges Cup Final v Surrey (Lord's) 1974. Benson & Hedges Gold awards: 1. HS: 98 v Northants (Leicester) 1977. HSTC: 63 England v West Indies (Oval) 1966. HSGC: 25 Lancs v Somerset (Taunton) 1966. HSJPL: 17* v Notts (Nottingham) 1975. BB: 7–19 Lancs v Leics (Manchester) 1965. BBTC: 6–91 v West Indies (Lord's) 1966. BBC: 7–44 v Middlesex (Lord's) 1978. BBGC: 5–20 v Staffs (Longton) 1975. BBJPL: 6–17 v Glamorgan (Leicester) 1973. BBBH: 4–10 v Surrey (Lord's) 1974. Soccer for Port Vale.

Gordon James PARSONS B Slough (Bucks) 17/10/1959. LHB, RM. Played for county 2nd XI since 1976 and also for Buckinghamshire in 1977. Debut 1978 (two matches). HS: 7 v Notts (Nottingham) 1978.

Martin SCHEPENS (Rawlins School, Quorn) B Barrow-upon-Soar (Leics) 12/8/1955. RHB, LB. Played for 2nd XI since 1971. Debut 1973 aged 17 years 8 months. HS: 39 v Middlesex (Lord's) 1976 and 39 v Northants (Leicester) 1978.

Kenneth (Ken) SHUTTLEWORTH B St Helens 13/11/1944. RHB, RFM. Debut for Lancs 1964. Cap 1968. Joint testimonial (£12,500) with J. Sullivan in 1975. Did not play in 1976. Not re-engaged at end of season and made debut for county in 1977. Cap 1977. Tests: 5 in 1970–71 and 1971. Played in one match v Rest of World 1970. Tour: Australia and New Zealand 1970–71. Hat-trick v Surrey (Oval) 1977. HS: 71 Lancs v Glos (Cheltenham) 1967. HSTC: 21 v Pakistan (Birmingham) 1971. HSC: 30* v Somerset (Leicester) 1977. HSGC: 23 Lancs v Somerset (Manchester) 1967. HSJPL: 19* Lancs v Notts (Manchester) 1969. HSBH: 12* Lancs v Derbyshire (Manchester) 1974. BB: 7–41 Lancs v Essex (Leyton) 1968. BBTC: 5–47 v Australia (Brisbane) 1970–71. BBC: 6–17 v Essex (Leicester) 1977. BBGC: 4–26 Lancs v Essex (Chelmsford) 1971. BBJPL: 5–13 Lancs v Notts (Nottingham) 1972. BBBH: 3–15 Lancs v Notts (Manchester) 1972.

John Frederick STEELE B Stafford 23/7/1946. Younger brother of D. S. Steele of Northants. RHB, SLA. Debut 1970. Was 12th man for England v Rest of World (Lord's) a month after making debut. Cap 1971. Played for Natal in 1973–74 and 1977–78 Currie cup competition. 1,000 runs (5)— 1,347 (av 31.32) in 1972 best. Gillette Man of Match awards: 2. Benson & Hedges Gold awards: 4. HS: 195 v Derbyshire (Leicester) 1971. HSGC: 108* v Staffs (Longton) 1975. HSJPL: 92 v Essex (Leicester) 1973. HSBH: 91 v Somerset (Leicester) 1974. BB: 7–29 Natal B v Griqualand West (Umzinto) 1973–74. BBUK: 6–33 v Northants (Northampton) 1975. BBGC: 5–19 v Essex (Southend) 1977. BBJPL: 4–27 v Derbyshire (Burton-on-Trent) 1973. BBBH: 3–17 v Cambridge U (Leicester) 1972.

Leslie Brian TAYLOR (Heathfield HS, Earl Shilton) B Earl Shilton (Leics) 25/10/1953. 6ft 3½ins tall. RHB, RM. Debut 1977. HS: 15 v Kent (Canterbury) 1978. BB: 4–32 v Derbyshire (Derby) 1978. BBGC: 3–11 v Hants (Leicester) 1978. BBJPL: 5–23 v Notts (Nottingham) 1978.

Roger William TOLCHARD (Malvern College) B Torquay 15/6/1946. RHB, WK. Played for Devon in 1963 and 1964. Also played for Hants 2nd XI and Public Schools v Combined Services (Lord's) in 1964. Debut 1965. Cap 1966. Appointed vice-captain in 1970. Relinquished appointment in 1973. Tests: 4 in 1976–77. Tours: India, Pakistan, and Sri Lanka 1972–73, India, Sri Lanka and Australia 1976–77, Australia 1978–79. Scored 998 runs (av 30.24) in 1970. Benson & Hedges Gold awards: 4. HS: 126* v Cambridge U (Cambridge) 1970. HSGC: 86* v Glos (Leicester) 1975. HSJPL: 103 v Middlesex (Lord's) 1972 and was dismissed obstructing the field. HSBH: 92* v Worcs (Worcester) 1976. Had soccer trial for Leicester City.

Alan WARD B Dronfield (Derbyshire) 10/8/1947. RHB, RF. Debut for Derbyshire 1966. Cap 1969. Elected Best Young Cricketer of the Year in 1969 by the Cricket Writers Club. Played for Border in 1971–72 Currie Cup competition. Was sent off the field for refusing to bowl against Yorks at Chesterfield in June 1973. Left staff afterwards, but rejoined in 1974. Not re-engaged after 1976 season and made debut for Leics in 1977. Cap 1977. Tests: 5 between 1969 and 1976. Also played in 1 match v Rest of World in 1970. Tour: Australia 1970–71 returning home early owing to injury. Took 4 wickets in 4 balls in John Player League match Derbyshire v Sussex (Derby) 1970. Benson & Hedges Gold awards: 1 (for Derbyshire). HS: 44 Derbyshire v Notts (Ilkeston) 1969. HSTC: 21 v New Zealand (Oval) 1969. HSC: 19 v Surrey (Oval) 1977. HSGC: 17 Derbyshire v Yorks (Lord's) 1969. HSJPL: 21* Derbyshire v Somerset (Buxton) 1969. BB: 7–42 Derbyshire v Glamorgan (Burton-on-Trent) 1974. BBTC: 4–61 v New Zealand (Nottingham) 1969. BBC: 4–37 v Notts (Leicester) 1977. BBGC: 3–31 Derbyshire v Yorks (Lord's) 1969. BBJPL: 6–24 Derbyshire v Essex (Ilkeston) 1976. BBBH: 4–14 Derbyshire v Lancs (Manchester) 1974.

NB. The following players whose particulars appeared in the 1978 annual have been omitted: G. F. Cross, R. Illingworth (retired), N. M. McVicker and J. G. Tolchard.

The career record of Illingworth will be found elsewhere in this annual.

COUNTY AVERAGES

Schweppes Championship: Played 22, won 4, drawn 13, lost 5
All first-class matches: Played 24, won 5, drawn 14, lost 5

BATTING AND FIELDING

Cap		M	I	NO	Runs	HS	Avge	100	50	Ct	St
1971	B. F. Davison	23	35	3	1644	180*	51.37	4	9	8	—
1966	R. W. Tolchard	24	35	16	841	103*	44.26	1	5	39	7
1971	J. F. Steele	22	34	3	1182	133	38.12	3	6	28	—
1965	J. Birkenshaw	22	26	9	506	70*	29.76	—	1	10	—
	N. E. Briers	16	24	2	601	116*	27.31	2	2	6	—
1977	D. I. Gower	11	17	2	405	61	27.00	—	1	5	—
1973	J. C. Balderstone	24	36	1	931	101	26.60	1	5	9	—
	M. Schepens	5	8	2	147	39	24.50	—	—	3	—
1976	P. B. Clift	22	26	7	465	61	24.47	—	3	13	—
1977	K. Shuttleworth	6	5	2	70	27*	23.33	—	—	11	—
1969	B. Dudleston	15	22	1	454	75	21.61	—	2	4	—
1969	R. Illingworth	17	15	5	209	39*	20.90	—	—	5	—
1976	P. Booth	18	10	2	99	25*	12.37	—	—	2	—
1972	K. Higgs	18	11	6	51	13*	10.20	—	—	13	—
	L. B. Taylor	11	6	1	27	15	5.40	—	—	4	—
	J. P. Agnew	4	1	0	1	1	1.00	—	—	—	—

Played in two matches: N. G. B. Cook 2*, 31 (1 ct); G. J. Parsons 7, 3
A. Ward did not bat.

BOWLING

	Type	O	M	R	W	Avge	Best	5 wI	10 wM
K. Higgs	RFM	381	112	923	41	22.51	7-44	1	—
P. B. Clift	RM	519.4	156	1209	51	23.70	6-29	1	—
J. C. Balderstone	SLA	368.5	104	914	38	24.05	6-25	2	—
R. Illingworth	OB	261.4	86	635	25	25.40	6-38	2	—
J. F. Steele	SLA	229.5	62	566	22	25.72	5-54	1	—
L. B. Taylor	RM	278.2	47	962	36	26.72	4-32	—	—
J. Birkenshaw	OB	344.2	83	874	30	29.13	3-23	—	—
P. Booth	RFM	293.2	63	870	29	30.00	6-93	1	—
K. Shuttleworth	RFM	159.4	45	436	13	33.53	3-27	—	—
J. P. Agnew	RF	67.4	13	215	6	36.83	3-51	—	—

Also bowled: N. E. Briers 16-2-40-1; N. G. B. Cook 38-16-83-3;
B. F. Davison 5-0-29-0; B. Dudleston 2-0-11-0; G. J. Parsons 17-1-78-0;
A. Ward 29-7-70-4.

County Records

First-class cricket

Highest innings totals:	For	701-4d v Worcestershire (Worcester)	1906
	Agst.	739-7d by Nottinghamshire (Nottingham)	1903
Lowest innings totals:	For	25 v Kent (Leicester)	1912
	Agst.	24 by Glamorgan (Leicester)	1971

Highest individual innings:	For	252* S. Coe v Northants (Leicester)	1914
	Agst	341 G. H. Hirst for Yorkshire (Leicester)	1905
Best bowling in an innings:	For	10–18 G. Geary v Glamorgan (Pontypridd)	1929
	Agst	10–32 H. Pickett for Essex (Leyton)	1958
Best bowling in a match:	For	16–96 G. Geary v Glamorgan (Pontypridd)	1929
	Agst	16–102 C. Blythe for Kent (Leicester)	1909

Most runs in a season:	2446 (av 52.04) L. G. Berry	1937
runs in a career:	30143 (av 30.32) L. G. Berry	1924–1951
100s in a season:	7 by L. G. Berry and	
	W. Watson 1937 and 1959	
100s in a career:	45 by L. G. Berry	1924–1951
wickets in a season:	170 (av 18.96) J. E. Walsh	1948
wickets in a career:	2130 (av 23.19) W. E. Astill	1906–1939

RECORD WICKET STANDS

1st	380	C. J. B. Wood & H. Whitehead v Worcestershire (Worcester)	1906
2nd	287	W. Watson & A. Wharton v Lancashire (Leicester)	1961
3rd	316*	W. Watson & A. Wharton v Somerset (Taunton)	1961
4th	270	C. S. Dempster & G. S. Watson v Yorkshire (Hull)	1937
5th	226*	R. MacDonald & F. Geeson v Derbyshire (Glossop)	1901
6th	262	A. T. Sharpe & G. H. S. Fowke v Derbyshire (Chesterfield)	1911
7th	206	B. Dudleston & J. Birkenshaw v Kent (Canterbury)	1969
8th	164	M. R. Hallam & C. T. Spencer v Essex (Leicester)	1964
9th	160	W. W. Odell & R. T. Crawford v Worcestershire (Leicester)	1902
10th	228	R. Illingworth & K. Higgs v Northamptonshire (Leicester)	1977

One-day cricket

Highest innings totals:	Gillette Cup	313–5 v Hertfordshire (Leicester)	1977
	John Player League	262–6 v Somerset (Frome)	1970
	Benson & Hedges Cup	327–4 v Warwickshire (Coventry)	1972
Lowest innings totals:	Gillette Cup	56 v Northamptonshire (Leicester)	1964
	John Player League	36 v Sussex (Leicester)	1973
	Benson & Hedges Cup	82 v Hampshire (Leicester)	1973
Highest individual innings:	Gillette Cup	119* J. C. Balderstone v Somerset (Taunton)	1973
	John Player League	152 B. Dudleston v Lancs (Manchester)	1975
	Benson & Hedges Cup	158* B. F. Davison v Warwicks (Coventry)	1972
Best bowling figures:	Gillette Cup	6–20 K. Higgs v Staffs (Longton)	1975
	John Player League	6–17 K. Higgs v Glamorgan (Leicester)	1973
	Benson & Hedges Cup	5–20 R. Illingworth v Somerset (Leicester)	1974

101

MIDDLESEX

Formation of present club: 1863.
Colours: Blue.
Badge: Three seaxes.
County Champions (6): 1866, 1903, 1920, 1921, 1947
and 1976.
Joint Champions (2): 1949 and 1977.
Gillette Cup Winners: 1977.
Gillette Cup finalists: 1975.
Best position in John Player League: 3rd in 1977.
Benson & Hedges Cup finalists: 1975.
Gillette Man of the Match awards: 21,
Benson & Hedges Gold awards: 14.

Secretary: A. W. Flower, Lord's Cricket Ground, St John's Wood Road,
London NW8 8QN.
Captain: J. M. Brearley, OBE.

Prospects of play Telephone No.: (01) 286 8011.

Graham Derek BARLOW (Ealing GS) B Folkestone 26/3/1950. LHB,
RM. Played in MCC Schools matches at Lord's 1968. Debut 1969. Cap
1976. Tests: 3 in 1976–77 and 1977. Tour: India, Sri Lanka and Australia
1976–77. 1,000 runs (2)—1,478 runs (av 49.26) in 1976 best. Gillette Man
of Match awards: 1. Benson & Hedges Gold awards: 1. HS: 160* v
Derbyshire (Lord's) 1976. HSTC: 7* v India (Calcutta) 1976–77. HSGC:
76* v Warwickshire (Birmingham) 1975. HSJPL: 104 v Somerset (Bath)
1976. HSBH: 129 v Northants (Northampton) 1977. Studied at Loughborough College for whom he played rugby.

John Michael (Mike) BREARLEY (City of London School and
Cambridge) B Harrow 28/4/1942. RHB. Occasional WK. Debut 1961
scoring 1,222 runs (av 35.94) in first season. Blue 1961–62–63–64 (capt
1963–64). Cap 1964. Elected Best Young Cricketer of the Year in 1964 by
the Cricket Writers' Club. Did not play in 1966 or 1967, but reappeared in
latter half of each season between 1968 and 1970. Appointed county captain in 1971. *Wisden* 1976. Awarded OBE in 1978 New Year Honours List.
Benefit in 1978. Tests: 21 between 1976 and 1978, captaining England in
8 tests in 1977–78 and 1978. Tours: South Africa 1964–65, Pakistan 1966–
67 (captain), India, Sri Lanka and Australia (vice-captain) 1976–77,
Pakistan and New Zealand 1977–78 (captain). Returned home early owing
to injury, Australia 1978–79 (captain). 1,000 runs (8)—2,178 runs (av
44.44) in 1964 best. Holds record for most runs scored for Cambridge
University (4,310 runs, av38.48). Gillette Man of Match awards: 2. Benson
& Hedges Gold awards: 2. HS: 312* MCC under-25 v North Zone
(Peshawar) 1966–67. HSUK: 173* v Glamorgan (Cardiff) 1974. HSTC:
91 v India (Bombay) 1976–77. HSGC: 124* v Bucks (Lord's) 1975.
HSJPL: 75* v Glamorgan (Lord's) 1974. HSBH: 88 v Notts (Newark)
1976.

Roland Orlando BUTCHER B East Point, St Philip, Barbados 14/10/1953. RHB, RM. Debut 1974. Played for Barbados in 1974–75 Shell Shield competition. HS: 142 v Glos (Bristol) 1978. HSJPL: 33 v Northants (Lord's) 1974.

Wayne Wendell DANIEL B St Philip, Barbados 16/1/1956. RHB, RF. Toured England with West Indies Schoolboys team 1974. Played for 2nd XI in 1975. Debut for Barbados 1975–76. Debut for county and cap 1977. Tests: 5 for West Indies in 1975–76 and 1976. Tour: West Indies to England 1976. Gillette Man of Match awards: 1. Benson & Hedges Gold awards: 2. HS: 30 West Indians v Sussex (Hove) 1976 and 30* v Notts (Lord's) 1978. HSTC: 11 West Indies v India (Kingston) 1975–76. HSBH: 20* v Derbyshire (Derby) 1978. BB: 6–21 West Indians v Yorks (Sheffield) 1976. BBC: 6–33 v Sussex (Lord's) 1977. BBTC: 4–53 West Indies v England (Nottingham) 1976. BBGC: 4–24 v Somerset (Lord's) 1977. BBJPL: 4–31 v Yorks (Lord's) 1978. BBBH: 7–12 v Minor Counties (East) (Ipswich) 1978. Record for competition.

Phillippe Henri (Phil) EDMONDS (Gilbert Rennie HS, Lusaka, Skinner's School, Tunbridge Wells, Cranbrook School and Cambridge) B Lusaka, Northern Rhodesia (now Zambia) 8/3/1951. RHB, SLA. Debut for Cambridge U and county 1971. Blue 1971–73 (capt in 1973). Cap 1974. Elected Best Young Cricketer of the Year in 1974 by the Cricket Writers' Club. Played for Eastern Province in 1975–76 Currie Cup competition. Tests: 13 between 1975 and 1978. Tours: Pakistan and New Zealand 1977–78, Australia 1978–79. HS: 103* T. N. Pearce's XI v West Indians (Scarborough) 1976. HSC: 93 v Northants (Lord's) 1976. HS1C: 50 v New Zealand (Christchurch) 1977–78. HSGC: 35 v Kent (Canterbury) 1977. HSJPL: 43 v Leics (Lord's) 1977. HSBH: 44* v Notts (Newark) 1976. BB: 8–132 (14–150 match) v Glos (Lord's) 1977. BBTC: 7–66 v Pakistan (Karachi) 1977–78. BBGC: 3–47 v Bucks (Lord's) 1975. BBJPL: 3–19 v Leics (Lord's) 1973. BBBH: 4–11 v Kent (Lord's) 1975. Has also played rugby for University and narrowly missed obtaining Blue.

John Ernest EMBUREY B Peckham 20/8/1952. RHB, OB. Played for Surrey Young Cricketers 1969–70. Joined county staff 1972. Debut 1973. Cap 1977. Tests: 1 in 1978. Tour: Australia 1978–79. HS: 48 v Warwickshire (Lord's) 1977. HSGC: 36* v Lancs (Manchester) 1978. HSJPL: 30 v Lancs (Lord's) 1978. BB: 7–36 v Cambridge U (Cambridge) 1977. BBJPL: 4–43 v Worcs (Worcester) 1976.

Norman George FEATHERSTONE (King Edward VII High School, Johannesburg) B Que Que, Rhodesia 20/8/1949. RHB, OB. Member of South African Schools Team to England 1967. Debut for Transvaal B 1967–68 in Currie Cup competition. Debut for county 1968. Cap 1971. Asked to be released from contract after 1972 season, but subsequently changed his decision. Benefit in 1979. 1,000 runs (2)—1,156 runs (av 35.03) in 1975 best. Scored two centuries in match (127* and 100*) v Kent (Canterbury) 1975. Gillette Man of Match awards: 1. Benson & Hedges Gold awards: 1. HS: 147 v Yorks (Scarborough) 1975. HSGC: 72* v Worcs (Worcester) 1975. HSJPL: 82* v Notts (Lord's) 1976. HSBH: 56* v Sussex (Hove) 1975 and 56 v Kent (Lord's) 1975. BB: 5–32 v Notts (Nottingham) 1978. BBGC: 3–17 v Glamorgan (Lord's) 1977. BBJPL: 4–10 v Worcs (Worcester) 1978. BBBH: 4–35 v Minor Counties (East) (Lord's) 1976.

MIDDLESEX

Paul Bernard FISHER (St Ignatius College, Enfield and Oxford). B Edmonton, 19/12/1954. RHB, WK. Debut for Oxford U 1974. Blue 1975–76–77–78. Played for county in one Fenner Trophy match and in last John Player League Match in 1978. HS: 42 Oxford U v Warwickshire (Oxford) 1975.

Michael William (Mike) GATTING (John Kelly Boys HS, Cricklewood) B Kingsbury (Middlesex) 6/6/1957. RHB, RM. Represented England Young Cricketers 1974. Debut 1975. Toured West Indies with England Young Cricketers 1976. Cap 1977. Tests: 2 in 1977–78. Tour: Pakistan and New Zealand 1977–78.1,000 runs (2)—1,166 runs (av 33.31) in 1978 best. HS: 128 v Derbyshire (Lord's) 1978. HSTC: 6 v Pakistan (Karachi) 1977–78. HSGC: 62 v Kent (Canterbury) 1977 and 62 v Lancs (Manchester) 1978. HSJPL: 85 v Notts (Lord's) 1976. HSBH: 50 v Derbyshire (Derby) 1978. BB: 5–59 v Leics (Lord's) 1978. BBJPL: 4–32 v Kent (Lord's) 1978. BBBH: 3–35 v Minor Counties (East) (Lord's) 1976.

Ian James GOULD B Slough (Bucks) 19/8/1957. LHB, WK. Joined staff 1972. Debut 1975. Toured West Indies with England Young Cricketers 1976. Cap 1977. HS: 128 v Worcs (Worcester) 1978. HSGC: 58 v Derbyshire (Derby) 1978. HSJPL: 36* v Yorks (Lord's) 1975. HSBH: 10 v Derbyshire (Derby) 1978.

Robin HERKES (Lincoln GS) B Lincoln 30/6/1957. 6ft 4ins tall. RHB, RM. Played for Lincolnshire in 1977. Debut 1978. One match v MCC (Lord's) and also played in one John Player League match v Leics (Leicester).

Allan Arthur JONES (St John's College, Horsham) B Horley (Surrey) 9/12/1947. RHB, RFM. 6ft 4ins tall. Debut for Sussex 1966. Left staff in 1969 and made debut for Somerset in 1970. Cap 1972. Played for Northern Transvaal in 1972–73 Currie Cup competition and for Orange Free State in 1976–77. Left Somerset after 1975 season and made debut for Middlesex in 1976. Cap 1976. Took 3 wkts in 4 balls v Somerset Notts (Nottingham) 1972. Hat-trick in Benson & Hedges Cup v Essex (Lord's) 1977. Benson & Hedges Gold awards: 3 (1 for Somerset). HS: 33 v Kent (Canterbury) 1978. HSJPL: 18* Somerset v Sussex (Hove) 1973. HSBH: 13 Somerset v Glos (Bristol) 1973. BB: 9–51 Somerset v Sussex (Hove) 1972. BBC: 6–89 v Kent (Canterbury) 1978. BBGC: 5–23 v Kent (Canterbury) 1977. BJPL: 6–34 Somerset v Essex (Westcliff) 1971. BBBH: 5–16 v Minor Counties (East) (Lakenham) 1977.

Roger Peter MOULDING (Haberdashers' Aske's School, Elstree and Oxford) B Enfield 3/1/1958. RHB, LB. Debut 1977. Blue 1978. University Secretary for 1979. Did not play for county in 1978. HS: 77* Oxford U v Worcs (Worcester) 1978. HSC: 26* v Cambridge U (Cambridge) 1977.

Ashok Sitaram PATEL (Willesden Lane GS) B Nairobi, Kenya 23/9/1956. LHB, SLA. Toured West Indies with England Young Cricketers 1976. Played in two John Player League matches in 1977. Debut 1978 (two matches). Also played in one John Player League Match. HS: 25* v Glos (Bristol) 1978. HSJPL: 27* v Northants (Lord's) 1977. BBJPL: 3–26 v Northants (Lord's) 1977. Is studying at Durham University.

104

Stephen John **POULTER** B Hornsey 9/9/1956. RHB. Played for 2nd XI since 1975. Debut 1978. HS: 36 v Notts (Nottingham) 1978. HSJPL: 13 v Sussex (Hove) 1978.

Clive Thornton **RADLEY** (King Edward VI GS, Norwich) B Hertford 13/5/1944. RHB, LB. Debut 1964. Cap 1967. Benefit (£26,000) in 1977. *Wisden* 1978. Tests: 8 in 1977–78 and 1978. Tours: Pakistan and New Zealand 1977–78 (as replacement for J. M. Brearley), Australia 1978–79. 1,000 runs (11)—1,414 runs (av 38.21) in 1969 and 1,413 runs (av 41.55) in 1972 best. Shared in 6th wkt partnership record for county, 227 with F. J. Titmus v South Africans (Lord's) 1965. Gillette Man of Match awards: 2. Benson & Hedges Gold awards: 2. HS: 171 v Cambridge U (Cambridge) 1976. HSTC: 158 v New Zealand (Auckland) 1977–78. HSGC: 105* v Worcs (Worcester) 1975. HSJPL: 133* v Glamorgan (Lord's) 1969. HSBH: 121* v Minor Counties (East) (Lord's) 1976.

Michael Walter William (Mike) **SELVEY** (Battersea GS and Manchester and Cambridge Universities) B Chiswick 25/4/1948. RHB, RFM. Debut for Surrey 1968. Debut for Cambridge U and Blue 1971. Debut for Middlesex 1972. Cap 1973. Played for Orange Free State in 1973–74 Currie Cup competition. Tests: 3 in 1976 and 1976–77. Tour: India, Sri Lanka and Australia 1976–77. Took 101 wkts (av 19.09) in 1978. Benson & Hedges Gold awards: 1. HS: 42 Cambridge U v Pakistanis (Cambridge) 1971. HSC: 37* v Worcs (Worcester) 1974. HSGC: 14 v Derbyshire (Derby) 1978. HSJPL: 38 v Essex (Southend) 1977. HSBH: 27* v Surrey (Lord's) 1973. BB: 7–20 v Glos (Gloucester) 1976. BBTC: 4–41 v West Indies (Manchester) 1976. BBGC: 3–32 v Somerset (Lord's) 1977. BBJPL: 5–18 v Glamorgan (Cardiff) 1975. BBBH: 5–39 v Glos (Lord's) 1972. Played soccer for University.

Wilfred Norris **SLACK** B Troumaca, St. Vincent, 12/12/1954. LHB, RM. Played for Buckinghamshire in 1976. Debut 1977. HS: 52 v Cambridge U (Cambridge) 1978. HSJPL: 57 v Kent (Lord's) 1978.

Michael John (Mike) **SMITH** (Enfield GS) B Enfield 4/1/1942. RHB, SLA. Debut 1959. Cap 1967. Benefit (£20,000) in 1976. 1,000 runs (10)—1,705 runs (av 39.65) in 1970 best. Gillette Man of Match awards: 2. Benson & Hedges Gold awards: 1. HS: 181 v Lancs (Manchester) 1967. HSGC: 123 v Hants (Lord's) 1977. HSJPL: 101 v Lancs (Lord's) 1971. HSBH: 105 v Minor Counties (East) (Lord's) 1976. BB: 4–13 v Glos (Lord's) 1961.

Keith Patrick **TOMLINS** (St. Benedict's School, Ealing) B Kingston-upon-Thames 23/10/1957. RHB, RM. Debut 1977. HS: 94 v Worcs (Worcester) 1978. HSJPL: 15 v Sussex (Hove) 1978. BBJPL: 4–24 v Notts (Lord's) 1978. Is studying at Durham University.

NB   M. O. C. Sturt who re-appeared in two matches has not been included.

His career record will be found elsewhere in this annual.

COUNTY AVERAGES

Schweppes Championship: Played 21, won 11, drawn 5, lost 5, abandoned 1
All first-class matches: Played 24, won 11, drawn 7, lost 6, abandoned 1

BATTING AND FIELDING

Cap		M	I	NO	Runs	HS	Avge	100	50	Ct	St
1967	C. T. Radley	12	18	1	615	105	36.17	2	3	13	—
—	R. O. Butcher	10	14	0	464	142	33.14	1	3	18	—
1977	M. W. Gatting	24	36	4	1024	128	32.00	2	5	19	—
1976	G. D. Barlow	24	35	2	1016	102*	30.78	1	6	15	—
1971	N. G. Featherstone	19	27	1	740	108	28.46	1	3	15	—
1964	J. M. Brearley	11	17	3	394	79	28.14	—	3	6	—
1977	I. J. Gould	22	31	4	706	128	26.14	1	2	50	5
1967	M. J. Smith	23	34	1	726	63	22.00	—	3	3	—
—	K. P. Tomlins	11	16	2	295	94	21.07	—	2	8	—
1974	P. H. Edmonds	11	14	2	233	43*	19.41	—	—	10	—
—	W. N. Slack	10	16	1	268	52	17.86	—	1	7	—
—	S. J. Poulter	3	3	0	47	36	15.66	—	—	—	—
1977	J. E. Emburey	22	29	6	284	33	12.34	—	—	13	—
1977	W. W. Daniel	21	24	12	132	30*	11.00	—	—	3	—
1973	M. W. W. Selvey	24	28	8	164	19*	8.20	—	—	8	—
1976	A. A. Jones	12	17	2	80	33	5.33	—	—	2	—

Played in two matches: A. S. Patel 25*, 22, 9 (1 ct); M. O. C. Sturt 2, 9 (6 ct, 1 st).

Played in one match: R. Herkes 0*.

BOWLING

	Type	O	M	R	W	Avge	Best	5 wI	10 wM
M. W. Gatting	RM	144.3	33	350	24	14.58	5-59	1	—
W. W. Daniel	RF	453.3	113	1114	76	14.65	5-42	3	—
P. H. Edmonds	SLA	315	97	649	42	15.45	7-34	2	—
M. W. W. Selvey	RFM	743.5	199	1929	101	19.09	6-26	8	1
J. E. Emburey	OB	684.2	201	1455	71	20.49	6-25	3	—
N. G. Featherstone	OB	140.3	39	365	13	28.07	5-32	1	—
A. A. Jones	RFM	247.4	45	840	29	28.96	6-89	2	—

Also bowled: J. M. Brearley 1-1-0-0; R. Herkes 5-3-9-0; A. S. Patel 12-0-55-2; C. T. Radley 1-1-0-0; K. P. Tomlins 8-2-16-0.

County Records

Highest innings totals:	For —642-3d v Hampshire (Southampton)	1923
	Agst—655 by West Indians (Lord's)	1939
Lowest innings totals:	For —20 v MCC (Lord's)	1864
	Agst—31 by Gloucestershire (Bristol)	1924
Highest individual innings:	For —331* J. D. Robertston v Worcs (Worcester)	1949
	Agst—316* J. B. Hobbs for Surrey (Lord's)	1926
Best bowling in an innings:	For —10-40 G. O. Allen v Lancs (Lord's)	1929
	Agst—9-38 R. C. Robertson-Glasgow for Somerset (Lord's)	1924

Best bowling in a match:	For —16–114 { G. Burton v Yorks (Sheffield)	1888
	{ J. T. Hearne v Lancs (Manchester)	1898
	Agst.—16–109 C.W.L.Parker for Glos (Cheltenham)	1930

Most runs in a season:	2650 (av 85.48) W. J. Edrich	1947
runs in a career:	40302 (av 49.81) E. H. Hendren	1907–1937
100s in a season:	13 by D. C. S. Compton	1947
100s in a career:	119 by E. H. Hendren	1907–1937
wickets in a season:	158 (av 14.63) F. J. Titmus	1955
wickets in a career:	2343 (av 21.18) F. J. Titmus	1949–1976

RECORD WICKET STANDS

1st	310	W. E. Russell & M. J. Harris v Pakistanis (Lord's)	1967
2nd	380	F. A. Tarrant & J. W. Hearne v Lancashire (Lord's)	1914
3rd	424*	W. J. Edrich & D. C. S. Compton v Somerset (Lord's)	1948
4th	325	J. W. Hearne & E. H. Hendren v Hampshire (Lord's)	1919
5th	338	R. S. Lucas & T. C. O'Brien v Sussex (Hove)	1895
6th	227	C. T. Radley & F. J. Titmus v South Africans (Lord's)	1965
7th	271*	E. H. Hendren & F. T. Mann v Nottinghamshire (Nottingham)	1925
8th	182*	M. H. C. Doll & H. R. Murrell v Nottinghamshire (Lord's)	1913
9th	160*	E. H. Hendren & T. J. Durston v Essex (Leyton)	1927
10th	230	R. W. Nicholls & W. Roche v Kent (Lord's)	1899

One-day cricket

Highest innings totals:	Gillette Cup	280–8 v Sussex (Lord's)	1965
	John Player League	256–9 v Worcestershire (Worcester)	1976
	Benson & Hedges Cup	303–7 v Northants (Northampton)	1977
Lowest innings totals:	Gillette Cup	41 v Essex (Westcliff)	1972
	John Player League	23 v Yorkshire (Leeds)	1974
	Benson & Hedges Cup	97 v Northamptonshire (Lord's)	1976
Highest individual innings:	Gillette Cup	124* J. M. Brearley v Buckinghamshire (Lord's)	1975
	John Player League	133* C. T. Radley v Glamorgan (Lord's)	1969
	Benson & Hedges Cup	129 G. D. Barlow v Northants (Northampton)	1977
Best bowling figures:	Gillette Cup	6–28 K. V. Jones v Lancashire (Lord's)	1974
	John Player League	6–6 R. W. Hooker v Surrey (Lord's)	1969
	Benson & Hedges Cup	7–12 W. W. Daniel v Minor Counties (East) (Ipswich)	1978

NORTHAMPTONSHIRE

Formation of present club: 1820, reorganised 1878.
Colours: Maroon.
Badge: Tudor Rose.
County Championship runners-up (4):
 1912, 1957, 1965 and 1976.
Gillette Cup winners: 1976.
Best final position in John Player League: 4th in 1974.
Benson & Hedges Cup semi-finalists: 1977.
Fenner Trophy Winners: 1978.
Gillette Man of the Match awards: 14.
Benson & Hedges Gold awards: 9.

Secretary: K. C. Turner, County Ground, Wantage Rd, Northampton,
NN1 4TJ.
Captain: P. J. Watts.

Prospects of play Telephone No: Northampton (0604) 32697.

 Robert Michael CARTER B King's Lynn 25/5/1960. RHB, RM.
Played for 2nd XI since 1976. Debut 1978. HS: 8* v Worcs (Northampton)
1978. BBJPL: 3–35 v Worcs (Milton Keynes) 1978. Has played soccer for
Norwich City.

 Geoffrey (Geoff) COOK (Middlesbrough HS) B Middlesbrough
9/10/1951. RHB, SLA. Debut 1971. Cap 1975. Gillette Man of Match
awards: 1. Benson & Hedges Gold awards: 1. 1,000 runs (4)—1,226 runs
(av 32.26) in 1978 best. HS: 155 v Derbyshire (Northampton) 1978.
HSGC: 95 v Leics (Northampton) 1977. HSJPL: 85 v Leics (Leicester)
1976. HSBH: 96 v Minor Counties (East) (Northampton) 1978.

 Vincent Anthony FLYNN (Aylesbury GS) B Aylesbury (Bucks) 3/10/
1955. RHB, WK. Debut 1976. HS: 15 v Yorks (Northampton) 1978.
Studied at Leeds University.

 Brian James (Jim) GRIFFITHS B Wellingborough 13/6/1949. RHB,
RM. Debut 1974. Cap 1978. HS: 11 v Middlesex (Lord's) 1978. BB: 5–66 v
Surrey (Northampton) 1978. BBJPL: 4–22 v Somerset (Weston-super-
Mare) 1977. BBBH: 4–36 v Warwickshire (Northampton) 1977.

 Alan HODGSON (Annfield Plain GTS) B Moorside Consett, County
Durham 27/10/1951. 6ft 4½ins tall. LHB, RFM. Joined staff 1969. Debut
1970. Cap 1976. Hat-trick in John Player League v Somerset (Northampton) 1976. HS: 41 v New Zealanders (Northampton) 1973 and 41* v
Glos (Northampton) 1976. HSGC: 20 v Kent (Canterbury) 1971. HSJPL:
26 v Middlesex (Lord's) 1973. HSBH: 17 v Worcs (Northampton) 1975.
BB: 5–30 v Oxford U (Oxford) 1976. BBGC: 4–32 v Leics (Northampton)
1977. BBJPL: 7–39 v Somerset (Northampton) 1976. BBBH: 3–30 v
Minor Counties (East) (Northampton) 1978.

Allan Joseph LAMB (Wynberg Boys' High School) B Langebaanweg, Cape Province, South Africa 20/6/1954. RHB, Debut for Western Province in Currie Cup 1972–73. Debut for county and cap 1978. HS: 109 Western Province v Rhodesia (Bulawayo) 1976–77 and 109 Western Province v Natal (Durban) 1977–78. HSC: 106* v Essex (Northampton) 1978. HSJPL: 31 v Sussex (Northampton) and 31 v Notts (Nottingham) 1978. HSBH: 34 v Middlesex (Lord's) 1978.

Hon. Timothy Michael LAMB (Shrewsbury School and Oxford) B Hartford (Cheshire) 24/3/1953. Younger son of Lord Rochester. RHB, RM. Debut for Oxford U 1973. Blue 1973–74. Debut for Middlesex 1974. Left county and made debut for Northants in 1978, cap 1978. HS: 77 Middlesex v Notts (Lord's) 1976. HSC: 33 v Notts (Northampton) 1978. HSGC: 11* Middlesex v Lancs (Lord's) 1975. HSJPL: 27 Middlesex v Hants (Basingstoke) 1976. BB: 6–49 Middlesex v Surrey (Lord's) 1975. BBC: 6–71 v Warwickshire (Northampton) 1978. BBJPL: 3–24 Middlesex v Essex (Chelmsford) 1975. BBBH: 5–44 Middlesex v Yorks (Lord's) 1975.

Wayne LARKINS B Roxton (Beds) 22/11/1953. RHB, RM. Joined staff 1969. Debut 1972. Cap 1976. Scored 1,448 runs (av. 37.12) in 1978. Benson & Hedges Gold awards: 1. HS: 170* v Worcs (Northampton) 1978. HSGC: 24 v Kent (Northampton) 1978. HSJPL: 107* v Surrey (Tring) 1978. HSBH: 73* v Essex (Chelmsford) 1977. BB: 3–34 v Somerset (Northampton) 1976. BBJPL: 5–32 v Essex (Ilford) 1978. BBBH: 3–13 v Essex (Chelmsford) 1977.

Ian Michael RICHARDS (Grangefield GS and Stockton VIth Form College) B Stockton-on-Tees 9/12/1957. LHB, RM. Debut 1976. HS: 50 v Notts (Northampton) 1976. HSJPL: 18 v Worcs (Milton Keynes) 1978. BB: 4–57 v Warwickshire (Birmingham) 1978.

Sarfraz NAWAZ (Government College, Lahore) B Lahore, Pakistan 1/12/1948. RHB, RFM. Debut 1967–68 for West Pakistan Governor's XI v Punjab University at Lahore and subsequently played for various Lahore sides and United Bank 1978. Debut for county 1969. Not re-engaged after 1971 season, but rejoined staff in 1974, Cap 1975. Tests: 26 for Pakistan between 1968–69 and 1978. Tours: Pakistan to England 1971, 1974 and 1978. Australia and New Zealand 1972–73, Australia and West Indies 1976–77. Took 101 wkts (av 20.30) in 1975. Gillette Man of Match awards: 1. Benson & Hedges Gold awards: 1. HS: 86 v Essex (Chelmsford) 1975. HSTC: 53 Pakistan v England (Leeds) 1974. HSGC: 22 v Cambs (March) 1975. HSJPL: 43* v Lancs (Manchester) 1975. HSBH: 50 v Kent (Northampton) 1977. BB: 8–27 Pakistanis v Notts (Nottingham) 1974. BBC: 7–37 v Somerset (Weston-super-Mare) 1977. BBTC: 6–89 Pakistan v West Indies (Lahore) 1974–75. BBGC: 4–17 v Herts (Northampton) 1976 BBJPL: 5–15 v Yorks (Northampton) 1975. BBBH: 3–11 v Minor Counties (East)(Horton) 1977.

George SHARP B West Hartlepool 12/3/1950. RHB, WK. Can also bowl LM. Debut 1968. Cap 1973. HS: 85 v Warwickshire (Birmingham) 1976. HSGC: 35* v Durham (Northampton) 1977. HSJPL: 47 v Sussex (Hove) 1974 and 47* v Worcs (Milton Keynes) 1978. HSBH: 36 v Warwickshire (Coventry) 1973.

NORTHAMPTONSHIRE

Patrick James (Jim) WATTS (Stratton School, Biggleswade) B Henlow (Beds) 16/6/1940. Brother of P. D. Watts who also played for county. LHB, RM. Debut 1959, scoring 1,118 runs (av 28.66) in his first season. Cap 1962. Left staff after 1966 season, but rejoined staff in 1970. County captain from 1971 to 1974. Benefit (£6,351) in 1974. Left staff after 1974 season to train as a teacher. Played occasionally in 1975, but did not appear in 1976 and 1977. Re-appointed county captain in 1978. 1,000 runs (7)—1,798 runs (av 43.85) in 1962 best. Benson & Hedges Gold awards: 1. HS: 145 v Hants (Bournemouth) 1962. HSGC: 40 v Glamorgan (Northampton) 1972. HSJPL: 83 v Lancs (Bedford) 1971. HSBH: 40 v Middlesex (Lord's) 1974. BB: 6–18 v Somerset (Taunton) 1965. BBGC: 4–58 v Warwickshire (Northampton) 1964. BBJPL: 5–24 v Notts (Peterborough) 1971. BBBH: 4–11 v Middlesex (Lord's) 1974 .

Peter WILLEY B Sedgefield (County Durham) 6/12/1949. RHB, OB. Debut 1966 aged 16 years 5 months scoring 78 in second innings of first match v Cambridge U (Cambridge). Cap 1971. Tests: 2 in 1976. Scored 1,115 runs (av 41.29) in 1976. Shared in 4th wkt partnership record for county, 370 with R. T. Virgin v Somerset (Northampton) 1976. Gillette Man of Match awards: 3. HS: 227 v Somerset (Northampton) 1976. HSTC: 45 v West Indies (Leeds) 1976. HSGC: 77 v Kent (Northampton) 1978. HSJPL: 107 v Warwickshire (Birmingham) 1975 and 107 v Hants (Tring) 1976. HSBH: 58 v Warwickshire (Northampton) 1974. BB: 7–37 v Oxford U (Oxford) 1975. BBGC: 3–37 v Cambs (March) 1975. BBJPL: 4–59 Kent (Northampton) 1971. BBBH: 3–12 v Minor Counties (East) (Horton) 1977.

Richard Grenville WILLIAMS (Ellesmere Port GS) B Bangor (Caernarvonshire) 10/8/1957. RHB, OB. Debut for 2nd XI in 1972, aged 14 years 11 months. Debut 1974 aged 16 years 10 months. Toured West Indies with England Young Cricketers 1976. HS: 64 v Oxford U (Oxford) 1974. HSGC: 51 v Durham (Northampton) 1977. HSJPL: 65* v Glamorgan (Cardiff) 1976. HSBH: 10* v Minor Counties (East) (Longton) 1976. BB: 4–48 v Derbyshire (Northampton) 1978.

Thomas James (Jim) YARDLEY (King Charles I GS, Kidderminster) B Chaddesley Corbett (Worcs) 27/10/1946. LHB, RM. Occasional WK. Debut for Worcs 1967. Cap 1972. Not re-engaged after 1975 season and made debut for Northants in 1976. Cap 1978. Scored 1,066 runs (av 30.45) in 1971. HS: 135 Worcs v Notts (Worcester) 1973. HSC: 97 v Middlesex (Lord's) 1978. HSGC: 52 Worcs v Warwickshire (Birmingham) 1972 and 52* Worcs v Warwickshire (Birmingham) 1973. HSJPL: 66* v Middlesex (Lord's) 1977. HSBH: 75* Worcs v Warwickshire (Worcester) 1972.

COUNTY AVERAGES

Schweppes Championship: Played 20, won 2, drawn 12, lost 6, abandoned 2
All first-class matches: Played 21, won 2, drawn 13, lost 6, abandoned 2

BATTING AND FIELDING

Cap		M	I	NO	Runs	HS	Avge	100	50	Ct	St
1978	A. J. Lamb	17	27	8	883	106*	46.47	2	5	10	—
1976	W. Larkins	21	37	3	1343	170*	39.50	3	7	12	—
1965	D. S. Steele	21	36	5	1182	130	38.12	3	9	24	—
1971	P. Willey	21	33	8	893	112	35.72	1	6	7	—
1975	G. Cook	21	37	2	1177	155	33.62	1	7	20	—
1978	T. J. Yardley	18	26	6	611	97	30.55	—	3	22	—
—	R. G. Williams	16	20	5	399	60*	26.60	—	1	8	—
—	I. M. Richards	7	4	1	54	23	18.00	—	—	—	—
1962	P. J. Watts	13	15	1	185	57*	13.21	—	1	1	—
1973	G. Sharp	19	20	4	193	27*	12.06	—	—	32	3
1978	T. M. Lamb	21	20	4	139	33	9.92	—	—	6	—
1978	B. J. Griffiths	19	12	8	31	11	7.75	—	—	5	—
1975	Sarfraz Nawaz	9	11	3	61	20	7.62	—	—	2	—
1976	A. Hodgson	4	6	3	22	10	7.33	—	—	—	—

Played in two matches: R. G. Carter 8*; V. A. Flynn 15,6* (1 ct).

BOWLING

	Type	O	M	R	W	Avge	Best	5 wI	10 wM
I. M. Richards	RM	53	10	154	7	22.00	4–57	—	—
P. J. Watts	RM	73	18	182	8	22.75	3–32	—	—
D. S. Steele	SLA	378.3	110	976	37	26.37	6–36	3	1
T. M. Lamb	RM	492.5	115	1370	46	29.78	6–71	1	—
B. J. Griffiths	RM	554	103	1591	51	31.19	5–66	1	—
Sarfraz Nawaz	RFM	276.3	79	613	19	32.26	4–28	—	—
A. Hodgson	RFM	105.2	21	351	10	35.10	3–29	—	—
P. Willey	OB	635.1	181	1470	39	37.69	4–61	—	—
R. G. Williams	OB	148.1	34	429	10	42.90	4–48	—	—

Also bowled: R. G. Carter 15–3–43–0; G. Cook 2.2–0–18–0; A. J. Lamb 3.5–1–13–2; W. Larkins 44–9–142–3.

County Records

First-class cricket

Highest innings totals:	For —557–6d v Sussex (Hove)	1914
	Agst—670–9d by Sussex (Hove)	1921
Lowest innings totals:	For —12 v Gloucestershire (Gloucester)	1907
	Agst—43 by Leicestershire (Peterborough)	1968
Highest individual innings:	For —300 R. Subba Row v Surrey (The Oval)	1958
	Agst—333 K. S. Duleepsinhji for Sussex (Hove)	1930
Best bowling in an innings:	For —10–127 V. W. C. Jupp v Kent (Tunbridge Wells)	1932
	Agst—10–30 C. Blythe for Kent (Northampton)	1907
Best bowling	For —15–31 G. E. Tribe v Yorkshire	

NOTTINGHAMSHIRE

in a match:		(Northampton)		1958
	Agst—17–48 C. Blythe for Kent (Northampton)			1907
Most runs in a season:	2198 (av 51.11) D. Brookes			1952
runs in a career:	28980 (av 36.13) D. Brookes			1934–1959
100s in a season:	8 by R. Haywood			1921
100s in a career:	67 by D. Brookes			1934–1959
wickets in a season:	175 (av 18.70) G. E. Tribe			1955
wickets in a career:	1097 (av 21.31) E. W. Clark			1922–1947

RECORD WICKET STANDS

1st	361	N. Oldfield & V. Broderick v Scotland (Peterborough)	1953
2nd	299*	T. L. Livingston & D. Barrick v Sussex (Northampton)†	1953
3rd	320	T. L. Livingston & F. Jakeman v South Africans (Northampton)	1951
4th	370	R. T. Virgin & P. Willey v Somerset (Northampton)	1976
5th	347	D. Brookes & D. Barrick v Essex (Northampton)	1952
6th	376	R. Subba Row & A. Lightfoot v Surrey (The Oval)	1958
7th	229	W. W. Timms & F. A. Waldren v Warwickshire (Northampton)	1926
8th	155	F. R. Brown & A. E. Nutter v Glamorgan (Northampton)	1952
9th	156	R. Subba Row & S. Starkie v Lancashire (Northampton)	1955
10th	148	R. Bellamy & V. Murdin v Glamorgan (Northampton)	1925

†307 *runs in all were added for this wicket, N. Oldfield retiring hurt after 8 runs had been scored.*

One-day cricket

Highest innings totals:	Gillette Cup	275–5 v Nottinghamshire (Nottingham)	1976
	John Player League	239–3 v Kent (Dover)	1970
	Benson & Hedges Cup	249–3 v Warwickshire (Northampton)	1974
Lowest innings totals:	Gillette Cup	62 v Leics (Leicester)	1974
	John Player League	41 v Middlesex (Northampton)	1972
	Benson & Hedges Cup	85 v Sussex (Northampton)	1978
Highest individual innings:	Gillette Cup	109 D. S. Steele v Cambs (March)	1975
	John Player League	115* H. M. Ackerman v Kent (Dover)	1970
	Benson & Hedges Cup	131 Mushtaq Mohammad v Minor Counties (East) (Longton)	1976
Best bowling figures:	Gillette Cup	5–24 J. D. F. Larter v Leicestershire (Leicester)	1964
	John Player League	7–39 A. Hodgson v Somerset (Northampton)	1976
	Benson & Hedges Cup	5–30 J. C. J. Dye v Worcestershire (Northampton)	1975

NOTTINGHAMSHIRE

Formation of present club: 1841, reorganized 1866.
Colours: Green and gold.
Badge: County Badge of Nottinghamshire.
County Champions (12): 1865, 1868, 1871, 1872
  1875, 1880, 1883, 1884, 1885, 1886
  1907 and 1929
Joint Champions (5) 1869, 1873, 1879,
  1882 and 1889
Gillette Cup semi-finalists: 1969.
Best final position in John Player League: 5th in 1975.
Benson & Hedges Cup quarter-finalists (3): 1973,
  1976 and 1978.
Gillette Man of Match awards: 11.
Benson & Hedges Gold awards: 15.

Chief Executive: P. G. Carling, County Cricket Ground, Trent Bridge,
Nottingham, NG2 6AG.
Captain: M. J. Smedley.
Prospects of play Telephone No.: Nottingham (0602) 869607.

Mark Edward ALLBROOK (Tonbridge School and Cambridge) B
Frimley (Surrey) 15/11/1954. RHB, OB. Played for Kent 2nd XI 1974–75.
Debut for Cambridge U 1975. Blue 1975–76–77–78. Debut for county
1976. HS: 39 Cambridge U v Yorks (Cambridge) 1976. HSC: 13 v
Yorks (Bradford) 1976. BB: 7–79 Cambridge U v Notts (Cambridge)
1978. BBC: 4–106 v Northants (Northampton) 1976.

John Dennis BIRCH B Nottingham 18/6/1955. RHB, RM. Debut 1973.
HS: 86 v Glamorgan (Worksop) 1977. HSGC: 32 v Yorks (Bradford)
1978. HSJPL: 71 v Yorks (Scarborough) 1978. HSBH: 24* v Essex
(Chelmsford) 1978. BB: 6–64 v Hants (Bournemouth) 1975. BBJPL: 3–29 v
Glamorgan (Swansea) 1976.

Michael Kenneth (Mike) BORE B Hull 2/6/1947. RHB, LM. Debut
1969. Left to join Notts 1979. H.S: 37* v Notts (Bradford) 1973. HSJPL:
15 v Kent (Dover) 1973. BB: 7–63 v Derbyshire (Scarborough) 1977.
BBGC: 3–35 v Kent (Canterbury) 1971. BBJPL: 4–21 v Sussex (Middle-
brough) 1970 and 4–21 v Worcs (Worcester) 1970. BBBH: 3–29 v Minor
Counties (Leeds) 1974.

Kevin COOPER B Hucknall (Notts) 27/12/1957. LHB, RFM. Debut
1976. HS: 19 v Cambridge U (Cambridge) 1978. BB: 6–32 v Derbyshire
(Derby) 1978. BBJPL: 4–25 v Hants (Nottingham) 1976. BBBH: 3–51 v
Kent (Nottingham) 1978.

David Edward COOTE (Magnus GS, Newark) B Winkburn (Notts)
8/4/1955. LHB. Debut 1977. Played in one match and also one John
Player League match. Did not play in 1978. HS: 20 v Yorks (Nottingham)
1977. HSJPL: 13 v Glos (Nottingham) 1977.

Christopher Colin CURZON B Lenton, Nottingham 22/12/1958. RHB WK. Played for 2nd XI since 1976. Debut 1978. HS: 26 v Glos (Cheltenham) 1978. HSJPL: 18* v Yorks (Scarborough) 1978.

John Timothy CURZON (Bilborough GS, Nottingham) B Lenton, Nottingham 4/6/1954. Brother of C. C. Curzon. RHB, RM. Played for 2nd XI since 1976. Debut 1978. One match v Cambridge U (Cambridge) 1978.

Roy Evatt DEXTER (Nottingham High School) B Nottingham 13/4/1955. RHB. Debut 1975. HS: 48 v Derbyshire (Ilkeston) 1977.

Bruce Nicholas FRENCH (The Meden Comprehensive School, Warsop) B Warsop (Notts) 13/8/1959. RHB, WK. Debut 1976 aged 16 years 10 months. HS: 66 v Cambridge U (Cambridge) 1978. HSJPL: 25 v Northants (Nottingham) 1978.

Peter John HACKER B Lenton Abbey, Nottingham 16/7/1952. RHB, LFM. Debut 1974. HS: 35 v Kent (Canterbury) 1977. BB: 3–27 v Oxford U (Oxford) 1977.

Richard John HADLEE (Christchurch Boys' High School). B Christchurch, New Zealand 3/7/1951. Youngest son of W. A. Hadlee, former New Zealand Test cricketer, and brother of D. R. Hadlee. LHB, RFM. Debut for Canterbury 1971–72 in Plunket Shield Competition. Debut for county and cap 1978. Tests: 23 for New Zealand between 1972–73 and 1978. Tours: New Zealand to England 1973 and 1978. Australia 1973–74, Pakistan and India 1976–77. HS: 101* v Derbyshire (Nottingham) 1978. HSTC: 87 New Zealand v Pakistan (Karachi) 1976–77. HSJPL: 17 v Leics (Nottingham) 1978. HSBH: 41 v Kent (Canterbury) 1978. BB: 7–23 New Zealand v India (Wellington) 1975–76. BBUK: 7–77 New Zealanders v.Warwickshire (Birmingham) 1978. BBC: 6–39 v Yorks (Worksop) 1978. BBJPL: 3–35 v Derbyshire (Nottingham) 1978.

Michael John (Mike, Pasty) HARRIS B St Just-in-Roseland (Cornwall) 25/5/1944. RHB, WK. Can bowl LBG. Debut for Middlesex 1964. Cap 1967. Left staff after 1968 season and joined Notts by special registration in 1969. Cap 1970. Played for Eastern Province in 1971–72 Currie Cup competition. Played for Wellington in New Zealand Shell Shield competition in 1975–76. Had a benefit in 1977. 1,000 runs (10)—2,238 runs (av 50.86) in 1971 best. Scored 9 centuries in 1971 to equal county record. Scored two centuries in match twice in 1971, 118 and 123 v Leics (Leicester) and 107 and 131* v Essex (Chelmsford). Shared in 1st wkt partnership record for Middlesex, 312 with W. E. Russell v Pakistanis (Lord's) 1967. Benson & Hedges Gold awards: 2. HS: 201* v Glamorgan (Nottingham) 1973. HSGC: 101 v Somerset (Nottingham) 1970. HSJPL: 104* v Hants (Nottingham) 1970. HSBH: 101 v Yorks (Hull) 1973. BB: 4–16 v Warwickshire (Nottingham) 1969.

114

Basharat HASSAN (City HS, Nairobi) B Nairobi (Kenya) 24/3/1944.
RHB, RM, occasional WK. Debut for East Africa Invitation XI v MCC
1963–64. Played for Coast Invitation XI v Pakistan International Airways
1964. Also played for Kenya against these and other touring sides. Debut
for county 1966. Cap 1970. Benefit in 1978. 1,000 runs (5)—1,395 runs
(av 32.44) in 1970 best. Scored century with aid of a runner v Kent
(Canterbury) 1977—a rare achievement in first-class cricket. HS: 182* v
Glos (Nottingham) 1977. HSGC: 79 v Hants (Southampton) 1977.
HSJPL: 111 v Surrey (Oval) 1977. HSBH: 98* v Minor Counties (North)
(Nottingham) 1973. BB: 3–33 v Lancs (Manchester) 1976. BBGC: 3–20
v Durham (Chester-le-Street) 1967.

Edward Ernest (Eddie) HEMMINGS (Campion School, Leamington
Spa) B Leamington Spa 20/2/1949. RHB, OB. Debut for Warwickshire
1966. Cap 1974. Has joined Notts for 1979. Hat-trick Warwickshire v
Worcs (Birmingham) 1977. HS: 85 Warwickshire v Essex (Birmingham)
1977. HSGC: 20 Warwickshire v Worcs (Birmingham) 1973. HSJPL: 44*
Warwickshire v Kent (Birmingham) 1971. HSBH: 61* Warwickshire v
Leics (Birmingham) 1974. BB: 7–33 (12–64 match) Warwickshire v
Cambridge U (Cambridge) 1975. BBJPL: 5–22 Warwickshire v Northants
(Birmingham) 1974. BBBH: 3–18 Warwickshire v Oxford and Cambridge
Universities (Coventry) 1975.

Kevin Scott MACKINTOSH (Kingston-Upon-Thames) GS B Surbiton
(Surrey) 30/8/1957. RHB, RM. On Surrey staff from 1975 to 1977. Debut
for County 1978. HS: 23* v Essex (Nottingham) 1978. HSJPL: 12* v Lancs
(Nottingham) 1978. BB: 4–49 v Surrey (Oval) 1978.

Derek William RANDALL B Retford 24/2/1951. RHB, RM. Played in
one John Player League match in 1971. Debut 1972. Cap 1973. Tests: 16
between 1976–77 and 1977–78. Tours: India, Sri Lanka and Australia
1976–77, Pakistan and New Zealand 1977–78. Australia 1978–79. 1,000
runs (4)—1,546 runs (av 42.94) in 1976 best. Benson & Hedges Gold
awards: 3. HS: 204* v Somerset (Nottingham) 1976. HSTC: 174 v
Australia (Melbourne) 1976–77. HSGC: 73 v Northants (Nottingham)
1976. HSJPL: 107* v Middlesex (Lord's) 1976. HSBH: 60* v Minor
Counties (East) (Nottingham) 1976.

Clive Edward Butler RICE (St John's College, Johannesburg) B Johannesburg 23/7/1949. RHB, RFM. Debut for Transvaal 1969–70. Professional
for Ramsbottom in Lancashire League in 1973. Played for D. H. Robins'
XI v West Indians 1973 and Pakistanis 1974. Debut for county and cap
1975. Appointed county captain for 1978, but was relieved of appointment
when his signing for world series cricket was announced. 1,000 runs (4)—
1,871 runs (av 66.82) in 1978 best. Benson & Hedges Gold awards: 2.
HS: 246 v Sussex (Hove) 1976. HSGC: 71 v Yorks (Bradford) 1978.
Scored 157 for Transvaal v Orange Free State (Bloemfontein) 1975–76 in
South African Gillette Cup competition. HSJPL: 120* v Glamorgan
(Swansea) 1978. HSBH 94 v Middlesex (Newark) 1976. BB: 7–62 Transvaal
v Western Province (Johannesburg) 1975–76. BBUK: 6–16 v Worcs
(Worcester) 1977. BBGC: 3–29 v Sussex (Nottingham) 1975. BBJPL:
4–23 v Glamorgan (Nottingham) 1975. BBBH: 4–9 v Combined Univer-
sities (Nottingham) 1977.

NOTTINGHAMSHIRE

Robert Timothy (Tim) ROBINSON (High Pavement College, Nottingham). B Sutton-in-Ashfield (Notts) 21/11/1958. RHB, RM. Played for Northants 2nd XI in 1974 and 1975 and for county 2nd XI in 1977. Debut 1978. One match and one John Player League match v Lancs (Nottingham). HS: 27* v Lancs (Nottingham) 1978. Is studying at Sheffield University.

Kevin SAXELBY (Magnus GS, Newark) B Worksop 23/2/1959. RHB, RM. Debut 1978. Played in two matches and two John Player League matches in 1978.

Michael John (Mike) SMEDLEY (Woodhouse GS, Sheffield) B Maltby (Yorks) 28/10/1941. RHB, OB. Played for Yorkshire 2nd XI 1960 to 1962. Debut 1964. Cap 1966. Appointed county vice-captain in 1973 and county captain from 1975. Benefit (£8,500) in 1975. 1,000 runs in season (9)—1,718 runs (av 38.17) in 1971 best. Scored two centuries in match (119 and 109) v Lancs (Manchester) 1971. Shared in 7th wkt partnership record for county, 204 with R. A. White v Surrey (Oval) 1976. Gillette Man of Match awards: 1. Benson & Hedges Gold awards: 2. HS: 149 v Glamorgan (Cardiff) 1970. HSGC: 75 v Glos (Nottingham) 1968. HSJPL: 69 v Kent (Dover) 1975. HSBH: 66 v Minor Counties (North) (Nottingham) 1973.

Paul Adrian TODD B Morton (Notts) 12/3/1953. RHB, RM. Debut 1972. Cap 1977. 1,000 runs—(2), 1,181 runs (av 29.52) in 1978 best. HS: 178 v Glos (Nottingham) 1975. HSGC: 41 v Middlesex (Lord's) 1973. HSJPL: 79 v Hants (Nottingham) 1978. HSBH: 57 v Surrey (Oval) 1978.

Howard Trevor TUNNICLIFFE (Malvern College) B Derby 4/3/1950. RHB, RM. Debut 1973. HS: 87 v Derbyshire (Nottingham) 1974. HSGC: 53* v Yorks (Bradford) 1978. HSJPL: 52* v Somerset (Nottingham) 1978.: HSBH: 32 v Kent (Canterbury) 1976. BB: 3–48 v Leics (Nottingham) 1975. BBJPL: 3–17 v Sussex (Nottingham) 1975.

William Kenneth (Ken) WATSON (Dale College, Kingwilliamstown) B Port Elizabeth 21/5/1955. RHB, RFM. Debut for Border 1974–75. Played for Northern Transvaal 1975–76 and for Eastern Province from 1976–77. Debut for county 1976. Played only in John Player League matches in 1977. HS: 28* v Cambridge U. (Cambridge) 1978. BB: 6–102 v Kent (Nottingham) 1978. BBJPL: 3–20 v Hants (Bournemouth) 1977.

Robert Arthur (Bob) WHITE (Chiswick GS) B Fulham 6/10/1936. LHB, OB. Debut for Middlesex 1958. Cap 1963. Debut for Notts after special registration in 1966 and developed into useful off-break bowler. Cap 1966. Benefit (£11,000) in 1974. Scored 1,355 runs (av 33.87) in 1963. HS: 116* v Surrey (Oval) 1967, sharing in 7th wkt partnership record for county, 204 with M. J. Smedley. HSGC: 39 v Worcs (Worcester) 1966. HSJPL: 86* v Surrey (Guildford) 1973. HSBH: 52* v Worcs (Worcester) 1973. BB: 7–41 v Derbyshire (Ilkeston) 1971. BBGC: 3–43 v Worcs (Worcester) 1968. BBJPL: 4–15 v Somerset (Bath) 1975. BBBH: 3–27 v Northants (Northampton) 1976.

NB The following players whose particulars appeared in the 1978 annual have been omitted: D. R. Doshi (not re-engaged), W. H. Hare, N. Nanan, B. Stead (retired) and W. Taylor.

The career record of Doshi will be found elsewhere in this annual.

COUNTY AVERAGES

Schweppes Championship: Played 22, won 3, drawn 12, lost 7
All first-class matches: Played 24, won 3, drawn 14, lost 7

BATTING AND FIELDING

Cap		M	I	NO	Runs	HS	Avge	100	50	Ct	St
1975	C. E. B. Rice	22	35	7	1727	213*	61.67	5	7	22	—
1978	R. J. Hadlee	7	8	4	193	101*	48.25	1	—	1	—
1973	D. W. Randall	23	38	7	1461	157*	47.12	2	10	11	—
1970	M. J. Harris	24	36	4	1315	148*	41.09	3	6	13	—
1977	P. A. Todd	24	40	0	1181	89	29.52	—	10	6	—
1966	M. J. Smedley	23	31	4	660	83*	24.44	—	4	18	—
1970	S. B. Hassan	8	9	0	220	81	24.44	—	1	3	—
—	J. D. Birch	13	16	2	308	52*	22.00	—	2	6	—
—	W. K. Watson	5	3	1	44	28*	22.00	—	—	—	—
—	B. N. French	21	25	8	300	66	17.64	—	1	36	7
1966	R. A. White	17	16	3	220	44*	16.92	—	—	8	—
—	H. T. Tunnicliffe	9	12	3	148	69*	16.44	—	1	6	—
—	K. S. Mackintosh	14	14	5	124	23*	13.77	—	—	6	—
—	R. E. Dexter	4	7	2	65	22	13.00	—	—	2	—
1977	D. R. Doshi	14	13	7	51	23	8.50	—	—	7	—
—	K. E. Cooper	23	18	3	102	19	6.80	—	—	10	—
—	C. C. Curzon	4	4	0	26	26	6.50	—	—	2	1
—	M. E. Allbrook	5	5	3	8	3*	4.00	—	—	—	—

Played in two matches: K. Saxelby 0, 3*, 0 (1 ct).
Played in one match: J. T. Curzon 1 (1 ct); P. J. Hacker 0; R. T. Robinson 9, 27* (1 ct)

BOWLING

	Type	O	M	R	W	Avge	Best	5 wI	10 wM
R. J. Hadlee	RFM	216.3	48	555	37	15.00	6-39	4	1
C. E. B. Rice	RFM	322.3	82	835	41	20.36	4-25	—	—
K. E. Cooper	RFM	473.5	92	1439	53	27.15	6-32	2	—
D. R. Doshi	SLA	628.5	159	1585	57	27.80	6-33	3	1
W. K. Watson	RFM	151.3	34	486	15	32.40	6-142	1	—
K. S. Mackintosh	RM	239	47	693	16	43.31	4-49	—	—
H. T. Tunnicliffe	RM	100	26	304	7	43.42	3-93	—	—
M. E. Allbrook	OB	74	10	278	5	55.60	2-64	—	—
R. A. White	OB	541	145	1515	27	56.11	4-73	—	—

Also bowled: J. D. Birch 77–9–282–2; J. T. Curzon 5–1–22–0; P. J. Hacker 6–0–51–0; M. J. Harris 41–10–142–4; S. B. Hassan 14–4–52–0; D. W. Randall 1.4–0–8–0; K. Saxelby 28.2–1–123–1.

County Records
First-class Cricket

Highest innings totals:	For	739–7d v Leicestershire (Nottingham)	1903
	Agst	706–4d by Surrey (Nottingham)	1947
Lowest innings totals:	For	13 v Yorkshire (Nottingham)	1901
	Agst	16 by Derbyshire (Nottingham) and	
		Surrey (The Oval)	1879 & 1880
Highest individual innings:	For	312* W.W.Keeton v Middlesex (The Oval)	1939
	Agst	345 C.G.Macartney for Australians (Nottm)	1921
Best bowling in an innings:	For	10–66 K. Smales v Gloucestershire (Stroud)	1956
	Agst	10–10 H. Verity for Yorkshire (Leeds)	1932
Best bowling in a match:	For	17–89 F.C.L.Matthews v Northants (Nottm)	1923
	Agst	17–89 W. G. Grace for Glos (Cheltenham)	1877
Most runs in a season:		2620 (av 53.46) W. W. Whysall	1929
runs in a career:		31327 (av 36.71) G. Gunn	1902–1932
100s in a season:		9 by W. W. Whysall	1928
		and M. J. Harris	1971
100s in a career:		62 by J. Hardstaff	1930–1955
wickets in a season:		181 (av 14.96) B. Dooland	1954
wickets in a career:		1653 (av 20.40) T. Wass	1896–1914

RECORD WICKET STANDS

1st	391	A. O. Jones & A. Shrewsbury v Gloucestershire (Bristol)	1899
2nd	398	W. Gunn & A. Shrewsbury v Sussex (Nottingham)	1890
3rd	369	J. Gunn & W. Gunn v Leicestershire (Nottingham)	1903
4th	361	A. O. Jones & J. Gunn v Essex (Leyton)	1905
5th	266	A. Shrewsbury & W. Gunn v Sussex (Hove)	1884
6th	303*	H. Winrow & P. F. Harvey v Derbyshire (Nottingham)	1947
7th	204	M. J. Smedley & R. A. White v Surrey (Oval)	1967
8th	220	G. F. H. Heane & R. Winrow v Somerset (Nottingham)	1933
9th	167	W. McIntyre & G. Wootton v Kent (Nottingham)	1869
10th	152	E. Alletson & W. Riley v Sussex (Hove)	1911

One-day cricket

Highest innings totals:	Gillette Cup	271 v Gloucestershire (Nottingham)	1968
	John Player League	260–5 v Warwickshire (Birmingham)	1976
	Benson & Hedges Cup	245–7 v Essex (Ilford)	1976
Lowest innings totals:	Gillette Cup	123 v Yorkshire (Scarborough)	1969
	John Player League	66 v Yorks (Bradford)	1969
	Benson & Hedges Cup	94 v Lancashire (Nottingham)	1975
Highest individual innings:	Gillette Cup	107 M. Hill v Somerset (Taunton)	1964
	John Player League	120* C. E. B. Rice v Glamorgan (Swansea)	1978
	Benson & Hedges Cup	101 M. J. Harris v Yorks (Hull)	1973

Best bowling figures:	Gillette Cup	5–44 B. Stead v Worcestershire (Worcester)	1974
	John Player League	5–23 C. Forbes v Glos (Bristol)	1969
	Benson & Hedges Cup	5–26 B. Stead v Minor Counties (North) (Newark)	1975

SOMERSET

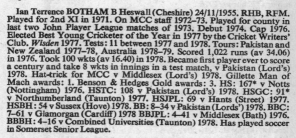

Formation of present club: 1875, reorganised 1885.
Colours: Black, white and maroon.
Badge: Wessex Wyvern.
Best final position in Championship: Third (4): 1892, 1958, 1963, and 1966.
Gillette Cup finalists (2): 1967 and 1978.
John Player League runners-up (3): 1974, 1976, and 1978.
Benson & Hedges Cup semi-finalists (2): 1974 and 1978.
Gillette Man of the Match awards: 22.
Benson & Hedges Gold awards: 17.
Secretary: R. Stevens, County Cricket Ground, St James's Street, Taunton, TA1 1JT.
Captain: B. C. Rose.

Ian Terrence BOTHAM B Heswall (Cheshire) 24/11/1955. RHB, RFM. Played for 2nd XI in 1971. On MCC staff 1972–73. Played for county in last two John Player League matches of 1973. Debut 1974. Cap 1976. Elected Best Young Cricketer of the Year in 1977 by the Cricket Writers' Club. *Wisden* 1977. Tests: 11 between 1977 and 1978. Tours: Pakistan and New Zealand 1977–78, Australia 1978–79. Scored 1,022 runs (av 34.06) in 1976. Took 100 wkts (av 16.40) in 1978. Became first player ever to score a century and take 8 wkts in innings in a test match, v Pakistan (Lord's) 1978. Hat-trick for MCC v Middlesex (Lord's) 1978. Gillette Man of Mach awards: 1. Benson & Hedges Gold awards: 3. HS: 167* v Notts (Nottingham) 1976. HSTC: 108 v Pakistan (Lord's) 1978. HSGC: 91* v Northumberland (Taunton) 1977. HSJPL: 69 v Hants (Street) 1977. HSBH: 54 v Sussex (Hove) 1978. BB: 8–34 v Pakistan (Lords') 1978. BBC: 7–61 v Glamorgan (Cardiff) 1978 BBJPL: 4–41 v Middlesex (Bath) 1976. BBBH: 4–16 v Combined Universities (Taunton) 1978. Has played soccer in Somerset Senior League.

Dennis BREAKWELL (Ounsdale Comprehensive School, Wombourne, Wolverhampton) B Brierley Hill (Staffs) 2/7/1948. LHB, SLA. Debut for Northants 1969 after being on staff for some years. Left county after 1972 season and joined Somerset by special registration in 1973. Cap 1976. HS: 100* v New Zealanders (Taunton) 1978. HSGC: 19* v Essex (Westcliff) 1974. HSJPL: 44* v Notts (Nottingham) 1976. HSBH: 28* v Minor Counties (West) (Chippenham) 1976. BB: 8–39 Northants v Kent (Dover) 1970. BBC: 6–45 v Worcs (Taunton) 1978. BBJPL: 4–10 Northants v Derbyshire (Northampton) 1970.

119

Graham Iefvion BURGESS (Millfield School) B Glastonbury 5/5/1943. RHB, RM. Debut 1966. Cap 1968. Testimonial (£24,800) in 1977. Gillette Man of Match awards: 2. HS: 129 v Glos (Taunton) 1973. HSGC: 73 v Leics (Taunton) 1967. HSJPL: 66* v Glos (Bristol) 1971. HSBH: 58 v Hants (Yeovil) 1972. BB: 7–43 (13–75 match) v Oxford U (Oxford) 1975. BBGC: 3–54 v Essex (Westcliff) 1974. BBJPL: 6–25 v Glamorgan (Glastonbury) 1972. BBBH: 4–12 v Glamorgan (Pontypridd) 1972. Plays soccer.

Peter William (Pete) DENNING (Millfield School) B Chewton Mendip (Somerset) 16/12/1949. LHB. OB. Debut 1969. Cap 1973. 1,000 runs (3) —1,199 runs (av 32.40) in 1975 best. Scored two centuries in match (122 and 107) v Glos (Taunton) 1977. Gillette Man of Match awards: 3. Benson & Hedges Gold awards: 2. HS: 122 v Glos (Taunton) 1977. HSGC: 145 v Glamorgan (Cardiff) 1978. HSJPL: 100 v Northants (Brackley) 1974. HSBH: 87 v Glos (Taunton) 1974. Trained as a teacher at St Luke's College, Exeter.

Colin Herbert DREDGE B Frome 4/8/1954. LHB, RM. 6ft. 5in. tall. Debut 1976. Cap 1978. Gillette Man of Match awards: 1. HS: 56* Yorks (Harrogate) 1977. HSJPL: 14 v Essex (Taunton) 1978. HSBH: 10* v Worcs (Taunton) 1978. BB: 5–53 v Kent (Taunton) 1978. BBGC: 4–23 v Kent (Canterbury) 1978. BBJPL: 3–19 v Middlesex (Taunton) 1978. Played soccer for Bristol City Reserves.

Trevor GARD (Huish Episcopi School, Langport) B West Lambrook, near South Petherton (Somerset) 2/6/1957. RHB, WK. Played for 2nd XI since 1972. Debut 1976. Played in two matches only in 1978. HS: 7 v West Indians (Taunton) 1976.

Joel GARNER B Barbados 16/12/1952. RHB, RFM. 6ft 8ins tall. Debut for Barbados in Shell Shield competition 1975–76. Debut for county 1977 plays in mid-week matches whilst playing as a professional for Littleborough in Central Lancashire League. Tests: 7 for West Indies in 1976–77 and 1977–78. HS: 44* Barbados v Guyana (Bridgetown) 1976–77. HSTC: 43 West Indies v Pakistan (Bridgetown) 1976–77. HSUK: 37 v Surrey (Weston-super-Mare) 1977. HSBH: 17 v Sussex (Hove) 1978. BB: 8–31 v Glamorgan (Cardiff) 1977. BBTC: 4–48 West Indies v Pakistan (Georgetown) 1977. BBGC: 5–30 v Derbyshire (Ilkeston) 1977.

David Roberts GURR (Aylesbury GS and Oxford) B Whitchurch (Bucks) 27/3/1956. RHB, RFM. 6ft 3½ins tall. Played for Middlesex 2nd XI in 1974. Debut for both Oxford U and county in 1976. Blue 1976–77. HS: 46* Oxford U v Cambridge U (Lord's) 1977. HSC: 21 v Glos (Bristol) 1976. HSBH: 29*. Combined Universities v Sussex (Oxford) 1977. BB: 6–82 Oxford U v Warwickshire (Birmingham) 1976. BBC: 5–30 v Lancs (Weston-super-Mare) 1977. BBBH: 3–42 Combined Universities v Kent (Oxford) 1976.

Keith Francis JENNINGS B Wellington (Somerset) 5/10/1953. RHB, RM. Formerly on MCC staff. Debut 1975. Cap 1978. HS: 49 v West Indians (Taunton) 1976. HSJPL: 51* v Notts (Nottingham) 1976. BB: 5–18 v Sussex (Hove) 1978. BBGC: 3–51 v Glamorgan (Cardiff) 1978. BBJPL: 4–33 v Hants (Portsmouth) 1976. BBBH: 3–20 v Sussex (Hove) 1978.

Mervyn John KITCHEN B Nailsea (Somerset) 1/8/1940. LHB, RM.
Joined staff 1957. Debut 1960. Cap 1966. Testimonial (£6,000) in 1973.
Left staff after 1974 season, but rejoined county in 1976. 1,000 runs (7)—
1,730 runs (av 36.04) in 1968 best. Gillette Man of Match awards: 2.
Benson & Hedges Gold awards: 1. HS: 189 v Pakistanis (Taunton) 1967.
HSGC: 116 v Lancs (Manchester) 1972. HSJPL: 82 v Glamorgan (Yeovil)
1977. HSBH: 70 v Minor Counties (West) (Chippenham) 1976.

Victor James (Vic) MARKS (Blundell's School and Oxford) B Middle
Chinnock (Somerset) 25/6/1955. RHB, OB. Debut for both Oxford U and
county 1975. Blue 1975–76–77–78 (captain in 1976–77). Scored 215 for
Oxford U v Army (Aldershot) in non-first class match. HS: 105 Oxford U
v Worcs (Oxford) 1976. HSC: 98 v Essex (Leyton) 1976. HSGC: 33* v
Essex (Taunton) 1978. HSJPL: 32* v Hants (Weston-super-Mare) 1975.
HSBH: 59 Combined Universities v Glamorgan (Oxford) 1978. BB: 5–50
v Surrey (Weston-super-Mare) 1977. Half blue for Rugby Fives.

Hallam Reynold MOSELEY B Christchurch, Barbados 28/5/1948.
RHB, RFM. Toured England with Barbados team in 1969 and made
debut v Notts (Nottingham). Subsequently played for Barbados in Shell
Shield. Joined county in 1970 and made debut in 1971. Cap 1972. Testimonial in 1979. HS: 67 v Leics (Taunton) 1972. HSGC: 15 v Lancs (Manchester) 1972. HSJPL: 24 v Notts (Torquay) 1972 and 24 v Hants (Weston-
super-Mare) 1975. HSBH: 33 v Hants (Bournemouth) 1973. BB: 6–34 v
Derbyshire (Bath) 1975 and 6–35 v Glos (Taunton) 1978. BBGC: 4–31 v
Surrey (Taunton) 1974. BBJPL: 5–30 v Middlesex (Lord's) 1973. BBBH:
3–17 v Leics (Taunton) 1977.

Martin OLIVE (Millfield School) B Watford (Herts) 18/4/1958. RHB,
RM. Played for 2nd XI since 1974. Debut 1977. Played in only one match
in 1978, v New Zealanders (Taunton). HS: 15 v Leics (Leicester) 1977.

Isaac Vivian Alexander (Viv) RICHARDS (Antigua Grammar School)
B St John's Antigua 7/3/1952. RHB, OB. Debut 1971–72 for Leeward
Islands v Windward Islands and subsequently played for Combined
Islands in Shell Shield tournament. Debut for county and cap 1974.
Wisden 1976. Played for Queensland in 1976–77 Sheffield Shield competi-
tion. Tests: 28 for West Indies between 1974–75 and 1977–78. Tours: West
Indies to India, Sri Lanka and Pakistan 1974–75, Australia 1975–76,
England 1976. 1,000 runs (2)—2,161 runs (av 65.48) in 1977 best. Also
scored 1,267 runs (av 60.33) on 1974–75 tour and 1,107 runs (av 58.26) on
1975–76 tour. Scored 1,710 in 11 Test matches in 1976 including 829 runs
in 4 Tests against England – record aggregate for a year and fourth highest
aggregate for a Test series. Shared in 4th wkt partnership record for
county, 251 with P. M. Roebuck v Surrey (Weston-super-Mare) 1977.
Scored 99 and 110 v Leics (Taunton) 1978. Gillette Man of Match awards:
2. Benson & Hedges Gold awards: 3. HS: 291 West Indies v England (Oval)
1976. HSC: 241* v Glos (Bristol) 1977. HSGC: 139* v Warwickshire
(Taunton) 1978. HSJPL: 126* v Glos (Bristol, Imperial Ground) 1975.
HSBH: 85 v Glamorgan (Cardiff) 1978. BB: 3–15 v Surrey (Weston-super-
Mare) 1977. BBJPL: 3–32 v Glos (Bristol) 1978.

SOMERSET

Peter James **ROBINSON** B Worcester 9/2/1943. Nephew of R. O. Jenkins, former Worcestershire player. LHB, SLA. Debut for Worcs 1963. Left county after 1964 season and made debut for Somerset in 1965. Cap 1966. Testimonial in 1974. Is now county coach and reappeared in one championship match in 1977 and one John Player League match in 1978. Scored 1,158 runs (av 26.93) in 1970. HS: 140 v Northants (Northampton) 1970. HSGC: 67 v Leics (Taunton) 1973. HSJPL: 71* v Warwickshire (Birmingham) 1973. HSBH: 15 v Minor Counties (South) (Taunton) 1973. BB: 7–10 v Notts (Nottingham) 1966. BBBH: 3–17 v Minor Counties (South) (Plymouth) 1972. Played soccer for Worcester City.

Peter Michael **ROEBUCK** (Millfield School and Cambridge) B Oxford 6/3/1956. RHB, LB. Played for 2nd XI in 1969 at age of 13. Debut 1974. Blue 1975–76–77. Cap 1978. Shared in 4th wkt partnership record for county. 251 with I. V. A. Richards v Surrey (Weston-super-Mare) 1977. HS 158 Cambridge U v Oxford U (Lord's) 1975. HSC: 131* v New Zealanders (Taunton) 1978. HSGC: 57 v Essex (Taunton) 1978. HSJPL: 30 v Essex (Taunton) 1978. HSBH: 48 Combined Universities v Kent (Oxford) 1976. BB: 6–50 Cambridge U. v Kent (Canterbury) 1977.

Brian Charles **ROSE** (Weston-super-Mare GS) B Dartford (Kent) 4/6/1950. LHB, LM. Played for English Schools CA at Lord's 1968. Debut 1969. Cap 1975. Appointed county captain in 1978. Tests: 5 in 1977–78. Tour: Pakistan and New Zealand 1977–78. 1,000 runs (4)—1,624 runs (av 46.40) in 1976 best. Gillette Man of Match awards: 1. HS: 205 v Northants (Weston-super-Mare) 1977. HSTC: 27 v Pakistan (Hyderabad) 1977–78. HSGC: 128 v Derbyshire (Ilkeston) 1977. HSJPL: 96 v Derbyshire (Heanor) 1976. HSBH: 68 v Glos (Street) 1975. BB: 3–9 v Glos (Taunton) 1975. BBJPL: 3–25 v Lancs (Manchester) 1975. Trained as a teacher at Borough Road College, Isleworth.

Neil **RUSSOM** (Huish's GS, Taunton) B Finchley, London 3/12/1958. RHB, RM. Played for 2nd XI since 1975. Played in one Fenner Trophy match v Northants (Scarborough) 1978. Has yet to appear in first-class cricket. Entered Cambridge University in 1978.

Philip Anthony **SLOCOMBE** (Weston-super-Mare GS and Millfield School) B Weston-super-Mare 6/9/1954. RHB, RM. Played for 2nd XI in 1969 at age of 14. Joined staff 1974. Debut 1975. Cap 1978. 1,000 runs (2)—1,221 runs (av 38.15) in 1978 best. Scored 106* & 98 v Worcs (Worcester) 1978. HS: 132 v Notts (Taunton) 1975. HSGC: 42 v Surrey (Oval) 1975. HSJPL: 39 v Glamorgan (Yeovil) 1977. HSBH: 11 v Minor Counties (West) (Chippenham) 1976. Plays soccer for Weston-super-Mare in Western League.

Derek John Somerset **TAYLOR** (Amersham College) B Amersham (Bucks) 12/11/1942. Twin brother of M. N. S. Taylor of Hants. RHB, WK. Debut for Surrey 1966. Cap 1969. Left staff after 1969 season and made debut for Somerset in 1970. Cap 1971. Benefit in 1978. Played for Griqualand West in Currie Cup competition 1970–71 and 1971–72. Scored 1,121 runs (av 28.02) in 1975. HS: 179 v Glamorgan (Swansea) 1974. HSGC: 49 v Kent (Canterbury) 1974. HSJPL: 93 v Surrey (Guildford) 1975. HSBH: 83* v Glos (Street) 1975. Has played soccer for Corinthian Casuals.

NB The following player whose particulars appeared in the 1978 annual has been omitted: R. J. Clapp.

COUNTY AVERAGES

Schweppes Championship: Played 22, won 9, drawn 9, lost 4
All first-class matches: Played 24, won 9, drawn 11, lost 4

BATTING AND FIELDING

Cap		M	I	NO	Runs	HS	Avge	100	50	Ct	St
1974	I. V. A. Richards	21	38	4	1558	118	45.82	2	10	22	—
1978	P. A. Slocombe	23	40	8	1221	128*	38.15	3	5	12	—
1975	B. C. Rose	24	41	5	1263	122	35.08	4	3	11	—
1978	P. M. Roebuck	23	37	8	944	131*	32.55	1	6	10	—
1976	D. Breakwell	16	23	5	579	100*	32.16	1	4	5	—
1973	P. W. Denning	22	39	3	925	78*	25.69	—	5	13	—
—	V. J. Marks	11	18	3	304	51	20.26	—	1	6	—
1966	M. J. Kitchen	13	20	2	359	50	19.94	—	1	12	—
1976	I. T. Botham	10	14	0	275	86	19.64	—	1	5	—
1968	G. I. Burgess	16	23	5	336	55	18.66	—	1	12	—
1971	D. J. S. Taylor	23	29	5	424	78	17.66	—	2	55	9
1978	K. F. Jennings	17	19	10	152	31*	16.88	—	—	11	—
1972	H. R. Moseley	14	9	3	62	30	10.33	—	—	7	—
1978	C. H. Dredge	20	19	3	148	23	9.25	—	—	6	—
—	D. R. Gurr	4	5	3	12	4	6.00	—	—	1	—
—	J. Garner	4	4	2	12	6*	4.00	—	—	2	—

Played in two matches: T. Gard did not bat (2 ct).
Played in one match: M. Olive 3, 1.

BOWLING

	Type	O	M	R	W	Avge	Best	5 wI	10 wM
J. Garner	RF	170.1	61	351	22	15.95	5–50	3	—
I. T. Botham	RFM	369.5	77	1051	58	18.12	7–61	5	—
H. R. Moseley	RFM	348.1	103	813	41	19.82	6–35	1	—
D. Breakwell	SLA	445.1	135	1007	41	24.56	6–45	1	—
K. F. Jennings	RM	442.3	147	1041	40	26.02	5–18	1	—
C. H. Dredge	RM	573.1	137	1473	56	26.30	5–53	2	—
D. R. Gurr	RFM	104	25	296	11	26.90	4–65	—	—
V. J. Marks	OB	349.4	99	945	31	30.48	4–48	—	—
G. I. Burgess	RM	363	136	890	27	32.96	5–45	1	—
I. V. A. Richards	OB	89.5	16	268	8	33.50	2–11	—	—

Also bowled: P. W. Denning 7–2–25–0; P. M. Roebuck 101–28–272–4;
B. C. Rose 8.2–1–31–1; P. A. Slocombe 4–1–11–0.

County Records

First-class cricket

Highest innings totals:	For....675–9d v Hampshire (Bath)	1924
	Agst....811 by Surrey (The Oval)	1899
Lowest innings totals:	For ...25 v Gloucestershire (Bristol)	1947
	Agst....22 by Gloucestershire (Bristol)	1920
Highest individual innings:	For ...310 H. Gimblett v Sussex (Eastbourne)	1948
	Agst....424 A. C. MacLaren for Lancs (Taunton)	1895
Best bowling in an innings:	For ...10–49 E. J. Tyler v Surrey (Taunton)	1895
	Agst....10–35 A. Drake for Yorkshire (Weston-super-Mare)	1914

SOMERSET

Best bowling: For —16–83 J. C. White v Worcestershire (Bath) 1919
in a match: Agst—17–137 W. Brearley for Lancashire
                      (Manchester)   1905

Most runs in a season: 2761 (av 56.82) W. E. Alley   1961
    runs in a career: 21108 (av 37.09) H. Gimblett 1935–1954
    100s in a season: 10 by W. E. Alley   1961
    100s in a career: 49 by H. Gimblett   1935–1954
    wickets in a season: 169 (av 19.24) A. W. Wellard   1938
    wickets in a career: 2153 (av 18.10) J. C. White 1909–1937

RECORD WICKET STANDS

1st	346	H. T. Hewett & L. C. H. Palairet v Yorkshire (Taunton)	1892
2nd	286	J. C. W. MacBryan & M. D. Lyon v Derbyshire (Buxton)	1924
3rd	300	G. Atkinson & P. B. Wight v Glamorgan (Bath)	1960
4th	251	I. V. A. Richards & P. M. Roebuck v Surrey (Weston-super-Mare)	1977
5th	235	J. C. White & C. C. C. Case v Gloucestershire (Taunton)	1927
6th	265	W. E. Alley & K. E. Palmer v Northamptonshire (Northampton)	1961
7th	240	S. M. J. Woods & V. T. Hill v Kent (Taunton)	1898
8th	143*	E. F. Longrigg & C. J. P. Barnwell v Gloucestershire (Bristol)	1938
9th	183	C. Greetham & H. W. Stephenson v Leicestershire (Weston-super-Mare)	1963
10th	143	J. J. Bridges & H. Gibbs v Surrey (Weston-super-Mare)	1919

One-day cricket

Highest innings totals:	Gillette Cup	330–4 v Glamorgan (Cardiff)	1978
	John Player League	270–4 v Gloucestershire (Bristol, Imperial)	1975
	Benson & Hedges Cup	265–8 v Gloucestershire (Taunton)	1974
Lowest innings totals:	Gillette Cup	59 v Middlesex (Lord's)	1977
	John Player League	58 v Essex (Chelmsford)	1977
	Benson & Hedges Cup	105 v Hampshire (Bournemouth)	1975
Highest individual innings:	Gillette Cup	145 B. C. Rose v Glamorgan (Cardiff)	1978
	John Player League	131 D. B. Close v Yorkshire (Bath)	1974
	Benson & Hedges Cup	95 R. C. Cooper v Minor Counties (Plymouth)	1972
Best bowling figures:	Gillette Cup	5–18 R. Palmer v Lancashire (Taunton)	1966
	John Player League	6–25 G. I. Burgess v Glamorgan (Glastonbury)	1972
	Benson & Hedges Cup	4–12 G. I. Burgess v Glamorgan (Pontypridd)	1972

SURREY

Formation of present club: 1845.
Colours: Chocolate.
Badge: Prince of Wales' Feathers.
County Champions (18): 1864, 1887, 1888, 1890,
1891, 1892, 1894, 1895, 1899, 1914, 1952, 1953,
1954, 1955, 1956, 1957, 1958, and 1971.
Joint Champions (2): 1889 and 1950.
Gillette Cup finalist: 1965.
Best final position in John Player League: 5th in
1969.
Benson & Hedges Cup winners: 1974.
Gillette Man of the Match awards: 14.
Benson & Hedges Gold awards: 21.
Secretary: I. F. B. Scott-Browne, Kennington Oval, London, SE11 5SS.
Captain: R. D. V. Knight.
Prospects of play Telephone No: (01) 735 4911.

Alan Raymond BUTCHER (Heath Clark GS, Croydon) B Croydon
7/1/1954. LHB, LM. Played in two John Player League matches in 1971.
Debut 1972. Cap 1975. Scored 977 runs (av 25.71) in 1976 and 994 runs
(av 32.06) in 1978. Benson & Hedges Gold awards: 3. HS: 188 v Sussex
(Hove) 1978. HSGC: 51 v Derbyshire (Ilkeston) 1976. HSJPL: 113* v
Warwickshire (Birmingham) 1978. HSBH: 61 v Kent (Canterbury) 1976.
BB: 6–48 v Hants (Guildford) 1972. BBJPL: 5–19 v Glos (Bristol) 1975.
BBBH: 3–11 v Lancs (Manchester) 1974.

Sylvester Theophilus CLARKE B Barbados 11/12/1954. RHB, RFM.
Debut for Barbados 1977–78. Has joined County for 1979. Tests: 1 for
West Indies in 1977–78. Tour: West Indies to India and Sri Lanka 1978–79.
HS: 15 Barbados v Australians (Bridgetown) 1977–78. BB: 6–39 Barbados
v Trinidad (Bridgetown) 1977–78. BBTC: 3–58 West Indies v Australia
(Georgetown) 1977–78.

Grahame Selvey CLINTON (Chislehurst and Sidcup GS) B Sidcup
5/5/1953. LHB, RM. Toured West Indies v England Young Cricketers
1972. Debut for Kent 1974. Left county after 1978 season and has joined
Surrey for 1979. Benson & Hedges Gold awards: 1. (For Kent). HS:
88 Kent v Leics (Leicester) 1977. HSJPL: 26 Kent v Sussex (Canterbury)
1978. HSBH: 66 Kent v Surrey (Canterbury) 1976.

John Hugh EDRICH B Blofield (Norfolk) 21/6/1937. LHB, RM. Cousin
of W. J. Edrich. Played for Norfolk in 1954 and Surrey 2nd XI in 1955.
Debut 1956 for Combined Services. Debut for Surrey 1958. Cap 1959.
Wisden 1965. Benefit (£10,551) in 1968. County captain from 1973 to 1977.
Testimonial (£20,000) in 1975. Awarded MBE in 1977 Birthday Honours
list. Tests: 77 between 1963 and 1976. Scored century (120) on debut v
Australia at Lord's 1964. Tours: India 1963–64, Australia and New
Zealand 1965–66, 1970–71 and 1974–75 (vice-captain), West Indies 1967–

125

68, Ceylon and Pakistan 1968–69. 1,000 runs (19)—2,482 runs (av 51.70) in 1962 best. Also scored 1,060 runs (av 44.16) on 1965–66 tour and 1,136 runs (av 56.80) in 1970–71. Scored 1,799 runs (av 52.91) in 1959 in first full season, despite absence through injury for a few matches) Scored two centuries in match v Notts (Nottingham) 1959 (171 and 124 v. Worcs (Worcester) 1970 (143 and 113*), v Warwickshire (Oval) 1971 (111 and 124) and v Kent (Oval) 1977 (140 and 115). Scored 1,311 runs in 9 consecutive innings all over 50 including three consecutive centuries in 1965. Completed 30,000 runs in 1971 and scored 100th century in 1977. Gillette Man of Match awards: 3. Benson & Hedges Gold awards: 9. HS: 310* England v New Zealand (Leeds) 1965 sharing in 2nd wkt partnership of 369 with K. F. Barrington. HSC: 226* v Middlesex (Oval) 1971. HSGC: 96 v Glos (Oval) 1964. HSJPL: 108* v Derbyshire (Derby) 1972. HSBH: 83* v Sussex (Oval) 1973.

Geoffrey Philip (Geoff) HOWARTH (Auckland GS) B Auckland 29/3/1951. Younger brother of H. J. Howarth, New Zealand Test cricketer. RHB, OB. Debut for New Zealand under-23 XI v Auckland (Auckland) 1968–69. Joined Surrey staff 1969. Debut 1971. Cap 1974. Tests: 14 between 1974–75 and 1978. Tours: New Zealand to Pakistan and India 1976–77, England 1978. 1,000 runs (2)—1,554 runs (av 37.90) in 1976 best. Scored two centuries in match (122 and 102) New Zealand v England (Auckland) 1977–78. Benson & Hedges Gold awards: 1. HS: 179* v Cambridge U (Cambridge) 1978. HSTC: 123 New Zealand v England (Lord's) 1978. HSGC: 34 v Lancs (Manchester) 1977. HSJPL: 122 v Glos (Oval) 1976. HSBH: 80 v Yorks (Oval) 1974. BB: 5–32 Auckland v Central Districts (Auckland) 1973–74. BBUK: 3–20 v Northants (Northampton) 1976.

INTIKHAB ALAM B Hoshiarpur, India 28/12/1941. RHB, LBG. Debut for Karachi 1957–58 aged 16 years 9 months and has played continuously for various Karachi sides and Pakistan International Airways since. Professional for West of Scotland Club in Scottish Western Union for some seasons. Debut for county and cap 1969. Benefit in 1978. Tests: 47 for Pakistan between 1959–60 and 1976–77, captaining country in 17 Tests: Played in 5 matches for Rest of World in 1970 and 5 in 1971–72. Took wkt of C. C. McDonald with first ball he bowled in Test cricket. Tours: Pakistan to India 1960–61, England 1962, 1967, 1971 and 1974 (captain on last two tours), Ceylon 1964. Australia and New Zealand 1964–65, 1972–73 (captain), Australia and West Indies 1976–77, Pakistan Eaglets to England 1963, Pakistan International Airways to East Africa 1964, Rest of World to Australia 1971–72 (vice-captain). Took 104 wkts (av 28.36) in 1971. Hat-trick v Yorks (Oval) 1972. Benson & Hedges Gold awards: 1. HS: 182 Karachi Blues v Pakistan International Airways B (Karachi) 1970–71. HSUK: 139 v Glos (Oval) 1973. HSTC: 138 Pakistan v England (Hyderabad) 1972–73. HSGC: 50 v Somerset (Oval) 1975. HSJPL: 62 v Northants (Tolworth) 1973. HSBH: 32 v Middlesex (Lord's) 1973. BB: 8–54 Pakistanis v Tasmania (Hobart) 1972–73. BBUK: 8–61 Pakistanis v Minor Counties (Swindon) 1967. BBTC: 7–52 Pakistan v. New Zealand (Dunedin) 1972–73. BBC: 8–74 v Middlesex (Oval) 1970. BBJPL: 6–25 v Derbyshire (Oval) 1974. BBBH: 3–42 v Essex (Chelmsford) 1973.

Robin David JACKMAN (St Edmund's School, Canterbury) B Simla (India) 13/8/1945. RHB, RFM. Debut 1964. Cap 1970. Played for Western Province in 1971–72 and Rhodesia from 1972–73 to 1976–77 in Currie Cup competition. Hat-tricks (3): v Kent (Canterbury) 1971, Western Province v Natal (Pietermaritzburg) 1971–72 and v Yorks (Leeds) 1973. Gillette Man of Match awards: 1. HS: 92* v Kent (Oval) 1974. HSGC: 18* v Glamorgan (Cardiff) 1977. HSJPL: 43 v Kent (Maidstone) 1977. HSBH: 36 v Leics (Lord's) 1974. BB: 8–40 Rhodesia v Natal (Durban) 1972–73. BBUK: 8–79 v Hants (Oval) 1976. BBGC: 7–33 v Yorks (Harrogate) 1970. BBJPL: 6–34 v Derbyshire (Derby) 1973. BBBH: 4–31 v Kent (Canterbury) 1973.

Roger David Verdon KNIGHT (Dulwich College and Cambridge) B Streatham 6/9/1946. LHB, RM. Debut for Cambridge U 1967. Blues 1967–70. Debut for Surrey 1968. Left county after 1970 season and made debut for Glos by special registration 1971. Cap 1971. Left county after 1975 season and made debut for Sussex in 1976. Cap 1976. Left county after 1977 season. and rejoined Surrey for 1978 as county captain. Cap 1978. 1,000 runs (8)—1,350 runs (av 38.57) in 1974 best. Gillette Man of Match awards: 3 (for Glos). Benson & Hedges Gold awards: 3 (1 for Sussex, 2 for Glos). HS: 165* Sussex v Middlesex (Hove) 1976. HSC: 128 v Lancs (Oval) 1978. HSGC: 75 Glos v Glamorgan (Cardiff) 1973. HSJPL: 127 Sussex v Hants (Hove) 1976. HSBH: 117 Sussex v Surrey (Oval) 1977. BB: 6–44 Glos v Northants (Northampton) 1974. BBC: 3–22 v Cambridge U (Cambridge) 1978. BBGC: 5–39 Glos v Surrey (Bristol) 1971. BBJPL: 5–42 Sussex v Notts (Nottingham) 1977. BBBH: 3–19 Sussex v Surrey (Oval) 1977.

Monte Alan LYNCH (Ryden's School, Walton-on-Thames) B Georgetown, British Guiana 21/5/1958. RHB, RM/OB. Debut 1977. HS: 101 v Pakistanis (Oval) 1978. HSJPL: 45* v Glamorgan (Oval) 1978.

Andrew NEEDHAM (Paisley GS and Watford GS) B Calow (Derbyshire) 23/3/1957. RHB, OB. Debut 1977. HS: 21 v Sussex (Hove) 1978. BB: 3–25 v Oxford U (Oxford) 1977.

Ian Roger PAYNE (Emanuel School) B Lambeth Hospital, Kennington 9/5/1958. RHB, RM. Debut 1977. HS: 29 v Kent (Oval) 1977. HSJPL: 20 v Kent (Maidstone) 1977. BBJPL: 4–31 v Northants (Guildford) 1977.

Patrick Ian (Pat) POCOCK (Wimbledon Technical School) B Bangor (Caernarvonshire) 24/9/1946. RHB, OB. Debut 1964. Benefit (£18,500) in 1977. Played for Northern Transvaal in 1971–72 Currie Cup competition. Tests: 17 between 1967–68 and 1976. Tours: Pakistan 1966–67, West Indies 1967–68 and 1973–74, Ceylon and Pakistan 1968–69, India, Pakistan and Sri Lanka 1972–73. Took 112 wkts (av 18.22) in 1967. Took 4 wkts in 4 balls, 5 in 6, 6 in 9, and 7 in 11 (the last two being first-class records) v Sussex (Eastbourne) 1972. Hat-tricks (2): as above and v Worcs (Guildford) 1971. Benson & Hedges Gold awards: 2. HS: 75* v Notts (Oval) 1968. HSTC: 33 v Pakistan (Hyderabad) 1972–73. HSGC: 14 v Essex (Colchester) 1978. HSJPL: 22 v Notts (Nottingham) 1971. HSBH: 19 v Middlesex (Oval) 1972. BB: 7–57 v Essex (Romford) 1968. BBTC: 6–79 v Australia (Manchester) 1968. BBGC: 3–34 v Somerset (Oval) 1975. BBJPL: 4–27 v Essex (Chelmsford) 1974. BBBH: 4–11 v Yorks (Barnsley) 1978.

Clifton James (Jack) **RICHARDS** (Humphrey Davy GS, Penzance) B Penzance 10/8/1958. RHB, WK. Debut 1976. Cap 1978. HS: 50 v Notts (Oval) 1978. HSGC: 14 v Essex (Colchester) 1978. HSJPL: 18* v Glos (Cheltenham) 1977.

Graham Richard James **ROOPE** (Bradfield College) B Fareham (Hants) 12/7/1946. RHB, RM. Played for Public Schools XI v Comb. Services (Lord's) 1963 and 1964. Played for Berkshire 1963 scoring century against Wiltshire. Joined county staff and debut 1964. Cap 1969. Played for Griqualand West in 1973–74 Currie Cup competition. Tests: 21 between 1972–73 and 1978. Tours: India, Pakistan and Sri Lanka 1972–73, Pakistan and New Zealand 1977–78. 1,000 runs (8)—1,641 runs (av 44.35) in 1971 best. Scored two centuries in match (109 and 103*) v Leics (Leicester) 1971. Held 59 catches in 1971. Benson & Hedges Gold awards: 3. HS: 171 v Yorks (Oval) 1971. HSTC: 77 v Australia (Oval) 1975. HSGC: 66 v Somerset (Oval) 1975. HSJPL: 120* v Worcs (Byfleet) 1973. HSBH: 115* v Essex (Chelmsford) 1973. BB: 5–14 v West Indians (Oval) 1969. BBGC: 5–23 v Derbyshire (Oval) 1967. BBJPL: 4–31 v Glamorgan (Oval) 1974. BBBH: 3–31 v Essex (Chelmsford) 1978. Soccer (goalkeeper) for Corinthian Casuals, Wimbledon, and Guildford City.

David Mark **SMITH** (Battersea GS) B Balham 9/1/1956. LHB, RM. Played for 2nd XI in 1972. Debut 1973 aged 17 years 4 months, whilst still at school. HS: 115 v Hants (Portsmouth) 1978. HSGC: 19 v Derbyshire (Ilkeston) 1978. HSJPL: 39 v Essex (Southend) 1978. HSBH: 40 v Kent (Oval) 1976. BB: 3–40 v Sussex (Oval) 1976. BBGC: 3–39 v Derbyshire (Ilkeston) 1976.

Stuart Spicer **SURRIDGE** (Westminster School) B Westminster 28/10/1951. Son of W. S. Surridge. RHB, WK. Has played for county 2nd XI since 1971 and for Derbyshire 2nd XI in 1976. Debut 1978. One match v Pakistanis (Oval).

David James **THOMAS** (Licensed Victuallers School, Slough) B Solihull (Warwickshire) 30/6/1959. LHB, LM. Debut 1977. HS: 14 v Lancs (Oval) 1977. BB: 4–47 v Pakistanis (Oval) 1978. BBJPL: 4–13 v Sussex (Oval) 1978.

Peter Hugh **L'Estrange WILSON** (Wellington College) B Guildford 17/8/1958. 6ft 5ins tall. RHB, RFM. Played for Hants 2nd XI 1976–77. Debut 1978. HS: 9* v Hants (Oval) 1978. BB: 4–56 v Hants (Oval) 1978. BBGC: 3–59 v Essex (Colchester) 1978.

NB The following players whose particulars appeared in the 1978 annual have been omitted: R. P. Baker (left staff), L. E. Skinner (left staff), F. J. Titmus (resigned appointment as coach) and Younis Ahmed (left staff).

The career records of Baker, Titmus and Younis Ahmed will be found elsewhere in this section.

COUNTY AVERAGES

Schweppes Championship: Played 22, won 3, drawn 12, lost 7
All first-class matches: Played 24, won 3, drawn 13, lost 8

BATTING AND FIELDING

Cap		M	I	NO	Runs	HS	Avge	100	50	Ct	St
1969	G. R. J. Roope	15	24	6	752	113*	41.77	2	5	22	—
1978	R. D. V. Knight	23	39	6	1247	128	37.78	3	7	16	—
1974	G. P. Howarth	9	17	1	559	179*	34.93	1	3	4	—
1975	A. R. Butcher	19	33	2	994	188	32.06	2	4	4	—
1959	J. H. Edrich	18	29	5	733	114	30.54	1	4	9	—
1969	Younis Ahmed	15	23	4	514	72	27.05	—	4	9	—
—	D. M. Smith	17	27	6	463	115	22.04	1	—	6	—
—	M. A. Lynch	13	23	0	437	101	19.00	1	2	7	—
—	R. P. Baker	11	17	3	249	91	17.78	—	1	4	—
1978	C. J. Richards	23	29	10	310	50	16.31	—	1	24	7
1970	R. D. Jackman	23	30	7	319	42	13.86	—	—	13	—
1969	Intikhab Alam	23	32	2	266	34	8.86	—	—	10	—
—	A. Needham	5	5	0	33	21	6.60	—	—	1	—
—	I. R. Payne	5	6	0	33	28	5.50	—	—	8	—
—	D. J. Thomas	13	16	3	70	12	5.38	—	—	5	—
1967	P. I. Pocock	21	22	4	91	17*	5.05	—	—	7	—
—	P. H. L. Wilson	9	4	4	9	9*	—	—	—	1	—

Played in one match: S. S. Surridge 2* (1 ct); F. J. Titmus 0*, 4* (1 ct).

BOWLING

	Type	O	M	R	W	Avge	Best	5 wI	10 wM
P. I. Pocock	OB	662.4	201	1615	67	24.10	6–73	5	—
R. D. Jackman	RFM	590.2	134	1707	70	24.38	5–26	3	—
Intikhab Alam	LBG	623.2	197	1570	59	26.61	6–126	3	—
R.D.V. Knight	RM	161.2	41	432	14	30.85	3–22	—	—
P. H. L. Wilson	RFM	105.2	22	355	11	32.27	4–56	—	—
R. P. Baker	RM	166.4	28	573	17	33.70	3–54	—	—
D. J. Thomas	LM	272.1	60	844	16	52.75	4–47	—	—

Also bowled: A. R. Butcher 53–7–192–1; G. P. Howarth 9–3–22–1;
M. A. Lynch 14.1–1–59–2; A. Needham 33.2–9–103–2; I. R. Payne
34–4–133–2; G. R. J. Roope 47–10–141–2; D. M. Smith 11–2–50–1;
F. J. Titmus 14–1–35–1; Younis Ahmed 9–2–27–0.

County Records

First-class cricket

Highest innings totals:	For	811 v Somerset (The Oval)	1899
	Agst	705–8d by Sussex (Hastings)	1902
Lowest innings totals:	For	16 v Nottinghamshire (The Oval)	1880
	Agst	15 by MCC (Lord's)	1839
Highest Individual innings:	For	357* R. Abel v Somerset (The Oval)	1899
	Agst	300* F.Watson for Lancashire (Manchester)	1928
		300 R. Subba Row for Northamptonshire (The Oval)	1958

Best bowling in an innings:	For	10–43 T. Rushby v Somerset (Taunton)	1921
	Agst	10–28 W. P. Howell for Australians (The Oval)	1899
Best bowling in a match:	For	16–83 G. A. R. Lock v Kent (Blackheath)	1956
	Agst	15–57 W. P. Howell for Australians (The Oval)	1899
Most runs in a season:		3246 (av 72.13) T. W. Hayward	1906
runs in a career:		43703 (av 49.77) J. B. Hobbs	1905–1934
100s in a season:		13 by T. W. Hayward	1906
		J. B. Hobbs	1925
100s in a career:		144 by J. B. Hobbs	1905–1934
wickets in a season:		250 (av 14.06) T. Richardson	1895
wickets in a career:		1775 (av 17.91) T. Richardson	1892–1905

RECORD WICKET STANDS

1st	428	J. B. Hobbs & A. Sandham v Oxford U (The Oval) 1926
2nd	371	J. B. Hobbs & E. G. Hayes v Hampshire (The Oval) 1909
3rd	353	A. Ducat & E. G. Hayes v Hampshire (Southampton) 1919
4th	448	R. Abel & T. W. Hayward v Yorkshire (The Oval) 1899
5th	308	J. N. Crawford & F. C. Holland v Somerset (The Oval) 1908
6th	298	A. Sandham & H. S. Harrison v Sussex (The Oval) 1913
7th	200	T. F. Shepherd & J. W. Hitch v Kent (Blackheath) 1921
8th	204	T. W. Hayward & L. C. Braund v Lancashire (The Oval) 1898
9th	168	E. R. T. Holmes & E. W. J. Brooks v Hampshire (The Oval) 1936
10th	173	A. Ducat & A. Sandham v Essex (Leyton) 1921

One-day cricket

Highest innings totals:	Gillette Cup	280–5 v Middlesex (Oval)	1970
	John Player League	248–2 v Gloucestershire (Oval)	1976
	Benson & Hedges Cup	264 v Kent (Oval)	1976
Lowest innings totals:	Gillette Cup	74 v Kent (Oval)	1967
	John Player League	64 v Worcestershire (Worcester)	1978
	Benson & Hedges Cup	125 v Sussex (Hove)	1972
Highest individual innings:	Gillette Cup	101 M. J. Stewart v Durham (Chester-le-Street)	1972
	John Player League	122 G. P. Howarth v Gloucestershire (Oval)	1976
	Benson & Hedges Cup	115 G. R. J. Roope v Essex (Chelmsford)	1973
Best bowling figures:	Gillette Cup	7–33 R. D. Jackman v Yorkshire (Harrogate)	1970
	John Player League	6–25 Intikhab Alam v Derbyshire (Oval)	1974
	Benson & Hedges Cup	4–11 P. I. Pocock v Yorkshire (Barnsley)	1978

SUSSEX

Formation of present club: 1839, reorganised 1857.
Colours: Dark blue, light blue, and gold.
Badge: County Arms of six martlets (in shape of inverted pyramid.
County Championship runners-up (6): 1902, 1903, 1932, 1933, 1934, and 1953.
Gillette Cup winners (3): 1963, 1964, and 1978.
Gillette Cup finalists (3): 1968, 1970, and 1973.
John Player League runners-up: 1976.
Benson & Hedges Cup quarter-finalists (2): 1972 and 1977.
Gillette Man of the Match awards: 26.
Benson & Hedges Gold awards: 17.

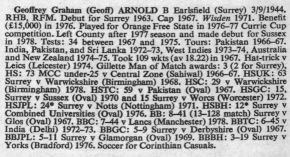

Secretary: S. R. Allen, MBE, County Ground, Eaton Road, Hove, BN3 3AN.
Captain: A. Long.
Prospects of Play Telephone No.: Hove (0273) 772766.

Geoffrey Graham (Geoff) ARNOLD B Earlsfield (Surrey) 3/9/1944. RHB, RFM. Debut for Surrey 1963. Cap 1967. *Wisden* 1971. Benefit (£15,000) in 1976. Played for Orange Free State in 1976-77 Currie Cup competition. Left County after 1977 season and made debut for Sussex in 1978. Tests: 34 between 1967 and 1975. Tours: Pakistan 1966-67. India, Pakistan, and Sri Lanka 1972-73, West Indies 1973-74, Australia and New Zealand 1974-75. Took 109 wkts (av 18.22) in 1967. Hat-trick v Leics (Leicester) 1974. Gillette Man of Match awards: 3 (2 for Surrey), HS: 73 MCC under-25 v Central Zone (Sahiwal) 1966-67. HSUK: 63 Surrey v Warwickshire (Birmingham) 1968. HSC: 29 v Warwickshire (Birmingham) 1978. HSTC: 59 v Pakistan (Oval) 1967. HSGC: 15, Surrey v Sussex (Oval) 1970 and 15 Surrey v Worcs (Worcester) 1972. HSJPL: 24* Surrey v Notts (Nottingham) 1971. HSBH: 12* Surrey v Combined Universities (Oval) 1976. BB: 8-41 (13-128 match) Surrey v Glos (Oval) 1967. BBC: 7-44 v Lancs (Manchester) 1978. BBTC: 6-45 v India (Delhi) 1972-73. BBGC: 5-9 Surrey v Derbyshire (Oval) 1967. BBJPL: 5-11 Surrey v Glamorgan (Oval) 1969. BBBH: 3-19 Surrey v Yorks (Bradford) 1976. Soccer for Corinthian Casuals.

John Robert Troutbeck BARCLAY (Eton College) B Bonn, West Germany 22/1/1954. RHB, OB. Debut 1970 age 16½, whilst still at school. Was in XI at school from age of 14 and scored the record number of runs for school in a season in 1970. Played in MCC Schools matches at Lord's in 1969-71. Vice-captain of English Schools Cricket Association team to India 1970-71. Captain of England Young Cricketers team to West Indies 1972. Cap 1976. Played for Orange Free State in 1978-79 Currie Cup Competition. 1,000 runs (3)—1,090 runs (av 30.27) in 1977 best. Benson & Hedges Gold awards: 2. HS: 112 v Warwickshire (Hove) 1977. HSGC: 44 v Derbyshire (Hove) 1977, and 44 v Somerset (Lord's) 1978. HSJPL: 48 v Derbyshire (Derby) 1977. HSBH: 93* v Surrey (Oval) 1976. BB: 6-94 v Lancs (Manchester) 1976. BBGC: 3-27 v Lancs (Hove) 1978. BBJPL: 3-11 v Worcs (Eastbourne) 1978

Robert Giles Lenthall CHEATLE (Stowe School) B London 31/7/1953. LHB, SLA. Debut 1974. HS: 34 v Kent (Hove) 1977. HSJPL: 13* v Essex (Hove) 1978. BB: 6–54 v Kent (Canterbury) 1976. BBJPL: 4–33 v Glamorgan (Eastbourne) 1977.

Peter John GRAVES (Hove Manor School) B Hove 19/5/1946. LHB, SLA. Close field. Debut 1965. Cap 1969. Is vice-captain of county. Benefit in 1978. Played for Orange Free State in 1969–70, 1970–71 (captain), 1973–74 to 1976–77 Currie Cup competitions whilst appointed as coach. Missed most of 1978 season through injury. 1,000 runs (5)—1,282 runs (av 38.84) in 1974 best. Scored two centuries in match (119 and136*) for Orange Free State v Border (Bloemfontein) 1976–77. Gillette Man of Match awards: 1. Benson & Hedges Gold awards: 2. HS: 145* v Glos (Gloucester) 1974. HSGC: 84* v Derbyshire (Chesterfield) 1973. HSJPL: 101* v Middlesex (Eastbourne) 1972. HSBH: 114* v Cambridge U (Hove) 1974. BB: 3–69 Orange Free State v Australians (Bloemfontein) 1969–70. BBUK: 3–75 v Glos (Cheltenham) 1965. Soccer player.

Timothy John (Tim) HEAD (Lancing College) B Hammersmith 22/9/1957. RHB, WK. Debut 1976. HS: 31 v Oxford U (Oxford) 1978. Held 7 catches in his first match.

Simon Peter HOADLEY (Uckfield School) B Eridge (Sussex) 16/8/1956. Brother of Stephen Hoadley who played previously for county. RHB, OB. Debut 1978. HS: 112 v Glamorgan (Swansea) 1978. HSJPL: 17 v Middlesex (Hove) 1978.

IMRAN KHAN NIAZI (Aitchison College and Cathedral School, Lahore, Worcester RGS and Oxford) B Lahore, Pakistan 25/11/1952. RHB, RF. Cousin of Majid Jahangir Khan. Debut for Lahore A 1969–70 and has played subsequently for various Lahore teams. Debut for Worcs 1971. Blue 1973–74–75 (capt in 1974). Cap 1976. Left Worcs in 1977 and joined Sussex by special registration. Cap 1978. Tests: 15 for Pakistan between 1971 and 1976–77. Tours: Pakistan to England 1971 and 1974, Australia and West Indies 1976–77. 1,000 runs (3)—1,339 runs (av 41.84) in 1978 best. Scored two centuries in match (117* and 106), Oxford U v Notts (Oxford) 1974. Had match double of 111* and 13–99 (7–53 & 6–46) v Lancs (Worcester) 1976. Gillette Man of Match awards: 2 (1 for Worcs). Benson & Hedges Gold awards: 4 (1 for Oxford and Cambridge Universities, 1 for Worcs). HS: 170 Oxford U v Northants (Oxford) 1974. HSC: 167 v Glos (Hove) 1978. HSTC: 59 Pakistan v New Zealand (Karachi) 1976–77. HSGC: 55* Worcs v Essex (Worcester) 1975. HSJPL: 75 Worcs v Warwickshire (Worcester) 1976. HSBH: 72 Worcs v Warwickshire (Birmingham) 1976. BB: 7–52 v Glos (Bristol) 1978. BBTC: 6–63 (12–165 match) Pakistan v Australia (Sydney) 1976–77. BBGC: 4–27 v Staffs (Stone) 1978. BBJPL: 5–29 Worcs v Leics (Leicester) 1973. BBBH: 5–8 v Northants (Northampton) 1978.

JAVED MIANDAD KHAN B Karachi 12/6/1957. RHB, LBG. Debut 1973–74 for Karachi Whites in Patron Trophy tournament aged 16 years 5 months. Has subsequently played for various Karachi, Sind and Habib Bank sides. Vice-captain of Pakistan Under-19 side in England 1974 and captain of Under-19 side in Sri Lanka 1974–75. Scored 227 for county 2nd XI v Hants (Hove) 1975 whilst qualifying for county. Debut for county 1976. Cap 1977. Tests: 13 for Pakistan between 1976–77 and 1978. Tours:

Pakistan to Australia and West Indies 1976–77, England 1978. Scored 1,326 runs (av 40.18) in 1977. Scored 163 for Pakistan v New Zealand (Lahore) 1976–77 on Test debut and 206 v New Zealand (Karachi) in third Test becoming youngest double-century maker in Test cricket at age of 19 years 4 months. Gillette Man of Match awards: 1. HS: 311 Karachi Whites v National Bank (Karachi) 1974–75. HSUK: 162 v Kent (Canterbury) 1976. HSTC: 206 Pakistan v New Zealand (Karachi) 1976–77. HSGC: 75 v Lancs (Hove) 1978. HSJPL: 62* v Middlesex (Hove) 1978. HSBH: 76 v Surrey (Oval) 1977. BB: 6–93 Sind v Railways (Lahore) 1974–75. BBUK: 4–10 v Northants (Northampton) 1977. BBTC: 3–74 Pakistan v New Zealand (Hyderabad) 1976–77.

Garth Stirling LE ROUX (Wynberg Boys High School) B Cape Town 4/9/1955. 6ft 3ins tall. RHB, RF. Debut for Western Province B in 1975–76 Currie Cup competition. Played for Derbyshire 2nd XI in 1977. Debut for county 1978. One match v New Zealanders (Hove). HS: 47* Western Province v Transvaal (Cape Town) 1977–78. HSUK: 17* v New Zealanders (Hove) 1978. BB: 7–40 Western Province v Eastern Province (Port Elizabeth) 1977–78.

Arnold LONG (Wallington CGS) B Cheam 18/12/1940. LBH, WK. Debut for Surrey 1960. Cap 1962. Benefit (£10,353) in 1971. Appointed county vice-captain in 1973. Left staff after 1975 season and made debut for Sussex in 1976. Cap 1976. Appointed county captain in 1978. Dismissed 7 batsmen in innings and 11 in match (all ct) v Sussex (Hove) 1964, world record for most catches in match and only one short of record for most dismissals in match. Dismissed 89 batsmen (72 ct 17 st) in 1962. HS: 92 Surrey v Leics (Leicester) 1970. HSC: 60 v Hants (Basingstoke) 1976. HSGC: 42 Surrey v Sussex (Oval) 1970. HSJPL: 71 Surrey v Warwickshire (Birmingham) 1971. HSBH: 46 Surrey v Kent (Oval) 1973. Soccer for Corinthian Casuals.

Gehan Dixon MENDIS (St Thomas College, Colombo and Brighton, Hove and Sussex GS) B Colombo, Celyon 20/4/1955. RHB, WK. Played for 2nd XI since 1971. Played in one John Player League match in 1973. Debut 1974. Scored 979 runs (av 30.39) in 1978. HS: 128 v Essex (Hove) 1978. HSGC: 44 v Somerset (Lord's) 1978. HSJPL: 56 v Glos (Bristol) 1978. HSBH: 31 v M Counties (East) (Eastbourne) 1978.

Paul William Giles PARKER (Collyers' GS, Horsham and Cambridge) B Bulawayo, Rhodesia 15/1/1956. RHB, RM. Debut for both Cambridge U and county 1976. Blue 1976–77/–78. University Secretary for 1977 and 1978. 1,000 runs (2)—1,192 runs (av 37.25) in 1978 best. Gillette Man of Match awards: 2. HS: 215 Cambridge U v Essex (Cambridge) 1976. HSC: 112 v Glamorgan (Swansea) 1978. HSGC: 69 v Lancs (Hove) 1978 HSJPL: 31 v Glamorgan (Hastings) 1978. HSBH: 36* Combined Universities v Sussex (Cambridge) 1976. Selected for University rugby match in 1977, but had to withdraw through injury.

Christopher Paul PHILLIPSON (Ardingly College) B Brindaban, India 10/2/1952. RHB, RM. Debut 1970. Benson & Hedges Gold awards: 1. HS: 70 v Oxford U (Oxford) 1978. HSC: 34 v Lancs (Hove) 1978. HSJPL: 37* v Northants (Northampton) 1978. HSBH: 21 v Leics (Leicester) 1978. BB: 6–56 v Notts (Hove) 1972. BBJPL: 4–25 v Middlesex (Eastbourne) 1972. BBBH: 5–32 v Combined Universities (Oxford) 1977. Trained as a teacher at Loughborough College of Education.

Anthony Charles Shackleton PIGOTT (Harrow School) B London 4/6/1958. RHB, RFM. Played for 2nd XI since 1975. Debut 1978. Hattrick v Surrey (Hove) 1978. HS: 11 v Kent (Hove) 1978. BB: 4–62 v Middlesex (Hove) 1978.

Kevin Brian SMITH B Lewes 28/8/1957. LHB, SLA. Played for 2nd XI since 1975. Debut 1978. HS: 43 v Kent (Hove) 1978.

John SPENCER (Brighton, Hove and Sussex GS, and Cambridge) B Brighton 6/10/1949. RHB, RM. Debut 1969. Blues 1970–71–72. Cap 1973. Benson & Hedges Gold awards: 3. HS: 79 v Hants (Southampton) 1975. HSGC: 14 v Glos (Hove) 1971. HSJPL: 35 v Northants (Northampton) 1977. HSBH: 18 Cambridge U v Warwickshire (Birmingham) 1972. BB: 6–19 v Glos (Gloucester) 1974. BBGC: 4–25 v Derbyshire (Chesterfield) 1973. BBJPL: 4–16 v Somerset (Hove) 1973. BBBH: 4–19 v Minor Counties (Hove) 1975.

Stewart James STOREY (Purley CGS) B. Worthing 6/1/1941. RHB RM. Debut for Surrey 1960. Cap 1964. Benefit (£9,500) in 1973. Retired after 1974 season. Re-appeared for Sussex in 1978. 1,000 runs (5)—1,184 runs (av 35.87) in 1971 best. Scored 1,013 runs (av 24.70), and took 104 wkts (av 18.39) in 1966 to achieve 'double', the first by a Surrey player since F. R. Brown in 1932. 'Hat-trick' Surrey v Glamorgan (Swansea) 1965. Gillette Man of Match awards: 2 (for Surrey). HS: 164 Surrey v Derbyshire (Oval) 1971. HSC: 57 v Somerset (Hove) 1978. HSGC: 40 Surrey v Middlesex (Lord's) 1968. HSJPL: 56 Surrey v Northants (Luton) 1974. HSBH: 43 Surrey v Yorks (Oval) 1974. BB: 8–22 Surrey v Glamorgan (Swansea) 1965. BBC: 3–12 v Glos (Bristol) 1978. BBGC: 5–35 Surrey v Middlesex (Oval) 1964. BBJPL: 3–23 Surrey v Northants (Northampton) 1971, 3–23 Surrey v Hants (Southampton) 1973 and 3–23 Surrey v Essex (Oval) 1973. BBBH: 3–18 Surrey v Sussex (Hove) 1974.

Christopher Edward (Chris) WALLER B Guildford 3/10/1948. RHB, SLA. Debut for Surrey 1967. Cap 1972. Left staff after 1973 season and made debut for Sussex in 1974. Cap 1976. HS: 47 Surrey v Pakistanis (Oval) 1971. HSC: 38 v Worcs (Worcester) 1975. HSGC: 14* v Notts (Nottingham) 1975. HSJPL: 18* v Glamorgan (Hove) 1975. HSBH: 11* v Essex (Chelmsford) 1975. BB: 7–64 Surrey v Sussex (Oval) 1971. BBC: 6–40 v Surrey (Hove) 1975. BBJPL: 4–28 v Essex (Hove) 1976. BBBH: 4–25 v Minor Counties (South) (Hove) 1975.

Colin Mark WELLS (Tideway School, Newhaven) B Newhaven 3/3/1960. RHB, RM. Played in three John Player League matches in 1978. Has yet to appear in first-class cricket.

Kepler Christoffel WESSELS (Greys College, Bloemfontein) B Bloemfontein, South Africa 14/9/1957. LHB, OB. Debut for Orange Free State 1973–74 in Currie Cup competition, aged 16 years 4 months. Debut for county 1976. Cap 1977. Benson & Hedges Gold awards: 1. HS: 146 Northern Transvaal v Western Province B (Cape Town) 1977–78. HSUK: 138* v Kent (Tunbridge Wells) 1977. HSGC: 43 v Staffs (Stone) 1978. HSJPL: 88 v Notts (Nottingham) 1977. HSBH: 106 v Notts (Hove) 1977.

NB The following players whose particulars appeared in the 1978, Annual have been omitted: M. A. Buss (retired), A. W. Greig (retired) J. J. Groome (left staff) and J. A. Snow (not re-engaged). In addition R. P. T. Marshall who re-appeared has not been included.

The career records of Buss, Greig, Groome and Marshall will be found elsewhere in this Annual.

COUNTY AVERAGES

Schweppes Championship: Played 22, won 4, drawn 11, lost 7
All first-class matches: Played 24, won 4, drawn 12, lost 8

BATTING AND FIELDING

Cap		M	I	NO	Runs	HS	Avge	100	50	Ct	St
1977	Javed Miandad	8	12	2	586	127	58.60	2	4	5	—
1978	Imran Khan	22	37	5	1339	167	41.84	3	6	8	—
—	P. W. G. Parker	14	25	2	781	112	33.95	1	3	3	—
—	T. J. Head	3	5	2	92	31	30.66	—	—	6	1
—	G. D. Mendis	20	36	4	979	128	30.59	3	1	14	—
1976	J. R. T. Barclay	22	40	4	979	103	27.19	1	4	9	—
1967	M. A. Buss	14	20	3	398	79*	23.41	—	2	9	—
—	C. P. Phillipson	22	36	4	749	70	23.40	—	5	11	—
1976	A. Long	21	28	7	410	56*	19.52	—	1	47	3
—	S. P. Hoadley	7	12	0	232	112	19.33	1	1	4	—
—	R. G. L. Cheatle	15	14	4	182	49	18.20	—	—	19	—
1967	A. W. Greig	5	8	1	122	32	17.42	—	—	4	—
—	S. J. Storey	16	23	4	331	57	16.55	—	1	7	—
1977	K. C. Wessels	4	8	0	123	29	15.37	—	—	6	—
—	J. J. Groome	9	17	1	229	50	14.31	—	1	2	—
1973	J. Spencer	17	22	8	189	30	13.50	—	—	8	—
—	K. B. Smith	4	8	1	90	43	12.85	—	—	1	—
—	G. G. Arnold	17	23	4	237	29	12.47	—	—	3	—
1976	C. E. Waller	13	13	7	55	14*	9.16	—	—	11	—
—	A. C. S. Pigott	6	6	0	33	11	5.50	—	—	1	—

Played in two matches: P. J. Graves 31, 21, 5; R. P. T. Marshall 4*, 4*, 2*, 0*.

Played in one match: G. S. le Roux 17*, 0.

BOWLING

	Type	O	M	R	W	Avge	Best	5 wI	10 wM
G. G. Arnold	RFM	401	102	910	49	18.57	7–44	2	—
C. E. Waller	SLA	371	125	861	46	18.71	5–30	3	—
J. Spencer	RM	496.5	143	1158	46	25.17	5–53	1	—
M. A. Buss	LM	179.2	52	473	18	26.27	3–47	—	—
J. R. T. Barclay	OB	200	48	532	19	28.00	5–72	1	—
Imran Khan	RF	543	128	1391	49	28.38	7–52	2	—
A. C. S. Pigott	RFM	69	8	306	9	34.00	4–62	—	—
S. J. Storey	RM	97	27	235	6	39.16	3–12	—	—
R. G. L. Cheatle	SLA	314.2	85	968	24	40.33	4–89	—	—
C. P. Phillipson	RM	193	37	702	16	43.87	3–72	—	—
A. W. Greig	RM	111	21	321	6	53.50	2–47	—	—

Also bowled: Javed Miandad 25–2–101–3; G. S. le Roux 31–7–107–1; R. P. T. Marshall 48–6–216–2; G. D. Mendis 1–0–9–0.

County Records
First-class cricket

Highest innings totals:	For	705–8d v Surrey (Hastings)	1902
	Agst.	726 by Nottinghamshire (Nottingham)	1895
Lowest innings totals:	For	19 v Surrey (Godalming)	1830
		19 v Nottinghamshire (Hove)	1873
	Agst.	18 by Kent (Gravesend)	1867
Highest individual innings:	For	333 K. S. Duleepsinhji v Northants (Hove)	1930
	Agst.	322 E. Paynter for Lancashire (Hove)	1937
Best bowling in an innings:	For	10–48 C. H. G. Bland v Kent (Tonbridge)	1899
	Agst.	9–11 A. P. Freeman for Kent (Hove)	1922
Best bowling in a match:	For	17–106 G. R. Cox v Warwicks (Horsham)	1926
	Agst.	17–67 A. P. Freeman for Kent (Hove)	1922
Most runs in a season:		2850 (av 64.77) John Langridge	1949
runs in a career:		34152 (av 37.69) John Langridge	1928–1955
100s in a season:		12 by John Langridge	1949
100s in a career:		76 by John Langridge	1928–1955
wickets in a season:		198 (av 13.45) M. W. Tate	1925
wickets in a career:		2223 av 16.34) M. W. Tate	1912–1937

RECORD WICKET STANDS

1st	490	E. H. Bowley & John Langridge v Middlesex (Hove)	1933
2nd	385	E. H. Bowley & M. W. Tate v Northamptonshire (Hove)	1921
3rd	298	K. S. Ranjitsinhji & E. H. Killick v Lancashire (Hove)	1901
4th	326*	G. Cox & James Langridge v Yorkshire (Leeds)	1949
5th	297	J. H. Parks & H. W. Parks v Hampshire (Portsmouth)	1937
6th	255	K. S. Duleepsinhji & M. W. Tate v Northamptonshire (Hove)	1930
7th	344	K. S. Ranjitsinhji & W. Newham v Essex (Leyton)	1902
8th	229*	C. L. A. Smith & G. Brann v Kent (Hove)	1902
9th	178	H. W. Parks & A. F. Wensley v Derbyshire (Horsham)	1930
10th	156	G. R. Cox & H. R. Butt v Cambridge U (Cambridge)	1908

One-day cricket

Highest innings totals:	Gillette Cup	314–7 v Kent (Tunbridge Wells)	1963
	John Player League	288–6 v M'sex (Hove)	1969
	Benson & Hedges Cup	280–5 v Cambridge U (Hove)	1974
Lowest innings totals:	Gillette Cup	49 v Derbyshire (Chesterfield)	1969
	John Player League	61 v Derbyshire (Derby)	1978
	Benson & Hedges Cup	61 v Middlesex (Hove)	1978
Highest individual innings:	Gillette Cup	115 E. R. Dexter v Northants (Northampton)	1963
	John Player League	129 A. W. Greig v Yorks (Scarborough)	1976
	Benson & Hedges Cup	114* P. J. Graves v Cambridge U (Hove)	1974
Best bowling figures:	Gillette Cup	6–30 D. L. Bates v Glos (Hove)	1968
	John Player League	6–14 M. A. Buss v Lancashire (Hove)	1973
	Benson & Hedges Cup	5–8 Imran Khan v Northamptonshire (Northampton)	1978

WARWICKSHIRE

Formation of present club: 1884.
Colours: Blue, gold, and silver.
Badge: Bear and ragged staff.
County Champions (3): 1911, 1951 and 1972.
Gillette Cup winners (2): 1966 and 1968.
Gillette Cup finalists (2): 1964 and 1972.
Best final position in John Player League: 5th in
1970 and 1975.
Benson & Hedges Cup semi-finalists (4): 1972,
1975, 1976 and 1978.
Gillette Man of the Match awards: 20.
Benson & Hedges Gold awards: 21.

Secretary: A. C. Smith, County Ground, Edgbaston, Birmingham,
B5 7QU.
Captain: J. Whitehouse.
Prospects of play Telephone No.: (021) 440 3624.

Robert Neal ABBERLEY (Saltley GS) B Birmingham 22/4/1944.
RHB, OB. Debut 1964. Cap 1966, Benefit in 1979. Tour: Pakistan 1966–67
(returning home early owing to injury). 1,000 runs (3)—1,315 runs (av
28.58) in 1966 best. Benson & Hedges Gold awards: 1. HS: 117* v Essex
(Birmingham) 1966. HSGC: 47 v Lincs (Birmingham) 1971. HSJPL: 76 v
Glamorgan (Birmingham) 1974. HSBH: 113* v Hants (Bournemouth)
1976.

Dennis Leslie AMISS B Birmingham 7/4/1943. RHB, SLC. Joined
county staff 1958. Debut 1960. Cap 1965. *Wisden* 1974. Benefit (£34,947)
in 1975. Tests: 50 between 1966 and 1977. Played in one match v Rest of
World in 1970. Tours: Pakistan 1966–67, India, Pakistan, and Sri Lanka
1972–73, West Indies 1973–74, Australia and New Zealand 1974–75,
India, Sri Lanka and Australia 1976–77. 1,000 runs (14)—2,110 runs
(av 65.93) in 1976 best. Also scored 1,120 runs (av 74.66) in West Indies
1973–74. Scored two centuries in match (155* and 112) v Worcs (Birmingham) 1978. Gillette Man of the Match awards: 2. Benson & Hedges Gold
awards: 2. HS: 262* England v West Indies (Kingston) 1973–74. HSUK:
203 England v West Indies (Oval) 1976. HSC: 195 v Middlesex (Birmingham) 1974. HSGC: 113 v Glamorgan (Swansea) 1966. HSJPL: 110 v
Surrey (Birmingham) 1974. HSBH: 73* v Minor Counties (West) (Coventry) 1977. BB: 3–21 v Middlesex (Lord's) 1970.

David John (Dave) BROWN (Queen Mary GS, Walsall) B Walsall
30/1/1942. RHB, RFM. 6ft 4ins tall. Debut 1961. Cap 1964. Benefit
(£21,109) in 1973. County captain from 1975 to 1977. Tests: 26 between
1965 and 1969. Played in 2 matches v Rest of World 1970. Tours: South
Africa 1964–65, Australia and New Zealand 1965–66. Pakistan 1966–67
(vice-captain), West Indies 1967–68, Ceylon and Pakistan 1968–69.
Gillette Man of the Match awards: 1. Benson & Hedges Gold awards: 1.
HS: 79 v Derbyshire (Birmingham) 1972. HSTC: 44 v New Zealand
(Christchurch) 1965–66 and 44* v Pakistan (Lahore) 1968–69. HSGC: 41
v Middlesex (Lord's) 1977. HSJPL: 38* v Worcs (Birmingham) 1972.
HSBH: 20* v Northants (Coventry) 1973. BB: 8–60 v Middlesex (Lord's)

137

1975. BBTC: 5–42 v Australia (Lord's) 1968. BBGC: 5–18 v Glamorgan (Swansea) 1966. BBJPL: 5–13 v Worcs (Birmingham) 1970. BBBH: 3–17 v Lancs (Coventry) 1978.

Christopher Craven (Chris) CLIFFORD (Malton G.S.). B Hoveringham (Yorks) 5/7/1942. RHB, OB. Played for Yorks 2nd XI in 1963 and made debut for county in 1972. Did not play again until making debut for Warwickshire in 1978. HS: 20 v Somerset (Weston-super-Mare) 1978. BB: 6–89 v Somerset (Weston-super-Mare) 1978.

Anthome Michal (Yogi) FERREIRA (Hillview High School, Pretoria) B Pretoria 13/4/1955. RHB, RM. Debut for Northern Transvaal 1974–75. Played for D. H. Robin's XI v both Oxford and Cambridge Universities at Eastbourne in 1978. Has joined county for 1979. HS: 76 Northern Transvaal v Western Province B (Cape Town) 1977–78. BB: 8–38 Northern Transvaal v Transvaal B (Pretoria) 1977–78.

Russell William FLOWER B Stone (Staffs) 6/11/1942. LHB, SLA. Played for Staffordshire since 1964. Debut 1978. HS: 10* v Yorks (Bradford) 1978. BB: 3–45 v Northants (Northampton) 1978.

David Charles HOPKINS (Moseley GS) B Birmingham 11/2/1957. RHB, RM. 6ft 6½ins tall. Played for 2nd XI since 1975. Debut 1977. HS: 13* v Somerset (Birmingham) 1977. BB: 3–27 v Lancs (Manchester) 1978.

Geoffrey William (Geoff) HUMPAGE (Golden Hillock Comprehensive School, Birmingham) B Birmingham 24/4/1954. RHB, WK. Debut 1974. Cap 1976. 1,000 runs (2)—1,329 runs (av 44.30) in 1976 best. HS: 125* v Sussex (Birmingham) 1976. HSGC: 58 v Somerset (Taunton) 1978. HSJPL: 55* v Northants (Birmingham) 1978 and 55* v Essex (Colchester) 1978. HSBH: 7 v Derbyshire (Derby) 1978.

Alvin Isaac (Kalli) KALLICHARRAN B Port Mourant. Berbice Guyana 21/3/1949. LHB, LBG. 5ft 4in tall. Debut 1966–67 for Guyana in Shell Shield competition. Debut for county 1971. Cap 1972. Played for Queensland in 1977–78 Sheffield Shield competition. Tests: 45 for West Indies between 1971–72 and 1977–78, scoring 100* and 101 in first two innings in Tests v New Zealand and captaining country in 3 Tests. Tours: West Indies to England 1973 and 1976. India, Sri Lanka and Pakistan 1974–75, Australia 1975–76, India and Sri Lanka 1978–79 (captain). 1,000 runs (5)—1,343 runs (av 41.96) in 1977 best. Also scored 1,249 runs (av 56.77) on 1974–75 tour. Benson & Hedges Gold awards: 2. HS: 197 Guyana v Jamaica (Kingston) 1973–74. HSUK: 164 v Notts (Coventry) 1972. HSTC: 187 West Indies v India (Bombay) 1978–79. HSGC: 88 v Glamorgan (Birmingham) 1972. HSJPL: 101* v Derbyshire (Chesterfield) 1972. HSBH: 109 v Glos (Bristol) 1978. BB: 4–48 v Derbyshire (Birmingham) 1978.

Timothy Andrew (Andy) LLOYD (Oswestry Boys' HS) B Oswestry (Shropshire) 5/11/1956. LHB. Played for both Shropshire and county 2nd XI in 1975. Appeared in one John Player League match in 1976, v Yorks (Leeds). Debut 1977. HS: 93 v Worcs (Birmingham) 1978. HSJPL: 54* v Middlesex (Birmingham) 1978. HSBH: 35* v Glamorgan (Birmingham) 1978.

Christopher William MAYNARD (Bishop Vesey's GS, Sutton Coldfield) B Haslemere (Surrey) 8/4/1958. RHB, WK. Played for 2nd XI since 1976. Debut 1978. Played in two matches and three John Player League matches. HS: 9 v Derbyshire (Birmingham) 1978.

Philip Robert OLIVER B West Bromwich (Staffs) 9/5/1956. RHB, RM. Played for Shropshire 1972–74. Debut 1975. HS: 59 v Glamorgan (Swansea) 1975. HSGC: 12* v Glamorgan (Birmingham) 1976. HSJPL: 78* v Hants (Southampton) 1978. HSBH: 39* v Worcs (Worcester) 1977. BBJPL: 3–36 v Middlesex (Lord's) 1977. Plays soccer for Telford in Southern League.

Stephen Peter (Steve) PERRYMAN (Sheldon Heath Comprehensive School) B Yardley, Birmingham 22/10/1955. RHB, RM. Debut 1974. Cap 1977. Benson & Hedges Gold awards: 1. HS: 43 v Somerset (Birmingham) 1977. HSJPL: 17* v Worcs (Birmingham) 1975. BB: 7–49 v Hants (Bournemouth) 1978. BBGC: 3–35 v Middlesex (Lord's) 1977. BBJPL: 4–19 v Surrey (Oval) 1975. BBBH: 4–17 v Minor Counties (West) (Birmingham) 1978.

Stephen John (Mic) ROUSE (Moseley County School) B Merthyr Tydfil (Glamorgan) 20/1/1949. LHB, LM. Debut 1970. Cap 1974. Benson & Hedges Gold awards: 2. HS: 93 v Hants (Bournemouth) 1976. HSGC: 34 v Middlesex (Lord's) 1977. HSJPL: 36 v Somerset (Weston-super-Mare) 1978. HSBH: 34* v Glamorgan (Birmingham) 1978. BB: 6–34 v Leics (Leicester) 1976. BBGC: 4–27 v Sussex (Hove) 1976. BBJPL: 5–20 v Kent (Canterbury) 1976. BBBH: 5–21 v Worcs (Worcester) 1974.

Richard Le Quesne SAVAGE (Marlborough College and Oxford) B Waterloo, London 10/12/1955. RHB, RM/OB. Played for county 2nd XI since 1974. Debut for both county and University 1976. Blue 1976–77–78. HS: 22* Oxford U v Worcs (Oxford) 1977. HSC: 13* v Northants (Northampton) 1977. BB: 7–50 v Glamorgan (Nuneaton) 1977.

Kenneth David SMITH (Heaton GS) B Jesmond, Newcastle upon Tyne 9/7/1956. RHB. Son of Kenneth D. Smith, former Northumberland and Leics player. Played for 2nd XI 1972. Debut 1973. Cap 1978. 1,000 runs (2)—1,187 runs (av 33.91) in 1978 best. HS: 135 v Lancs (Manchester) 1977. HSGC: 28 v Somerset (Taunton) 1978. HSJPL: 56 v Middlesex Lord's) 1977. HSBH: 59* v Minor Counties (West) (Coventry) 1977.

Gary Philip THOMAS (George Dixon GS, Birmingham) B Birmingham 8/11/1958. RHB, RM. Played for 2nd XI since 1975. Debut 1978. One match and one John Player League match v Lancs (Manchester). HSJPL: 16 v Lancs (Manchester) 1978.

John WHITEHOUSE (King Edward VI School, Nuneaton and Bristol University) B Nuneaton 8/4/1949. RHB, OB. Played for county against Scotland in 1970, a match no longer counted as first-class. Debut 1971, scoring 173 v Oxford U (Oxford) in first innings of debut match, in 167 minutes with 35 4's. Elected Best Young Cricketer of the Year in 1971 by Cricket Writers' Club. Cap 1973. Appointed county captain in 1978. 1,000 runs (3)—1,543 runs (av 42.86) in 1977 best. HS: as above. HSGC: 109 v Glamorgan (Birmingham) 1976. HSJPL: 92 v Surrey (Birmingham) 1976. HSBH: 71* v Lancashire (Birmingham) 1976.

Robert George Dylan (Bob) WILLIS (Guildford RGS) B Sunderland 30/5/1949. RHB, RF. Debut for Surrey 1969. Left staff after 1971 season and made debut for Warwickshire in 1972. Cap 1972. *Wisden* 1977. Tests: 41 between 1970–71 and 1978. Tours: Australia and New Zealand 1970–71 (flown out as replacement for A. Ward) and 1974–75. West Indies 1973–74,

India, Sri Lanka and Australia 1976–77. Pakistan and New Zealand 1977–78, Australia 1978–79 (vice-captain). Hat-tricks (2) v Derbyshire (Birmingham) 1972 and v West Indians (Birmingham) 1976. Also in John Player League v Yorks (Birmingham) 1973. Gillette Man of Match awards: 1 (for Surrey). Benson & Hedges Gold awards: 2. HS: 43 v Middlesex (Birmingham) 1976. HSTC: 24 v India (Manchester) 1974 and 24* v Australia (Oval) 1977. HSGC: 12* Surrey v Sussex (Oval) 1970. HSJPL: 52* v Derbyshire (Birmingham) 1975. HSBH: 25* v Northants (Northampton) 1977. BB: 8–32 v Glos (Bristol) 1977. BBTC: 7–78 v Australia (Lord's) 1977. BBGC: 6–49 Surrey v Middlesex (Oval) 1970. BBJPL: 4–12 v Middlesex (Lord's) 1973. BBBH: 5–27 v Lancs (Birmingham) 1976. Has played soccer (goalkeeper) for Guildford City.

NB The following players whose particulars appeared in the 1978 annual have been omitted: R. J. Davies and R. B. Kanhai (retired).

COUNTY AVERAGES

Schweppes Championship: Played 22, won 4, drawn 13, lost 5
All first-class matches: Played 24, won 4, drawn 14, lost 6

BATTING AND FIELDING

Cap		M	I	NO	Runs	HS	Avge	100	50	Ct	St
1965	D. L. Amiss	23	41	3	2030	162	53.42	7	11	14	—
1972	A. I. Kallicharran	16	29	5	1041	129	43.37	3	5	10	—
1978	K. D. Smith	23	39	4	1187	132*	33.91	3	5	6	—
1966	R. N. Abberley	15	25	2	625	81	27.17	—	6	6	—
—	T. A. Lloyd	15	23	3	526	93	26.30	—	3	15	—
1976	G. W. Humpage	21	31	3	663	110	23.67	1	2	29	3
1973	J. Whitehouse	24	40	8	740	102*	23.12	1	—	9	—
1974	E. E. Hemmings	14	18	4	275	51	19.64	—	1	8	—
—	P. R. Oliver	17	22	1	322	47	15.33	—	—	7	—
1964	D. J. Brown	16	19	6	171	38	13.15	—	—	6	—
1974	S. J. Rouse	10	12	1	137	40	12.45	—	—	1	—
—	C. C. Clifford	11	12	5	76	20	10.85	—	—	7	—
1972	R. G. D. Willis	12	12	2	88	23*	8.80	—	—	9	—
—	C. Maynard	3	3	1	17	9	8.50	—	—	4	—
—	R. W. Flower	9	8	4	23	10*	5.75	—	—	—	—
1977	S. P. Perryman	24	24	6	97	17*	5.38	—	—	10	—
—	D. C. Hopkins	9	9	0	33	11	3.66	—	—	4	—

Played in one match: R. Savage 5*; G. P. Thomas 4, 1.

BOWLING

	Type	O	M	R	W	Avge	Best	5 wI	10 wM
R. G. D. Willis	RF	286.2	67	735	40	18.37	7–63	3	1
D. J. Brown	RFM	405	80	1160	40	29.00	5–53	1	—
S. P. Perryman	RM	591.3	172	1527	50	30.54	7–49	3	—
C. C. Clifford	OB	431.3	115	1220	38	32.60	6–89	2	—
E. E. Hemmings	OB	376.1	88	1142	28	40.78	4–51	—	—
S. J. Rouse	LM	142.4	27	565	12	47.08	4–63	—	—
R. W. Flower	SLA	173	42	554	10	55.40	3–45	—	—
P. R. Oliver	RM/OB	222	41	657	7	93.85	2–28	—	—

Also bowled: D. L. Amiss 3–0–20–0; D. C. Hopkins 123.3–31–361–4; A. I. Kallicharran 19–5–48–4; T. A. Lloyd 15–5–35–1; R. Savage 4–0–18–0 J. Whitehouse 1–1–0–0.

County Records
First-class cricket

Highest innings totals:	For	657–6d v Hampshire (Birmingham)	1899
	Agst	887 by Yorkshire (Birmingham)	1896
Lowest innings totals:	For	16 v Kent (Tonbridge)	1913
	Agst	15 by Hampshire (Birmingham)	1922
Highest individual innings:	For	305* F. R. Foster v Worcestershire (Dudley)	1914
	Agst	316 R. H. Moore for Hants (Bournemouth)	1937
Best bowling in an innings:	For	10–41 J. D. Bannister v Combined Services (Birmingham)	1959
	Agst	10–36 H. Verity for Yorkshire (Leeds)	1931
Best bowling in a match:	For	15–76 S. Hargreave v Surrey (The Oval)	1903
	Agst	17–92 A. P. Freeman for Kent (Folkestone)	1932
Most runs in a season:		2417 (av 60.42) M. J. K. Smith	1959
runs in a career:		34172 (av 35.31) W. G. Quaife	1894–1928
100s in a season:		8 by R. E. S. Wyatt	1937
		and R. B. Kanhai	1972
100s in a career:		71 by W. G. Quaife	1894–1928
wickets in a season:		180 (av 15.13) W. E. Hollies	1946
wickets in a career:		2201 (av 20.45) W. E. Hollies	1932–1957

RECORD WICKET STANDS

1st	377*	N. F. Horner & K. Ibadulla v Surrey (The Oval)	1960
2nd	465*	J. A. Jameson & R. B. Kanhai v Gloucestershire (Birmingham)	1974
3rd	327	S. P. Kinneir & W. G. Quaife v Lancashire (Birmingham)	1901
4th	402	R. B. Kanhai & K. Ibadulla v Notts (Nottingham)	1968
5th	268	W. Quaife & W. G. Quaife v Essex (Leyton)	1900
6th	220	H. E. Dollery & J. Buckingham v Derbyshire (Derby)	1938
7th	250	H. E. Dollery & J. S. Ord v Kent (Maidstone)	1953
8th	228	A. J. Croom & R. E. S. Wyatt v Worcestershire (Dudley)	1925
9th	154	G. W. Stephens & A. J. Croom v Derbyshire (Birmingham)	1925
10th	128	F. R. Santall & W. Sanders v Yorkshire (Birmingham)	1930

One-day cricket

Highest innings totals:	Gillette Cup	307–8 v Hampshire (Birmingham)	1964
	John Player League	261–8 v Nottinghamshire (Birmingham)	1976
	Benson & Hedges Cup	269–9 v Worcestershire (Birmingham)	1976
Lowest innings totals:	Gillette Cup	109 v Kent (Canterbury)	1971
	John Player League	85 v Glamorgan (Swansea)	1972
		85 v Gloucestershire (Cheltenham)	1973
	Benson & Hedges Cup	96 v Leics (Leicester)	1972
Highest individual innings	Gillette Cup	126 R. B. Kanhai v Lincs (Birmingham)	1971
	John Player League	123* J. A. Jameson v Notts (Nottingham)	1973
	Benson & Hedges Cup	119* R. B. Kanhai v Northants (Northampton)	1975

141

Best bowling figures:	Gillette Cup	6–32 K. Ibadulla v Hants (Birmingham)	1965
	John Player League	5–13 D. J. Brown v Worcs (Birmingham)	1970
	Benson & Hedges Cup	5–21 S. J. Rouse v Worcestershire (Worcester)	1974

WORCESTERSHIRE

Formation of present club: 1865.
Colours: Dark green and black.
Badge: Shield, *Argent* bearing *Fess* between three *Pears Sable*.
County Champions (3): 1964, 1965 and 1974.
Gillette Cup finalists (2): 1963 and 1966.
John Player League champions: 1971.
Benson & Hedges Cup finalists (2): 1973 and 1976.
Gillette Man of the Match awards: 16.
Benson & Hedges Gold awards: 17.

Secretary: M. D. Vockins, County Ground, New Road, Worcester, WR2 4QQ.
Captain: N. Gifford, MBE.
Prospects of play Telephone No.: (0905) 422011.

Cedric Nigel BOYNS (Adams' GS, Newport, Shropshire and Cambridge) B Harrogate 14/8/1954. RHB, RM. Played for county 2nd XI since 1972 and also for Shropshire. Debut for county and University 1976. HS: 95 v Yorks (Scarborough) 1976. HSJPL: 41* v Yorks (Middlesbrough) 1978. HSBH: 15 v Kent (Lord's) 1976. BB: 3–24 v Oxford U (Oxford) 1977. BBGC: 3–36 v Glamorgan (Worcester) 1977. BBJPL: 4–34 v Leics (Worcester) 1978. Obtained degree at London University.

James (Jimmy) CUMBES (Didsbury Secondary Technical School) B East Didsbury (Lancs) 4/5/1944. RHB. RFM. Debut for Lancs 1963. Not re-engaged at end of 1967 season and made debut for Surrey in 1968. Not re-engaged after 1970 season and rejoined Lancs in 1971. Made debut for Worcs in 1972 by special registration. Cap 1978. Hat-trick v Northants (Worcester) 1977. HS: 25* Surrey v West Indians (Oval) 1969. HSC: 22 v Middlesex (Lord's) 1977. HSJPL: 14* v Sussex (Eastbourne) 1978. BB: 6–24 v Yorks (Worcester) 1977. BBGC: 4–23 v Sussex (Hove) 1974. BBJPL: 3–13 v Middlesex (Worcester) 1978. BBBH: 3–34 v Somerset (Taunton) 1978. Soccer (goalkeeper) for Tranmere Rovers, West Bromwich Albion, and Aston Villa.

Basil Lewis D'OLIVEIRA B Cape Town 4/10/1031. RHB, RM/OB. Played for Middleton in Central Lancashire League from 1960 to 1963. Made first-class debut on Commonwealth tour of 1961–62 playing in two matches in Rhodesia. Took part in further tour of Rhodesia in 1962–63. Toured Pakistan with Commonwealth XI 1963–64. Joined Worcestershire in 1964, becoming eligible for Championship matches in 1965. Cap 1965. *Wisden* 1966. Played for Kidderminster in Birmingham League whilst qualifying. Awarded OBE in 1969 Birthday Honours list. Benefit (£27,000) in 1975. Tests: 44 between 1966 and 1972. Played in 4 matches against Rest of World 1970. Tours: West Indies 1967–68, Ceylon and Pakistan 1968–69, Australia and New Zealand 1970–71, 1,000 runs (9)—1,691 runs (av 43.35) in 1965 best. Gillette Man of Match awards: 6. Benson & Hedges Gold awards: 2. HS: 227 v Yorks (Hull) 1974. HSTC: 158 v Australia (Oval) 1968. HSGC: 102 v Sussex (Hove) 1974. HSJPL: 100 v Surrey (Byfleet) 1973. HSBH: 84 v Middlesex (Lord's) 1974. BB: 6–29 v Hants (Portsmouth) 1968. BBTC: 3–46 v Pakistan (Leeds) 1971. BBGC: 4–18 v Notts (Worcester) 1974. BBJPL: 5–26 v Glos (Lydney) 1972. BBBH: 4–23 v Oxford and Cambridge Universities (Cambridge) 1975.

Norman **GIFFORD** B Ulverston (Lancs) 30/3/1940. LHB, SLA .Joined staff 1958 and made debut 1960. Cap 1961. Appointed county captain in 1971 after being vice-captain since 1969. Benefit (£11,047) in 1974. *Wisden* 1974. Tests: 15 between 1964 and 1973. Played in one match for Rest of World v Australia 1971–72. Tours: Rest of World to Australia 1971–72, India, Pakistan and Sri Lanka 1972–73. 100 wkts (3)—133 wkts (av 19.66) in 1961 best. Hat-trick v Derbyshire (Chesterfield) 1965. Took 4 wkts in 6 balls v Cambridge U (Cambridge) 1972. Gillette Man of Match awards: 1. Benson & Hedges Gold awards: 2. HS: 89 v Oxford U (Oxford) 1963. HSTC: 25* v New Zealand (Nottingham) 1973. HSGC: 38 v Warwickshire (Lord's) 1966. HSJPL: 29 v Essex (Worcester) 1974. HSBH: 33 v Kent (Lord's) 1973. BB: 8–28 v Yorks (Sheffield) 1968. BBTC: 5–55 v Pakistan (Karachi) 1972–73. BBGC: 4–7 v Surrey (Worcester) 1972. BBJPL: 4–18 v Middlesex (Worcester) 1974. BBBH: 5–32 v Northants (Worcester) 1973. Awarded MBE in 1979.

Edward John Orton (Ted) **HEMSLEY** (Bridgnorth GS) B Norton, Stoke-on-Trent 1/9/1943. RHB, RM. Debut 1963. Cap 1969. Shared in 6th wkt partnership record for county, 227 with D. N. Patel v Oxford U (Oxford) 1976. Scored 1,168 runs (av 38.93) in 1978. Benson & Hedges Gold awards: 2. HS: 176* v Lancs (Worcester) 1977. HSGC: 73 v Sussex (Hove) 1972. HSJPL: 72 v Notts (Nottingham) 1969. HSBH: 73 v Warwickshire (Birmingham) 1973. BB: 3–5 v Warwickshire (Worcester) 1971. BBJPL: 4–42 v Essex (Worcester) 1971. Soccer for Shrewsbury Town, Sheffield United and Doncaster Rovers.

Stephen Peter **HENDERSON** (Downside School) B Oxford 24/9/1958. Son of D. Henderson, former Oxford Blue. LHB, RM. Debut 1977. HS: 52 v Northants (Worcester) 1977. HSGC: 33 v Glamorgan (Worcester) 1977. HSJPL: 19 v Hants (Worcester) 1977. Is studying at Durham University.

Vanburn Alonza (Van) **HOLDER** B St Michael, Barbados 8/10/1945. RHB, RFM. Debut 1966–67 for Barbados in one match in Shell Shield tournament. Debut for county 1968. Cap 1970. Benefit in 1979. Tests: 34 for West Indies between 1969 and 1977–78. Tours: West Indies to England 1969, 1973 and 1976. India, Sri Lanka, and Pakistan 1974–75, Australia 1975–76, India and Sri Lanka 1978–79 (vice-captain). HS: 122 Barbados v Trinidad (Bridgetown) 1973–74. HSUK: 52 v Glos (Dudley) 1970. HSTC: 42 West Indies v New Zealand (Port of Spain) 1971–72. HSGC: 25* v Notts (Worcester) 1974. HSJPL: 35* v Middlesex (Lord's) 1970. HSBH: 15* v Leics (Leicester) 1973. BB: 7–40 v Glamorgan (Cardiff) 1974. BBTC: 6–28 West Indies v Australia (Port of Spain) 1977–78. BBGC: 3–14 v Oxfordshire (Cowley) 1970. BBJPL: 6–33 v Middlesex (Lord's) 1972. RBBH: 5–12 v Northants (Northampton) 1974.

WORCESTERSHIRE

David John **HUMPHRIES** B Alveley (Shropshire) 6/8/1953. LHB, WK. Played for Shropshire 1971–73. Debut for Leics 1974. Left county after 1976 season and made debut for Worcs in 1977. Cap 1978. HS: 111* v Warwickshire (Worcester) 1978. HSGC: 58 v Glamorgan (Worcester) 1977. HSJPL: 62 v Notts (Dudley) 1977. HSBH: 22* v Minor Counties (West) (Worcester) 1977.

John Darling **INCHMORE** (Ashington GS) B Ashington (Northumberland) 22/2/1949. RHB, RFM. Played for Northumberland in 1970. Played for both Warwickshire and Worcs 2nd XIs in 1972 and for Stourbridge in Birmingham League. Debut 1973. Cap 1976. Played for Northern Transvaal in 1976–77 Currie Cup competition. Benson & Hedges Gold awards: 1. HS: 113 v Essex (Worcester) 1974. HSGC: 12 v Glos (Bristol) 1976. HSJPL: 30* v Essex (Dudley) 1976. HSBH: 49* v Somerset (Taunton) 1976. BB: 8–58 v Yorks (Worcester) 1977. BBGC: 3–11 v Essex (Worcester) 1975. BBJPL: 4–9 v Northants (Dudley) 1975.

Barry John Richardson **JONES** (Wrekin College) B Shrewsbury 2/11/1955. LHB, RM. Debut 1976. HS: 65 v Warwickshire (Birmingham 1977. HSJPL: 36* v Warwickshire (Worcester) 1978.

Philip Anthony (Phil) **NEALE** (Frederick Gough Comprehensive School, Bottesford and John Leggott Sixth Form College, Scunthorpe) B Scunthorpe (Lincs) 5/6/1954. RHB, RM. Played for Lincolnshire 1973–74. Debut 1975. Cap 1978. Scored 1,182 runs (av 34.76) in 1978. HS: 143 v West Indians (Worcester) 1976. HSGC: 68 v Glos (Bristol) 1976. HSJPL: 79* v Somerset (Worcester) 1976. HSBH: 52* v Combined Universities (Worcester) 1978. Soccer for Lincoln City. Studied at Leeds University and obtained degree in Russian.

Joseph **Alan** **ORMROD** (Kirkcaldy HS) B Ramsbottom (Lancs) 22/12/1942. RHB, OB. Debut 1962. Cap 1966. Benefit (£19,000) in 1977. Tour: Pakistan 1966–67. 1,000 runs (10)—1,535 runs (av 45.14) in 1978 best. Benson & Hedges Gold awards: 3. HS: 204* v Kent (Dartford) 1973. HSGC: 59 v Essex (Worcester) 1975. HSJPL: 110* v Kent (Canterbury) 1975. HSBH: 124* v Glos (Worcester) 1976. BB: 5–27 v Glos (Bristol) 1972. BBJPL: 3–51 v Hants (Worcester) 1972.

Dipak Narshibhai **PATEL** (George Salter Comprehensive School, West Bromwich) B Nairobi, Kenya 25/10/1958. Has lived in UK since 1967. RHB, OB. Debut 1976. Shared in 6th wkt partnership record for county, 227 with E. J. O. Hemsley v Oxford U (Oxford) 1976. HS: 107 v Surrey (Worcester) 1976. HSJPL: 28 v Sussex (Eastbourne) 1976. HSBH: 26 v Somerset (Taunton) 1978. BB: 5–22 v Sussex (Eastbourne) 1978. BBJPL: 3–22 v Glos (Moreton-in-Marsh) 1978.

Alan **Paul** **PRIDGEON** B Wall Heath (Staffs) 22/2/1954. RHB, RM. 6ft 3ins tall. Joined staff 1971. Debut 1972. HS: 32 v Yorks (Middlesbrough) 1978. HSJPL: 16* v Essex (Dudley) 1976. HSBH: 10 v Leics (Leicester) 1976. BB: 7–35 v Oxford U (Oxford) 1976. BBJPL: 6–26 v Surrey (Worcester) 1978. BBBH: 3–57 v Warwickshire (Birmingham) 1976. Plays amateur soccer.

Glenn Maitland TURNER (Otago Boys' HS) B Dunedin (New Zealand) 26/5/1947. RHB, OB. Debut for Otago in Plunket Shield competition 1964–65 whilst still at school. Debut for county 1967. Cap 1968. *Wisden* 1970. Benefit in 1978. Tests: 39 for New Zealand between 1968–69 and 1976–77 captaining country in 10 Tests. Tours: New Zealand to England 1969 and 1973 (vice-captain), India and Pakistan 1969–70, Australia 1969–70 and 1973–74 (vice-captain), West Indies 1971–72, Pakistan and India 1976–77 (captain). 1,000 runs (11)—2,416 runs (av 67.11) in 1973 best. including 1,018 runs (av 78.30) by 31 May—the first occasion since 1938. Scored 1,284 runs (av 85.60) in West Indies and Bermuda 1971–72. Scored 1,244 runs (av 77.75) in 1975–76—record aggregate for New Zealand season. Scored 10 centuries in 1970, a county record. Scored two centuries in a match on four occasions (122 and 128*) v Warwickshire (Birmingham) 1972, (101 and 110*) New Zealand v Australia (Christchurch) 1973–74, (135 and 108) Otago v Northern Districts (Gisborne. 1974–75 and (105 and 186*) Otago v Central Districts (Dunedin) 1974–75. Scored 141* out of 169—83.4% of total—v Glamorgan (Swansea) 1977 —a record for first-class cricket. Benson & Hedges Gold awards: 2. HS: 259 twice in successive innings, New Zealanders v Guyana and New Zealand v West Indies (Georgetown) 1971–72. HSUK: 214* v Oxford U (Worcester) 1975. HSGC: 117* v Lancs (Worcester) 1971. HSJPL: 129* v Glamorgan (Worcester) 1973. HSBH: 143* v Warwickshire (Birmingham) 1976. BB: 3–18 v Pakistanis (Worcester) 1967. Has played hockey for Worcs and had trial for Midlands.

Gregory George (Greg) WATSON (Mudgee High School and University of New South Wales) B Gulgong, New South Wales, Australia 29/1/1955. RHB, RFM. Toured England with old collegians team in 1977 and played for Smethwick in Birmingham League. Debut for New South Wales in 1977–78. Debut for county 1978. Benson & Hedges Gold awards: 1. HS: 38 v Somerset (Taunton) 1978. BB: 6–45 v Sussex (Eastbourne) 1978. BBJPL: 4–30 v Somerset (Taunton) 1978. BBBH: 5–22 v Combined Universities (Worcester) 1978.

NB The following player whose particulars appeared in the 1978 annual has been omitted: H. G. Wilcock (left staff).
His career record will be found elsewhere in this annual.

COUNTY AVERAGES

Schweppes Championship: Played 22, won 2, drawn 15, lost 5
All first-class matches: Played 25, won 3, drawn 16, lost 6

BATTING AND FIELDING

Cap		M	I	NO	Runs	HS	Avge	100	50	Ct	St
1968	G. M. Turner	22	38	7	1711	202*	55.19	6	4	20	—
1976	J. D. Inchmore	4	2	1	48	34	48.00	—	—	—	—
1966	J. A. Ormrod	24	41	7	1535	173	45.14	5	4	21	—
1965	B. L. D'Oliveira	17	22	5	728	146*	42.82	1	2	4	—
1969	E. J. O. Hemsley	24	37	7	1168	141*	38.93	3	6	17	—
1978	P. A. Neale	24	40	6	1182	103*	34.76	1	9	10	—
1978	D. J. Humphries	24	32	5	743	111*	27.51	1	3	44	8
—	C. N. Boyns	10	13	2	255	71	23.18	—	1	8	—
1961	N. Gifford	22	24	12	278	37*	23.16	—	—	10	—
—	D. N. Patel	23	29	0	544	104	18.75	1	1	8	—
—	G. G. Watson	21	24	5	266	38	14.00	—	—	7	—
—	S. P. Henderson	4	6	1	65	32*	13.00	—	—	5	—
—	B. J. R. Jones	10	16	0	182	61	11.37	—	1	8	—
—	A. P. Pridgeon	21	22	7	93	32	6.20	—	—	7	—
1970	V. A. Holder	5	5	0	30	23	6.00	—	—	1	—
1978	J. Cumbes	19	16	8	46	11	5.75	—	—	5	—

Played in one match: H. G. Wilcock 0 (4 ct).

BOWLING

	Type	O	M	R	W	Avge	Best	5 wI	10 wM
B. L. D'Oliveira	RM/OB	193.2	48	483	17	28.41	5–48	1	—
N. Gifford	SLA	667.3	210	1557	54	28.83	6–68	2	—
A. P. Pridgeon	RM	587.2	115	1771	59	30.01	4–38	—	—
V. A. Holder	RFM	179	31	468	15	31.20	4–52	—	—
G. G. Watson	RFM	503	83	1535	48	31.97	6–45	1	—
D. N. Patel	OB	398.1	94	1126	35	32.17	5–22	1	—
J. Cumbes	RFM	435	95	1207	31	38.93	4–52	—	—
C. N. Boyns	RM	152.2	21	566	12	47.16	3–92	—	—

Also bowled: E. J. O. Hemsley 21.5–3–81–0; S. P. Henderson 5–0–21–0;
J. D. Inchmore 86–23–223–4; P. A. Neale 9–0–46–0.

County Records

First-class cricket

Highest innings totals:	For......633 v Warwickshire (Worcester)	1906
	Agst......701-4d by Leicestershire (Worcester)	1906
Lowest innings totals:	For......24 v Yorkshire (Huddersfield)	1903
	Agst......30 by Hampshire (Worcester)	1903
Highest individual innings:	For......276 F. L. Bowley v Hampshire (Dudley)	1914
	Agst......331*J.D. Robertson for Middx (Worcester)	1949
Best bowling in an innings:	For......9–23 C. F. Root v Lancashire (Worcester)	1931
	Agst......10–51 J. Mercer for Glamorgan (Worcester)	1936
Best bowling in a match:	For......15–87 A. J. Conway v Gloucestershire (Moreton-in-Marsh)	1914
	Agst......17–212 J. C. Clay for Glamorgan (Swansea)	1937

146

Most runs in a season: 2654 (av 52.03) H. H. I. H. Gibbons 1934
runs in a career: 34490 (av 34.04) D. Kenyon 1946–1967
100s in a season: 10 by G. M. Turner 1970
100s in a career: 70 by D. Kenyon 1946–1967
wickets in a season: 207 (av 17.52) C. F. Root 1925
wickets in a career: 2143 (av 23.73) R. T. D. Perks 1930–1955

RECORD WICKET STANDS

1st 309 F. L. Bowley & H. K. Foster v Derbyshire (Derby) 1901
2nd 274 { H. H. I. H. Gibbons & Nawab of Pataudi v Kent (Worcester) 1933
H. H. I. H. Gibbons and Nawab of Pataudi v Glamorgan (Worcester) 1934
3rd 314 M. J. Horton & T. W. Graveney v Somerset (Worcester) 1962
4th 277 H. H. I. H. Gibbons & B. W. Quaife v Middlesex (Birmingham) 1931
5th 393 E. G. Arnold & W. B. Burns v Warwickshire (Worcester) 1909
6th 227 E. J. O. Hemsley & D. N. Patel v Oxford U (Oxford) 1976
7th 197 H. H. I. H. Gibbons & R. Howorth v Surrey (The Oval) 1938
8th 145* F. Chester & W. H. Taylor v Essex (Worcester) 1914
9th 181 J. A. Cuffe & R. O. Burrows v Gloucestershire (Worcester) 1907
10th 119 W. B. Burns & G. A. Wilson v Somerset (Worcester) 1906

One-day cricket

Category	Competition	Record
Highest innings:	Gillette Cup	261–7 v Essex (Worcester) 1975
	John Player League	307–4 v Derbyshire (Worcester) 1975
	Benson & Hedges Cup	281–4 v Warwickshire (Birmingham) 1976
Lowest innings totals:	Gillette Cup	98 v Durham (Chester-le-Street) 1968
	John Player League	86 v Yorkshire (Leeds) 1969
	Benson & Hedges Cup	92 v Oxford and Cambridge Universities (Cambridge) 1975
Highest individual innings:	Gillette Cup	117* G. M. Turner v Lancashire (Worcester) 1971
	John Player League	129* G. M. Turner v Glamorgan (Worcester) 1973
	Benson & Hedges Cup	143* G. M. Turner v Warwickshire (Birmingham) 1976
Best bowling figures:	Gillette Cup	6–14 J. A. Flavell v Lancs (Worcester) 1963
	John Player League	6–26 A. P. Pridgeon v Surrey (Worcester) 1978
	Benson & Hedges Cup	5–12 V. A. Holder v Northants (Northam'ton) 1974

147

YORKSHIRE

Formation of present club: 1863, reorganised 1891.
Colours: Oxford blue, Cambridge blue, and gold.
Badge: White rose.
County Champions (31): 1867, 1870, 1893, 1896,
1898, 1900, 1901, 1902, 1905, 1908, 1912,
1919, 1922, 1923, 1924, 1925, 1931, 1932,
1933, 1935, 1937, 1938, 1939, 1946, 1959,
1960, 1962, 1963, 1966, 1967, and 1968.
Joint Champions (2): 1869 and 1949.
Gillette Cup Winners (2): 1965 and 1969.
John Player League runners-up: 1973.
Benson & Hedges Cup finalists: 1972.
Fenner Trophy Winners (2): 1972 and 1974.
Gillette Man of the Match awards: 11.
Benson & Hedges Gold awards: 17.

Secretary: J. Lister, Headingley Cricket Ground, Leeds, LS6 3BU.

Captain: J. H. Hampshire.

Charles William Jeffrey (Bill) ATHEY (Acklam Hall High School,
Middlesbrough) B Middlesbrough 27/9/1957. RHB, OB. Toured West
Indies with England Young Cricketers 1976. Debut 1976. HS: 131* v
Sussex (Leeds) 1976 and 131 v Somerset (Taunton) 1978. HSGC: 29 v
Notts (Bradford) 1978. HSJPL: 118 v Leics (Leicester) 1978. HSBH: 31 v
Minor Counties (East) (Jesmond) 1977. BB: 3–38 v Surrey (Oval) 1978.
BBJPL: 3–10 v Kent (Canterbury) 1978.

David Leslie BAIRSTOW (Hanson GS, Bradford) B Bradford 1/9/1951.
RHB, WK. Debut 1970 whilst still at school. Played for MCC Schools at
Lord's in 1970. Cap 1973. Played for Griqualand West in 1976–77 and
1977–78 (captain) Currie Cup competition. Dismissed 70 batsmen (64 ct
6 st) in 1971, including 9 in match and 6 in innings (all ct) v Lancs (Manchester). Benson & Hedges Gold awards: 2. HS: 106 v Glamorgan (Middlesbrough) 1976 and 106 Griqualand West v Natal B (Pietermaritzburg)
1976–77. HSGC: 31* v Durham (Middlesbrough) 1978. HSJPL: 76 v
Sussex (Scarborough) 1976. HSBH: 35* v Essex (Middlesbrough) 1978.
BB: 3–82 Griqualand West v Transvaal B (Johannesburg) 1976–77.
Soccer for Bradford City.

Geoffrey (Geoff) BOYCOTT (Hemsworth GS) B Fitzwilliam (Yorks)
21/10/1940. RHB, RM. Plays in contact lenses. Debut 1962. Cap 1963.
Elected Best Young Cricketer of the Year in 1963 by the Cricket Writers'
Club. Wisden 1964. County captain from 1971 to 1978. Played for N.
Transvaal in 1971–72. Benefit (£20,639) in 1974. Tests: 66 between 1964
and 1977. Played in 2 matches against Rest of World in 1970. Tours:
South Africa 1964–65, Australia and New Zealand 1965–66 and 1970–71
(returned home early through broken arm injury), West Indies 1967–68
and 1973–74, Pakistan and New Zealand 1977–78 (vice-captain), Australia

148

1978–79. 1,000 runs (16)—2,503 runs (av 100.12) in 1971 best. Only English batsman ever to have an average of 100 for a season. Also scored 1,000 runs in South Africa 1964–65 (1,135 runs, av 56.75), West Indies 1967–68 (1,154 runs, av 82.42), Australia 1970–71 (1,535 runs, av 95.93). Scored two centuries in match (103 and 105) v Notts (Sheffield) 1966 and (160* and 116) England v The Rest (Worcester) 1974. Completed 30,000 runs in 1977 and scored his 100th century in Leeds Test of that year—only player to have done so in a Test match. Gillette Man of Match awards: 1. Benson & Hedges Gold awards: 6. HS: 261* MCC v President's XI (Bridgetown) 1973–74. HSUK: 260* v Essex (Colchester) 1970. HSTC: 246 v India (Leeds) 1967. HSGC: 146 v Surrey (Lord's) 1965. HSJPL: 108* v Northants (Huddersfield) 1974. HSBH: 102 v Northants (Middlesbrough) 1977. BB: 3–47 England v South Africa (Cape Town) 1964–65.

Philip (Phil) CARRICK B Armley, Leeds 16/7/1952. RHB, SLA. Debut 1970. Cap 1976. Played for Eastern Province in 1976–77 Currie Cup competition. HS: 105 v Lancs (Leeds) 1978. HSGC: 18 v Durham (Harrogate) 1973 and 18 v Notts (Bradford) 1978. HSJPL: 16 v Hants (Bournemouth) 1976. HSBH: 10 v Middlesex (Lord's) 1977. BB: 8–33 v Cambridge U (Cambridge) 1973. BBJPL: 3–32 v Hants (Bournemouth) 1976.

Howard Pennett COOPER (Buttershaw Comprehensive School, Bradford) B Bradford 17/4/1949. LHB, RM. Debut 1971. Played for Northern Transvaal in 1973–74 Currie Cup competition. HS: 56 v Notts (Worksop) 1976. HSGC: 17 v Hants (Bournemouth) 1977. HSJPL: 29* v Hants (Bournemouth) 1976. HSBH: 20* v Minor Counties (East) (Jesmond) 1977. BB: 8–62 v Glamorgan (Cardiff) 1975. BBGC: 4–18 v Leics (Leeds) 1975. BBJPL: 6–14 v Worcs (Worcester) 1975. BBBH: 3–23 v Surrey (Barnsley) 1978.

Geoffrey Alan (Geoff) COPE (Temple Moor School, Leeds) B Leeds 23/2/1947. RHB, OB. Wears glasses. Debut 1966. Cap 1970. Suspended from playing in second half of 1972 season by TCCB, owing to unsatisfactory bowling action. Action cleared in 1973 by TCCB sub-committee after watching film of him bowling. Suspended again in 1978. Tours: India, Sri Lanka and Australia 1976–77, Pakistan and New Zealand 1977–78. Hat-trick v Essex (Colchester) 1970. HS: 78 v Essex (Middlesbrough) 1977. HSJPL: 16* v Sussex (Bradford) 1974. HSBH: 18* v Surrey (Bradford) 1976. BB: 8–73 v Glos (Bristol) 1975. BBJPL: 3–24 v Northants (Bradford) 1969.

John Harry HAMPSHIRE (Oakwood Technical HS, Rotherham) B Thurnscoe (Yorks) 10/2/1941. RHB, LB. Debut 1961. Cap 1963. Played for Tasmania in 1967–68, 1968–69, 1977–78 and 1978–79. Benefit (£28,425) in 1976. Appointed county captain for 1979. Tests: 8 between 1969 and 1975. Scored 107 in his first Test v West Indies (Lord's) and is only English player to have scored a century on debut in Test cricket when this has occurred at Lord's. Tour: Australia and New Zealand 1970–71. 1,000 runs (13)—1,596 runs (av 53.20) in 1978 best. Gillette Man of Match awards: 4. HS: 183* v Sussex (Hove) 1971. HSTC: 107 v West Indies (Lord's) 1969. HSGC: 110 v Durham (Middlesbrough) 1978. HSJPL: 119 v Leics (Hull) 1971. HSBH: 47 v Sussex (Hove) 1976. BB: 7–52 v Glamorgan (Cardiff) 1963.

Stuart Neil HARTLEY (Beckfoot GS) B Shipley (Yorks) 18/3/1956. RHB, RM. Played for 2nd XI since 1975. Debut 1978. One match v Derbyshire (Sheffield). HS: 20 v Derbyshire (Sheffield) 1978.

Colin JOHNSON (Pocklington School) B Pocklington (Yorks) 5/9/1947. RHB, OB. Played in MCC Schools matches at Lord's 1966. Debut 1969. Benson & Hedges Gold awards: 1. HS: 107 v Somerset (Sheffield) 1973. HSGC: 44 v Durham (Harrogate) 1973. HSJPL: 67* v Glamorgan (Ebbw Vale) 1978. HSBH: 73* v Middlesex (Lord's) 1977.

Barrie LEADBEATER B Harehills, Leeds 14/8/1943. RHB, RM. Distant cousin of E. Leadbeater who played for county from 1949 to 1956 and subsequently for Warwickshire. Debut 1966. Cap 1969. Scored maiden century in 1976 in 208th innings in first-class cricket. Gillette Man of Match awards: 1 (in 1969 final). HS: 140* v Hants (Portsmouth) 1976. HSGC: 76 v Derbyshire (Lord's) 1969. HSJPL: 86* v Northants (Sheffield) 1972. HSBH: 90 v Lancs (Bradford) 1974.

James Derek LOVE B Leeds 22/4/1955. RHB. Debut 1975. HS: 163 v Notts (Bradford) 1976. HSJPL: 60 v Lancs (Leeds) 1977. HSBH: 18 v Notts (Nottingham) 1978.

Richard Graham LUMB (Percy Jackson GS, Doncaster and Mexborough GS) B Doncaster 27/2/1950. RHB, RM. Played in MCC Schools matches at Lord's 1968. Debut 1970 after playing in one John Player League match in 1969. Cap 1974. 1,000 runs (3)—1,532 runs (av 41.40) in 1975 best. HS: 132 v Glos (Leeds) 1976. HSGC: 56 v Shropshire (Wellington) 1976. HSJPL: 101 v Notts (Scarborough) 1976. HSBH: 60* v Kent (Canterbury) 1976.

Christopher Middleton (Chris) OLD (Acklam Hall Secondary GS, Middlesbrough) B Middlesbrough 22/12/1948. LHB, RFM. Debut 1966. Cap 1969. Elected Best Young Cricketer of the Year in 1970 by the Cricket Writers' Club. *Wisden* 1978. Benefit in 1979. Tests: 40 between 1972–73 and 1978. Played in 2 matches against Rest of World 1970. Tours: India, Pakistan, and Sri Lanka 1972–73, West Indies 1973–74, Australia and New Zealand 1974–75, India, Sri Lanka and Australia 1976–77, Pakistan and New Zealand 1977–78, Australia 1978–79. Scored century in 37 minutes v Warwickshire (Birmingham) 1977—second fastest ever in first-class cricket. Benson & Hedges Gold awards: 3. HS: 116 v Indians (Bradford) 1974. HSTC: 65 v Pakistan (Oval) 1974. HSGC: 29 v Lancs (Leeds) 1974. HSJPL: 82 v Somerset (Bath) 1974 and 82* v Somerset (Glastonbury) 1976. HSBH: 72 v Sussex (Hove) 1976. BB: 7–20 v Glos (Middlesbrough) 1969. BBTC: 7–50 v Pakistan (Birmingham) 1978. BBGC: 4–9 v Durham (Middlesbrough) 1978. BBJPL: 5–53 v Sussex (Hove) 1971. BBBH: 4–17 v Derbyshire (Bradford) 1973. Took 4 wkts in 5 balls, England v Pakistan (Birmingham) 1978.

Stephen (Steve) OLDHAM B High Green, Sheffield 26/7/1948. RHB, RFM. Debut 1974. Benson & Hedges Gold awards: 1. HS: 19 v Middlesex (Bradford) 1976. HSJPL: 38* v Glamorgan (Cardiff) 1977. BB: 5–40 v Surrey (Oval) 1978. BBGC: 3–45 v Lancs (Leeds) 1978. BBJPL: 4–21 v Notts (Scarborough) 1974. BBBH: 5–32 v Minor Counties (North) (Scunthorpe) 1975.

Arthur Leslie (Rocker) ROBINSON B Brompton (Yorks) 17/8/1946. LHB, LFM. Debut 1971. Cap 1976. Did not play in 1978 owing to injury. Hat-trick v Notts (Worksop) 1974. HS: 30* v Glamorgan (Cardiff) 1977. HSGC: 18* v Lancs (Leeds) 1974. HSJPL: 14 v Surrey (Oval) 1971. BB: 6–61 v Surrey (Oval) 1974. BBGC: 3–17 v Shropshire (Wellington) 1976. BBJPL: 4–25 v Surrey (Oval) 1974. BBBH: 3–20 v Notts (Nottingham) 1974.

Kevin SHARP (Abbey Grange C.E. High School, Leeds) B Leeds 6/4/1959. LHB, OB. Debut 1976. Captained England under-19 v West Indies under-19 in 1978 and scored 260* in match at Worcester. HS: 91 v Middlesex (Bradford) 1978. HSGC: 21 v Sussex (Leeds) 1978. HSJPL: 40 v Surrey (Oval) 1978. HSBH: 14 v Essex (Middlesbrough) 1978 and 14 v Surrey (Barnsley) 1978.

Arnold SIDEBOTTOM (Broadway GS, Barnsley) B Barnsley 1/4/1954. RHB, RFM. Played for 2nd XI since 1971 and in Schools matches at Lord's in that year. Debut 1973. HS: 124 v Glamorgan (Cardiff) 1977. HSGC: 45 v Hants (Bournemouth) 1977. HSJPL: 31 v Sussex (Hove) 1975. HSBH: 11 v Middlesex (Lord's) 1975. BB: 4–47 v Derbyshire (Chesterfield) 1975. BBGC: 4–36 v Hants (Bournemouth) 1977. BBJPL: 4–24 v Surrey (Scarborough) 1975. Soccer for Manchester United and Huddersfield Town.

Graham Barry STEVENSON (Minsthorpe GS) B Ackworth (Yorks) 16/12/1955. RHB, RM. Played for 2nd XI in 1972. Debut 1973. Cap 1978. HS: 83 v Derbyshire (Chesterfield) 1976. HSGC: 27 v Glos (Leeds) 1976. HSJPL: 33* v Derbyshire (Huddersfield) 1978. BB: 8–65 v Lancs (Leeds) 1978. BBGC: 4–57 v Lancs (Leeds) 1974. BBJPL: 5–41 v Leics (Leicester) 1976. BBBH: 5–28 v Kent (Canterbury) 1978.

Stephen STUCHBURY (Ecclesfield GS) B Sheffield 22/6/1954. LHB, LFM. Played for 2nd XI since 1975. Debut 1978. One match v New Zealanders (Leeds) and also played in six John Player League matches.

John Peter WHITELEY (Ashville College, Harrogate) B Otley (Yorks) 28/2/1955. RHB, OB. Played for 2nd XI since 1972. Debut 1978. HS: 8 v Middlesex (Lord's) 1978. BB: 4–14 v Notts (Scarborough) 1978. Studied at Bristol University.

NB The following players whose particulars appeared in the 1978 annual have been omitted: M. K. Bore, A. Ramage and S. Silvester.

COUNTY AVERAGES

Schweppes Championship: Played 22, won 10, drawn 9, lost 3
All first-class matches: Played 24, won 10, drawn 11, lost 3, abandoned 1

BATTING AND FIELDING

Cap		M	I	NO	Runs	HS	Avge	100	50	Ct	St
1963	J. H. Hampshire	22	36	6	1596	132	53.20	3	9	12	—
1963	G. Boycott	14	22	1	1074	129	51.14	5	3	3	—
1969	C. M. Old	9	10	5	197	100*	39.40	1	—	4	—
1976	P. Carrick	24	30	11	670	105	35.26	1	3	10	—
	K. Sharp	16	24	4	656	91	32.80	—	3	2	—
1974	R. G. Lumb	23	37	3	1070	107	31.47	2	8	19	—
1978	G. B. Stevenson	15	18	4	416	70*	29.71	—	1	6	—
	J. D. Love	14	19	2	461	107	27.11	1	3	8	—
1969	B. Leadbeater	4	7	1	155	61	25.83	—	1	3	—
—	C. W. J. Athey	21	35	2	846	131	25.63	2	4	21	—
—	C. Johnson	7	14	3	276	61	25.09	—	2	4	—
1973	D/ L. Bairstow	24	36	7	725	60	25.00	—	4	61	10
—	H. P. Cooper	19	16	5	186	40	16.90	—	—	11	—
—	A. Sidebottom	6	4	2	27	16	13.50	—	—	1	—
1970	G. A. Cope	15	17	6	133	44	12.09	—	—	7	—
—	J. P. Whiteley	9	4	2	14	8	7.00	—	—	6	—
—	S. Oldham	20	11	7	22	7*	5.50	—	—	3	—

Played in one match: S. N. Hartley 11, 20. S. Stuchbury did not bat.

BOWLING

	Type	O	M	R	W	Avge	Best	5 wI	10 wM
C. M. Old	RFM	353.5	101	807	44	18.34	6–34	2	—
J. P. Whiteley	OB	172.5	46	475	22	21.59	4–14	—	—
C. W. J. Athey	RM	93	26	268	11	24.36	3–38	—	—
G. A. Cope	OB	342.3	114	784	32	24.50	4–34	—	—
G. B. Stevenson	RM	331.3	69	1034	42	24.61	8–65	3	—
S. Oldham	RFM	485	115	1326	53	25.01	5–40	1	—
P. Carrick	SLA	648.2	221	1449	52	27.86	7–35	4	1
H. P. Cooper	RM	447	113	1191	37	32.18	6–26	1	—
A. Sidebottom	RFM	84	11	309	7	44.14	2–15	—	—

Also bowled: D. L. Bairstow 9–2–15–1; G. Boycott 12–6–13–0; J. H. Hampshire 9–0–45–2; S. N. Hartley 2–0–6–0; C. Johnson 2–0–5–0; J. D. Love 6–2–16–0; S. Stuchbury 15.5–1–60–2.

County Records

First-class cricket

Highest innings totals:	For	.....887 v Warwickshire (Birmingham)	1896
	Agst	.....630 by Somerset (Leeds)	1901
Lowest innings totals:	For	.....23 v Hampshire (Middlesbrough)	1965
	Agst	.....13 by Nottinghamshire (Nottingham)	1901
Highest individual innings:	For	.....341 G. H. Hirst v Leicestershire (Leicester)	1905
	Agst	.....318* W. G. Grace for Glos (Cheltenham)	1876
Best bowling in an innings:	For	.....10–10 H. Verity v Nottinghamshire (Leeds)	1932
	Agst	.....10–37 C. V. Grimmett for Australians (Sheffield)	1930

Best bowling	For ___17–91 H. Verity v Essex (Leyton)	1933
in a match:	Agst ___17–91 H. Dean for Lancashire (Liverpool)	1913
Most runs in a season:	2883 (av 80.08) H. Sutcliffe	1932
runs in a career:	38561 (av 50.21) H. Sutcliffe	1919–1945
100s in a season:	12 by H. Sutcliffe	1932
100s in a career:	112 by H. Sutcliffe	1919–1945
wickets in a season:	240 (av 12.72) W. Rhodes	1900
wickets in a career:	3608 (av 16.00) W. Rhodes	1898–1930

RECORD WICKET STANDS

1st	555	P. Holmes & H. Sutcliffe v Essex (Leyton)	1932
2nd	346	W. Barber & M. Leyland v Middlesex (Sheffield)	1932
3rd	323*	H. Sutcliffe & M. Leyland v Glamorgan (Huddersfield)	1928
4th	312	G. H. Hirst & D. Denton v Hampshire (Southampton)	1914
5th	340	E. Wainwright & G. H. Hirst v Surrey (The Oval)	1899
6th	276	M. Leyland & E. Robinson v Glamorgan (Swansea)	1926
7th	254	D. C. F. Burton & W. Rhodes v Hampshire (Dewsbury)	1919
8th	292	Lord Hawke & R. Peel v Warwickshire (Birmingham)	1896
9th	192	G. H. Hirst & S. Haigh v Surrey (Bradford)	1898
10th	148	Lord Hawke & D. Hunter v Kent (Sheffield)	1898

One-day cricket

Highest innings totals:	Gillette Cup	317–4 v Surrey (Lord's)	1965
	John Player League	244–5 v Leicestershire (Leicester)	1978
	Benson & Hedges Cup	218–3 v Minor Counties (North) (Scunthorpe)	1975
		218–9 v Minor Counties (East) (Jesmond)	1977
Lowest innings totals:	Gillette Cup	76 v Surrey (Harrogate)	1970
	John Player League	74 v Warwickshire (Birmingham)	1972
	Benson & Hedges Cup	114 v Kent (Canterbury)	1978
Highest individual innings:	Gillette Cup	146 G. Boycott v Surrey (Lord's)	1965
	John Player League	119 J. H. Hampshire v Leicestershire (Hull)	1971
	Benson & Hedges Cup	102 G. Boycott v Northamptonshire (Middlesbrough)	1977
Best bowling figures:	Gillette Cup	6–15 F. S. Trueman v Somerset (Taunton)	1965
	John Player League	7–15 R. A. Hutton v Worcestershire (Leeds)	1969
	Benson & Hedges Cup	6–27 A. G. Nicholson v Minor Counties (North) (Middlesbrough)	1972

153

THE FIRST-CLASS UMPIRES FOR 1979

NB The abbreviations used below are identical with those given at the beginning of the section 'The Counties and their Players'.

William Edward (Bill) ALLEY B Sydney (Australia) 3/2/1919. LHB, RM. Played for New South Wales 1945–46 to 1947–48. Subsequently came to England to play League cricket and then for Somerset from 1957 to 1968. *Wisden* 1961. Testimonial (£2,700) in 1961. Tours: India and Pakistan 1949–50, Pakistan 1963–64 with Commonwealth team. Scored 3,019 runs (av 56.96) in 1961 including 2,761 runs and 10 centuries for county, both being records. Won Man of the Match award in Gillette Cup Competition on three occasions. HS: 221* v Warwickshire (Nuneaton) 1961. BB: 8–65 v Surrey (Oval) 1962. Career record: 19,612 runs (av 31.88), 31 centuries, 768 wkts (av 22.68). Appointed 1969. Umpired in 7 Tests between 1974 and 1977.

Ronald (Ron) ASPINALL B Almondbury (Yorks) 26/10/1918. RHB, RFM. Played for Yorkshire from 1946 to 1950 (retiring early through injury) and for Durham from 1951 to 1957. HS: 57* v Notts (Nottingham) 1948. BB: 8–42 v Northants (Rushden) 1949. Career record: 763 runs (av 19.07), 131 wkts (av 20.38). Appointed 1960.

Harold Denis BIRD B Barnsley 19/4/1933. RHB, RM. Played for Yorks from 1956 to 1959 and for Leics from 1960 to 1964. Has since been professional at Paignton CC. HS: 181* Yorks v Glamorgan (Bradford) 1959. Career record: 3,315 runs (av 20.71), 2 centuries. Appointed 1970. Umpired in 15 Tests between 1973 and 1978.

William Lloyd BUDD B Hawkley (Hants) 20/10/1913. RHB, RFM. Played for Hampshire from 1934 to 1946. HS: 77* v Surrey (Oval) 1937. BB: 4–22 v Essex (Southend) 1937. Career record: 941 runs (av 11.47). 64 wkts (av 39.15). Was on Minor Counties list for some years. Appointed 1969. Umpired in 4 Tests between 1976 and 1978.

David John CONSTANT B Bradford-on-Avon (Wilts) 9/11/1941. LHB, SLA. Played for Kent from 1961 to 1963 and for Leics from 1965 to 1968. HS: 80 v Glos (Bristol) 1966. Career record: 1,517 runs (av 19.20), 1 wkt (av 36.00). Appointed 1969. Umpired in 16 Tests between 1971 and 1978.

Cecil (Sam) COOK B Tetbury (Glos) 23/8/1921. RHB, SLA. Played for Gloucestershire from 1946 to 1964. Benefit (£3,067) in 1957. Took wicket with first ball in first-class cricket. Tests: 1 v SA 1947. HS: 35* v Sussex (Hove) 1957. BB: 9–42 v Yorks (Bristol) 1947. Career record: 1,964 runs (av 5.39), 1,782 wkts (av 20.52). Appointed 1971, after having withdrawn from appointment in 1966.

Derek James DENNIS B Swansea 1/1/1929. Has not played first-class cricket. Has umpired in Minor Counties matches since 1975. Appointed 1979.

David Gwilliam Lloyd EVANS B Lambeth (London) 27/7/1933. RHB. WK. Played for Glamorgan from 1956 to 1969. Benefit (£3,500) in 1969. HS: 46* v Oxford U (Oxford) 1961. Career record: 2,875 runs (av 10.53). 558 dismissals (502 ct 56 st). Appointed 1971.

John Vesey Claude GRIFFITHS B Blackheath (London) 19/1/1931, LHB, SLA. Played for Gloucestershire from 1952 to 1957. HS: 32 v Combined Services (Bristol) 1953. BB: 4–74 v Cambridge U (Bristol) 1955. Career record: 396 runs (av 9.20), 48 wkts (av 24.31). Appointed 1979.

David John HALFYARD B Winchmore Hill (Middlesex) 3/4/1931. RHB, RM. Played for Kent from 1956 to 1964 retiring through leg injury. Testimonial (£3,216) in 1965. Played for Notts from 1968 to 1970. Not re-engaged and has subsequently played in Minor Counties competition for Durham in 1971 and 1972, Northumberland in 1973 and Cornwall from 1974. HS: 79 Kent v Middlesex (Lord's) 1960. BB: 9–39 Kent v Glamorgan (Neath) 1957. Career record: 3,242 runs (av 10.91), 963 wkts (av 25.77). Appointed 1977, after having been on list in 1967.

Arthur JEPSON B Selston (Notts) 12/7/1915. RHB, RFM. Played for Notts from 1938 to 1959. Benefit (£2,000) in 1951. HS: 130 v Worcs (Nottingham) 1950. BB: 8–45 v Leics (Nottingham) 1958. Career record: 6,369 runs (av 14.31),1 century, 1,051 wkts (av 29.08). Soccer (goalkeeper) for Port Vale, Stoke City and Lincoln City. Appointed 1960. Umpired in 4 Tests between 1966 and 1969.

Raymond (Ray) JULIAN B Cosby (Leics) 23/8/1936. RHB, WK. Played for Leicestershire from 1953 (debut at age of 16) to 1971, but lost regular place in side to R. W. Tolchard in 1966. HS: 51 v Worcs (Worcester) 1962. Career record: 2,581 runs (av 9.73), 421 dismissals (382 ct 39 st). Appointed 1972.

John George LANGRIDGE B Chailey (Sussex) 10/2/1910. Younger brother of late James Langridge. Opening RHB and outstanding slip field. Played for Sussex from 1928 to 1955. *Wisden* 1949. Shared joint benefit (£1,930) with H. W. Parks in 1948. Testimonial (£3,825) in 1953. Scored more runs and centuries in first-class cricket than any other player who never appeared in a Test match. Only F. E. Woolley, W. G. Grace, W. R. Hammond, G. A. R. Lock and D. B. Close have held more catches than his total of 786. HS: 250* v Glamorgan (Hove) 1933. Career record: 34,380 runs (av 37.45), 76 centuries, 44 wkts (av 42.00). Appointed 1956. Umpired in 7 Tests between 1960 and 1963.

Barrie John MEYER B Bournemouth 21/8/1932. RHB, WK. Played for Gloucestershire from 1957 to 1971. Benefit 1971. HS: 63 v Indians (Cheltenham) 1959 v Oxford U (Bristol) 1962 and v Sussex (Bristol) 1964. Career record: 5,367 runs (av 14.19), 826 dismissals (707 ct 119 st). Soccer, for Bristol Rovers, Plymouth Argyle, Newport County and Bristol City. Appointed 1973. Umpired in 2 Tests in 1978.

Donald Osmund OSLEAR B Cleethorpes (Lincs) 3/3/1929. Has not played first-class cricket. Played soccer for Grimsby Town, Hull City, and Oldham Athletic. Also played ice hockey. Has umpired in county second XI matches since 1972. Appointed in 1975.

Kenneth Ernest (Ken) PALMER B Winchester 22/4/1937. RHB, RFM. Played for Somerset from 1955 to 1969. Testimonial (£4,000) in 1968. Tour: Pakistan with Commonwealth team 1963–64. Coached in Johannesburg 1964–65 and was called upon by MCC to play in final Test v South Africa owing to injuries to other bowlers. Tests (1): 1 v SA 1964–65. HS: 125* v Northants (Northampton) 1961. BB: 9–57 v Notts (Nottingham) 1963. Career record: 7,771 runs (av 20.66), 2 centuries, 866 wkts (av 21.34). Appointed 1972. Umpired in 2 Tests in 1978.

Cecil George (Cec) PEPPER B Forbes, New South Wales (Australia) 15/9/1918. RHB, LBG. Played for New South Wales 1938–39 to 1940–41, Australian Services 1945 and 1945–46. Returned to England to play in League cricket from 1947 and appeared in the Hastings Festivals in 1956 and 1957. Tours: India and Ceylon 1945–46 with Australian Services Team and India and Pakistan 1949–50 with Commonwealth Team. HS: 168 Australian Services v H. D. G. Leveson-Gower's XI (Scarborough) 1945. BB: 6–33 Commonwealth XI v Holkar Cricket Association (Indore) 1949–50. Career record: 1,927 runs (av 29.64), 1 century, 169 wkts (av 29.31). Appointed 1964.

Albert Ennion Growcott (Dusty) RHODES B Tintwistle (Cheshire) 10/10/1916. Father of H. J. Rhodes. RHB, LBG. Played for Derbyshire from 1937 to 1954. Testimonial (£2,096) in 1952. Tour: India 1951–52 returning home early owing to injury. Achieved 5 hat-tricks. HS: 127 v Somerset (Taunton) 1949. BB: 8–162 v Yorks (Scarborough) 1947. Career record: 7,363 runs (av 18.97), 3 centuries, 661 wkts (av 28.22). Appointed 1959. Has umpired in 8 Tests between 1963 and 1973. Also umpired in 2 matches between England and Rest of World 1970.

Derek SHACKLETON B Todmorden (Yorks) 12/8/1924. RHB, RM. Played for Hampshire from 1948 to 1969. *Wisden* 1958. Benefit (£5,000) in 1958. Testimonial (£5,000) in 1967. Played for Dorset from 1971 to 1974. Tests: 7 between 1950 and 1963. Tours: India with Commonwealth XI 1950–51 and MCC 1951–52. Took 100 wkts in 20 consecutive seasons from 1949 to 1968, to create record. Only W. Rhodes has taken 100 wkts in more seasons (23). Took more wkts (2,669, av 18.22) than any other bowler. HS: 87* v Essex (Bournemouth) 1949. BB: 9–30 v Warwickshire (Portsmouth) 1960. Career record: 9,561 runs (av 14.59), 2,857 wkts (av 18.65). The eighth highest aggregate by a bowler in first-class cricket. Appointed 1979.

Charles Terry SPENCER B Leicester 18/8/1931. RHB, RFM. Played for Leicestershire from 1952 to 1974. Benefit (£3,500) in 1964. HS: 90 v Essex (Leicester) 1964. BB: 9–63 v Yorks (Huddesersfield) 1954. Career record: 5,871 runs (av 10.77), 1,367 wkts (av 26.69). Appointed 1979.

Thomas William (Tom) SPENCER B Deptford 22/3/1914. RHB, RM. Played for Kent from 1935 to 1946. HS: 96 v Sussex (Tunbridge Wells) 1946. Career record: 2,152 runs (av 20.11), 1 wkt (av 19.00). Appointed 1950 (longest serving umpire on list). Has umpired in 17 Tests between 1954 and 1978.

Jack **VAN GELOVEN** B Leeds 4/1/1934. RHB, RM. Played for Yorkshire in 1955 and for Leicestershire from 1956 to 1965. Subsequently played for Northumberland in Minor Counties competition from 1966 to 1973. HS: 157* v Somerset (Leicester) 1960. BB: 7–56 v Hants (Leicester) 1959. Career record: 7,522 runs (av 19.43), 5 centuries, 486 ≉ kts (av 28.62). Appointed 1977.

Alan Geoffrey Thomas **WHITEHEAD** B Butleigh (Somerset) 28/10/1940. LHB, SLA. Played for Somerset from 1957 to 1961. HS: 15 v Hants (Southampton) 1959 and 15 v Leics (Leicester) 1960. BB: 6–74 v Sussex (Eastbourne) 1959. Career record: 137 runs (av 5.70), 67 wkts (av 34.41). Served on Minor Counties list in 1969. Appointed 1970.

Peter Bernard **WIGHT** B Georgetown (British Guiana) 25/6/1930. RHB, OB. Played for British Guiana in 1950–51 and for Somerset from 1953 to 1965. Benefit (£5,000) in 1963. HS: 222* v Kent (Taunton) 1959. BB: 6–29 v Derbyshire (Chesterfield) 1957. Career record: 17,773 runs (av 33.09), 28 centuries, 68 wkts (av 33.26). Appointed 1966.

NB The Test match panel for 1979 is H. D. Bird, D. J. Constant, B. J. Meyer and K. E. Palmer.

Young Cricketer of the Year

At the end of each season the members of the Cricket Writers' Club select by ballot the player they consider the best young cricketer of the season.

D. I. Gower (Leicestershire) was elected last year.

The selections to date are:

1950 R. Tattersall (Lancashire)
1951 P. B. H. May (Surrey)
1952 F. S. Trueman (Yorkshire)
1953 M. C. Cowdrey (Kent)
1954 P. J. Loader (Surrey)
1955 K. F. Barrington (Surrey)
1956 B. Taylor (Essex)
1957 M. J. Stewart (Surrey)
1958 A. C. D. Ingleby-
        Mackenzie (Hampshire)
1959 G. Pullar (Lancashire)
1960 D. A. Allen
        (Gloucestershire)
1961 P. H. Parfitt (Middlesex)
1962 P. J. Sharpe (Yorkshire)
1963 G. Boycott (Yorkshire)

1964 J. M. Brearley (Middlesex)
1965 A. P. E. Knott (Kent)
1966 D. L. Underwood (Kent)
1967 A. W. Greig (Sussex)
1968 R. H. M. Cottam
        (Hampshire)
1969 A. Ward (Derbyshire)
1970 C. M. Old (Yorkshire)
1971 J. Whitehouse (Warwickshire)
1972 D. R. Owen-Thomas (Surrey)
1973 M. Hendrick (Derbyshire)
1974 P. H. Edmonds (Middlesex)
1975 A. Kennedy (Lancashire)
1976 G. Miller (Derbyshire)
1977 I. T. Botham (Somerset)
1978 D. I. Gower (Leicestershire)

FIRST-CLASS AVERAGES 1978

The following averages include everyone who appeared in first-class cricket during the season. There were 233 first-class matches as follows: Test matches (6); Pakistan touring team (10); New Zealand touring team (13); Schweppes Championship (184); Oxford and Cambridge Universities (18); MCC v Middlesex (1); Scotland v Ireland (1). Matches abandoned without a ball being bowled are excluded.

† *Indicates left-handed batsman.*

BATTING AND FIELDING

	Cap	M	I	NO	Runs	HS	Avge	100	50	Ct	St
Aamer Hameed (Pak)	—	6	3	1	26	13	13.00	—	—	—	—
Abberley, R. N. (Wa)	1966	15	25	2	625	81	27.17	—	6	6	—
Abdul Qadir (Pak)	—	7	6	0	16	9	2.66	—	—	4	—
†Abrahams, J. (La)	—	19	30	2	654	126	23.35	1	4	12	—
Acfield, D. L. (Ex)	1970	22	15	9	44	12*	7.33	—	—	8	—
Agnew, J. P. (Le)	—	4	1	0	1	1	1.00	—	—	—	—
Allbrook, M. E. (CU/Nt)	—	14	14	5	76	18	8.44	—	—	—	—
Allott, P. J. W. (La)	—	4	2	1	1	1	1.00	—	—	1	—
Amiss, D. L. (Wa)	1965	23	41	3	2030	162	53.42	7	11	14	—
Anderson, I. J. (Ire)	—	1	—	—	—	—	—	—	—	—	—
Anderson, I. S. (D)	—	6	10	1	140	75	15.55	—	1	3	—
Anderson, R. W. (NZ)	—	14	24	3	739	155	35.19	2	2	6	—
Arnold, G. G. (Sx)	—	17	23	4	237	29	12.47	—	—	3	—
Arrowsmith, R. (La)	—	13	10	4	96	24*	16.00	—	—	4	—
Arshad Pervaiz (Pak)	—	3	5	0	59	30	11.80	—	—	1	—
Asif Iqbal (K)	1968	18	25	6	934	171	49.15	3	2	18	—
Athey, C. W. J. (Y/DHR/YE)	—	23	38	2	906	131	25.16	2	4	22	—
Bainbridge, P. (Gs)	—	3	5	2	233	76*	77.66	—	3	1	—
Bairstow, D. L. (Y)	1973	24	36	7	725	60	25.00	—	4	61	10
Baker, R. P. (Sy)	—	11	17	3	249	41	17.78	—	1	6	—
Balderstone, J. C. (Le)	1973	24	36	1	931	101	26.60	1	5	9	—
Barclay, J. R. T. (Sx/DHR)	1976	23	41	4	1006	103	27.18	1	4	9	—
Barlow, E. J. (D)	1976	16	25	4	765	127	36.42	1	3	25	—
†Barlow, G. D. (M)	1976	24	35	2	1016	102*	30.78	1	6	15	—
Beaumont, D. J. (CU)	—	4	6	1	90	31	18.00	—	—	2	—
Birch, J. D. (Nt)	—	13	16	2	308	52*	22.00	—	2	6	—
†Birkenshaw, J. (Le)	1965	22	26	9	506	70*	29.76	—	1	10	—
Bishop, M. M. (CU)	—	2	2	1	0	0*	0.00	—	—	1	—
Boock, S. L. (NZ)	—	13	14	10	57	14*	14.25	—	—	4	—
Booth, P. (Le)	1976	18	10	2	99	25*	12.37	—	—	4	—
Borrington, A. J (D)	1977	17	27	3	669	137	27.87	1	2	3	—
Botham, I. T. (E/So/MCC)	1976	17	20	0	538	108	26.90	2	1	11	—
Boycott, G. (E/Y)	1963	16	25	1	1233	131	51.37	6	3	1	—
Boyns, C. N. (Wo)	—	10	13	2	255	71	23.18	—	1	8	—
Bracewell, B. P. (NZ)	—	9	10	3	18	10*	2.57	—	—	4	—
Brain, B. M. (Gs)	1977	23	27	7	268	35	13.40	—	—	5	—
Brassington, A. J. (Gs)	1978	21	30	8	192	22	7.11	—	—	42	3

	Cap	M	I	NO	Runs	HS	Avge	100	50	Ct	St
†Breakwell, D. (So)	1976	16	23	5	579	100*	32.16	1	4	5	—
Brearley, J. M. (E/M/MCC)	1964	18	27	4	558	70*	24.26	—	4	18	—
†Brettell, D. N. (OU)	—	3	4	0	49	30	12.25	—	—	1	—
†Briers, N. E. (Le)	—	16	24	2	601	116*	27.31	2	2	6	—
Brown, A. (Sc)	—	2	3	0	13	7	4.33	—	—	1	—
Brown, D. J. (Wa)	1964	16	19	6	171	38	13.15	—	—	6	—
Burgess, G. I. (So)	1968	16	23	5	336	55	18.66	—	1	12	—
Burgess, M. G. (NZ)	—	15	24	1	552	68	24.00	—	5	8	—
†Buss, M. A. (Sx)	1967	14	20	3	398	79*	23.41	—	2	9	—
†Butcher, A. R. (Sy)	1975	19	33	2	994	188	32.06	2	4	4	—
Butcher, R. O. (M)	—	10	14	0	464	142	33.14	1	3	18	—
Cairns, B. L. (NZ)	—	11	16	2	239	41	17.07	—	—	7	—
Carrick, P. (Y/YB)	1976	25	32	11	679	105	32.33	1	3	11	—
Carter, R. M. (NO)	—	2	1	1	8	8*	—	—	—	—	—
Cartwright, H. (D)	1978	24	37	4	644	77*	19.51	—	2	8	—
†Cheatle, R. G. L. (Sx)	—	15	14	4	182	49	18.20	—	—	19	—
†Childs, J. H. (Gs)	1977	19	16	11	28	4*	5.60	—	—	8	—
Claughton, J. A. (OU)	—	10	15	0	366	130	24.40	1	1	5	—
Clifford, C. C. (Wa)	—	11	12	5	76	20	10.85	—	—	7	—
Clift, P. B. (Le)	1976	22	26	7	465	61	24.47	—	3	13	—
†Clinton, G. S. (K)	—	6	8	2	113	33	18.83	—	—	2	—
†Close, D. B. (TNP)	—	1	2	0	9	8	4.50	—	—	2	—
Colhoun, O. D. (Ire)	—	1	—	—	—	—	—	—	—	2	—
Collinge, R. O. (NZ)	—	6	5	1	91	63*	22.75	—	1	—	—
Congdon, B. E. (NZ)	—	13	21	5	556	110*	34.75	1	1	10	—
Cook, G. (No/MCC/TNP)	1975	23	40	2	1226	155	32.26	1	7	23	—
Cook, N. G. B. (Le)	—	2	2	1	33	31	33.00	—	—	1	—
†Cooper, H. P. (Y)	—	19	16	5	186	40	16.90	—	—	11	—
†Cooper, K. E. (Nt)	—	24	18	3	102	19	6.80	—	—	10	—
†Cooper, N. H. C. (Gs)	—	6	12	0	219	94	18.25	—	1	4	—
Cope, G. A. (Y)	1970	15	17	6	133	44	12.09	—	—	7	—
Cordle, A. E. (Gm)	1967	15	15	3	161	33*	13.41	—	—	8	—
Corlett, S. C. (Ire)	—	1	—	—	—	—	—	—	—	2	—
Cowdrey, C. S. (K)	—	17	17	4	291	69*	22.38	—	1	11	—
Cowley, N. G. (H)	1978	23	38	5	650	64	19.69	—	2	16	—
Crawford, I. C. (Gs)	—	2	3	0	89	73	29.66	—	1	—	—
Crawford, N. C. (CU)	—	5	6	0	71	30	11.83	—	—	1	—
Croft, C. E. H. (La)	—	18	22	3	124	19*	6.52	—	—	1	—
Crowther, P. G. (Gm)	—	4	7	0	47	27	6.71	—	—	1	—
Cumbes, J. (Wo)	1978	19	16	8	46	11	5.75	—	—	5	—
Curzon, C. C. (Nt)	—	4	4	0	26	26	6.50	—	—	2	1
Curzon, J. T. (Nt)	—	1	1	0	1	1	1.00	—	—	1	—
Dalrymple, J. J. H. (OU)	—	3	4	2	27	15	13.50	—	—	1	—
Daniel, W. W. (M)	1977	21	24	12	132	30*	11.00	—	—	3	—
†Davey, J. (Gs)	1971	15	19	6	135	20*	10.38	—	—	4	—
Davison, B. F. (Le)	1971	23	35	3	1644	180*	51.37	4	9	8	—
†Dean, P. J. (OU)	—	2	4	0	75	39	18.75	—	—	1	—
Denness, M. H. (Ex)	1977	22	37	2	870	126	24.85	1	4	10	—
†Denning, P. W. (So)	1973	22	39	3	925	78*	25.69	—	5	13	—
Dewes, A. R. (CU)	—	5	8	0	99	32	12.37	—	—	1	—
Dexter, R. E. (Nt)	—	4	7	2	65	22	13.00	—	—	2	—

	Cap	M	I	NO	Runs	HS	avge	100	50	Ct	St
†Dilley, G. R. (K)	—	4	4	2	11	8	5.50	—	—	—	3
D'Oliveira, B. L. (Wo)	1965	17	22	5	728	146*	42.82	1	2	4	—
†Donald, P. C. G. (OU)	—	1	1	0	1	1	1.00	—	—	—	—
Donald, W. A. (Sc)	—	1	1	0	0	0	0.00	—	—	—	—
†Doshi, D. R. (Nt/TNP)	1977	15	13	7	51	23	8.50	—	—	3	—
Downton, P. R. (K/MCC/YE)	—	27	21	6	147	31	9.80	—	—	59	4
†Dredge, C. H. (So)	—	20	19	3	148	23	9.25	—	—	6	—
Dudleston, B. (Le/TNP)	1969	16	24	1	608	90	26.43	—	4	5	—
Ealham, A. G. E. (K)	1970	23	32	4	856	102*	30.57	1	5	15	—
East, R. E. (Ex)	1967	23	26	5	391	57	18.61	—	1	14	—
†Edgar, B. A. (NZ)	—	15	24	2	823	113	37.40	1	8	19	—
Edmonds, P. H. (E/M/MCC)	1974	18	21	6	359	46*	23.93	—	—	15	—
†Edrich, J. H. (Sy)	1959	18	29	5	733	114	30.54	1	4	9	—
Edwards, G. N. (NZ)	—	14	21	3	401	83	22.27	—	3	22	1
Elder, J. W. G. (Ire)	—	1	—	—	—	—	—	—	—	—	—
Elms, R. B. (H)	—	3	2	0	48	48	24.00	—	—	—	—
Emburey, J. E. (E/M/MCC/YE)	1977	25	33	7	338	42	13.00	—	—	16	—
Featherstone, N. G. (M)	1971	19	27	1	740	108	28.46	1	3	15	—
Fisher, P. B. (OU)	—	10	14	1	138	35	10.61	—	—	8	3
Fletcher, K. W. R. (Ex)	1963	24	35	8	1127	89	41.74	—	10	27	—
†Flower, R. W. (Wa)	—	9	8	4	23	10*	5.75	—	—	—	—
Flynn, V. A. (No)	—	2	2	1	21	15	21.00	—	—	1	—
Foat, J. C. (Gs)	—	19	29	4	722	102*	28.88	2	3	7	—
†Fosh, M. K. (CU/Ex)	—	10	15	1	341	99	24.35	1	1	2	—
Francis, D. A. (Gm)	—	7	10	1	154	56	17.11	—	2	5	—
French, B. N. (Nt/DHR)	—	22	26	8	308	60	17.11	—	1	37	7
Gard, T. (So)	—	2	—	—	—	—	—	—	—	2	—
†Gardiner, S. J. (CU)	—	8	9	3	59	14	9.83	—	—	3	—
Garner, J. (So)	—	4	5	2	12	6*	4.00	—	—	2	—
Gatting, M. W. (M/MCC/YE)	1977	26	39	4	1166	128	33.31	2	6	19	—
†Gifford, N. (Wo)	1961	22	24	12	278	37*	23.16	—	—	10	—
Gilliat, R. M. C. (H)	1969	16	27	9	453	54	25.16	—	1	13	—
Goddard, G. F. (Sc)	—	2	3	1	46	29	23.00	—	—	—	—
Gooch, G. A. (E Ex/DHR)	1975	21	33	3	1254	129	41.80	2	9	23	—
†Gould, I. J. (M)	1977	22	31	4	706	128	26.14	1	2	50	5
†Gower, D. I. (E/Le/MCC/DHR/YE)	1977	21	31	2	1098	111	37.86	2	5	6	—
Graham-Brown, J. M. H. (D)	—	11	17	2	209	43	13.93	—	—	1	—
Graveney, D. A. (Gs/MCC/DHR)	1976	26	35	8	740	92	27.40	—	4	16	—
†Graves, P. J. (Sx)	1969	—	3	0	57	31	19.00	—	—	1	—
Greenidge, C. G. (H)	1972	19	34	1	1771	211	53.66	5	9	34	—
Greig, A. W. (Sx)	1967	5	8	1	122	32	17.42	—	—	4	—
Greig, I. A. (CU)	—	5	5	0	26	10	5.20	—	—	1	—
Griffiths, B. J. (No)	1978	19	12	8	31	11	7.75	—	—	5	—
Groome, J. J. (Sx)	—	9	17	1	229	50	14.31	—	1	2	—
Gurr, D. R. (So)	—	4	5	3	12	6	6.00	—	—	1	—

	Cap	M	I	NO	Runs	HS	Avge	100	50	Ct	St
Hacker, P. J. (Nt)	—	1	1	0	0	0	0.00	—	—	—	—
Hadlee, D. R. (NZ)	—	1	1	0	8	8	8.00	—	—	—	—
†Hadlee, R. J. (NZ/Nt)	1978	17	21	4	342	101*	20.11	1	—	10	—
Halliday, M. (Ire)	—	1	—								
Hampshire, J. H. (Y)	1963	22	36	6	1596	132	53.20	3	9	12	—
Hardie, B. R. (Ex)	1974	23	33	7	1044	109	40.15	1	6	28	—
Haroon Rashid (Pak)	—	10	15	0	268	78	17.86	—	1	2	—
Harris, M. J. (Nt)	1970	23	36	4	1315	148*	41.09	3	6	13	—
Harrison, D. (Ire)	—	1	—								
Hartley, S. N. (Y)	—	1	2	0	31	20	15.50	—	—	—	—
Harvey-Walker, A. J. (D)	—	9	13	2	230	80	20.90	—	2	4	—
†Hasan Jamil (Pak)	—	1	2	1	9	7	9.00	—	—	—	—
Hassan, S. B. (Nt)	1970	8	9	0	220	81	24.44	—	1	5	—
Hayes, F. C. (La/MCC)	1972	21	35	5	1055	136*	35.16	2	4	15	—
Head, T. J. (Sx)	—	3	5	2	92	31	30.66	—	—	6	1
Hemmings, E. E. (Wa)	1974	14	18	4	275	51	19.64	—	1	8	—
Hemsley, E. J. O. (Wo)	1969	24	37	7	1168	141*	38.93	3	6	17	—
†Henderson, S. P. (Wo)	—	4	6	1	65	32*	13.00	—	—	5	—
Hendrick, M. (E/D/MCC)	1972	17	15	6	127	33	14.11	—	—	9	—
Herkes, R. (M)	—	1	1	1	0	0*					
†Higgs, K. (Le)	1972	18	11	6	51	13*	10.20	—	—	13	—
Hignell, A. J. (CU/Gs)	1977	20	32	1	661	145	21.32	2	1	17	—
Hill, A. (D)	1976	24	41	1	928	153*	23.20	1	2	12	—
Hills, R. W. (K)	1977	14	13	2	122	31*	11.09	—	—	3	—
Hoadley, S. P. (Sx)	—	7	12	0	232	112	19.33	1	1	4	—
†Hodgson, A. (Nt)	1976	4	6	3	22	10	7.33	—	—	—	—
Hogg, W. (La)	—	11	14	5	50	19	5.55	—	—	—	—
Holder, V. A. (Wo)	1970	5	5	0	30	23	6.00	—	—	1	—
Holmes, G. C. (Gm)	—	2	4	2	37	17*	18.50	—	—	1	—
Hopkins, D. C. (Wa)	—	9	9	0	33	11	3.66	—	—	4	—
Hopkins, J. A. (Gm/MCC)	1977	25	44	3	1371	116	33.43	3	7	18	—
Howarth, G. P. (NZ/Sy)	1974	21	37	3	1375	179*	40.44	2	8	15	—
Howat, M. G. (CU)	—	7	8	1	118	31	16.85	—	—	2	—
Hughes, D. P. (La)	1970	13	17	2	243	72	16.20	—	1	13	—
Humpage, G. W. (Wa)	1976	21	31	3	663	110	23.67	1	2	29	3
†Humphries, D. J. (Wo)	1978	24	32	5	743	111*	27.51	1	3	44	8
Illingworth, R. (Le)	1969	17	15	5	209	39*	20.90	—	—	5	—
Imran Khan (Sx)	1978	22	37	5	1339	147	41.84	3	6	8	—
Inchmore, J. D. (Wo)	1976	4	2	1	48	34	48.00	—	—	10	—
Intikhab Alam (Sy)	1969	23	32	2	266	34	8.86	—	—	10	—
†Iqbal Qasim (Pak)	—	9	9	2	16	8*	2.28	—	—	4	—
Jackman, R. D. (Sy)	1970	23	30	7	319	42	13.86	—	—	13	—
Jarvis, K. B. S. (K/YE)	1977	25	14	7	22	12	3.14	—	—	5	—
Javed Miandad (Pak/Sx)	1977	21	32	6	983	127	37.80	2	6	10	—
Jennings, K. F. (So)	—	17	19	10	152	31*	16.88	—	—	11	—
Jesty, T. E. (H/MCC)	1971	24	43	6	1174	125*	31.72	5	2	11	—
Johnson, C. (Y)	—	7	14	3	276	61	25.09	—	2	4	—
Johnson, G. W. (K)	1970	24	31	6	685	95	27.40	—	3	19	—
†Jones, A. (Gm)	1962	24	39	1	1133	147	29.81	3	3	4	—
Jones, A. A. (M)	1976	12	17	2	80	33	5.33	—	—	2	—
†Jones, A. L. (Gm)	—	9	16	2	213	54	15.21	—	1	5	—
†Jones, B. J. R. (Wo)	—	10	16	0	182	61	11.37	—	1	8	—

	Cap	M	I	NO	Runs	HS	Avge	100	50	Ct	St
Jones, E. W. (Gm)	1967	22	25	5	232	58	11.60	—	1	40	1
†Kallicharran, A. I. (Wa)	1972	16	29	5	1041	129	43.37	3	5	10	—
Kayum, D. A. (OU)	—	5	7	0	194	57	27.71	—	2	6	—
Kemp, N. J. (K)	—	3	2	1	8	8*	8.00	—	—	—	—
†Kennedy, A. (La)	1975	19	31	2	859	100	29.62	1	4	8	—
Ker, J. E. (Sc)	—	2	3	1	54	50	27.00	—	1	—	—
Kirsten, P. N. (D)	1978	20	35	4	1133	206*	36.54	1	7	11	—
†Kitchen, M. J. (So)	1966	13	20	2	359	50	19.94	—	1	12	—
Knight, J. M. (OU)	—	6	8	1	61	19	8.71	—	—	1	—
†Knight, R. D. V. (Sy)	1978	22	38	6	1233	128	38.53	3	7	16	—
†Laing, J. R. (Sc)	—	1	2	0	20	20	10.00	—	—	1	—
Lamb, A. J. (No)	1978	17	27	8	883	106*	46.47	2	5	10	—
Lamb, T. M. (No)	1978	21	18	4	139	33	9.92	—	—	6	—
Larkins, W. (No/ MCC/DHR/YE/TNP)	1976	25	44	5	1448	170*	37.12	3	7	14	—
Leadbeater, B. (Y)	1969	4	7	1	155	61	25.83	—	1	3	—
Lee, P. G. (La)	1972	1	1	0	1	1	1.00	—	—	—	—
Le Roux, G. S. (Sx)	—	1	2	1	17	17*	17.00	—	—	—	—
†L'Estrange, M. G. (OU)	—	2	2	0	32	16	16.00	—	—	2	—
Lever, J. K. (Ex/MCC)	1970	22	15	7	85	30	10.62	—	—	9	—
Liaquat Ali (Pak)	—	8	7	5	18	9	9.00	—	—	—	—
Lilley, A. W. (Ex)	—	1	2	1	122	100*	122.00	1	—	1	—
Lister, J. W. (D)	—	3	6	0	137	48	22.83	—	—	1	—
Littlewood, D. J. (CU)	—	9	10	3	95	51	13.57	—	1	10	5
†Llewellyn, M. J. (Gm)	1977	21	31	6	849	82	33.96	—	7	9	—
Lloyd, B. J. (Gm)	—	24	28	8	245	27	12.25	—	—	10	—
†Lloyd, C. H. (La)	1969	21	36	6	1116	120	37.20	4	6	21	—
†Lloyd, D. (La)	1968	22	37	2	1113	185	31.80	3	3	18	—
†Lloyd, T. A. (Wa)	—	15	23	3	526	93	26.30	—	3	15	—
†Long, A. (Sx)	1976	21	28	7	410	56*	19.52	—	1	47	3
Love, J. D. (Y/MCC)	—	15	20	3	483	107	28.41	1	3	8	—
Lumb, R. G. (Y)	1974	23	37	3	1070	107	31.47	2	8	19	—
Lynch, M. A. (Sy)	—	14	24	0	451	101	18.79	1	2	7	—
Lyon, J. (La)	1975	21	25	3	267	74*	12.13	—	1	49	3
McEvoy, M. S. A. (Ex)	—	4	6	0	87	51	14.50	—	1	2	—
McEwan, K. S. (Ex)	1974	24	37	3	1682	186	49.47	5	8	21	—
†McIntyre, J. M. (NZ)	—	9	9	4	85	24*	17.00	—	—	3	—
†Mack, A. J. (Gm)	—	5	4	2	8	8*	4.00	—	—	2	—
Mackintosh, K. S. (Nt)	—	14	14	5	124	23*	13.77	—	—	6	—
McLellan, A. J. (D)	—	14	14	5	27	11*	3.00	—	—	17	—
†McPherson, T. I. (Sc)	—	2	2	0	9	5	5.00	—	—	—	—
Malone, S. J. (Ex)	—	1	—	—	—	—	—	—	—	—	—
Marie, G. V. (OU)	—	9	11	0	87	27	7.90	—	—	1	—
Marks, V. J. (OU/So)	—	15	25	3	456	60	20.72	—	2	18	—
Marshall, R. P. T. (Sx)	—	2	4	4	10	4*	—	—	—	—	—
Masood Iqbal (Pak)	—	1	1	0	8	8	8.00	—	—	3	—
Maynard, C. W. (Wa)	—	3	3	1	17	9	8.50	—	—	4	—
Mellor, A. J. (D)	—	5	7	2	19	10*	3.80	—	—	—	—
Mendis, G. D. (Sx)	—	20	36	4	979	128	30.59	3	1	14	—
Miller, G. (E/D/MCC)	1976	18	25	5	674	95	33.70	—	5	15	—
Mohsin Khan (Pak)	—	11	16	0	386	79	24.12	—	1	4	—
Monteith, I. D. (Ire)	—	1	—	—	—	—	—	—	—	—	—
Morrill, N. D. (OU)	—	5	7	1	83	20*	13.83	—	—	3	—

	Cap	M	I	NO	Runs	HS	Avge	100	50	Ct	St
Morris, A. (D)	—	5	7	0	116	55	16.57	—	1	4	—
Moseley, H. R. (So)	1972	14	9	3	62	30	10.33	—	—	7	—
Moulding, R. P. (OU)	—	8	11	2	276	77*	30.66	—	3	5	—
Mubarak, A. M. (CU)	—	6	11	0	205	77	18.63	—	1	3	—
Mudassar Nazar (Pak)	—	13	21	1	677	107	33.85	1	3	5	—
Naeem Ahmed (Pak)	—	2	1	0	2	2	2.00	—	—	—	—
†Nash, M. A. (Gm)	1969	23	34	5	794	124*	27.37	1	5	10	—
Neale, P. A. (Wo)	1978	24	40	6	1182	103*	34.76	1	9	10	—
Needham, A. (Sy)	—	5	5	0	33	21	6.60	—	—	1	—
Nicholas, M. C. J. (H)	—	3	5	2	77	40*	25.66	—	—	2	—
O'Brien, B. A. (Ire)	—	1	—								
†Old, C. M. (E/Y/MCC)	1969	14	15	5	236	100*	23.60	1	—	5	—
Oldham, S. (Y)	—	20	11	7	22	7*	5.50	—	—	3	—
Olive, M. (So)	—	1	2	0	4	3	2.00	—	—	—	—
Oliver, P. R. (Wa)	—	17	22	1	322	47	15.33	—	—	7	—
Ontong, R. C. (Gm)	—	21	34	4	969	116*	32.30	2	5	7	—
†Orders, J. O. D. (OU)	—	8	13	1	335	79	27.91	—	2	2	—
Ormrod, J. A. (Wo)	1966	24	41	7	1535	173	45.14	5	4	21	—
Parker, J. M. (NZ)	—	12	17	2	549	104*	36.60	2	1	7	1
Parker, P. W. G. (CU/Sx)	—	22	36	4	1192	112	35.25	1	7	11	—
Parsons, G. J. (Le)	—	2	2	0	10	7	5.00	—	—	—	—
†Partridge, M. D. (Gs)	—	7	10	3	133	50	19.00	—	1	2	—
†Patel, A. S. (M)	—	2	3	1	56	25*	28.00	—	—	1	—
Patel, D. N. (Wo)	—	23	29	0	544	104	18.75	1	1	8	—
Pathmanathan, G. (OU)	—	7	9	0	166	55	18.44	—	1	7	—
Payne, I. R. (Sy)	—	5	6	0	33	28	5.50	—	—	8	—
Pearce, J. P. (OU)	—	2	3	3	6	5*		—	—	—	—
Peck, I. G. (CU)	—	5	6	0	22	11	3.66	—	—	1	—
Perryman, S. P. (Wa)	1977	24	24	6	97	17*	5.38	—	—	10	—
Phillip, N. (Ex)	1978	20	28	4	645	134	26.87	1	3	4	—
Phillipson, C. P. (Sx)	—	22	36	4	749	70	23.40	—	5	11	—
Pigott, A. C. S. (Sx)	—	6	6	0	33	11	5.50	—	—	1	—
Pilling, H. (La)	1965	8	13	1	203	49	16.91	—	—	2	—
Pocock, N. E. J. (H)	—	5	8	1	71	18	10.14	—	—	8	—
Pocock, P. I. (Sy)	1967	21	22	4	91	17*	5.05	—	—	7	—
Pont, K. R. (Ex)	1976	12	18	2	366	101	22.87	1	2	8	—
Popplewell, N. F. M. (CU)	—	9	11	2	157	46	17.44	—	—	1	—
Poulter, S. J. (M)	—	3	3	0	47	36	15.66	—	—	—	—
Price, D. H. (OU)	—	4	8	0	93	27	11.62	—	—	3	—
Pridgeon, A. P. (Wo)	—	21	22	7	93	32	6.20	—	—	7	—
Pringle, D. R. (Ex/TNP)	—	4	5	1	60	50*	15.00	—	1	1	—
Procter, M. J. (Gs)	1968	21	36	3	1655	203	50.15	3	7	11	—
Racionzer, T. B. (Sc)	—	2	3	0	12	5	4.00	—	—	—	—
Radley, C. T. (E/M)	1967	18	26	1	923	106	36.92	3	5	17	—
Randall, D. W. (Nt/TNP)	1973	24	40	7	1525	157*	46.21	2	11	11	—
Ratcliffe, R. M. (La)	1976	20	23	5	318	48	17.66	—	—	8	—
†Reidy, B. W. (La)	—	10	15	3	360	88	30.00	—	1	2	—
†Reith, M. S. (Ire)	—	1	—						—	1	—
Rhind, P. A. (Sc)	—	2	2	1	3	3*	3.00	—	—	—	—
Rice, C. E. B. (Nt/TNP)	1975	23	37	9	1871	213*	66.82	5	9	24	—

	Cap	M	I	NO	Runs	HS	Avge	100	50	Ct	St
Rice, J. M. (H)	1975	19	31	2	630	63	21.72	—	3	15	—
Richards, B. A. (H)	1968	6	11	0	337	73	30.63	—	2	8	—
Richards, C. J. (Sy)	1978	23	29	10	310	50	16.31	—	1	24	7
Richards, G. (Gm)	1976	22	36	10	768	74	29.53	—	5	6	—
†Richards, I. M. (No)	—	7	4	1	54	23	18.00	—	—	1	—
Richards, I. V. A. (So)	1974	21	38	4	1558	118	45.82	2	10	21	—
Roberts, A. M. E. (H)	1974	9	14	5	209	37*	23.22	—	—	1	—
Robertson, F. (Sc)	—	2	3	1	34	14*	17.00	—	—	1	—
Robinson, R. T. (Nt)	—	1	2	1	36	27*	36.00	—	—	1	—
Rock, D. J. (H)	—	7	13	0	231	54	17.76	—	2	6	—
Roebuck, P. M. (So)	—	23	37	8	944	131*	32.55	1	6	10	—
Roope, G. R. J. (E/Sy)	1969	19	29	7	888	113*	40.36	2	6	28	—
†Rose, B. C. (So)	1975	24	41	5	1263	122	35.08	4	3	12	—
Ross, C. J. (OU)	—	6	7	1	7	4	1.16	—	—	1	—
†Rouse, S. J. (Wa)	1974	10	12	1	137	40	12.45	—	—	1	—
Rowe, C. J. C. (K)	1977	20	35	5	1065	85	35.50	—	7	7	—
Russell, P. E. (D)	1975	15	12	2	90	22	9.00	—	—	15	—
†Sadiq Mohammad (Pak/Gs)	1973	26	42	4	1449	176	38.13	2	6	10	—
Sarfraz Nawaz (Pak/No/TNP)	1975	18	19	7	151	32*	12.58	—	—	6	—
Savage, R. L. G. (OU/Wa)	—	5	8	5	39	12	13.00	—	—	2	—
Saxelby, K. (Nt)	—	2	3	1	3	3*	1.50	—	—	1	—
Schepens, M. (Le)	—	5	8	2	147	39	24.50	—	—	3	—
†Scott, C. J. (La)	—	2	2	1	9	8	9.00	—	—	3	—
Selvey, M. W. W. (M)	1973	24	28	8	164	19*	8.20	—	—	8	—
Shackleton, J. H. (Gs)	—	7	9	4	49	22	9.80	—	—	5	—
†Shantry, B. K. (Gs)	—	2	—	—	—	—	—	—	—	—	—
Sharp, G. (No/TNP)	1973	20	21	5	204	27*	12.75	—	—	33	3
†Sharp, K. (Y/DHR/YE)	—	18	27	5	695	91	31.59	—	3	2	—
Shepherd, D. R. (Gs)	1969	16	24	1	446	72	19.39	—	3	4	—
Shepherd, J. N. (K)	1967	20	28	6	785	101	35.68	2	3	12	—
Short, J. F. (Ire)	—	1	—	—	—	—	—	—	—	—	—
Shuttleworth, K. (Le)	1977	6	5	2	70	27*	23.33	—	—	11	—
Sidebottom, A. (Y)	—	6	4	2	27	16	13.50	—	—	4	—
Sikander Bakht (Pak)	—	6	6	1	11	4	2.20	—	—	—	—
Simmons, J. (La)	1971	22	30	7	663	106	28.82	1	2	22	—
†Slack, W. N. (M)	—	10	16	1	268	52	17.86	—	1	7	—
Slocombe, P. A. (So)	1978	23	40	8	1221	128*	38.15	3	5	11	—
Smedley, M. J. (Nt)	1966	23	31	4	660	83*	24.44	—	4	18	—
†Smith, A. V. (Ire)	—	1	—	—	—	—	—	—	—	1	—
†Smith, D. M. (Sy)	—	17	27	6	463	115	22.04	1	—	6	—
†Smith, K. B. (Sx)	—	4	8	1	90	43	12.85	—	—	1	—
Smith, K. D. (Wa)	1978	23	39	4	1187	132*	33.91	3	5	6	—
Smith, M. J. (M)	1967	23	34	1	726	63	22.00	—	3	3	—
Smith, N. (Ex)	1975	24	24	6	323	59*	17.94	—	1	50	8
Southern, J. W. (H)	1978	23	22	8	148	51	10.57	—	1	7	—
Spencer, J. (Sx)	1973	17	22	8	189	30	13.50	—	—	8	—
Steele, A. (Sc)	—	2	3	0	100	48	33.33	—	—	2	—
Steele, D. S. (No)	1965	21	36	5	1182	130	38.12	3	9	24	—
Steele, J. F. (Le)	1971	22	34	3	1182	133	38.12	3	6	28	—
Stephenson, G. R. (H)	1969	23	30	5	350	66	14.00	—	1	46	9

164

	Cap	M	I	NO	Runs	HS	Avge	100	50	Ct	St
Stevenson, G. B. (Y/MCC/YE)	1978	17	19	4	426	70*	28.40	—	1	5	—
Stevenson, K. (H)	—	21	21	4	111	19	6.52	—	—	8	—
Stewart, D. E. R. (Sc)	—	2	3	0	30	26	10.00	—	—	1	—
Storey, S. J. (Sx)	—	16	23	3	331	57	16.55	—	1	7	—
Stovold, A. W. (Gs)	1976	21	35	2	962	139	29.15	1	5	9	3
Sturt, M. O. C. (M)	1967	2	2	0	11	9	5.50	—	—	6	1
†Stuchbury, S. (Y)	—	1	—								
Surridge, S. S. (Sy)	—	1	1	1	2	2*	—	—	—	1	—
Sutcliffe, R. J. (La)	—	1	2	1	10	10*	—	—	—	—	—
†Swarbrook, F. W. (D)	1975	12	16	6	240	60*	24.00	—	1	5	—
Swart, P. D. (Gm)	—	23	37	2	1078	115	31.70	3	5	19	—
†Tait, A. (Gs)	—	11	19	1	348	53	19.33	—	2	2	—
Talat Ali (Pak)	—	8	14	3	278	60	25.27	—	1	1	—
Tavare, C. J. (K/YE)	1978	25	39	5	1534	105	45.11	2	11	49	—
Taylor, D. J. S. (So)	1971	23	29	7	424	78	17.66	—	2	55	9
Taylor, L. B. (Le/DHR)	—	12	6	1	27	15	5.40	—	—	4	—
Taylor, M. N. S. (H)	1973	22	29	9	770	103*	38.50	1	6	8	—
Taylor, R. W. (E/D)	1962	16	17	1	179	32	11.18	—	—	44	3
Terry, V. P. (H)	—	2	3	0	16	8	5.33	—	—	—	—
†Thomas, D. J. (Sy/DHR)	—	14	16	3	70	12	5.38	—	—	5	—
Thomas, G. P. (Wa)	—	1	2	0	5	4	2.50	—	—	—	—
†Thomson, G. B. (NZ)	—	7	3	2	13	9	13.00	—	—	2	—
Titmus, F. J. (Sy)	—	1	2	2	4	4*	—	—	—	1	—
Todd, P. A. (Nt)	1977	24	40	0	1181	89	29.52	—	10	6	—
Tolchard, R. W. (Le)	1966	24	35	16	841	103*	44.26	1	5	39	7
Tomlins, K. P. (M)	—	11	16	2	295	94	21.07	—	2	8	—
Tremlett, T. M. (H)	—	6	10	2	183	50	22.87	—	1	1	—
Troup, G. B. (NZ)	—	1	1	0	19	19	19.00	—	—	1	—
Tunnicliffe, C. J. (D)	1977	19	23	4	146	45	7.68	—	—	7	—
Tunnicliffe, H. T. (Nt)	—	9	12	3	148	69*	16.44	—	1	6	—
†Turner, D. R. (H)	1970	23	42	3	1255	148*	32.17	3	2	9	—
Turner, G. M. (Wo)	1968	22	38	7	1711	202*	55.19	6	4	20	—
Turner, S. (Ex)	1970	23	29	8	636	89*	30.28	—	3	13	—
Underwood, D. L. (K)	1964	22	17	6	145	25	13.18	—	—	7	—
Waller, C. E. (Sx)	1976	13	13	7	55	14*	9.16	—	—	11	—
†Walters, J. (D)	—	14	22	4	482	90	26.77	—	2	2	—
Ward, A. (Le)	1977	2	—								
†Warner, C. J. (Sc)	—	2	3	0	41	28	13.66	—	—	—	—
Wasim Bari (Pak)	—	12	11	2	123	38*	13.66	—	—	13	—
†Wasim Raja (Pak)	—	12	17	5	324	56*	27.00	—	2	3	—
Watson, G. G. (WO)	—	21	24	5	266	38	14.00	—	—	7	—
Watson, W. K. (Nt)	—	5	3	1	44	28*	22.00	—	—	4	—
†Watts, P. J. (No)	1962	13	15	1	185	57*	13.21	—	1	1	—
Wells, R. R. C. (OU)	—	4	6	0	54	29	9.00	—	—	1	—
†Wessels, K. C. (Sx)	1977	4	8	0	123	29	15.37	—	—	6	—
†White, R. A. (Nt)	1966	17	16	3	220	44*	16.92	—	—	8	—
Whitehouse, J. (Wa/MCC)	1973	25	42	8	744	102*	21.88	1	—	9	—
Whiteley, J. P. (Y)	—	9	5	3	14	8	7.00	—	—	4	—
Wilcock, H. G. (Wo)	—	1	1	0	0	0	0.00	—	—	2	—
Wilkins, A. H. (Gm)	—	18	21	10	61	17	5.54	—	—	10	—

	Cap	M	I	NO	Runs	HS	Avge	100	50	Ct	St
Willey, E. (No/TNP)	1971	22	35	9	921	112	35.42	1	6	7	—
Williams, R. G. (No)	—	16	20	5	399	60*	26.60	—	1	8	—
Williams, S. (Gs	—	1	1	0	0	0	0.00	—	—	—	—
Willis, R. G. D. (E/Wa)	1972	18	16	5	117	23*	10.63	—	—	10	—
Wilson, P. H. L. (Sy)	—	9	4	4	9	9*	—	—	—	1	—
†Wincer, R. C. (D)	—	10	10	4	43	16*	7.16	—	—	5	—
Wood, E. (E/La	1968	9	13	1	228	103	19.00	1	—	5	—
Wookey S. M. (OU)	—	7	8	1	44	15*	6.28	—	—	2	—
Woolmer, R. A. (K)	1970	21	34	3	1245	137	40.16	2	9	25	—
†Wright, J. G. (NZ/D)	1977	18	31	3	901	164	32.17	2	4	8	—
†Yardley, T. J. (Wo)	1978	18	26	6	611	97	30.55	—	3	22	—
†Younis Ahmed (Sy)	1969	15	23	4	514	72	27.05	—	4	9	—
Zaheer Abbas (Gs)	1975	22	35	1	1535	213	45.14	6	4	15	—

BOWLING

*N.B.: Players who did not bowl in first-class cricket 1978
are omitted from this list*

	Type	Overs	Mds	Runs	Wkt	Avge	Best	5 wI	10 wM
Aamer Hameed (Pak)	RFM	95	28	237	6	39.50	3–71	—	—
Abdul Qadir (Pak)	LBG	123	22	396	6	66.00	2–29	—	—
Abrahams, J. (La)	OB	1	1	0	0	—	—	—	—
Acfield, D. L. (Ex)	OB	454.1	125	1013	36	28.13	3–33	—	—
Agnew, J. P. (Le)	RF	67.4	13	215	6	35.83	3–51	—	—
Allbrook, M. E. (CU/Nt)	OB	324.2	76	991	29	34.17	7–79	2	—
Allott, P. J. W. (La)	RFM	129	12	456	14	32.57	5–98	1	—
Amiss, D. L. (Wa)	SLA	3	0	20	0	—	—	—	—
Anderson, I. S. (D)	OB	43	10	150	2	75.00	1–24	—	—
Arnold, G. G. (Sx)	RFM	401	102	910	49	18.57	7–44	2	—
Arrowsmith, R. (La)	SLA	320.1	106	889	27	32.92	4–49	—	—
Asif Iqbal (K)	RM	73	15	228	8	28.50	4–47	—	—
Athey, C. W. J. (Y/DER/YE)	RM	93	26	268	11	24.36	3–38	—	—
Bainbridge, P. (Gs)	RM	25	8	59	0	—	—	—	—
Bairstow, D. L. (Y)	RM	9	2	15	1	15.00	1–15	—	—
Baker, E. P. (Sy)	RM	166.4	28	573	17	33.70	3–54	—	—
Balderstone, J. C. (Le)	SLA	368.5	104	914	38	24.05	6–25	2	—
Barclay, J. R. T. (Sx/D=IR)	OB	207	49	554	20	27.70	5–72	1	—
Barlow, E. J. (D)	RM	214.5	58	528	24	22.00	4–34	—	—
Birch, J. D. (Nt)	RM	77	9	282	2	141.00	1–6	—	—
Birkenshaw, J. (Le)	OB	344.2	83	874	30	29.13	3–23	—	—
Bishop, M. M. (CU)	RM	40	10	119	2	59.50	1–13	—	—
Boock, S. L. (NZ)	SLA	388.3	156	865	39	22.17	5–9	1	—
Booth, P. (Le)	RFM	293.2	63	870	29	30.00	6–93	1	—
Botham I. T. (E/So/MCC)	RFM	605.2	143	1640	100	16.40	8–34	10	1
Boycott, G. (E/Y)	RM	12	6	13	0	—	—	—	—
Boyns, C. N. (Wo)	RM	152.2	21	566	12	47.16	3–92	—	—
Bracewell, B. P. (NZ)	RFM	221.2	38	694	24	28.91	3–38	—	—

166

	Type	Overs	Mds	Runs	Wkts	Avge	Best	5 wI	10 wM
Brain, B. M. (Gs)	RFM	573.2	138	1589	76	20.90	5–48	2	—
Breakwell, D. (So)	SLA	445.1	135	1007	41	24.56	6–45	1	—
Brearley, J. M. (E/M/MCC)	RM	1	1	0	0	—	—	—	—
Brettell, D. N. (OU)	SLA	28	14	39	3	13.00	3–22	—	—
Briers, N. E. (Le)	RM	16	2	40	1	40.00	1–22	—	—
Brown, D. J. (Wa)	RFM	405	80	1160	40	29.00	5–53	1	—
Burgess, G. I. (So)	RM	363	136	890	27	32.96	5–25	1	—
Buss, M. A. (Sx)	LM	179.2	52	473	18	26.27	3–47	—	—
Butcher, A. R. (Sy)	LM	53	7	192	1	192.00	1–15	—	—
Cairns, B. L. (NZ)	RM	370	101	882	35	25.20	5–51	2	1
Carrick, P. (Y/YE)	SLA	682	227	1529	56	27.30	7–35	4	1
Carter, R. M. (No)	RM	15	3	43	0	—	—	—	—
Cartwright, H. (D)	RM	1	0	1	0	—	—	—	—
Cheatle, R. G. L. (Sx)	SLA	314.2	85	968	24	40.33	4–89	—	—
Childs, J. H. (Gs)	SLA	520.2	154	1440	59	24.40	8–34	5	2
Clifford, C. C. (Wa)	OB	431.3	115	1220	38	32.10	6–89	2	—
Clift, P. B. (Le)	RM	519.4	156	1209	51	23.70	6–29	1	—
Clinton, G. S. (K)	SLA	1	0	8	2	4.00	2–8	—	—
Close, D. B. (TNP)	RM/OB	8	1	31	1	31.00	1–31	—	—
Collinge, R. O. (NZ)	LFM	158	35	455	13	35.00	3–43	—	—
Congdon, B. E. (NZ)	RM	288.2	85	650	23	28.26	5–40	1	—
Cook, G. (No/MCC/TNP)	SLA	2.2	0	18	0	—	—	—	—
Cook, N. G. B. (Le)	SLA	38	16	83	3	27.66	1–16	—	—
Cooper, H. P. (Y)	RM	447	113	1191	37	32.18	6–26	1	—
Cooper, K. E. (Nt/DHR)	RFM	481.5	93	1467	53	27.67	6–32	2	—
Cooper, N. H. C. (Gs)	RM	3	0	26	0	—	—	—	—
Cope, G. A. (Y)	OB	342.3	114	784	32	24.50	4–34	—	—
Cordle, A. E. (Gm)	RFM	307.5	73	864	21	41.14	5–33	1	—
Corlett, S. C. (Ire)	RM	7	3	8	0	—	—	—	—
Cowdrey, C. S. (K)	RM	12	5	20	0	—	—	—	—
Cowley, N. G. (H)	OB	672.3	192	1700	56	30.35	5–93	1	—
Crawford, I. C. (Gs)	OB	17	8	37	0	—	—	—	—
Crawford, N. C. (CU)	RM	8	1	33	0	—	—	—	—
Croft, C. E. H. (La)	RF	431.3	101	1266	56	22.60	5–58	1	—
Cumbes, J. (Wo)	RFM	435	95	1207	31	38.93	4–52	—	—
Curzon, J. T. (Nt)	RFM	5	1	22	0	—	—	—	—
Dalrymple, J. J. H. (OU)	RM	81	12	260	7	37.14	3–34	—	—
Daniel, W. W. (M)	RF	453.3	113	1114	76	14.65	5–42	3	—
Davey, J. (Gs)	LFM	309.3	65	900	30	30.00	4–52	—	—
Davison, B. F. (Le)	RM	5	0	29	0	—	—	—	—
Denning, P. W. (So)	RM	7	2	25	0	—	—	—	—
Dewes, A. R. (CU)	LB	33	3	146	1	146.00	1–52	—	—
Dilley, G. R. (K)	RM	75	19	197	8	24.62	5–32	1	—
D'Oliveira, B. L. (Wo)	RM/OB	193.2	48	483	17	28.41	5–48	1	—
Doshi, D. R. (Nt/TNP)	SLA	675.1	170	1763	60	29.38	6–33	3	1
Dredge, C. H. (So)	RM	573.1	137	1473	56	26.30	5–53	2	—
Dudleston, B. (Le)	SLA	2	0	11	0	—	—	—	—

167

	Type	Overs	Mds	Runs	Wkts	Avge	Best	wI	wM
Ealham, A. G. E. (K)	OB	0.2	0	4	0	—	—	—	—
East, R. E. (Ex)	SLA	700.2	226	1506	92	16.36	8-41	6	1
Edmonds, P. H. (E/M/MCC)	SLA	503	174	912	60	15.20	7-34	2	—
Elder, J. W. G. (Ire)	RFM	13	4	16	1	16.00	1-16	—	—
Elms, R. E. (H)	LFM	27	6	89	1	89.00	1-38	—	—
Emburey, J. E. (E/M/MCC/YE)	OB	799.3	243	1641	79	20.77	6-25	3	—
Featherstone, N. G. (M)	OB	140.3	39	365	13	28.07	5-32	1	—
Flower, R. W. (Wa)	SLA	173	42	554	10	55.40	3-45	—	—
Foat, J. C. (Gs)	RM	1	0	7	0	—	—	—	—
Gardiner, S. J. (CU)	LM	161.1	53	459	11	41.72	4-52	—	—
Garner, J. (So)	RF	170.1	61	351	22	15.95	5-50	3	—
Gatting, M. W. (M/MCC/YE)	RM	168.3	36	411	26	15.80	5-59	1	—
Gifford, N. (Wo)	SLA	667.3	210	1557	54	28.83	6-68	2	—
Goddard, G. F. (Sc)	OB	21	2	98	1	98.00	1-98	—	—
Gooch, G. A. (E/Ex/DHR)	RM	36	6	90	2	45.00	2-33	—	—
Gower, D. I. (E/Le/MCC/DHR/YE)	OB	1	0	2	0	—	—	—	—
Graham-Brown, J. M. E. (D)	RM	114.2	28	338	7	48.28	2-23	—	—
Graveney D. A. (Gs/MCC/DHR)	SLA	558	175	1492	35	42.62	4-47	—	—
Greenidge, C. G. (H)	RM	4	2	8	1	8.00	1-8	—	—
Greig, A. W. (Sx)	RM	111	21	321	6	53.50	2-47	—	—
Greig, I. A. (CU)	RM	87	17	283	8	35.37	3-73	—	—
Griffiths, B. J. (No)	RM	554	103	1591	51	31.19	5-66	1	—
Gurr, D. R. (So)	RFM	104	25	296	11	26.90	4-65	—	—
Hacker, E. J. (Nt)	LM	6	0	51	0	—	—	—	—
Hadlee, D. R. (NZ)	RM	16	0	70	1	70.00	1-70	—	—
Hadlee, E. J. (NZ/Nt)	RFM	497.1	120	1269	78	16.26	7-77	6	2
Halliday, M. (Ire)	OB	19	8	25	2	12.50	2-25	—	—
Hampshire, J. H. (Y)	LBG	9	0	45	2	22.50	2-32	—	—
Harris, M. J. (Nt)	LB	41	10	142	4	35.50	3-28	—	—
Hartley, S. N. (Y)	RM	2	0	6	0	—	—	—	—
Harvey-Walker, A. J. (D)	OB	145	42	408	17	24.00	7-35	1	1
Hassan Jamil (Pak)	LM	24	3	77	2	38.50	2-32	—	—
Hassan, S. B. (Nt)	RM	14	4	52	0	—	—	—	—
Hemmings, E. E. (Wa)	OB	376.1	88	1142	28	40.78	4-51	—	—
Hemsley, E. J. O. (Wo)	RM	21.5	3	81	0	—	—	—	—
Henderson, S. P. (Wo)	RM	5	0	21	0	—	—	—	—
Hendrick, M. (E/D/MCC)	RFM	473.5	167	895	59	15.16	5-32	2	—
Herkes, E. (M)	RM	5	3	9	0	—	—	—	—
Higgs, K. (Le)	RFM	381	112	923	41	22.51	7-44	1	—
Hignell, A. J. (CU/Gs)	RM	30.5	5	118	0	—	—	—	—
Hill, A. (D)	OB	2	0	14	0	—	—	—	—

	Type	Overs	Mds	Runs	Wkts	Avge	Best	5 wI	10 wM
Hills, R. W. (K)	RM	263.2	63	803	24	33.45	6-64	1	—
Hodgson, A. (No)	RFM	105.2	21	351	10	35.10	3-29	—	—
Hogg, W. (La)	RFM	256.4	58	775	38	20.39	7-84	3	—
Holder, V. A. (Wo)	RFM	179	31	468	15	31.20	4-52	—	—
Holmes, G. C. (Gm)	RM	4	0	41	0	—	—	—	—
Hopkins, D. C. (Wa)	RM	123.3	31	361	4	90.25	3-27	—	—
Hopkins, J. A. (Gm/MCC)		2	0	10	0	—	—	—	—
Howarth, G. P. (NZ/Sy)	OB	21	5	69	4	17.25	2-12	—	—
Howat, M. G. (CU)	RM	140	33	370	9	41.11	2-31	—	—
Hughes, D. P. (La)	SLA	191.1	54	517	22	23.50	5-46	1	—
Illingworth, R. (Le)	OB	261.4	86	635	25	25.40	6-38	2	—
Imran Khan (Sx)	RF	543	128	1391	49	28.38	7-52	2	—
Inchmore, J. D. (Wo)	RFM	86	23	223	4	55.75	2-48	—	—
Intikhab Alam (Sy)	LBG	623.2	197	1570	59	26.61	6-126	3	—
Iqbal Qasim (Pak)	SLA	115.4	34	310	7	44.28	3-101	—	—
Jackman, R. D. (Sy)	RFM	590.2	134	1707	70	24.38	5-26	3	—
Jarvis, K.B.S.(K/YE)	RFM	598.5	139	1863	80	23.28	8-97	3	1
Javed Miandad (Pak/Sx)	LBG	68	6	238	5	47.60	2-55	—	—
Jennings, K. F. (So)	RM	442.3	148	1041	40	26.02	5-18	1	—
Jesty, T. E. (H/MCC)	RM	260.5	73	663	20	33.15	6-50	1	—
Johnson, C. (Y)	OB	2	0	5	0	—	—	—	—
Johnson, G. W. (K)	OB	510.4	173	1084	56	19.35	6-32	2	—
Jones, A. (Gm)	OB	2.3	0	10	0	—	—	—	—
Jones, A. A. (So)	RFM	247.4	45	840	29	28.96	6-89	2	—
Jones, A. L. (Gm)		0.2	0	4	0	—	—	—	—
Kallicharran, A. I. (Wa)	LBG	19	5	48	4	12.00	4-48	—	—
Kemp, N. J. (K)	RM	28	4	91	3	30.33	3-83	—	—
Kennedy, A. (La)	RM	26	10	59	2	29.50	2-29	—	—
Ker, J. E. (Sc)	RM	20	5	83	1	83.00	1-83	—	—
Kirsten, P. N. (D)	OB	207.4	55	581	18	32.27	4-51	—	—
Knight, J. M. (OU)	RM	93.3	22	237	6	39.50	3-36	—	—
Knight, R. D. V. (Sy)	RM	161.2	41	432	14	30.85	3-22	—	—
Lamb, A. J. (No)	RM	3.5	1	13	2	6.50	1-1	—	—
Lamb, T. M. (No)	RM	492.5	115	1370	46	29.78	6-71	1	—
Larkins, W. (No/MCC DHR/YE/TNP)	RM	47	11	147	3	49.00	2-29	—	—
Lee, P. G. (La)	RFM	8	2	26	2	13.00	2-26	—	—
Le Roux, G. S. (Sx)	RFM	31	7	107	1	107.00	1-64	—	—
Lever,J.K. (Ex/MCC)	LFM	681.1	160	1610	106	15.18	7-32	9	1
Liaquat Ali (Pak)	LM	188	45	510	18	28.33	3-26	—	—
Lloyd, B. J. (Gm)	OB	561.3	154	1590	40	39.75	4-82	—	—
Lloyd, D. (La)	SLA	3.5	1	11	0	—	—	—	—
Lloyd, T. A. (Wa)		15	5	35	1	35.00	1-14	—	—
Love, J. D. (Y)		6	2	16	0	—	—	—	—
Lynch, M. A. (Sy)	OB	14.1	1	59	2	29.50	1-14	—	—
McIntyre, J. M. (NZ)	SLA	204.4	71	546	14	39.00	3-40	—	—
Mack, A. J. (Gm)	LM	77.3	26	195	16	12.18	4-28	—	—

169

	Type	Overs	Mds	Runs	Wkts	Avge	Best	5 wI	10 wM
Mackintosh,K.S.(Nt)	RM	239	47	693	16	43.31	4-49	—	—
McPherson, T. I. (Sc)	SLA	36	8	110	4	27.50	4-110	—	—
Malone, S. J. (Ex)	RM	15	6	28	1	28.00	1-28	—	—
Marie, G. V. (OU)	RM	234	66	620	15	41.33	3-48	—	—
Marks, V. J. (OU/So)	OB	459.1	133	1217	45	27.04	4-48	—	—
Marshall,R.P.T. (Sx)	LM	48	6	216	2	108.00	2-93	—	—
Mellor, A J. (D)	SLA	106	33	305	9	33.88	5-52	1	—
Mendis, C. D. (Sx)	RM	1	0	0	0	—	—	—	—
Miller, G. (E/D/MCC)	OB	484.2	170	1020	37	27.56	5-43	2	—
Monteith, J. D. (Ire)	SLA	21	16	17	4	4.25	4-17	—	—
Morrill, N. D. (OU)	OB	76	18	251	4	62.75	2-55	—	—
Morris, A. (D)	LB	16	2	58	0	—	—	—	—
Moseley, H. R. (So)	RFM	348.1	103	813	41	19.82	6-35	1	—
Mudassar Nazar (Pak)	RM	100.1	23	253	8	31.62	2-28	—	—
Naeem Ahmed (Pak)	SLA	47	7	136	2	68.00	1-45	—	—
Nash, M. A. (Gm)	LM	519.2	133	1631	42	38.83	6-74	2	—
Neale, P. A. (Wo)	RM	9	0	46	0	—	—	—	—
Needham, A. (Sy)	OB	33.2	9	103	2	51.50	1-44	—	—
Old,C.M. (E/Y/MCC)	RFM	520.1	166	1108	64	17.31	7-50	4	—
Oldham, S (Y)	RFM	485	115	1326	53	25.01	5-40	1	—
Oliver, P. R. (Wa)	RM/OB	222	41	657	7	93.85	2-28	—	—
Ontong, R. C. (Gm)	RFM	262.5	57	856	22	38.90	4-95	—	—
Orders, J. O. D. (OU)	LM	73.1	12	244	5	48.80	2-16	—	—
Parker, J. M. (NZ)	LB	5	1	30	1	30.00	1-30	—	—
Parker, P. W. G. (CU/Sx)	RM	49.2	10	183	6	30.50	2-23	—	—
Parsons, G. J. (Le)	RM	17	1	78	0	—	—	—	—
Partridge, M. D. (Gs)	RM	85	15	312	3	104.00	2-77	—	—
Patel, A. S. (M)	SLA	12	0	55	2	27.50	2-55	—	—
Patel, D. N. (Wo)	OB	398.1	94	1126	35	32.17	5-22	1	—
Payne, I. R. (Sy)	RM	34	4	133	2	66.50	2-41	—	—
Pearce, J. E. (OU)	SLA	61.1	23	157	4	39.25	3-26	—	—
Perryman, S. P. (Wa)	RM	591.3	172	1527	50	30.54	7-49	3	1
Phillip, N. (Ex)	RFM	583.1	113	1591	71	22.40	6-33	4	—
Phillipson, C. P. (Sx)	RM	193	37	702	16	43.87	3-72	—	—
Pigott, A. C. S. (Sx)	RFM	69	8	306	9	34.00	4-62	—	—
Pocock, N. E. J. (H)	LM	3	0	5	0	—	—	—	—
Pocock, P. I. (Sy)	OB	662.4	201	1615	67	24.10	6-73	5	—
Pont, K. R. (Ex)	RM	65	17	193	3	64.33	1-28	—	—
Popplewell, N. F. M. (CU)	RM	166.1	38	540	5	108.00	2-118	—	—
Price, D. H (OU)	RM	55	15	174	2	87.00	1-22	—	—
Pridgeon, A. P. (Wo)	RFM	587.2	113	1771	59	30.01	4-38	—	—
Pringle,D.H.(Ex/TNP)	RM	35	13	101	1	101.00	1-31	—	—
Procter, M. J. (Gs)	RF/OB	665.2	185	1649	69	23.89	7-45	2	—
Radley, C. T. (M)	RM	1	1	0	0	—	—	—	—
Randall, D. W. (Nt/TNP)	RM	1.4	0	8	0	—	—	—	—
Ratcliffe, R. M. (La)	RM	571.3	151	1532	70	21.88	7-58	3	—
Reidy, B. W. (La)	LM	163	29	515	6	85.83	2-47	—	—
Rhind, P. A. (Sc)	RFM	17	2	81	1	81.00	1-81	—	—
Rice, C. E. B. (Nt/TNP)	RFM	322.3	82	835	41	20.36	4-25	—	—

	Type	Overs	Mds	Runs	Wkts	Avge	Best	5 wI	10 wM
Rice, J. M. (H)	RM	267.1	70	709	29	24.44	4-49	—	—
Richards, B. A. (H)	OB	1	0	1	0	—	—	—	—
Richards, G. (Gm)	OB	218.3	45	750	19	39.47	5-55	1	—
Richards, I. M. (No)	RM	53	10	154	7	22.00	4-57	—	—
Richards, I. V. A. (So)	OB	89.5	16	268	8	33.50	2-11	—	—
Roberts, A.M.E. (H)	RF	254.1	74	617	27	22.85	5-20	1	—
Robertson, F. (Sc)	RM	15	0	98	0	—	—	—	—
Roebuck, P. M. (So)	OB	101	28	272	4	68.00	1-8	—	—
Roope, G.R.J. (E/Sy)	RM	47	10	141	2	70.50	1-20	—	—
Rose, B. C. (So)	LM	8.2	1	31	1	31.00	1-21	—	—
Ross, C. J. (OU)	RM	86.1	24	224	8	28.00	4-34	—	—
Rouse, S. J. (Wa)	LM	142.4	27	565	12	47.08	4-63	—	—
Rowe, C. J. C. (K)	OB	84.3	29	211	3	70.33	1-12	—	—
Russell, P. E. (D)	RM/OB	235.4	88	423	21	20.14	4-23	—	—
Sadiq Mohammad (Pak/Gs)	LBG	16.3	7	33	1	33.00	1-13	—	—
Sarfraz Nawaz (Pak/No/TNP)	RFM	445	116	998	40	24.95	5-39	1	—
Savage, R.L.(OU/Wa)	RM/OB	117.1	28	384	11	34.90	4-97	—	—
Saxelby, K. (Nt)	RM	28.2	1	123	1	123.00	1-32	—	—
Selvey, M.W.W. (M)	RFM	743.5	199	1929	101	19.09	6-26	8	1
Shackleton, J.H. (Gs)	RM	96	22	275	4	68.75	2-17	—	—
Shantry, B. K. (Gs)	LFM	39	6	167	3	55.66	2-63	—	—
Sharp, K. (Y/DHR/YE)	OB	1	0	1	0	—	—	—	—
Shepherd, D. R. (Gs)	RM	4.5	0	26	0	—	—	—	—
Shepherd, J. N. (K)	RM	601.2	166	1573	44	35.75	5-70	1	—
Shuttleworth, K. (Le)	RFM	159.4	45	436	13	33.53	3-27	—	—
Sidebottom, A. (Y)	RFM	84	11	309	7	44.14	2-15	—	—
Sikander Bakht (Pak)	RFM	149	31	450	12	37.50	4-132	—	—
Simmons, J. (La)	OB	501	146	1203	35	34.37	3-33	—	—
Slocombe, P. A. (So)	OB	4	1	11	0	—	—	—	—
Smith, D. M. (Sy)	RM	11	2	50	1	50.00	1-30	—	—
Southern, J. W. (H)	SLA	762.3	247	1833	76	24.11	5-32	4	—
Spencer, J. (Sx)	RM	496.5	143	1158	46	25.17	5-53	1	—
Steele, D. S. (No)	SLA	378.3	110	976	37	26.37	6-36	3	1
Steele, J. F. (Le)	SLA	229.5	62	566	22	25.72	5-54	1	—
Stephenson, G.R. (H)	RM	0.1	0	1	0	—	—	—	—
Stevenson, G. B. (Y/MCC/YE)	RM	375.3	79	1144	44	26.00	8-65	3	—
Stevenson, K. (H)	RFM	515.5	101	1706	56	30.46	6-73	2	—
Storey, S. J. (Sx)	RM	97	27	235	6	39.16	3-12	—	—
Stuchbury, S. (Y)	LFM	15.5	1	60	2	30.00	2-39	—	—
Sutcliffe, R. J. (La)	RM	12	3	37	1	37.00	1-37	—	—
Swarbrook, F.W. (D)	SLA	134	43	344	12	28.66	4-22	—	—
Swart, P. D. (Gm)	RM	358	73	1112	43	25.86	4-24	—	—
Tait, A. (Gs)		0.1	0	0	0	—	—	—	—
Tavare, C. J. (K/YE)	RM	5	1	20	1	20.00	1-20	—	—
Taylor,L.B. (Le/DHR)	RM	300.2	50	1040	40	26.00	4-32	—	—
Taylor, M. N. S. (H)	RM	346.1	104	900	27	33.33	5-67	1	—
Thomas, D. J. (Sy/DHR)	LM	296	66	923	20	46.15	4-47	—	—

	Type	Overs	Mds	Runs	Wkts	Avge	Best	5wI	10wM
Thomson, G. B. (NZ)	LM	188	50	521	15	34.73	4–42	—	—
Titmus, F. J. (Sy)	OB	14	1	35	1	35.00	1–35	—	—
Tomlins, K. P. (M)	RM	8	2	16	0	—	—	—	—
Tremlett, T. M. (H)	RM	95	27	219	7	31.28	2–25	—	—
Troup, G. B. (NZ)	LFM	37	6	108	2	54.00	1–37	—	—
Tunnicliffe, C. J. (D)	LFM	456.4	127	1241	44	28.20	4–30	—	—
Tunnicliffe, H. T. (Nt)	RM	100	26	304	7	43.42	3–93	—	—
Turner, S. (Ex)	RFM	531	149	1183	48	24.64	4–9	—	—
Underwood, D. L. (K)	LM	815.1	359	1594	110	14.49	9–32	8	2
Waller, C. E. (Sx)	SLA	371	125	861	46	18.71	5–30	3	—
Walters, — (D)	RFM	166	31	497	16	31.06	3–70	—	—
Ward, A. (Le)	RF	29	7	70	4	17.50	2–49	—	—
Wasim Raja (Pak)	LBG	89.2	15	258	8	32.25	2–15	—	—
Watson, G. G. (Wo)	RFM	503	83	1535	48	31.97	6–45	1	—
Watson, W. K. (Nt)	RFM	151.3	34	486	15	32.40	6–102	1	—
Watts, P. J. (No)	RM	73	18	182	8	22.75	3–32	—	—
White, R. A. (Nt)	OB	541	145	1515	27	56.11	4–73	—	—
Whitehouse, J. (Wa/M=C)	OB	1	1	0	0	—	—	—	—
Whiteley, J. P. (Y)	OB	172.5	46	475	22	21.59	4–14	—	—
Wilkins, A. H. (Gm)	LM	370.3	74	1267	37	34.24	5–96	1	—
Willey, P. (No/TNP)	OB	691.1	197	1608	51	31.52	7–73	2	1
Williams, R. G. (No)	OB	148.1	34	429	10	42.90	4–48	—	—
Willis, R. C. D. (E/Wa)	RF	474.2	116	1197	65	18.41	7–63	5	1
Wilson, P. H. L. (Sy)	RFM	105.2	22	355	11	32.27	4–56	—	—
Wincer, R. C. (D)	RFM	203.2	40	680	19	35.78	4–42	—	—
Wood, B. (E/La)	RM	90	30	242	8	30.25	3–45	—	—
Wookey, S. M. (OU)	RM	144.1	32	427	11	38.81	3–61	—	—
Woolmer, R. A. (K)	RM	135.4	46	292	20	14.60	6–27	1	—
Younis Ahmed (Sy)	LM	9	2	27	0	—	—	—	—
Zaheer Abbas (Gs)	OB	8	1	26	0	—	—	—	—

Future Cricket Tours

TO ENGLAND
198_ West Indies
198_ Australia

MCC TOURS OVERSEAS
1979–80 Australia, New Zealand and India
1980–81 West Indies

OTHER TOURS

197_–80 West Indies to Pakistan and New Zealand
Australia to India
Australia to Pakistan
India to Australia and West Indies

1980–81 Pakistan to India
New Zealand to Australia
Australia to New Zealand
West Indies to Australia
New Zealand to West Indies

1982–83 India to Pakistan
Pakistan to West Indies

1983–84 Australia to West Indies
India to New Zealand

Why are fast bowlers becoming 'smoothies'?

GILLETTE FOAMY is an essential shaving requisite for modern fast-bowlers. Blue, intimidatory jowls are a relic of a past age of speed-merchants. Today's scientific paceman cannot afford the wind-resistance. So before each match he applies rich creamy lather from the FOAMY aerosol can—and gets a really smooth shave. As he accelerates to the wicket, the air slips over his sleek chin, the ball is a blur of red leather, and the batsman departs with the scent of Regular or Lemon-Lime FOAMY lingering in his nostrils, as a reminder of what hit him.

Gillette FOAMY (Regular and Lemon-Lime)
For a smooth shaving action

CAREER FIGURES FOR THE LEADING PLAYERS

The following are the abbreviated figures of the leading batsmen and bowlers based on their career averages, and fielders and wicket-keepers based on the number of their catches and dismissals. The figures are complete to the end of the 1978 season and the full career records will be found in the main table on pages 175 to 191. The qualification for inclusion for batsmen and bowlers are 100 innings and 100 wickets respectively.

Only those players likely to play in first-class county cricket in 1978 have been included.

BATTING AND FIELDING

BATSMEN	Runs	Avge	100s	BOWLERS	Wkts	Avge
G. Boycott	33,690	56.81	109	W. W. Daniel	224	17.52
C. H. Lloyd	21,521	49.93	57	M. J. Procter	1,132	19.22
Zaheer Abbas	19,804	49.75	61	D. L. Underwood	1,734	19.55
G. M. Turner	27,128	48.27	73	J. Garner	124	19.83
I. V. A. Richards	13,065	48.03	35	M. Hendrick	505	21.12
J. H. Edrich	39,790	45.47	103	G. S. Le Roux	119	21.20
Javed Miandad	7,655	44.50	21	N. Gifford	1,487	21.57
D. L. Amiss	28,366	43.24	68	G. G. Arnold	985	21.70
C. G. Greenidge	15,159	42.58	35	C. M. Old	698	21.89
A. I. Kallicharran	15,102	42.30	35	J. E. Emburey	201	22.62
P. N. Kirsten	4,077	40.36	12	I. T. Botham	381	22.66
B. L. D'Oliveira	18,625	39.79	42	A. Ward	460	22.81
B. F. Davison	15,571	38.73	29	G. Miller	326	22.97
K. W. R. Fletcher	27,515	38.59	47	N. Phillip	222	22.97
G. R. J. Roope	15,713	37.86	23	D. S. Steele	272	23.26
K. S. McEwan	9,918	37.85	24			
Sadiq Mohammad	15,923	37.73	32			

FIELDERS	Ct	WICKET-KEEPERS	Total	Ct	St
G. R. J. Roope	470	R. W. Taylor	1,241	1,108	133
K. W. R. Fletcher	467	A. P. E. Knott	1,032	928	104
D. S. Steele	407	A. Long	973	856	117
M. H. Denness	396	R. W. Tolchard	798	701	97
C. T. Radley	358	E. W. Jones	725	652	73
J. H. Hampshire	353	G. R. Stephenson	606	534	72
G. M. Turner	342	D. L. Bairstow	554	478	76
J. A. Ormrod	336	D. J. S. Taylor	523	463	60
J. M. Brearley	330	G. Sharp	389	327	62
S. J. Storey	325	D. Nicholls	339	326	13
J. H. Edrich	311	N. Smith	323	281	42
J. Birkenshaw	293	M. J. Harris	273	259	14
K. Higgs	290	G. W. Humpage	180	168	12
D. L. Amiss	284	A. W. Stovold	150	125	25
Asif Iqbal	279	J. Lyon	139	129	10
D. Lloyd	278				

CAREER RECORDS
Compiled by Michael Fordham

The following career records are for all players appearing in first-class cricket in the 1978 season, with the exception of the Pakistan touring team. Unfortunately it has not been possible to obtain all the scores of the matches played in Pakistan in 1977–78 and figures have therefore not been compiled on these players. The three members of the team playing county cricket – Javed Miandad, Sadiq Mohammad and Sarfraz Nawaz are however given in an incomplete basis.

A few cricketers who did not re-appear for their counties in 1978, but who may do so in 1979 are also included as well as others who appeared only in John Player League and overseas players who have joined counties for 1979.

†*Figures are incomplete for performances in Pakistan in 1977–78.*

BATTING AND FIELDING

	M	I	NO	Runs	HS	Avge	100s	1000 runs S	Ct	St
Abberley, R. N.	255	430	25	10003	117*	24.69	3	3	168	—
Abrahams, J.	83	123	17	2541	126	23.97	2	—	50	—
Acfield, D. L.	248	262	127	1229	42	9.10	—	—	87	—
Agnew, J. P.	4	1	0	1	1	1.00	—	—	—	—
Allbrook, M. E.	44	55	18	320	39	8.64	—	—	14	—
Allott, P. J. W.	4	2	1	1	1	1.00	—	—	1	—
Amiss, D. L.	437	746	90	28366	262*	43.24	68	14+1	284	—
Anderson, I. J.	14	24	6	668	147	37.11	2	—	7	—
Anderson, I. S.	6	10	1	140	75	15.55	—	—	3	—
Anderson, R. W.	89	158	11	4296	155	29.22	6	—	60	—
Arnold, G. G.	305	321	75	3443	73	13.99	—	—	104	—
Arrowsmith, R.	35	33	8	213	30*	8.52	—	—	10	—
Asif Iqbal	369	588	63	19541	196	37.22	36	6+2	279	—
Athey, C. W. J.	49	76	5	1658	131*	23.35	3	—	50	1
Bainbridge, P.	11	16	2	444	76*	31.71	—	—	7	—
Bairstow, D. L.	213	307	49	5307	106	20.56	2	—	478	76
Baker, R. P.	54	56	30	563	91	21.65	—	—	24	—
Balderstone, J. C.	209	313	31	8800	178*	31.20	13	4	101	—
Barclay, J. R. T.	113	198	13	4146	112	22.41	3	3	84	—
Barlow, E. J.	254	440	25	16330	217	39.34	39	2+1	304	—
Barlow, G. D.	111	176	20	4888	160*	31.33	7	2	62	—
Beaumont, D. J.	11	16	1	258	44	17.20	—	—	4	—
Birch, J. D.	49	71	9	1025	86	16.53	—	—	28	—
Birkenshaw, J.	457	627	114	12084	131	23.55	4	—	293	—
Bishop, M. M.	3	4	1	4	3	1.33	—	—	1	—
Boock, S. L.	46	56	19	301	35*	8.13	—	—	20	—
Booth, P.	69	60	16	512	58*	11.63	—	—	21	—
Bore, M. K.	74	78	21	481	37*	8.43	—	—	27	—
Borrington, A. J.	97	165	19	3574	137	24.47	3	—	48	—
Botham, I. T.	103	159	19	3720	167*	26.57	6	1	82	—
Boycott, G.	422	696	103	33690	261*	56.81	109	16+3	172	—
Boyns, C. N.	36	52	5	844	95	17.95	—	—	37	—

175

	M	I	NO	Runs	HS	Avge	100s	1000 runs in season	Ct	St
Bracewell, B. P.	12	14	3	63	27	5.72	—	—	7	—
Brain, B. M.	205	221	61	1337	57	8.35	—	—	41	—
Brassington, A. J.	55	76	21	518	28	9.41	—	—	105	20
Breakwell, D.	181	245	49	3650	100*	18.62	1	—	68	—
Brearley, J. M.	358	613	78	19776	312*	36.96	29	8	330	12
Brettell, D. N.	13	19	4	175	39	11.66	—	—	4	—
Briers, N. E.	32	54	5	1254	116*	25.59	2	—	10	—
Brown, A.	3	5	0	47	25	9.40	—	—	1	—
Brown, D. J.	378	438	109	4000	79	12.15	—	—	154	—
Burgess, G. I.	251	412	37	7109	129	18.95	2	—	119	—
Burgess, M. G.	174	290	33	9096	146	35.39	17	0+2	143	—
Buss, M. A.	316	547	47	11996	159	23.99	11	4	230	—
Butcher, A. R.	107	168	13	3839	188	24.76	4	—	27	—
Butcher, R. O.	41	69	3	1699	142	25.74	1	—	46	—
Cairns, B. L.	64	104	13	1918	92	21.07	—	—	33	—
Carrick, P.	125	155	28	2539	105	19.99	1	—	69	—
Carter, R. M.	2	1	1	8	8*	—	—	—	—	—
Cartwright, H.	80	126	16	2312	141*	21.01	1	—	31	—
Cheatle, R. G. L.	32	26	8	238	49	13.22	—	—	32	—
Childs, J. H.	59	54	34	98	12	4.90	—	—	25	—
Clarke, S. T.	6	9	4	56	15	11.20	—	—	—	—
Claughton, J. A.	30	52	2	1088	130	21.76	2	—	14	—
Clifford, C.C.	22	24	9	115	20	7.66	—	—	12	—
Clift, P. B.	113	163	41	2571	75*	21.07	—	—	60	—
Clinton, G. S.	32	50	3	1142	88	24.29	—	—	10	—
Close, D. B.	781	1217	169	34833	198	33.23	52	20	810	1
Colhoun, O. D.	27	35	18	74	9*	4.35	—	—	45	1
Collinge, R. O.	163	178	50	1848	68*	14.43	—	—	57	—
Congdon, B. E.	241	416	40	13101	202*	34.84	23	1+1	201	—
Cook, G.	166	290	22	7274	155	27.14	6	4	183	—
Cook, N. G. B.	2	2	1	33	31	33.00	—	—	1	—
Cooper, H. P.	88	103	28	1065	56	14.20	—	—	57	—
Cooper, K. E.	44	41	8	191	19	5.78	—	—	16	—
Cooper, N. H. C.	17	31	1	561	106	18.70	1	—	7	—
Coote, D. E.	1	1	0	20	20	20.00	—	—	—	—
Cope, G. A.	216	240	79	2206	78	13.70	—	—	65	—
Cordle, A. E.	285	401	69	4906	81	14.77	—	—	127	—
Corlett, S. C.	23	35	6	440	60	15.17	—	—	20	—
Cowdrey, C. S.	33	37	8	716	101*	24.68	1	—	19	—
Cowley, N. G.	67	104	18	1962	109*	22.81	1	—	33	—
Crawford, I. C.	5	7	0	104	73	14.85	—	—	5	—
Crawford, N. C.	5	6	0	71	30	11.83	—	—	1	—
Croft, C. E. H.	58	64	21	464	46*	10.79	—	—	15	—
Crowther, P. G.	9	14	0	185	99	13.21	—	—	4	—
Cumbes, J.	110	90	44	303	25*	6.58	—	—	25	—
Curzon, C. C.	4	4	0	26	26	6.50	—	—	2	1
Curzon, J. T.	1	1	0	1	1	1.00	—	—	1	—
Dalrymple, J. J. H.	3	4	2	27	15	13.50	—	—	1	—
Daniel, W. W.	66	59	25	335	30*	9.85	—	—	12	—
Davey, J.	175	208	90	918	53*	7.77	—	—	32	—
Davison, B. F.	271	444	42	15571	189	38.73	29	8	206	—

176

	M	I	NO	Runs	HS	Avge	100s	1000 runs in season	Ct	St
Dean, P. J.	2	4	0	75	39	18.75	—	—	1	—
Denness, M. H.	462	773	59	24049	195	33.68	31	13+1	396	—
Denning, P. W.	160	276	23	6601	122	26.09	4	3	71	—
Dewes, A. R.	5	8	0	99	32	12.37	—	—	1	—
Dexter, R. E.	8	13	2	171	48	15.54	—	—	3	—
Dilley, G. R.	5	6	2	42	16	10.50	—	—	3	—
D'Oliveira, B. L.	354	555	87	18625	227	39.79	42	9	211	—
Donald, P. C. G.	1	1	0	1	1	1.00	—	—	—	—
Donald, W. A.	1	1	0	0	0	0.00	—	—	—	—
Doshi, D. R.	116	122	30	729	34	7.92	—	—	33	—
Downton, P. R.	38	30	9	243	31*	11.57	—	—	88	8
Dredge, C. H.	47	58	17	543	56*	13.24	—	—	19	—
Dudleston, B.	247	417	44	12331	172	33.05	29	7	198	6
Ealham, A. G. E.	257	397	61	9247	134*	27.52	5	3	155	—
East, R. E.	303	387	92	5242	113	17.76	1	—	196	—
Edgar, B. A.	34	62	4	1968	113	33.93	1	—	30	1
Edmonds, P. H.	181	256	40	4049	103*	18.74	1	—	196	—
Edrich, J. H.	564	979	104	39790	310*	45.47	103	19+2	311	—
Edwards, G. N.	55	99	5	2565	115	27.28	1	—	81	11
Elder, J. W. G.	5	6	2	12	5	3.00	—	—	5	—
Elms, R. B.	72	73	23	558	48	11.16	—	—	17	—
Emburey, J. E.	62	77	27	745	48	14.90	—	—	66	—
Featherstone, N. G.	267	428	40	11318	147	29.17	9	2	221	—
Ferreira, A. M.	11	16	4	514	76	42.83	—	—	12	—
Finan, N. H.	5	3	1	22	18	11.00	—	—	1	—
Fisher, P. B.	41	65	6	534	42	9.05	—	—	60	9
Fletcher, K. W. R.	499	834	121	27515	228*	38.59	47	14	467	—
Flower, R. W.	9	8	4	23	10*	5.75	—	—	—	—
Flynn, V. A.	3	2	1	21	15	21.00	—	—	4	—
Foat, J. C.	81	133	13	2049	102	17.07	3	—	34	—
Fosh, M. K.	30	48	2	1069	109	23.23	1	—	9	—
Francis, D. A.	67	117	16	2143	110	21.21	1	—	38	—
French, B. N.	43	54	19	454	66	12.97	—	—	65	12
Gard, T.	5	4	1	12	7	4.00	—	—	7	1
Gardiner, S. J.	34	49	16	556	40*	16.84	—	—	13	—
Garner, J.	24	29	8	354	44*	16.85	—	—	19	—
Gatting, M. W.	77	118	17	2975	128	29.45	2	2	68	—
Gifford, N.	493	588	180	5408	89	13.25	—	—	243	—
Gilliat, R. M. C.	269	441	46	11589	223*	29.33	18	4	221	—
Goddard, G. F.	19	29	4	341	39	13.64	—	—	7	—
Gooch, G. A.	105	172	16	5166	136	33.11	8	3	72	—
Gould, I. J.	55	78	13	1283	128	19.73	1	—	107	17
Gower, D. I.	58	85	8	2307	144*	29.96	4	1	20	—
Graham-Brown, J.	30	37	7	368	43	12.26	—	—	8	—
Graveney, D. A.	131	187	39	2500	92	16.89	—	—	64	—
Graves, P. J.	271	471	49	11369	145*	26.94	14	5	217	—
Greenidge, C. G.	217	379	23	15159	273*	42.58	35	8	226	—
Greig, A. W.	350	579	45	16660	226	31.19	26	7+1	345	—
Greig, I. A.	19	27	2	549	96	21.96	—	—	5	—
Griffiths, B. J.	36	32	17	40	11	2.66	—	—	9	—

	M	I	NO	Runs	HS	Avge	100s	1000 runs in season	Ct	St
Groome, J. J.	40	74	3	1120	86	15.77	—	—	19	—
Gurr, D. R.	37	46	21	379	46*	15.16	—	—	9	—
Hacker, P. J.	27	35	13	283	35	12.86	—	—	6	—
Hadlee, D. R.	96	135	34	1718	63*	17.00	—	—	34	—
Hadlee, R. J.	84	115	20	2040	101*	21.47	1	—	36	—
Halliday, M.	4	3	1	22	13*	11.00	—	—	2	—
Hampshire, J. H.	451	722	83	21530	183*	33.69	34	13	353	—
Hansell, T. M. G.	14	26	5	319	54	15.19	—	—	2	—
Hardie, B. R.	115	198	24	5435	162	31.23	6	3	102	—
Harris, M. J.	301	510	46	17262	201*	37.20	39	10	259	14
Harrison, D.	1	—	—							
Hartley, S. N.	1	2	0	31	20	15.50	—	—	—	—
Harvey-Walker, A. J.	81	143	10	3186	117	23.95	3	—	31	—
Hassan, S. B.	232	386	35	10308	182*	29.36	13	5	205	1
Hayes, F. C.	194	307	42	9566	187	36.09	18	5	144	—
Head, T. J.	5	8	3	105	31	21.00	—	—	14	1
Hemmings, E. E.	179	257	59	4306	85	21.74	—	—	87	—
Hemsley, E. J. O.	166	274	41	7137	176*	30.63	8	1	118	—
Henderson, S. P.	12	19	3	237	52	14.81	—	—	6	—
Hendrick, M.	179	175	66	1041	46	9.55	—	—	115	—
Herbert, R.	3	5	0	33	12	6.60	—	—	2	—
Herkes, R.	1	1	1	0	0*	—	—	—	—	—
Higgs, K.	486	513	198	3586	98	11.38	—	—	290	—
Hignell, A. J.	82	141	8	3406	149	25.60	5	2	85	—
Hill, A.	125	224	16	5862	160*	28.18	7	2	49	—
Hills, R. W.	64	68	17	840	45	16.47	—	—	18	—
Hoadley, S. P.	7	12	0	232	112	19.33	1	—	4	—
Hobbs, R. N. S.	399	502	119	4694	100	12.25	2	—	275	—
Hodgson, A.	88	107	21	870	41*	10.11	—	—	27	—
Hogg, W.	18	19	6	69	19	5.30	—	—	2	—
Holder, V. A.	279	318	72	3081	122	12.52	1	—	87	—
Holmes, G. C.	2	4	2	37	17*	18.50	—	—	1	—
Hopkins, D. C.	11	11	1	56	13*	5.60	—	—	4	—
Hopkins, J. A.	92	161	12	4071	230	27.32	5	2	66	1
Howarth, G. P.	164	294	18	8444	179*	30.59	13	2	109	—
Howat, M. G.	15	16	3	133	31	10.23	—	—	3	—
Hughes, D. P.	226	277	56	4075	101	18.43	1	—	137	—
Humpage, G. W.	78	121	8	3457	125*	32.92	4	2	168	12
Humphries, D. J.	51	73	13	1330	111*	22.16	1	—	81	14
Illingworth, R.	753	1051	207	23977	162	28.40	22	8	432	—
Imran Khan	157	256	30	7065	170	31.26	13	3	62	—
Inchmore, J. D.	79	96	21	1054	113	14.05	1	—	27	—
Intikhab Alam	445	661	68	13301	182	22.43	9	—	217	—
Jackman, R. D.	304	365	118	4104	92*	16.61	—	—	137	—
Jarvis, K. B. S.	78	53	29	80	12*	3.33	—	—	24	—
Javed Miandad	118	198	26	7655	311	44.50	21	1+2	124	2
Jennings, K. F.	36	51	15	394	49	10.94	—	—	24	—
Jesty, T. E.	228	358	46	8660	159*	27.75	12	3	133	1
Johnson, C.	99	150	14	2946	107	21.66	2	—	49	—

178

	M	I	NO	Runs	HS	Avge	100s	1000 runs in season	Ct	St
Johnson, G. W.	232	380	28	8886	168	25.24	10	3	188	—
Jones, A.	532	966	59	29716	187*	32.76	46	18	257	—
Jones, A. A.	184	191	60	706	33	5.38	—	—	42	—
Jones, A. L.	32	57	3	987	57	18.27	—	—	10	—
Jones, B. J. R.	30	52	3	675	65	13.77	—	—	17	—
Jones, E. W.	309	459	99	6752	146*	18.75	2	—	651	73
Kallicharran, A. I.	238	393	36	15102	197	42.30	35	6+1	165	—
Kayum, D. A.	12	18	1	423	57	24.88	—	—	8	—
Kemp, N. J.	6	5	1	24	14	6.00	—	—	1	—
Kennedy, A.	86	140	13	3683	176*	29.00	4	1	61	—
Ker, J. E.	3	5	1	60	50	15.00	—	—	—	—
Kirsten, P. N.	62	110	9	4077	206*	40.36	12	1+1	43	—
Kitchen, M. J.	347	602	32	15084	189	26.46	17	7	149	—
Knight, J. M.	6	8	1	61	19	8.71	—	—	1	—
Knight, R. D. V.	246	441	33	12666	165*	31.04	19	8	184	—
Knott, A. P. E.	379	560	102	14000	156	30.56	16	2	928	104
Laing, J. R.	6	11	1	251	127*	25.10	1	—	5	—
Lamb, A. J.	44	73	13	2446	180	40.76	5	—	32	—
Lamb, T. M.	73	81	25	761	77	13.58	—	—	21	—
Larkins, W.	103	170	15	3843	170*	24.79	8	1	51	—
Leadbeater, B.	145	237	28	5307	140*	25.39	1	—	82	—
Lee, P. G.	163	132	56	647	26	8.51	—	—	28	—
Le Roux, G. S.	26	34	19	285	47*	19.00	—	—	16	—
L'Estrange, M. G.	12	18	2	243	45	15.18	—	—	6	—
Lever, J. K.	284	300	131	1848	91	10.93	—	—	125	—
Lilley, A. W.	1	2	1	122	100*	122.00	1	—	—	—
Lister, J. W.	3	6	0	137	48	22.83	—	—	1	—
Littlewood, D. J.	10	10	3	95	51	13.57	—	—	12	6
Llewellyn, M. J.	103	168	22	3477	129*	23.81	2	—	70	—
Lloyd, B. J.	58	73	22	503	45*	9.86	—	—	32	—
Lloyd, C. H.	325	502	71	21521	242*	49.93	57	8+3	236	—
Lloyd, D.	312	502	57	14364	214*	32.27	24	8	278	—
Lloyd, T. A.	17	27	5	648	93	29.45	—	—	15	—
Long, A.	420	505	116	6436	92	16.54	—	—	856	117
Love, J. D.	47	76	9	1892	163	28.23	3	—	28	—
Lumb, R. G.	144	242	20	6623	132	29.83	11	3	95	—
Lynch, M. A.	19	34	0	621	101	18.26	1	—	7	—
Lyon, J.	65	69	10	703	74*	11.91	—	—	129	10
McEvoy, M. S. A.	9	14	1	296	67*	22.76	—	—	7	—
McEwan, K. S.	166	285	23	9918	218	37.85	24	5	175	7
McIntyre, J. M.	80	101	36	1095	87*	16.84	—	—	38	—
Mack, A. J.	15	13	2	50	16	4.54	—	—	2	—
Mackintosh, K. S.	14	14	5	124	23*	13.77	—	—	6	—
McLellan, A. J.	14	14	5	27	11*	3.00	—	—	17	—
McPherson, T. I.	3	4	1	57	28	19.00	—	—	—	—
Malone, S. J.	2	—	—	—	—	—	—	—	—	—
Marie, G. V.	9	11	0	87	27	7.90	—	—	1	—
Marks, V. J.	66	113	7	2814	105	26.54	1	—	30	—
Marshall, M. D.	1	1	0	0	0	0.00	—	—	—	—

	M	I	NO	Runs	HS	Avge	100s	1000 runs in season	Ct	St
Marshall, R. P. T.	24	37	15	315	37	14.31	—	—	6	—
Maynard, C. W.	3	3	1	17	9	8.50	—	—	4	—
Mellor, A. J.	5	7	2	19	10*	3.80	—	—	—	—
Mendis, G. D.	39	70	8	1688	128	27.22	3	—	23	1
Miller, G.	126	187	22	4051	98*	24.55	—	—	73	—
Monteith, J. D.	13	19	2	240	78	14.11	—	—	10	—
Morrill, N. D.	5	7	1	83	20*	13.83	—	—	3	—
Morris, A.	47	77	4	1174	74	16.08	—	—	29	—
Moseley, H. R.	150	163	67	1178	67	12.27	—	—	57	—
Moulding, R. P.	9	12	3	302	77*	33.55	—	—	5	—
Mubarak, A. M.	6	11	0	205	77	18.63	—	—	3	—
Murtagh, A. J.	27	47	5	640	65	15.23	—	—	9	—
Nash, M. A.	265	381	58	6137	130	19.00	2	—	110	—
Neale, P. A.	58	103	9	2796	413	29.74	3	1	29	—
Needham, A.	12	12	1	81	21	7.36	—	—	3	—
Nicholas, M. C. J.	3	5	2	77	40*	25.66	—	—	2	—
Nicholls, D.	202	342	24	7072	211	22.23	2	1	326	13
O'Brien, B. A.	7	10	0	155	45	15.50	—	—	4	—
Old, C. M.	242	308	59	5582	116	22.41	6	—	152	—
Oldham, S.	36	25	13	66	19	5.50	—	—	10	—
Olive, M.	4	7	1	28	15	4.66	—	—	4	—
Oliver, P. R.	36	52	7	816	59	18.13	—	—	17	—
Ontong, R. C.	72	116	9	2480	116*	23.17	3	—	35	—
Orders, J. O. D.	8	13	1	335	79	27.91	—	—	2	—
Ormrod, J. A.	380	641	77	17104	204*	30.32	22	10	336	—
Parker, J. M.	154	267	24	8174	195	33.63	16	2	125	5
Parker, P. W. G.	60	104	9	2993	215	31.50	5	2	30	—
Parsons, G. J.	2	2	0	10	7	5.00	—	—	—	—
Partridge, M. D.	12	17	5	199	50	16.58	—	—	4	—
Patel, A. S.	2	3	1	56	25*	28.00	—	—	1	—
Patel, D. N.	54	78	3	1407	107	18.76	3	—	25	—
Pathmanathan, G.	36	62	2	1255	82	20.91	—	—	32	—
Payne, I. A.	12	15	1	96	29	6.85	—	—	10	—
Pearce, J. P.	2	3	3	6	5*	—	—	—	—	—
Peck, I. G.	5	6	0	22	11	3.66	—	—	1	—
Perryman, S. P.	84	88	35	563	43	10.62	—	—	30	—
Phillip, N.	70	111	14	2710	134	27.93	1	—	22	—
Phillipson, C. P.	182	106	39	1103	70	16.46	—	—	39	—
Pigott, A. C. S.	6	6	0	33	11	5.50	—	—	1	—
Pilling, H.	329	536	67	15199	149*	32.40	25	8	88	—
Pocock, N. E. J.	15	26	4	445	68	20.22	—	—	10	—
Pocock, P. I.	388	434	100	3907	75*	11.69	—	—	135	—
Pont, K. R.	101	159	21	3324	113	24.08	5	—	56	—
Popplewell, N. F. N.	16	20	5	195	46	13.00	—	—	3	—
Poulter, S. J.	3	3	0	47	36	15.66	—	—	—	—
Price, D. H.	5	10	0	104	27	10.40	—	—	4	—
Pridgeon, A. P.	70	69	1	277	32	7.28	—	—	20	—
Pringle, D. R.	4	5	1	60	50*	15.00	—	—	1	—
Procter, M. J.	316	528	47	17997	254	37.41	42	7	266	—

	M	I	NO	Runs	HS	Avge	100s	1000 runs in season	Ct	St
Racionzer, T. B.	41	72	9	1282	91	20.34	—	—	33	—
Radley, C. T.	352	568	76	17038	171	34.63	28	11	358	—
Randall, D. W.	174	299	27	8813	204*	32.40	11	4	94	—
Ratcliffe, R. M.	61	65	17	699	48	14.56	—	—	20	—
Reidy, B. W.	49	73	11	1600	88	25.80	—	—	27	—
Reith, M. S.	6	10	0	206	82	20.60	—	—	3	—
Rhind, P. A.	5	6	3	21	10	7.00	—	—	3	—
Rice, C. E. B.	163	274	41	8692	246	37.30	10	4	112	—
Rice, J. M.	102	151	12	2577	96*	18.53	—	—	98	—
Richards, B. A.	319	543	53	27293	356	55.70	79	9+6	354	—
Richards, C. J.	36	44	14	447	50	14.90	—	—	49	13
Richards, G.	297	160	24	3215	102*	23.63	1	—	33	—
Richards, I. M.	12	10	3	155	50	22.14	—	—	2	—
Richards, I. V. A.	171	293	21	13065	291	48.03	35	5+2	161	—
Roberts, A. M. E.	131	160	44	1409	56*	12.14	—	—	25	—
Robertson, F.	8	12	1	94	14*	8.54	—	—	2	—
Robinson, A. L.	84	69	31	365	30*	9.60	—	—	46	—
Robinson, P. A.	6	6	2	80	25*	20.00	—	—	1	—
Robinson, P. J.	185	287	55	4936	140	21.27	3	1	171	—
Robinson, R. T.	1	2	1	36	27*	36.00	—	—	1	—
Rock, D. J.	21	38	0	754	144	19.84	2	—	11	—
Roebuck, P. M.	69	119	19	2880	158	28.80	4	—	33	—
Roope, G. R. J.	321	517	102	15713	171	37.86	23	8	470	1
Rose, B. C.	135	235	23	6591	205	31.08	15	4	62	—
Ross, C. J.	13	14	4	28	7*	2.80	—	—	3	—
Rouse, S. J.	108	130	26	1582	93	15.21	—	—	49	—
Rowe, C. J. C.	79	121	26	2600	103	27.36	1	1	26	—
Russell, P. E.	162	203	44	2007	72	12.62	—	—	123	—
†Sadiq Mohammad	259	448	26	15923	184*	37.73	32	5+2	204	—
†Sarfraz Nawaz	193	254	52	3829	86	18.95	—	—	108	—
Savage, R. L.	37	44	20	157	22*	6.54	—	—	11	—
Saxelby, K.	2	3	1	3	3*	1.50	—	—	1	—
Schepens, M.	13	19	3	267	39	16.68	—	—	6	—
Scott, C. J.	5	5	1	25	10	6 25	—	—	6	2
Selvey, M. W. W.	167	169	68	938	42	9.28	—	—	45	—
Shackleton, J. H.	48	64	20	596	41*	13.54	—	—	36	—
Shantry, B. K.	2	—	—	—	—	—	—	—	1	—
Sharp, G.	170	238	50	3546	85	18.86	—	—	327	62
Sharp, K.	28	47	7	1019	91	25.47	—	—	9	—
Shepherd, D. R.	274	466	38	10449	153	24.41	12	2	95	—
Shepherd, J. N.	301	441	69	9746	170	26.19	7	1	227	—
Short, J. P.	5	7	—	228	114	32.57	1	—	1	—
Shuttleworth, K.	217	219	76	2304	71	16.11	—	—	110	—
Sidebottom, A.	35	44	6	646	124	17.00	1	—	13	—
Simmons, J.	236	279	80	4243	112	21.32	2	—	184	—
Slack, W. N.	13	21	1	333	52	16.65	—	—	7	—
Slocombe, P. A.	75	131	19	3452	132	30.82	5	2	40	—
Smedley, M. J.	348	588	75	16131	149	31.44	28	9	249	—
Smith, A. V.	1	—	—	—	—	—	—	—	1	—
Smith, D. M.	56	84	20	1397	115	21.82	2	—	28	—
Smith, K. B.	4	8	1	90	43	12.85	—	—	1	—

	M	I	NO	Runs	HS	Avge	1000 runs in 100s season	Ct	St
Smith, K. D.	63	109	9	3008	135	30.08	5	2	16	—
Smith, M. J.	398	664	74	18622	181	31.56	35	10	214	—
Smith, N.	133	173	37	2438	126	17.92	2	—	281	42
Southern, J. W.	79	86	37	448	51	9.14	—	—	22	—
Spencer, J.	190	261	73	2576	79	13.70	—	—	69	—
Stead, B.	232	253	77	2166	58	12.30	—	—	59	—
Steele, A.	11	21	0	547	97	26.04	—	—	8	1
Steele, D. S.	358	599	74	17375	140*	33.09	27	9	407	—
Steele, J. F.	223	371	39	9746	195	29.35	14	5	254	—
Stephenson, G. R.	232	301	58	4144	100*	17.05	1	—	534	72
Stevenson, G. B.	63	75	9	1437	83	21.77	—	—	30	—
Stevenson, K.	68	81	23	485	33	8.36	—	—	23	—
Stewart, D. E. R.	30	47	3	839	69	19.06	—	—	15	—
Storey, S. J.	332	492	62	10776	164	25.06	12	5	325	—
Stovold, A. W.	113	203	10	5474	196	28.36	5	2	125	25
Stuchbury, S.	1	—	—	—	—	—	—	—	—	—
Sturt, M. O. C.	33	35	9	202	26	7.76	—	—	62	10
Surridge, S. S.	1	1	1	2	2*	—	—	—	1	—
Sutcliffe, R. J.	1	2	2	10	10*	—	—	—	—	—
Swarbrook, F. W.	214	314	85	4696	90	20.50	—	—	133	—
Swart, P. D.	99	151	16	3210	115	23.77	5	1	56	—
Tait, A.	63	104	1	1897	99	18.41	—	—	15	—
Tavare, C. J.	75	126	16	3819	124*	34.71	5	2	93	—
Taylor, D. J. S.	221	320	64	5639	179	22.02	4	1	463	60
Taylor, L. B.	14	8	3	29	15	5.80	—	—	4	—
Taylor, M. N. S.	344	473	111	7257	105	20.04	3	—	202	—
Taylor, R. W.	479	675	124	9306	97	16.88	—	—	1108	133
Terry, V. P.	2	3	0	16	8	5.33	—	—	—	—
Thomas, D. J.	16	19	4	84	14	5.60	—	—	5	—
Thomas, G. P.	1	2	0	5	4	2.50	—	—	—	—
Thomson, G. B.	35	39	12	254	34*	9.40	—	—	20	—
Titmus, F. J.	784	1133	204	21534	137*	23.17	6	8	471	—
Todd, P. A.	85	149	5	3770	178	26.18	3	2	63	—
Tolchard, R. W.	376	506	149	11192	126*	31.35	9	—	701	97
Tomlins, K. P.	14	19	2	296	94	17.41	—	—	9	—
Tremlett, T. M.	8	13	3	202	50	20.20	—	—	2	—
Trim, G. E.	2	4	0	36	15	9.00	—	—	—	—
Troup, G. B.	25	27	9	291	58*	16.16	—	—	13	—
Tunnicliffe, C. J.	56	61	16	445	82*	9.88	—	—	23	—
Tunnicliffe, H. T.	33	54	12	937	87	22.30	—	—	14	—
Turner, D. R.	241	402	35	10569	181*	28.79	17	6	142	—
Turner, G. M.	373	650	88	27128	259	48.27	73	11+3	342	—
Turner, S.	243	354	68	6203	121	21.68	3	—	164	—
Underwood, D. L.	447	482	125	3266	80	9.14	—	—	191	—
Waller, C. E.	126	141	47	811	47	8.62	—	—	65	—
Walters, J.	19	26	4	545	90	24.77	—	—	2	—
Ward, A.	163	157	47	928	44	8.43	—	—	51	—
Warner, C. J.	2	3	0	41	28	13.66	—	—	—	—
Watson, G. G.	28	35	9	384	38	14.76	—	—	10	—
Watson, W. K.	33	38	18	234	28*	11.70	—	—	8	—

	M	I	NO	Runs	HS	Avge	100s	1000 runs in season	Ct	St
Watts, P. J.	343	568	80	13906	145	28.49	10	7	255	—
Wells, R. R. C.	11	17	1	212	85	13.25	—	—	4	—
Wessels, K. C.	44	77	11	2725	146	41.28	4	—	27	—
White, R. A.	411	639	105	12442	116*	23.29	5	1	188	—
Whitehouse, J.	149	256	26	7344	173	31.93	14	3	107	—
Whiteley, J. P.	9	5	3	14	8	7.00	—	—	6	—
Wilcock, H. G.	99	137	31	1697	70	16.00	—	—	177	17
Wilkins, A. H.	41	46	17	236	70	8.13	—	—	15	—
Willey, P.	241	393	56	8584	227	25.47	10	1	102	—
Williams, R. G.	41	63	9	966	64	17.88	—	—	18	—
Williams, S.	1	1	0	0	0	0.00	—	—	—	—
Willis, R. G. D.	183	190	91	1413	43	14.27	—	—	88	—
Wilson, P. H. L.	9	4	4	9*	—	—	—	—	1	—
Wincer, R. C.	10	10	4	43	16*	7.16	—	—	5	—
Wood, B.	272	449	55	13117	198	33.29	22	6	214	—
Wookey, S. M.	16	24	5	239	48	12.57	—	—	4	—
Woolmer, R. A.	244	365	59	10028	149	32.77	19	4	171	—
Wright, J. G.	63	112	7	3332	164	31.73	4	1	42	—
Yardley, T. J.	190	288	49	6065	135	25.37	4	1	167	2
Younis Ahmed	307	525	70	16267	183*	35.75	23	7	174	—
Zaheer Abbas	262	444	46	19804	274	49.75	61	7+3	197	—

BOWLING

	Runs	Wkts	Avge	BB	5 WI	10 Wm	100 WS
Abberley, R. N.	285	4	71.25	2–19	—	—	—
Abrahams, J.	28	0	—	—	—	—	—
Acfield, D. L.	16315	578	28.22	7–36	19	2	—
Agnew, J. P.	215	6	35.83	3–51	—	—	—
Allbrook, M. E.	3373	75	44.97	7–79	2	—	—
Allott, P. J. W.	456	14	32.57	5–98	1	—	—
Amiss, D. L.	700	18	38.88	3–21	—	—	—
Anderson, I. J.	180	16	11.25	5–21	1	—	—
Anderson, I. S.	150	2	75.00	1–24	—	—	—
Anderson, R. W.	149	5	29.80	4–49	—	—	—
Arnold, G. G.	21381	985	21.70	8–41	42	3	1
Arrowsmith, R.	2480	89	27.86	6–29	4	—	—
Asif Iqbal	8459	286	29.57	6–45	5	—	—
Athey, C. W. J.	277	12	23.08	3–38	—	—	—
Bainbridge, P.	59	0	—	—	—	—	—
Bairstow, D. L.	151	4	37.75	3–82	—	—	—
Baker, R. P.	2942	104	28.28	6–29	1	—	—
Balderstone, J. C.	6005	245	24.51	6–25	5	—	—
Barclay, J. R. T.	3176	102	31.13	6–94	4	1	—
Barlow, E. J.	12750	512	24.90	7–24	14	2	—
Barlow, G. D.	13	1	13.00	1–6	—	—	—
Beaumont, D. J.							
Birch, J. D.	1716	35	49.02	6–64	1	—	—
Birkenshaw, J.	27877	1038	26.85	8–94	44	4	2

183

	Runs	Wkts	Avge	BB	5 Wi	10 Wm	100 WS
Bishop, M. M.	165	2	82.50	1–13	—	—	—
Boock, S. L.	3357	165	20.34	7–57	10	—	—
Booth, P.	3628	133	27.27	6–93	1	—	—
Bore, M. K.	4866	162	30.03	7–63	4	—	—
Borrington, A. J.	19	0	—	—	—	—	—
Botham, I. T.	8637	381	22.66	8–34	25	4	1
Boycott, G.	1011	23	43.95	3–47	—	—	—
Boyns, C. N.	1604	35	45.82	3–24	—	—	—
Bracewell, B. P.	861	31	27.77	4–49	—	—	—
Brain, B. M.	16621	702	23.67	8–55	28	6	—
Brassington, A. J.	10	0	—	—	—	—	—
Breakwell, D.	9947	334	29.78	8–39	10	1	—
Brearley, J. M.	103	1	103.00	1–21	—	—	—
Brettell, D. N.	549	18	30.50	3–22	—	—	—
Briers, N. E.	40	1	40.00	1–22	—	—	—
Brown, A.	—	—	—	—	—	—	—
Brown, D. J.	28104	1140	24.65	8–60	44	5	—
Burgess, G. I.	13535	474	28.55	7–43	18	2	—
Burgess, M. G.	997	27	36.92	3–23	—	—	—
Buss, M. A.	15349	547	28.06	7–58	18	—	—
Butcher, A. R.	2853	77	37.05	6–48	1	—	—
Butcher, R. O.	30	0	—	—	—	—	—
Cairns, B. L.	5406	201	26.89	6–62	11	2	—
Carrick, P.	9342	355	26.31	8–33	18	2	—
Carter, R. M.	43	0	—	—	—	—	—
Cartwright, H.	11	0	—	—	—	—	—
Cheatle, R. G. L.	1942	56	34.67	6–54	2	—	—
Childs, J. H.	4429	154	28.75	8–34	8	2	—
Clarke, S. T.	554	22	24.72	6–39	1	1	—
Claughton, J. A.	4	0	—	—	—	—	—
Clifford, C. C.	1886	64	29.46	6–89	3	—	—
Clift, P. B.	7655	312	24.53	8–17	11	—	—
Clinton, G. S.	9	2	4.50	2–8	—	—	—
Close, D. B.	30836	1167	26.42	8–41	43	3	2
Colhoun, O. D.	—	—	—	—	—	—	—
Collinge, R. O.	12792	524	24.41	8–64	21	4	—
Congdon, B. E.	6152	204	30.15	6–42	4	—	—
Cook, G.	68	0	—	—	—	—	—
Cook, N. G. B.	83	3	27.66	1–16	—	—	—
Cooper, H. P.	5711	211	27.06	8–62	4	1	—
Cooper, K.	3006	106	28.35	6–32	3	—	—
Cooper, N. H. C.	61	1	61.00	1–4	—	—	—
Coote, D. E.	—	—	—	—	—	—	—
Cope, G. A.	14900	631	23.61	8–73	34	6	—
Cordle, A. E.	17307	635	27.25	9–49	18	2	—
Corlett, S. C.	1515	38	39.86	5–62	1	—	—
Cowdrey, C. S.	111	2	55.50	1–18	—	—	—
Cowley, N. G.	3654	102	35.82	5–93	2	—	—
Crawford, I. C.	174	3	58.00	1–18	—	—	—
Crawford, N. C.	33	0	—	—	—	—	—
Croft, C. E. H.	4885	201	24.30	8–29	8	1	—
Crowther, P. G.	22	1	22.00	1–22	—	—	—

184

	Runs	Wkts	Avge	BB	5 Wi	10 Wm	100 WS
Cumbes, J.	7457	267	27.92	6–24	9	—	—
Curzon, C. C.	—	—	—	—	—	—	—
Curzon, J. T.	22	0	—	—	—	—	—
Dalrymple, J. J. H.	260	7	37.14	3–34	—	—	—
Daniel, W. W.	3925	224	17.52	6–21	12	3	—
Davey, J.	11720	411	28.51	6–95	9	—	—
Davison, B. F.	2526	81	31.18	5–52	1	—	—
Dean, P. J.	—	—	—	—	—	—	—
Denness, M. H.	62	2	31.00	1–7	—	—	—
Denning, P. W.	70	1	70.00	1–4	—	—	—
Dewes, A. R.	146	1	146.00	1–52	—	—	—
Dexter, R. E.	—	—	—	—	—	—	—
Dilley, G. R.	220	8	27.50	5–32	1	—	—
D'Oliveira, B. L.	14734	538	27.38	6–29	17	2	—
Donald, P. C. G.	—	—	—	—	—	—	—
Donald, W. A.	—	—	—	—	—	—	—
Doshi, D. R.	10499	473	22.19	7–29	23	3	—
Downton, P. R.	—	—	—	—	—	—	—
Dredge, C. H.	3317	102	32.51	5–53	2	—	—
Dudleston, B.	827	23	35.95	4–6	—	—	—
Ealham, A. G. E.	98	2	49.00	1–1	—	—	—
East, R. E.	19349	780	24.80	8–30	37	7	—
Edgar, B. A.	9	0	—	—	—	—	—
Edmonds, P. H.	14844	611	24.29	8–132	26	4	—
Edrich, J. H.	3	0	—	—	—	—	—
Edwards, G. N.	27	0	—	—	—	—	—
Elder, J. W. G.	147	8	18.37	3–56	—	—	—
Elms, R. B.	4060	116	39.70	5–38	4	—	—
Emburey, J. E.	4547	201	22.62	7–36	13	3	—
Featherstone, N. G.	3866	146	26.47	5–32	3	—	—
Ferreira, A. M.	802	37	21.67	8–38	3	1	—
Finan, N. H.	252	4	63.00	2–57	—	—	—
Fisher, P. B.	—	—	—	—	—	—	—
Fletcher, K. W. R.	1510	32	47.18	4–50	—	—	—
Flower, R. W.	554	10	55.40	3–45	—	—	—
Flynn, V. A.	—	—	—	—	—	—	—
Foat, J. C.	23	0	—	—	—	—	—
Fosh, M. K.	—	—	—	—	—	—	—
Francis, D. A.	6	0	—	—	—	—	—
French, B. N.	—	—	—	—	—	—	—
Gaird, T.	—	—	—	—	—	—	—
Gardiner, S. J.	2772	111	24.97	6–49	5	—	—
Garner, J.	2460	124	19.83	8–31	6	—	—
Gatting, M. W.	1217	52	23.40	5–59	1	—	—
Gifford, N.	32085	1487	21.57	8–28	73	11	3
Gilliat, R. M. C.	157	3	52.33	1–3	—	—	—
Goddard, G. F.	932	34	27.41	8–34	1	1	—
Gooch, G. A.	1035	25	41.40	5–40	1	—	—
Gould, I. J.	—	—	—	—	—	—	—

	Runs	Wkts	Avge	BB	5 Wl	10 Wm	100 WS
Gower, D. I.	61	3	20.33	3–47	—	—	—
Graham-Brown, J. M.	696	12	58.00	2–23	—	—	—
Graveney, D. A.	9135	317	28.81	8–85	12	2	—
Graves, P. J.	797	15	53.13	3–69	—	—	—
Greenidge, C. G.	421	16	26.31	5–49	1	—	—
Greig, A. W.	24702	856	28.85	8–25	33	8	—
Greig, I. A.	1110	29	38.27	4–76	—	—	—
Griffiths, B. J.	2609	81	32.20	5–66	2	—	—
Groome, J. J.	0	0			—	—	—
Gurr, D. R.	2890	108	26.75	6–82	5	—	—
Hacker, P. J.	1802	36	50.05	3–27	—	—	—
Hadlee, D. R.	7864	300	26.21	7–55	11	3	—
Hadlee, R. J.	7679	323	23.77	7–23	14	4	—
Halliday, M.	193	9	21.44	3–14	—	—	—
Hampshire, J. H.	1585	29	54.65	7–52	2	—	—
Hansell, T. M. G.	0	0			—	—	—
Hardie, B. R.	21	0			—	—	—
Harris, M. J.	3353	79	42.44	4–16	—	—	—
Harrison, D.	—	—			—	—	—
Hartley, S. N.	6	0			—	—	—
Harvey-Walker, A. J.	1150	34	33.82	7–35	1	1	—
Hassan, S. B.	407	6	67.83	3–33	—	—	—
Hayes, F. C.	15	0			—	—	—
Head, T. J.	—	—			—	—	—
Hemmings, E. E.	14197	445	31.90	7–33	19	5	—
Hemsley, E. J. O.	2283	67	34.07	3–5	—	—	—
Henderson, S. P.	30	0			—	—	—
Hendrick, M.	10669	505	21.12	8–45	18	3	—
Herbert, R.	—	—			—	—	—
Herkes, R.	9	0			—	—	—
Higgs, K.	35038	1477	23.72	7–19	45	5	5
Hignell, A. J.	154	0			—	—	—
Hill, A.	67	3	22.33	3–5	—	—	—
Hills, R. W.	3533	131	26.96	6–64	2	—	—
Hoadley, S. P.	—	—			—	—	—
Hobbs, R. N. S.	27806	1034	26.50	8–63	48	8	2
Hodgson, A.	5145	188	27.36	5–30	2	—	—
Hogg, W.	1142	46	24.82	7–84	3	—	—
Holder, V. A.	20963	886	23.66	7–40	38	3	—
Holmes, G. C.	41	0			—	—	—
Hopkins, D. C.	485	10	48.50	3–27	—	—	—
Hopkins, J. A.	27	0			—	—	—
Howarth, G. P.	2324	78	29.79	5–32	1	—	—
Howat, M. G.	765	17	45.00	3–39	—	—	—
Hughes, D. P.	14661	510	28.74	7–24	19	2	—
Humpage, G. W.	—	—			—	—	—
Humphries, D. J.	—	—			—	—	—
Illingworth, R.	40485	2031	19.93	9–42	104	11	10
Imran Khan	13150	496	26.51	7–52	26	5	—
Inchmore, J. D.	5640	206	27.37	8–58	7	1	—
Intikhab Alam	40119	1451	27.64	8–54	81	13	1

	Runs	Wkts	Avge	BB	5 Wl	10 Wm	100 WS
Jackman, R. D.	24384	1029	23.69	8–40	45	7	—
Jarvis, K. B. S.	5859	215	27.25	8–97	6	1	—
Javed Miandad	4376	145	30.17	6–93	5	—	—
Jennings, K. F.	2094	58	36.10	5–18	1	—	—
Jesty, T. E.	10438	368	28.36	7–75	12	—	—
Johnson, C.	265	4	66.25	2–22	—	—	—
Johnson, G. W.	9606	316	30.39	6–32	8	1	—
Jones, A.	329	3	109.66	1–24	—	—	—
Jones, A. A.	12927	483	26.76	9–51	22	3	—
Jones, A. L.	17	0	—	—	—	—	—
Jones, B. J. R.	—	—	—	—	—	—	—
Jones, E. W.	5	0	—	—	—	—	—
Kallicharran, A. I.	977	21	46.52	4–48	—	—	—
Kayum, D. A.	—	—	—	—	—	—	—
Kemp, N. J.	139	3	46.33	3–83	—	—	—
Kennedy, A.	59	2	29.50	2–29	—	—	—
Ker, J. E.	100	2	50.00	1–17	—	—	—
Kirsten, P. N.	753	23	32.73	4–51	—	—	—
Kitchen, M. J.	109	2	54.50	1–4	—	—	—
Knight, J. M.	237	6	39.50	3–36	—	—	—
Knight, R. D. V.	8514	231	36.85	6–44	2	—	—
Knott, A. P. E.	77	1	77.00	1–40	—	—	—
Laing, J. R.	—	—	—	—	—	—	—
Lamb, A. J.	13	2	6.50	1–1	—	—	—
Lamb, T. M.	4770	171	27.89	6–49	7	—	—
Larkins, W.	554	16	34.62	3–34	—	—	—
Leadbeater, B.	5	1	5.00	1–1	—	—	—
Lee, P. G.	13009	531	24.49	8–53	26	6	2
Le Roux, G. S.	2523	119	21.20	7–40	7	1	—
L'Estrange, M. G.	—	—	—	—	—	—	—
Lever, J. K.	19804	831	23.83	8–127	34	2	1
Lilley, A. W.	—	—	—	—	—	—	—
Lister, J. W.	—	—	—	—	—	—	—
Littlewood, D. J.	—	—	—	—	—	—	—
Llewellyn, M. J.	615	23	26.73	4–35	—	—	—
Lloyd, B. J.	3558	81	43.92	4–49	—	—	—
Lloyd, C. H.	4103	114	35.99	4–48	—	—	—
Lloyd, D.	4706	160	29.41	7–38	2	1	—
Lloyd, T. A.	35	1	35.00	1–14	—	—	—
Long, A.	2	0	—	—	—	—	—
Love, J. D.	16	0	—	—	—	—	—
Lumb, R. G.	—	—	—	—	—	—	—
Lynch, M. A.	59	2	29.50	1–14	—	—	—
Lyon, J.	—	—	—	—	—	—	—
McEvoy, M. S. A.	4	0	—	1–0	—	—	—
McEwan, K. S.	87	2	43.50	1–0	—	—	—
McIntyre, J. M.	5492	233	23.57	6–84	6	1	—
Mack, A. J.	955	23	41.52	4–28	—	—	—

187

	Runs	Wkts	Avge	BB	5 Wl	10 Wm	100 WS
Mackintosh, K. S.	693	16	43.31	4-49	—	—	—
McLellan, A. J.	—	—	—	—	—	—	—
McPherson, T. I.	184	9	20.44	4-74	—	—	—
Malone, S. J.	101	2	50.50	1-28	—	—	—
Marie, G. V.	620	15	41.33	3-48	—	—	—
Marks, V. J.	4072	119	34.21	5-50	2	—	—
Marshall, M. D.	97	7	13.85	6-77	1	—	—
Marshall, R. P. T.	1927	49	39.32	4-37	—	—	—
Maynard, C. W.	—	—	—	—	—	—	—
Mellor, A. J.	305	9	33.88	5-52	1	—	—
Mendis, G. D.	9	0	—	—	—	—	—
Miller, G.	7491	326	22.97	7-54	17	5	—
Monteith, J. D.	773	50	15.46	7-38	4	1	—
Morrill, N. D.	251	4	62.75	2-55	—	—	—
Morris, A.	118	0	—	—	—	—	—
Moseley, H. R.	9704	402	24.13	6-34	10	—	—
Moulding, R. P.	—	—	—	—	—	—	—
Mubarak, A. M.	—	—	—	—	—	—	—
Murtagh, A. J.	489	6	81.50	2-46	—	—	—
Nash, M. A.	20102	790	25.44	9-56	38	3	—
Neale, P. A.	61	1	61.00	1-15	—	—	—
Needham, A.	441	9	49.00	3-25	—	—	—
Nicholas, M. C. J.	—	—	—	—	—	—	—
Nicholls, D.	23	2	11.50	1-0	—	—	—
O'Brien, B. A.	—	—	—	—	—	—	—
Old, C. M.	15281	698	21.89	7-20	26	1	—
Oldham, S.	2241	86	26.05	5-40	2	—	—
Olive, M.	—	—	—	—	—	—	—
Oliver, P. R.	1125	11	102.27	2-28	—	—	—
Ontong, R. C.	4286	138	31.05	7-60	4	—	—
Orders, J. O. D.	244	5	48.80	2-16	—	—	—
Ormrod, J. A.	1075	25	43.00	5-27	1	—	—
Parker, J. M.	496	11	45.09	3-26	—	—	—
Parker, P. W. G.	303	7	43.28	2-23	—	—	—
Parsons, G. J.	78	0	—	—	—	—	—
Partridge, M. D.	432	9	48.00	2-9	—	—	—
Patel, A. S.	55	2	27.50	2-55	—	—	—
Patel, D. N.	1468	43	34.13	5-22	1	—	—
Pathmanathan, G.	26	0	—	—	—	—	—
Payne, I. A.	325	3	108.33	2-41	—	—	—
Pearce, J. P.	157	4	39.25	3-26	—	—	—
Peck, I. G.	—	—	—	—	—	—	—
Perryman, S. P.	5827	213	27.35	7-49	11	2	—
Phillip, N.	5101	222	22.97	6-33	9	1	—
Phillipson, C. P.	4522	131	34.51	6-56	4	—	—
Pigott, A. C. S.	306	9	34.00	4-62	—	—	—
Pilling, H.	195	1	195.00	1-42	—	—	—
Pocock, N. E. J.	73	1	73.00	1-40	—	—	—
Pocock, P. I.	30586	1187	25.76	7-57	44	5	1

	Runs	Wkts	Avge	BB	5 Wl	10 Wm	100 WS
Pont, K. R.	1626	47	34.59	4–100	—	—	—
Popplewell, N. F. M.	876	9	97.33	2–64	—	—	—
Poulter, S. J.	—	—	—	—	—	—	—
Price, D. H.	174	2	87.00	1–22	—	—	—
Pridgeon, A. P.	5132	134	38.29	7–35	2	1	—
Pringle, D. R.	101	1	101.00	1–31	—	—	—
Procter, M. J.	21758	1132	19.22	9–71	53	10	2
Racionzer, T. B.	5	0	—	—	—	—	—
Radley, C. T.	24	2	12.00	1–7	—	—	—
Randall, D. W.	91	0	—	—	—	—	—
Ratcliffe, R. M.	4070	165	24.66	7–58	12	1	—
Reidy, B. W.	604	7	86.28	2–47	—	—	—
Reith, M. S.	20	0	—	—	—	—	—
Rhind, P. A.	247	3	82.33	1–73	—	—	—
Rice, C. E. B.	9478	398	23.81	7–62	10	1	—
Rice, J. M.	6180	195	31.69	7–48	2	—	—
Richards, B. A.	2879	77	37.38	7–63	1	—	—
Richards, C. J.	—	—	—	—	—	—	—
Richards, G.	2093	39	53.66	5–55	1	—	—
Richards, I. M.	176	7	25.14	4–57	—	—	—
Richards, I. V. A.	2357	59	39.94	3–15	—	—	—
Roberts, A. M. E.	10745	530	20.27	8–47	26	2	1
Robertson, F.	491	24	20.45	6–58	1	—	—
Robinson, A. L.	4927	196	25.13	6–61	7	—	—
Robinson, P. A.	448	14	32.00	3–33	—	—	—
Robinson, P. J.	8101	297	27.27	7–10	10	1	—
Robinson, R. T.	—	—	—	—	—	—	—
Rock, D. J.	0	0	—	—	—	—	—
Roebuck, P. M.	1735	38	45.65	6–50	1	—	—
Roope, G. R. J.	7979	212	37.63	5–14	4	—	—
Rose, B. C.	165	6	27.50	3–9	—	—	—
Ross, C. J.	658	17	38.70	4–34	—	—	—
Rouse, S. J.	7173	246	29.15	6–34	5	—	—
Rowe, C. J. C.	1930	49	39.38	6–46	3	1	—
Russell, P. E.	9773	329	29.70	7–46	5	—	—
Sadiq Mohammad	5538	181	30.59	5–29	5	—	—
Sarfraz Nawaz	16365	700	23.37	8–27	35	3	1
Savage, R. L.	3221	116	27.76	7–50	6	1	—
Saxelby, K.	123	1	123.00	1–32	—	—	—
Schepens, M.	13	0	—	—	—	—	—
Scott, C. J.	—	—	—	—	—	—	—
Selvey, M. W. W.	13023	526	24.75	7–20	26	4	1
Shackleton, J. H.	2242	49	45.75	4–38	—	—	—
Shantry, B. K.	167	3	55.66	2–63	—	—	—
Sharp, G.	2	0	—	—	—	—	—
Sharp, K.	22	0	—	—	—	—	—
Shepherd, D. R.	106	2	53.00	1–1	—	—	—
Shepherd, J. N.	22206	847	26.21	8–40	45	2	—
Short, J. F.	—	—	—	—	—	—	—
Shuttleworth, K.	13857	577	24.01	7–41	21	1	—
Sidebottom, A.	1444	45	32.08	4–47	—	—	—
Simmons, J.	14152	518	27.32	7–64	16	2	—

189

	Runs	Wkts	Avge	BB	5 Wl	10 Wm	100 WS
Slack, W. N.	—	—	—	—	—	—	—
Slocombe, P. A.	25	0	—	—	—	—	—
Smedley, M. J.	4	0	—	—	—	—	—
Smith, A. V.	—	—	—	—	—	—	—
Smith, D. M.	1105	21	52.61	3–40	—	—	—
Smith, K. B.	—	—	—	—	—	—	—
Smith, K. D.	3	0	—	—	—	—	—
Smith, M. J.	1844	57	32.35	4–13	—	—	—
Smith, N.	—	—	—	—	—	—	—
Southern, J. W.	6570	230	28.56	6–46	9	—	—
Spencer, J.	13197	507	26.02	6–19	18	1	—
Stead, B.	18318	653	28.05	8–44	24	2	—
Steele, A.	—	—	—	—	—	—	—
Steele, D. S.	6327	272	23.26	8–29	6	1	—
Steele, J. F.	8262	310	26.65	7–29	7	—	—
Stephenson, G. R.	39	0	—	—	—	—	—
Stevenson, G. B.	4305	155	27.77	8–65	5	1	—
Stevenson, K.	4703	154	30.53	7–68	6	—	—
Stewart, D. E. R.	72	0	—	—	—	—	—
Storey, S. J.	13175	496	26.56	8–22	11	2	7
Stovold, A. W.	23	1	23.00	1–0	—	—	—
Stuchbury, S.	60	2	30.00	2–39	—	—	—
Sturt, M. O. C.	—	—	—	—	—	—	—
Surridge, S. S.	—	—	—	—	—	—	—
Sutcliffe, R. J.	37	1	37.00	1–37	—	—	—
Swarbrook, F. W	13837	467	29.62	9–20	15	2	—
Swart, P. D.	6121	235	26.04	6–85	4	1	—
Tait, A.	0	0	—	—	—	—	—
Tavare, C. J.	48	1	48.00	1–20	—	—	—
Taylor, D. J. S.	14	0	—	—	—	—	—
Taylor, L. B.	1180	43	27.44	4–32	—	—	—
Taylor, M. N. S.	21009	794	26.45	7–23	23	—	—
Taylor, R. W.	3346	0	—	—	—	—	—
Terry, V. P.	—	—	—	—	—	—	—
Thomas, D. J.	1024	21	48.76	4–47	—	—	—
Thomas, G. P.	—	—	—	—	—	—	—
Thomson, G. B.	2552	85	30.02	5–31	2	—	—
Titmus, F. J.	62731	2812	22.30	9–52	168	26	16
Todd, P. A.	3	0	—	—	—	—	—
Tolchard, R. W.	20	1	20.00	1–4	—	—	—
Tomlins, K. P.	16	0	—	—	—	—	—
Tremlett, T. M.	265	9	29.44	2–25	—	—	—
Trim, G. E.	—	—	—	—	—	—	—
Troup, G. B.	2012	61	32.98	4–55	—	—	—
Tunnicliffe, C. J.	3566	117	30.47	4–22	—	—	—
Tunnicliffe, H. T.	903	20	45.15	3–48	—	—	—
Turner, D. R.	135	2	67.50	1–14	—	—	—
Turner, G. M.	189	5	37.80	3–18	—	—	—
Turner, S.	14740	580	25.41	6–26	19	—	—
Underwood, D. L.	33917	1734	19.55	9–28	111	32	8

	Rnns	Wkts	Avge	BB	5 Wl	10 Wm	100 WS
Waller, C. E.	8763	323	27.13	7–64	15	1	—
Walters, J.	596	17	35.05	3–70	—	—	—
Ward, A.	10495	460	22.81	7–42	15	4	—
Warner, C. J.	—	—	—	—	—	—	—
Watson, G. G.	2223	65	34.20	6–45	1	—	—
Watson, W. K.	2876	109	26.38	6–102	2	—	—
Watts, P. J.	8352	326	25.61	6–18	7	—	—
Wells, R. R. C.	—	—	—	—	—	—	—
Wessels, K. C.	79	3	26.33	1–4	—	—	—
White, R. A.	21053	682	30.86	7–41	27	3	—
Whitehouse, J.	374	5	74.80	2–55	—	—	—
Whiteley, J. P.	475	22	21.59	4–14	—	—	—
Wilcock, H. G.	3	0	—	—	—	—	—
Wilkins, A. H.	2667	93	28.67	5–58	3	—	—
Willey, P.	8871	323	27.46	7–37	13	2	—
Williams, R. G.	619	14	44.21	4–48	—	—	—
Williams, S.	—	—	—	—	—	—	—
Willis, R. G. D.	13331	572	23.30	8–32	25	1	—
Wilson, P. H. L.	355	11	32.27	4–56	—	—	—
Wincer, R. C.	680	19	35.78	4–42	—	—	—
Wood, B.	6704	243	27.58	7–52	8	—	—
Wookey, S. M.	1050	26	40.38	3–61	—	—	—
Woolmer, R. A.	9834	385	25.54	7–47	12	1	—
Wright, J. G.	—	—	—	—	—	—	—
Yardley, T. J.	18	0	—	—	—	—	—
Younis Ahmed	1084	27	40.14	4–10	—	—	—
Zaheer Abbas	641	20	32.05	5–15	1	—	—

The lowest total ever made in a Test match was 26 by New Zealand against England at Auckland in 1954–55. After there had been very little in it, in the first innings – New Zealand 200 and England 246, New Zealand were 6 for no wicket in their second innings, and 26 all out. Of these Bert Sutcliffe, the opening bat, scored 11. Frank Tyson took 2 for 10, Brian Statham 3 for 9, Bob Appleyard 4 for 7 and Johnny Wardle 1 for 0.

Colin Cowdrey has played in more Test matches than any other English player – 114. Two other Kent players are second and third – Godfrey Evans (91) and Alan Knott (89).

FIRST-CLASS CRICKET RECORDS

COMPLETE TO 30 SEPTEMBER 1978

Highest Innings Totals

1107	Victoria v New South Wales (Melbourne)	1926–27
1059	Victoria v Tasmania (Melbourne)	1922–23
951–7d	Sind v Baluchistan (Karachi)	1973–74
918	New South Wales v South Australia (Sydney)	1900–01
912–8d	Holkar v Mysore (Indore)	1945–46
910–6d	Railways v Dera Ismail Khan (Lahore)	1964–65
903–7d	England v Australia (Oval)	1938
887	Yorkshire v Warwickshire (Birmingham)	1896
849	England v West Indies (Kingston)	1929–30

NB.   There are 22 instances of a side making 800 or more in an innings, the last occasion being 951–7 declared by Sind as above.

Lowest Innings Totals

12†	Oxford University v MCC and Ground (Oxford)	1877
12	Northamptonshire v Gloucestershire (Gloucester)	1907
13	Wellington v Nelson (Nelson)	1862–63
13	Auckland v Canterbury (Auckland)	1877–78
13	Nottinghamshire v Yorkshire (Nottingham)	1901
15	MCC v Surrey (Lord's)	1839
15†	Victoria v MCC (Melbourne)	1903–04
15†	Northamptonshire v Yorkshire (Northampton)	1908
15	Hampshire v Warwickshire (Birmingham)	1922
16	MCC and Ground v Surrey (Lord's)	1872
16	Derbyshire v Nottinghamshire (Nottingham)	1879
16	Surrey v Nottinghamshire (Oval)	1880
16	Warwickshire v Kent (Tonbridge)	1913
16	Trinidad v Barbados (Bridgetown)	1941–42
16	Border v Natal (East London)	1959–60

†*Batted one man short*

NB.   There are 26 instances of a side making less than 20 in an innings, the last occasion being 16 and 18 by Border v Natal at East London in 1959–60. The total of 34 is the lowest by one side in a match.

Highest Aggregates in a Match

2376	(38)	Bombay v Maharashtra (Poona)	1948–49
2078	(40)	Bombay v Holkar (Bombay)	1944–45
1981	(35)	England v South Africa (Durban)	1938–39
1929	(39)	New South Wales v South Australia (Sydney)	1925–26
1911	(34)	New South Wales v Victoria (Sydney)	1908–09
1905	(40)	Otago v Wellington (Dunedin)	1923–24

In England the highest are:

1723	(34)	England v Australia (Leeds) 5 day match	1948
1601	(29)	England v Australia (Lord's) 4 day match	1930
1507	(28)	England v West Indies (Oval) 5 day match	1976
1502	(28)	MCC v New Zealanders (Lord's)	1927
1499	(31)	T. N. Pearce's XI v Australians (Scarborough)	1961

1496	(24)	England v Australia (Nottingham) 4 day match	1938
1494	(37)	England v Australia (Oval) 4 day match	1934
1492	(33)	Worcestershire v Oxford U (Worcester)	1904
1477	(32)	Hampshire v Oxford U (Southampton)	1913
1477	(33)	England v South Africa (Oval) 4 day match	1947
1475	(27)	Northamptonshire v Surrey (Northampton)	1920

Lowest Aggregates in a Match

105	(31)	MCC v Australia (Lord's)	1878
134	(30)	England v The B's (Lord's)	1831
147	(40)	Kent v Sussex (Sevenoaks)	1828
149	(30)	England v Kent (Lord's)	1858
151	(30)	Canterbury v Otago (Christchurch)	1866–67
153	(37)	MCC v Sussex (Lord's)	1843
153	(31)	Otago v Canterbury (Dunedin)	1896–97
156	(30)	Nelson v Wellington (Nelson)	1885–86
158	(22)	Surrey v Worcestershire (Oval)	1954

Wickets that fell are given in parentheses.

Tie Matches

Due to the change of law made in 1948 for tie matches, a tie is now a rarity. The law states that only if the match is played out and the scores are equal is the result a tie.

The most recent tied matches are as follows:

Yorkshire (351–4d & 113) v Leicestershire (328 & 136) at Huddersfield	1954
Sussex (172 & 120) v Hampshire (153 & 139) at Eastbourne	1955
Victoria (244 & 197) v New South Wales (281 & 160) at Melbourne (St Kilda)	1956–57

(The first tie in Sheffield Shield cricket)

T. N. Pearce's XI (313–7d & 258) v New Zealanders (268 & 303–8d) at Scarborough	1958
Essex (364–6d & 176–8d) v Gloucestershire (329 & 211) at Leyton	1959
Australia (505 & 232) v West Indies (453 & 284) at Brisbane	1960–61

(The first tie in Test cricket)

Bahawalpur (123 & 282) v Lahore B (127 & 278) at Bahawalpur	1961–62
Middlesex (327–5d & 123–9d) v Hampshire (277 & 173) at Portsmouth	1967
England XI (312–8d & 190–3d) v England Under-25 XI (320–9d & 182) at Scarborough	1968
Yorkshire (106–9d & 207) v Middlesex (102 & 211) at Bradford)	1973
Sussex (245 & 173–5d) v Essex (200–8d & 218) at Hove	1974
South Australia (431 & 171–7d) v Queensland (340–8d & 262) at Adelaide	1976–77
England XI (296–6d & 104) v Central Districts (198 & 202) at New Plymouth	1977–78

Highest Individual Scores

499	Hanif Mohammad, Karachi v Bahawalpur (Karachi)	1958–59
452*	D. G. Bradman, New South Wales v Queensland (Sydney)	1929–30
443*	B. B. Nimbalkar, Maharashtra v Kathiawar (Poona)	1948–49
437	W. H. Ponsford, Victoria v Queensland (Melbourne)	1927–28
429	W. H. Ponsford, Victoria v Tasmania (Melbourne)	1922–23
428	Aftab Baloch, Sind v Baluchistan (Karachi)	1973–74
424	A. C. MacLaren, Lancashire v Somerset (Taunton)	1895
385	B. Sutcliffe, Otago v Canterbury (Christchurch)	1952–53
383	C. W. Gregory, New South Wales v Queensland (Brisbane)	1906–07
369	D. G. Bradman, South Australia v Tasmania (Adelaide)	1935–36
365*	C. Hill, South Australia v New South Wales (Adelaide)	1900–01
365*	G. S. Sobers, West Indies v Pakistan (Kingston)	1957–58
364	L. Hutton, England v Australia (Oval)	1938
359*	V. M. Merchant, Bombay v Maharashtra (Bombay)	1943–44
359	R. B. Simpson, New South Wales v Queensland (Brisbane)	1963–64
357*	R. Abel, Surrey v Somerset (Oval)	1899
357	D. G. Bradman, South Australia v Victoria (Melbourne)	1935–36
356	B. A. Richards, South Australia v Western Australia (Perth)	1970–71
355	B. Sutcliffe, Otago v Auckland (Dunedin)	1949–50
352	W. H. Ponsford, Victoria v New South Wales (Melbourne)	1926–27
350	Rashid Israr, National Bank v Habib Bank (Lahore)	1976–77

NB. There are 91 instances of a batsman scoring 300 or more in an innings, the last occasion being 350 by Rashid Israr as above.

Most Centuries in a Season

18	D. C. S. Compton	1947
16	J. B. Hobbs	1925
15	W. R. Hammond	1938
14	H. Sutcliffe	1932

Most Centuries in an Innings

6	for Holkar v Mysore (Indore)	1945–46
5	for New South Wales v South Australia (Sydney)	1900–01
5	for Australia v West Indies (Kingston)	1954–55

Most Centuries in Successive Innings

6	C. B. Fry	1901
6	D. G. Bradman	1938–39
6	M. J. Procter	1970–71
5	E. D. Weekes	1955–56

NB. The feat of scoring 4 centuries in successive innings has been achieved on 30 occasions.

Most Centuries in Succession in Test Matches

5	E. D. Weekes, West Indies	1947–48 and 1948–49
4	J. H. W. Fingleton, Australia	1935–36 and 1936–37
4	A. Melville, South Africa	1938–39 and 1947

Two Double Centuries in a Match

A. E. Fagg, 244 and 202* for Kent v Essex (Colchester)	1938

A Double Century and a Century in a Match

C. B. Fry, 125 and 229, Sussex v Surrey (Hove)	1900
W. W. Armstrong, 157* and 245, Victoria v South Australia (Melbourne)	1920–21
H. T. W. Hardinge, 207 and 102* for Kent v Surrey (Blackheath)	1921
C. P. Mead, 113 and 224, Hampshire v Sussex (Horsham)	1921
K. S. Duleepsinhji, 115 and 246, Sussex v Kent (Hastings)	1929
D. G. Bradman, 124 and 225, Woodfull's XI v Ryder's XI (Sydney)	1929–30
B. Sutcliffe, 243 and 100* New Zealanders v Essex (Southend)	1949
M. R. Hallam, 210* and 157, Leicestershire v Glamorgan (Leicester)	1959
M. R. Hallam, 203* and 143* Leicestershire v Sussex (Worthing)	1961
Hanumant Singh, 109 and 213*, Rajasthan v Bombay (Bombay)	1966–67
Salahuddin, 256 and 102*, Karachi v East Pakistan (Karachi)	1968–69
K. D. Walters, 242 and 103, Australia v West Indies (Sydney)	1968–69
S. M. Gavaskar, 124 and 220, India v West Indies (P. of Spain)	1970–71
L. G. Rowe, 214 and 100* West Indies v New Zealand (Kingston)	1971–72
G. S. Chappell, 247* and 133, Australia v New Zealand (Wellington)	1973–74
L. Baichan, 216* and 102, Berbice v Demerara (Georgetown)	1973–74
Zaheer Abbas, 216* and 156*, Gloucestershire v Surrey (Oval)	1976
Zaheer Abbas, 230* and 104*, Gloucestershire v Kent (Canterbury)	1976
Zaheer Abbas, 205* and 108*, Gloucestshire v Sussex (Cheltenham)	1977

Two Centuries in a Match on Most Occasions

7   W. R. Hammond   6   J. B. Hobbs   5   C. B. Fry

NB. 12 Batsmen have achieved the feat on four occasions, 21 batsmen on three occasions and 39 batsmen on two occasions.

Most Centuries

J. B. Hobbs, 197 (175 in England); E. H. Hendren 170 (151); W. R. Hammond, 167 (134); C. P. Mead 153 (145); H. Sutcliffe, 149 (135); F. E. Woolley, 145 (135); L. Hutton, 129 (105); W. G. Grace, 124 (123); D. C. S. Compton, 123 (92); T. W. Graveney, 122 (91); D. G. Bradman, 117 (41); G. Boycott 109 (87); M. C. Cowdrey, 107 (79); A. Sandham, 107 (87); T. W. Hayward, 104 (100); J. H. Edrich, 103 (90); L. E. G. Ames, 102 (89); E. Tyldesley, 102 (94).

Highest Individual Batting Aggregate in a Season

Runs		Season	M	Innings	NO	HS	Avge	100s
3,816	D. C. S. Compton	1947	30	50	8	246	90.85	18
3,539	W. J. Edrich	1947	30	52	8	267*	80.43	12

NB. The feat of scoring 3,000 runs in a season has been achieved on 28 occasions, the last instance being by W. E. Alley (3,019 runs, av. 59.96) in 1961.

Partnerships for First Wicket

561	Waheed Mirza and Mansoor Akhtar, Karachi Whites v Quetta (Karachi)	1976–77
555	H. Sutcliffe and P. Holmes, Yorkshire v Essex (Leyton)	1932
554	J. T. Brown and J. Tunnicliffe, Yorkshire v Derbyshire (Chesterfield)	1898
490	E. H. Bowley and John Langridge, Sussex v Middlesex (Hove)	1933

456	W. H. Ponsford and E. R. Mayne, Victoria v Queensland (Melbourne)	1923–24
451*	S. Desai and R. Binny, Karnataka v Kerala (Chikmala-galor)	1977–78
428	J. B. Hobbs and A. Sandham, Surrey v Oxford U (Oval)	1926
424	J. F. W. Nicholson and I. J. Siedle, Natal v Orange Free State (Bloemfontein)	1926–27
413	V. M. H. Mankad and P. Roy, India v New Zealand (Madras)	1955–56
405	C. P. S. Chauban and M. Gupte, Maharashtra v Vidarbha (Poona)	1972–73

Partnerships for Second Wicket

465*	J. A. Jameson and R. B. Kanhai, Warwickshire v Gloucestershire (Birmingham)	1974
455	K. V. Bhandarkar and B. B. Nimbalkar, Maharashtra v Kathiawar (Poona)	1948–49
451	D. G. Bradman and W. H. Ponsford, Australia v England (Oval)	1934
446	C. C. Hunte and G. S. Sobers, West Indies v Pakistan (Kingston)	1957–58
429*	J. G. Dewes and G. H. G. Doggart, Cambridge U v Essex (Cambridge)	1949
426	Arshad Pervez and Mohsin Khan, Habib Bank v Income Tax Department (Lahore)	1977–78
398	W. Gunn and A. Shrewsbury, Nottinghamshire v Sussex (Nottingham)	1890

Partnerships for Third Wicket

456	Aslam Ali and Khalid Irtiza, United Bank v Multan (Karachi)	1975–76
445	P. E. Whitelaw and W. N. Carson, Auckland v Otago (Dunedin)	1936–37
434	J. B. Stollmeyer and G. E. Gomez, Trinidad v British Guiana (Port of Spain)	1946–47
424*	W. J. Edrich and D. C. S. Compton, Middlesex v Somerset (Lord's)	1948
410	R. S. Modi and L. Amarnath, India v Rest (Calcutta)	1946–47
399	R. T. Simpson and D. C. S. Compton, MCC v NE Trans-vaal (Benoni)	1948–49

Partnerships for Fourth Wicket

577	Gul Mahomed and V. S. Hazare, Baroda v Holkar (Baroda)	1946–47
574*	C. L. Walcott and F. M. M. Worrell, Barbados v Trinidad (Port of Spain)	1945–46
502*	F. M. M. Worrell and J. D. C. Goddard, Barbados v Trinidad (Bridgetown)	1943–44
448	R. Abel and T. W. Hayward, Surrey v Yorkshire (Oval)	1899
424	I. S. Lee and S. O. Quin, Victoria v Tasmania (Melbourne)	1933–34
411	P. B. H. May and M. C. Cowdrey, England v West Indies (Birmingham)	1957
410	G. Abraham and B. Pandit, Kerala v Andhra (Pulghat)	1959–60

| 402 | W. Watson and T. W. Graveney, MCC v British Guiana (Georgetown) | 1953–54 |
| 402 | R. B. Kanhai and K. Ibadulla, Warwickshire v Nottinghamshire (Nottingham) | 1968 |

Partnerships for Fifth Wicket

405	D. G. Bradman and S. G. Barnes, Australia v England (Sydney)	1946–47
397	W. Bardsley and C. Kellaway, New South Wales v South Australia (Sydney)	1920–21
393	E. G. Arnold and W. B. Burns, Worcestershire v Warwickshire (Birmingham)	1909
360	V. M. Merchant and M. N. Raiji, Bombay v Hyderabad (Bombay)	1947–48
347	D. Brookes and D. Barrick, Northamptonshire v Essex (Northampton)	1952

Partnerships for Sixth Wicket

487*	G. A. Headley and C. C. Passailaigue, Jamaica v Lord Tennyson's XI (Kingston)	1931–32
428	W. W. Armstrong and M. A. Noble, Australians v Sussex (Hove)	1902
411	R. M. Poore and E. G. Wynyard, Hampshire v Somerset (Taunton)	1899
376	R. Subba Row and A. Lightfoot, Northamptonshire v Surrey (Oval)	1958
371	V. M. Merchant and R. S. Modi, Bombay v Maharashtra (Bombay)	1943–44

Partnerships for Seventh Wicket

347	D. Atkinson and C. C. Depeiza, West Indies v Australia (Bridgetown)	1954–55
344	K. S. Ranjitsinjhi and W. Newham, Sussex v Essex (Leyton)	1902
340	K. J. Key and H. Philipson, Oxford U v Middlesex (Chiswick Park)	1887
336	F. C. W. Newman and C. R. Maxwell, Cahn's XI v Leicestershire (Nottingham)	1935
335	C. W. Andrews and E. C. Bensted, Queensland v New South Wales (Sydney)	1934–35

Partnerships for Eighth Wicket

433	V. T. Trumper and A. Sims, Australians v Canterbury (Christchurch)	1913–14
292	R. Peel and Lord Hawke, Yorkshire v Warwickshire (Birmingham)	1896
270	V. T. Trumper and E. P. Barbour, New South Wales v Victoria (Sydney)	1912–13
263	D. R. Wilcox and R. M. Taylor, Essex v Warwickshire (Southend)	1946
255	E. A. V. Williams and E. A. Martindale, Barbados v Trinidad (Bridgetown)	1935–36

Partnerships for Ninth Wicket

283	A. R. Warren and J. Chapman, Derbyshire v Warwickshire (Blackwell)	1910
251	J. W. H. T. Douglas and S. N. Hare, Essex v Derbyshire (Leyton)	1921
245	V. S. Hazare and N. D. Nagarwalla, Maharashtra v Baroda (Poona)	1939–40
239	H. B. Cave and I. B. Leggat, Central Districts v Otago (Dunedin)	1952–53
232	C. Hill and E. Walkley, South Australia v New South Wales (Adelaide)	1900–01

Partnerships for Tenth Wicket

307	A. F. Kippax and J. E. H. Hooker, New South Wales v Victoria (Melbourne)	1928–29
249	C. T. Sarwate and S. N. Bannerjee, Indians v Surrey (Oval)	1946
235	F. E. Woolley and A. Fielder, Kent v Worcestershire (Stourbridge)	1909
230	R. W. Nicholls and W. Roche, Middlesex v Kent (Lord's)	1899
228	R. Illingworth and K. Higgs, Leicestershire v Northamptonshire (Leicester)	1977
218	F. H. Vigar and T. P. B. Smith, Essex v Derbyshire (Chesterfield)	1947

Most Wickets in a Season

W		Season	M	O	M	R	Avge
304	A. P. Freeman	1928	37	1,976.1	432	5,489	18.05
298	A. P. Freeman	1933	33	2,039	651	4,549	15.26

NB. The feat of taking 250 wickets in a season has been achieved on 12 occasions, the last instance being by A. P. Freeman in 1933 as above. 200 or more wickets in a season have been taken on 59 occasions, the last instance being by G. A. R. Lock (212 wkts, av 12.02) in 1957.

The most wickets taken in a season since the reduction of County Championship matches in 1969 are as follows:

W		Season	M	O	M	R	Avge
131	L. R. Gibbs	1971	23	1024.1	295	2475	18.89
119	A. M. E. Roberts	1974	21	727.4	198	1621	13.62
112	P. G. Lee	1975	21	799.5	199	2067	18.45

NB. 100 wickets in a season have been taken on 25 occasions since 1969

All Ten Wickets in an Innings

The feat has been achieved on 69 occasions.
On three occasions: A. P. Freeman, 1929, 1930 and 1931.
On two occasions: J. C. Laker, 1956, H. Verity, 1931 and 1932, V. E. Walker 1859 and 1865.
Instances since the war:
W. E. Hollies, Warwickshire v Nottinghamshire (Birmingham) 1946; J. M. Sims of Middlesex playing for East v West (Kingston) 1948; J. K. Graveney, Gloucestershire v Derbyshire (Chesterfield) 1949; T. E. Bailey, Essex v Lancashire (Clacton) 1949; R. Berry Lancashire v Worcestershire (Blackpool) 1953; S. P. Gupte, Bombay v Pakistan Services (Bombay), 1954–55; J. C. Laker, Surrey v Australians (Oval) 1956; J. C. Laker, England v Australia (Manchester) 1956; G. A. R. Lock, Surrey v Kent,

(Blackheath) 1956; K. Smales, Nottinghamshire v Gloucestershire (Stroud) 1956; P. Chatterjee, Bengal v Assam (Jorhat) 1956–57; J. D. Bannister, Warwickshire v Combined Services (Birmingham) 1959; A. J. G. Pearson, Cambridge U v Leicestershire (Loughborough) 1961; N. I. Thomson, Sussex v Warwickshire (Worthing) 1964; P. Allan, Queensland v Victoria (Melbourne) 1965–66; I. Brayshaw, Western Australia v Victoria (Perth) 1967–68; Shahid Mahmood, Karachi Whites v Khairpur (Karachi) 1969–70.

Nineteen Wickets in a Match

J. C. Laker 19–90 (9–37 and 10–53), England v Australia (Manchester) 1956.

Eighteen Wickets in a Match

H. A. Arkwright 18–96 (9–43 and 9–53), MCC v Gentlemen of Kent (Canterbury) 1861, (twelve-a-side match).

Seventeen Wickets in a Match

The feat has been achieved on 18 occasions. Instances between the two wars were: A. P. Freeman (for 67 runs), Kent v Sussex (Hove) 1922; F. C. L. Matthews (89 runs), Nottinghamshire v Northamptonshire (Nottingham) 1923; C. W. L. Parker (56 runs) Gloucestershire v Essex (Gloucester) 1925; G. R. Cox (106 runs), Sussex v Warwickshire (Horsham) 1926; A. P. Freeman (92 runs), Kent v Warwickshire (Folkestone) 1932; H. Verity (91 runs), Yorkshire v Essex (Leyton) 1933; J. C. Clay (212 runs), Glamorgan v Worcestershire (Swansea) 1937; T. W. Goddard (106 runs), Gloucestershire v Kent (Bristol) 1939. There has been no instance since the last war.

Most Hat-tricks in a Career

7 D. V. P. Wright.
6 T. W. Goddard, C. W. L. Parker.
5 S. Haigh, V. W. C. Jupp, A. E. G. Rhodes, F. A. Tarrant.

  NB. *Eight bowlers have achieved the feat on our occasions and 25 bowlers on three occasions.*

The 'Double' Event

3,000 and 100 wickets: J. H. Parks, 1937.
2,000 runs and 200 wickets: G. H. Hirst, 1906.
2,000 runs and 100 wickets: F. E. Woolley (4), J. W. Hearne (3), G. H. Hirst (2), W. Rhodes (2), T. E. Bailey, E. Davies, W. G. Grace, G. L. Jessop, V. W. C. Jupp, James Langridge, F. A. Tarrant, C. L. Townsend, L. F. Townsend.
1,000 runs and 200 wickets: M. W. Tate (3), A. E. Trott (2), A. S. Kennedy.
Most 'Doubles': W. Rhodes (16), G. H. Hirst (14), V. W. C. Jupp (10).
'Double' in first season: D. B. Close, 1949. At the age of 18, Close is the youngest player ever to perform this feat.
The feat of scoring 1,000 runs and taking 100 wickets has been achieved on 302 occasions, the last instance being F. J. Titmus in 1967.

FIELDING

Most catches in a season:	78 W. R. Hammond	1928
	77 M. J. Stewart	1957
Most catches in a match:	10 W. R. Hammond, Gloucestershire v Surrey (Cheltenham)	1928
Most catches in an innings:	7 M. J. Stewart, Surrey v Northamptonshire (Northampton)	1957
	7 A. S. Brown, Gloucestershire v Nottinghamshire (Nottingham)	1966

WICKET-KEEPING
Most Dismissals in a Season

127 (79 ct, 48 st), L. E. G. Ames   1929

NB. The feat of making 100 dismissals in a season has been achieved on 12 occasions, the last instance being by R. Booth (100 dismissals—91 ct 9 st) in 1964.

Most dismissals in a match:	12 E. Pooley (8 ct 4 st) Surrey v Sussex (Oval)	1868
	12 D. Tallon (9 ct 3 st), Queensland v New South Wales (Sydney)	1938–39
	12 H. B. Taber (9 ct 3 st), New South Wales v South Australia (Adelaide)	1968–69
Most catches in a match:	11 A. Long, Surrey v Sussex (Hove)	1964
	11 R. W. Marsh, Western Australia v Victoria (Perth)	1975–76
Most dismissals in an innings:	8 A. T. W. Grout (8 ct) Queensland v W. Australia (Brisbane)	1959–60

There have been 16 hat-tricks in Test matches, the most remarkable performance of all being that of T. J. Matthews who did the hat-trick in each innings on the second afternoon of the match, for Australia against South Africa at Old Trafford in the Triangular Tournament in 1912. They were the only 3 wickets that he took in each innings, batsmen 9, 10, and 11 in the first innings, and 1, 8, and 11 in the second.

The only case, until last season, of four wickets in five balls in a Test match by an England bowler is M. J. C. Allom, now President of Surrey, against New Zealand, in his first Test match in the winter of 1929–30 at Christchurch. Chris Old repeated the performance for England against Pakistan at Edgbaston.

TEST CRICKET RECORDS

COMPLETE TO 30 SEPTEMBER 1978

Matches between England and Rest of the World 1970 and between
Australia and Rest of the World 1971–72 are excluded

HIGHEST INNINGS TOTALS

903—7d	England v Australia (Oval)	1938
849	England v West Indies (Kingston)	1929–30
790—3d	West Indies v Pakistan (Kingston)	1957–58
758—8d	Australia v West Indies (Kingston)	1954–55
729—6d	Australia v England (Lord's)	1930
701	Australia v England (Oval)	1934
695	Australia v England (Oval)	1930
687—8d	West Indies v England (Oval)	1976
681—8d	West Indies v England (Port of Spain)	1953–54
674	Australia v India (Adelaide)	1947–48
668	Australia v West Indies (Bridgetown)	1954–55
659—8d	Australia v England (Sydney)	1946–47
658—8d	England v Australia (Nottingham)	1938
657—8d	Pakistan v West Indies (Bridgetown)	1957–58
656—8d	Australia v England (Manchester)	1964
654—5	England v South Africa (Durban)	1938–39
652—8d	West Indies v England (Lord's)	1973
650—6d	Australia v West Indies (Bridgetown)	1964–65

The highest innings for the countries not mentioned above are:

622—9d	South Africa v Australia (Durban)	1969–70
551—9d	New Zealand v England (Lord's)	1973
539—9d	India v Pakistan (Madras)	1960–61

*NB. There are 41 instances of a side making 600 or more in an innings
in a Test Match.*

LOWEST INNINGS TOTALS

26	New Zealand v England (Auckland)	1954–55
30	South Africa v England (Port Elizabeth)	1895–96
30	South Africa v England (Birmingham)	1924
35	South Africa v England (Cape Town)	1898–99
36	Australia v England (Birmingham)	1902
36	South Africa v Australia (Melbourne)	1931–32
42	Australia v England (Sydney)	1887–88
42	New Zealand v Australia (Wellington)	1945–46
42†	India v England (Lord's)	1974
43	South Africa v England (Cape Town)	1888–89
44	Australia v England (Oval)	1896
45	England v Australia (Sydney)	1886–87
45	South Africa v Australia (Melbourne)	1931–32
47	South Africa v England (Cape Town)	1888–89
47	New Zealand v England (Lord's)	1958

†Batted one man short.

The lowest innings for the countries not mentioned above are:

76	West Indies v Pakistan (Dacca)	1958–59
87	Pakistan v England (Lord's)	1954

HIGHEST INDIVIDUAL INNINGS

365*	G. S. Sobers: West Indies v Pakistan (Kingston)	1957–58
364	L. Hutton: England v Australia (Oval)	1938
337	Hanif Mohammad: Pakistan v West Indies (Bridgetown)	1957–58
336*	W. R. Hammond: England v New Zealand (Auckland)	1932–33
334	D. G. Bradman: Australia v England (Leeds)	1930
325	A. Sandham: England v West Indies (Kingston)	1929–30
311	R. B. Simpson: Australia v England (Manchester)	1964
310*	J. H. Edrich: England v New Zealand (Leeds)	1965
307	R. M. Cowper: Australia v England (Melbourne)	1965–66
304	D. G. Bradman: Australia v England (Leeds)	1934
302	L. G. Rowe: West Indies v England (Bridgetown)	1973–74
299*	D. G. Bradman: Australia v South Africa (Adelaide)	1931–32
291	I. V. A. Richards: West Indies v England (Oval)	1976
287	R. E. Foster: England v Australia (Sydney)	1903–04
285*	P. B. H. May: England v West Indies (Birmingham)	1957
278	D. C. S. Compton: England v Pakistan (Nottingham)	1954
274	R. G. Pollock: South Africa v Australia (Durban)	1969–70
274	Zaheer Abbas: Pakistan v England (Birmingham)	1971
270*	G. A. Headley: West Indies v England (Kingston)	1934–35
270	D. G. Bradman: Australia v England (Melbourne)	1936–37
266	W. H. Ponsford: Australia v England (Oval)	1934
262*	D. L. Amiss: England v West Indies (Kingston)	1973–74
261	F. M. M. Worrell: West Indies v England (Nottingham)	1950
260	C. C. Hunte: West Indies v Pakistan (Kingston)	1957–58
259	G. M. Turner: New Zealand v West Indies (Georgetown)	1971–72
258	T. W. Graveney: England v West Indies (Nottingham)	1957
258	S. M. Nurse: West Indies v New Zealand (Christchurch)	1968–69
256	R. B. Kanhai: West Indies v India (Calcutta)	1958–59
256	K. F. Barrington: England v Australia (Manchester)	1964
255*	D. J. McGlew: South Africa v New Zealand (Wellington)	1952–53
254	D. G. Bradman: Australia v England (Lord's)	1930
251	W. R. Hammond: England v Australia (Sydney)	1928–29
250	K. D. Walters: Australia v New Zealand (Christchurch)	1976–77

The highest individual innings for India is:

231	V. M. H. Mankad: India v New Zealand (Madras)	1955–56

NB. There are 111 instances of a double-century being scored in a Test Match.

HIGHEST RUN AGGREGATES IN A TEST RUBBER

R		Season	T	I	NO	HS	Avge	100s	50s
974	D. G. Bradman (A v E)	1930	5	7	0	334	139.14	4	—
905	W. R. Hammond (E v A)	1928–29	5	9	1	251	113.12	4	—
834	R. N. Harvey (A v SA)	1952–53	5	9	0	205	92.66	4	3
829	I. V. A. Richards (WI v E)	1976	4	7	0	291	118.42	3	2
827	C. L. Walcott (WI v A)	1954–55	5	10	0	155	82.70	5	2
824	G. S. Sobers (WI v P)	1957–58	5	8	2	365*	137.33	3	3
810	D. G. Bradman (A v E)	1936–37	5	9	0	270	90.00	3	1
806	D. G. Bradman (A v SA)	1931–32	5	5	1	299*	201.50	4	—
779	E. D. Weekes (WI v I)	1948–49	5	7	0	194	111.28	4	2
774	S. M. Gavaskar (I v WI)	1970–71	4	8	3	220	154.80	4	3
758	D. G. Bradman (A v E)	1934	5	8	0	304	94.75	2	1
753	D. C. S. Compton (E v SA)	1947	5	8	0	208	94.12	4	2

202

RECORD WICKET PARTNERSHIPS—ALL TEST CRICKET

1st	413	V. M. H. Mankad & P. Roy: I v NZ (Madras)	1955–56
2nd	451	W. H. Ponsford & D. G. Bradman: A v E (Oval)	1934
3rd	370	W. J. Edrich & D. C. S. Compton: E v SA (Lord's)	1947
4th	411	P. B. H. May & M. C. Cowdrey: E v WI (Birm'ham)	1957
5th	405	S. G. Barnes & D. G. Bradman: A v E (Sydney)	1946–47
6th	346	J. H. W. Fingleton & D. G. Bradman: A v E (Melbrne)	1936–37
7th	347	D. Atkinson & C. C. Depeiza: WI v A (Bridgetown)	1954–55
8th	246	L. E. G. Ames & G. O. Allen: E v NZ (Lord's)	1931
9th	190	Asif Iqbal & Intikhab Alam: P v E (Oval)	1967
10th	151	B. F. Hastings & R. O. Collinge: NZ v P (Auckland)	1972–73

WICKET PARTNERSHIPS OF OVER 300

451	2nd W. H. Ponsford & D. G. Bradman: A v E (Oval)	1934
446	2nd C. C. Hunte & G. S. Sobers: WI v P (Kingston)	1957–58
413	1st V. M. H. Mankad & P. Roy: I v NZ (Madras)	1955–56
411	4th P. B. H. May & M. C. Cowdrey: E v WI (Birm'ham)	1957
405	5th S. G. Barnes & D. G. Bradman: A v E (Sydney)	1946–47
399	4th G. S. Sobers & F. M. M. Worrell: WI v E (Bridgetown)	1959–60
388	4th W. H. Ponsford & D. G. Bradman: A v E (Leeds)	1934
387	1st G. M. Turner & T. W. Jarvis: NZ v WI (Georgetown)	1971–72
382	2nd L. Hutton & M. Leyland: E v A (Oval)	1938
382	1st W. M. Lawry & R. B. Simpson: A v WI (Bridgetown)	1964–65
370	3rd W. J. Edrich & D. C. S. Compton: E v SA (Lord's)	1947
369	2nd J. H. Edrich and K. F. Barrington: E v NZ (Leeds)	1965
359	1st L. Hutton & C. Washbrook: E v SA (Johannesburg)	1948–49
350	4th Mushtaq Mohammad & Asif Iqbal: P v NZ (Dunedin)	1972–73
347	7th D. Atkinson & C. C. Depeiza: WI v A (Bridgetown)	1954–55
346	6th J. H. W. Fingleton & D. G. Bradman: A v E (Melbourne)	1936–37
344*	2nd S. M. Gavaskar & D. B. Vengsarkar I v WI (Calcutta)	1978–79
341	3rd E. J. Barlow & R. G. Pollock: SA v A (Adelaide)	1963–64
338	3rd E. D. Weekes & F. M. M. Worrell: WI v E.P. of Spain)	1953–54
336	4th W. M. Lawry & K. D. Walters: A v WI (Sydney)	1968–69
323	1st J. B. Hobbs & W. Rhodes: E v A (Melbourne)	1911–12
319	3rd A. Melville & A. D. Nourse SA v E (Nottingham)	1947
308	7th Waqar Hasan & Imtiaz Ahmed: P v NZ (Lahore)	1955–56
303	3rd I. V. A. Richards & A. I. Kallicharran, WI v E (Nottingham)	1976
301	2nd A. R. Morris & D. G. Bradman: A v E (Leeds)	1948

HAT-TRICKS

F. R. Spofforth	Australia v England (Melbourne)	1878–79
W. Bates	England v Australia (Melbourne)	1882–83
J. Briggs	England v Australia (Sydney)	1891–92
G. A. Lohmann	England v South Africa (Port Elizabeth)	1895–96
J. T. Hearne	England v Australia (Leeds)	1899
H. Trumble	Australia v England (Melbourne)	1901–02
H. Trumble	Australia v England (Melbourne)	1903–04
T. J. Matthews (2)†	Australia v South Africa (Manchester)	1912
M. J. C. Allom‡	England v New Zealand (Christchurch)	1929–30
T. W. Goddard	England v South Africa (Johannesburg)	1938–39
P. J. Loader	England v West Indies (Leeds)	1957
L. F. Kline	Australia v South Africa (Cape Town)	1957–58
W. W. Hall	West Indies v Pakistan (Lahore)	1958–59

G. M. Griffin	South Africa v England (Lord's)	1960
L. R. Gibbs	West Indies v Australia (Adelaide)	1960–61
P. J. Petherick	New Zealand v Pakistan (Lahore)	1976–77

† *Matthews achieved the hat-trick in each innings.*
‡ *Allom took four wickets with five consecutive balls.*

NINE OR TEN WICKETS IN AN INNINGS

10—53	J. C. Laker: England v Australia (Manchester)	1956
9—28	G. A. Lohmann: England v South Africa (Johannesb'g)	1895–96
9—37	J. C. Laker: England v Australia (Manchester)	1956
9—69	J. M. Patel: India v Australia (Kanpur)	1959–60
9—95	J. M. Noreiga: West Indies v India (Port of Spain)	1970–71
9—102	S. P. Gupte: India v West Indies (Kanpur)	1958–59
9—103	S. F. Barnes: England v South Africa (Johannesburg)	1913–14
9—113	H. J. Tayfield: South Africa v England (Johannesburg)	1956–57
9—121	A. A. Mailey: Australia v England (Melbourne)	1920–21

NB. There are 35 instances of a bowler taking 8 wickets in an innings in a Test Match.

FIFTEEN OR MORE WICKETS IN A MATCH

19—90	J. C. Laker: England v Australia (Manchester)	1956
17—159	S. F. Barnes: England v South Africa (Johannesburg)	1913–14
16—137	R. A. L. Massie: Australia v England (Lord's)	1972
15—28	J. Briggs: England v South Africa (Cape Town)	1888–89
15—45	G. A. Lohmann: England v South Africa (Pt. Elizabeth)	1895–96
15—99	C. Blythe: England v South Africa (Leeds)	1907
15—104	H. Verity: England v Australia (Lord's)	1934
15—124	W. Rhodes: England v Australia (Melbourne)	1903–04

NB There are 7 instances of a bowler taking 14 wickets in a Test Match.

HIGHEST WICKET AGGREGATES IN A TEST RUBBER

W		Season	Tests	Balls	Mdns	Runs	Avge	5 wI	10 M
49	S. F. Barnes (E v SA)	1913–14	4	1356	56	536	10.93	7	3
46	J. C. Laker (E v A)	1956	5	1703	127	442	9.60	4	2
44	C. V. Grimmett (A v SA)	1935–36	5	2077	140	642	14.59	5	3
39	A. V. Bedser (E v A)	1953	5	1591	48	682	17.48	5	1
38	M. W. Tate (E v A)	1924–25	5	2528	62	881	23.18	5	1
37	W. J. Whitty (A v SA)	1910–11	5	1395	55	632	17.08	2	—
37	H. J. Tayfield (SA v E)	1956–57	5	2280	105	636	17.18	4	1
36	A. E. E. Vogler (SA v E)	1909–10	5	1349	33	783	21.75	4	1
36	A. A. Mailey (A v E)	1920–21	5	1463	27	946	26.27	4	2
35	G. A. Lohmann (E v SA)	1895–96	3	520	38	203	5.80	4	2
35	B. S. Chandrasekhar (I v E)	1972–73	5	1747	83	662	18.91	4	—

MOST WICKET-KEEPING DISMISSALS IN AN INNINGS

6 (6ct)	A. T. W. Grout, Australia v South Africa (Johannesburg)	1957–58
6 (6ct)	D. Lindsay, South Africa v Australia (Johannesburg)	1966–67
6 (6ct)	J. T. Murray, England v India (Lord's)	1967
6 (5ct 1 st)	S. M. H. Kirmani, India v New Zealand (Christchurch)	1975–76

MOST WICKET KEEPING DISMISSALS IN A MATCH

| 9 (8ct 1 st) | G. R. A. Langley, Australia v England (Lord's) | 1956 |

MOST WICKET-KEEPING DISMISSALS IN A SERIES

26 (23ct, 3st) J. H. B. Waite, South Africa v New Zealand — 1961–62
26 (26ct) R. W. Marsh, Australia v West Indies — 1975–76
24 (22ct, 2st) D. L. Murray, West Indies v England — 1963
24 (24ct) D. Lindsay, South Africa v Australia — 1966–67
24 (21ct, 3st) A. P. E. Knott, England v Australia — 1970–71

HIGHEST WICKET-KEEPING DISMISSAL AGGREGATES

Total		Tests	Ct	St
252	A. P. E. Knott (E)	89	233	19
219	T. G. Evans (E)	91	173	46
198	R. W. Marsh (A)	52	190	8
187	A. T. W. Grout (A)	51	163	24
158	D. L. Murray (WI)	51	150	8
141	J. H. B. Waite (SA)	50	124	17
130	W. A. Oldfield (A)	54	78	52
114	J. M. Parks (E)	46	103	11
109	Wasim Bari (P)	42	94	15

NB Parks' figures include 2 catches as a fielder.

HIGHEST RUN AGGREGATES

Runs			Tests	Inns	NO	HS	Avge	100s	50s
8032	G. S. Sobers	(WI)	93	160	21	365*	57.78	26	30
7624	M. C. Cowdrey	(E)	114	188	15	182	44.06	22	38
7249	W. R. Hammond	(E)	85	140	16	336*	58.45	22	24
6996	D. G. Bradman	(A)	52	80	10	334	99.94	29	13
6971	L. Hutton	(E)	79	138	15	364	56.67	19	33
6806	K. F. Barrington	(E)	82	131	15	256	58.67	20	35
6227	R. B. Kanhai	(WI)	79	137	6	256	47.53	15	28
6149	R. N. Harvey	(A)	79	137	10	205	48.41	21	24
5807	D. C. S. Compton	(E)	78	131	15	278	50.06	17	28
5675	G. Boycott	(E)	74	128	17	246*	51.12	16	32
5410	J. B. Hobbs	(E)	61	102	7	211	56.94	15	28
5234	W. M. Lawry	(A)	67	123	12	210	47.15	13	27
5187	I. M. Chappell	(A)	72	130	9	196	42.86	14	25
5138	J. H. Edrich	(E)	77	127	9	310*	43.54	12	24
4960	K. D. Walters	(A)	68	116	12	250	47.69	14	30
4882	T. W. Graveney	(E)	79	123	13	258	44.38	11	20
4869	R. B. Simpson	(A)	62	111	7	311	46.81	10	27
4737	I. R. Redpath	(A)	66	120	11	171	43.45	8	31
4594	C. H. Lloyd	(WI)	65	113	8	242*	43.75	11	22
4555	H. Sutcliffe	(E)	54	84	9	194	60.73	16	23
4537	P. B. H. May	(E)	66	106	9	285*	46.77	13	22
4502	E. R. Dexter	(E)	62	102	8	205	47.89	9	27
4455	E. D. Weekes	(WI)	48	81	5	207	58.61	15	19
4334	R. C. Fredericks	(WI)	59	109	7	169	42.49	8	26
4175	A. P. E. Knott	(E)	89	138	14	135	33.66	5	28
4097	G. S. Chappell	(A)	51	90	13	247*	53.20	14	20
3915	Hanif Mohammad	(P)	55	97	8	337	43.98	12	15
3860	F. M. M. Worrell	(WI)	51	87	9	261	49.48	9	22
3798	C. L. Walcott	(WI)	44	74	7	220	56.68	15	14
3631	P. R. Umrigar	(I)	59	94	8	223	42.22	12	14

3612	D. L. Amiss	(E)	50	88	10	262*	46.30	11	11
3599	A. W. Greig	(E)	58	93	4	148	40.43	8	20
3533	A. R. Morris	(A)	46	79	3	206	46.48	12	12
3525	E. H. Hendren	(E)	51	83	9	205*	47.63	7	21
3471	B. Mitchell	(SA)	42	80	9	189*	48.88	8	21
3448	B. E. Congdon	(NZ)	61	114	7	176	32.22	7	19
3428	J. R. Reid	(NZ)	58	108	5	142	33.28	6	22
3412	C. Hill	(A)	49	89	2	191	39.21	7	19
3331	A. I. Kallicharran	(WI)	45	76	7	158	48.27	10	17
3283	Mushtaq Mohammad	(P)	49	88	7	201	40.53	10	17
3283	F. E. Woolley	(E)	64	98	7	154	36.07	5	23
3245	C. C. Hunte	(WI)	44	78	6	260	45.06	8	13
3226	S. M. Gavaskar	(I)	37	71	5	220	48.87	13	14
3208	V. L. Manjrekar	(I)	55	92	10	189*	39.12	7	15
3163	V. T. Trumper	(A)	48	89	8	214*	39.04	8	13
3154	G. R. Viswanath	(I)	43	82	7	139	42.05	5	21
3106	C. C. McDonald	(A)	47	83	4	170	39.31	5	17
3104	B. F. Butcher	(WI)	44	78	6	209*	43.11	7	16
3073	A. L. Hassett	(A)	43	69	3	198*	46.56	10	11
3061	C. G. Borde	(I)	55	97	11	177*	35.59	5	18

HIGHEST WICKET AGGREGATES

Wkts			Tests	Balls	Mdns	Runs	Avge	wI 5	wM 10
309	L. R. Gibbs	(WI)	79	27115	1313	8989	29.09	18	2
307	F. S. Trueman	(E)	67	15178	522	6625	21.57	17	3
265	D. L. Underwood	(E)	74	18979	1063	6600	24.90	16	6
252	J. B. Statham	(E)	70	16056	595	6261	24.84	9	1
248	R. Benaud	(A)	63	19090	805	6704	27.03	16	1
246	B. S. Bedi	(I)	58	19135	1009	6615	26.89	14	1
246	G. D. McKenzie	(A)	60	17681	547	7238	29.78	16	3
236	A. V. Bedser	(E)	51	15923	572	5876	24.89	15	5
235	G. S. Sobers	(WI)	93	21599	995	7999	34.03	6	—
228	R. R. Lindwall	(A)	61	13666	418	5257	23.05	12	—
222	B. S. Chandrasekhar	(I)	50	14253	537	6270	28.24	15	2
216	C. V. Grimmett	(A)	37	14513	735	5231	24.21	21	7
202	J. A. Snow	(E)	49	12021	415	5387	26.66	8	1
193	J. C. Laker	(E)	46	12009	673	4099	21.23	9	3
192	W. W. Hall	(WI)	48	10415	312	5065	26.38	9	1
189	S. F. Barnes	(E)	27	7873	356	3106	16.43	24	7
187	E. A. S. Prasanna	(I)	47	13867	585	5491	29.36	10	2
186	A. K. Davidson	(A)	44	11665	432	3833	20.58	14	2
174	G. A. R. Lock	(E)	49	13147	819	4451	25.58	9	3
171	D. K. Lillee	(A)	32	8791	266	4017	23.49	12	4
170	K. R. Miller	(A)	55	10474	338	3906	22.97	7	1
170	F. J. Tayfield	(SA)	37	13568	602	4405	25.91	14	2
162	V. M. H. Mankad	(I)	44	14686	777	5235	32.31	8	2
160	W. A. Johnston	(A)	40	11048	370	3825	23.90	7	—
158	S. Ramadhin	(WI)	43	13939	813	4579	28.98	10	1
155	M. W. Tate	(E)	39	12523	581	4055	26.16	7	1
153	F. J. Titmus	(E)	53	15118	777	4931	32.22	7	—
151	R. G. D. Willis	(E)	41	7887	220	3653	24.19	10	—

MOST TEST APPEARANCES FOR EACH COUNTRY

NB The abandoned match at Melbourne in 1970–71 is excluded from these figures.

England

M. C. Cowdrey	114
T. G. Evans	91
A. P. E. Knott	89
W. R. Hammond	85
K. F. Barrington	82
T. W. Graveney	79
L. Hutton	79
D. C. S. Compton	78
J. H. Edrich	77
G. Boycott	74
D. L. Underwood	74
J. B. Statham	70
F. S. Trueman	67
P. B. H. May	66
F. E. Woolley	64
E. R. Dexter	62

Australia

R. N. Harvey	79
I. M. Chappell	72
K. D. Walters	68
W. M. Lawry	67
I. R. Redpath	66
R. Benaud	63
R. B. Simpson	62
R. R. Lindwall	61
G. D. McKenzie	60
S. E. Gregory	58
K. R. Miller	55
W. A. S. Oldfield	54
D. G. Bradman	52
R. W. Marsh	52
G. S. Chappell	51
A. T. W. Grout	51

South Africa

J. H. B. Waite	50
A. W. Nourse	45
B. Mitchell	42
H. W. Taylor	42
T. L. Goddard	41
R. A. McLean	40
H. J. Tayfield	37
D. J. McGlew	34
A. D. Nourse	34
E. J. Barlow	30
W. R. Endean	28
P. M. Pollock	28
K. G. Viljoen	27

West Indies

G. S. Sobers	93
L. R. Gibbs	79
R. B. Kanhai	79
C. H. Lloyd	65
R. C. Fredericks	59
D. L. Murray	51
F. M. M. Worrell	51
W. W. Hall	48
E. D. Weekes	48
A. I. Kallicharran	45
B. F. Butcher	44
C. C. Hunte	44
C. L. Walcott	44
S. Ramadhin	43

New Zealand

B. E. Congdon	61
J. R. Reid	58
M. G. Burgess	44
B. Sutcliffe	42
G. T. Dowling	39
G. M. Turner	39
R. O. Collinge	35
K. J. Wadsworth	33
R. C. Motz	32
V. Pollard	32
B. F. Hastings	31
H. J. Howarth	30
B. R. Taylor	30

India		Pakistan	
P. R. Umrigar	59	Hanif Mohammad	55
B. S. Bedi	58	Mushtaq Mohammad	49
C. G. Borde	55	Intikhab Alam	47
V. L. Manjrekar	55	Asif Iqbal	45
B. S. Chandrasekhar	50	Wasim Bari	42
E. A. S. Prasanna	47	Imtiaz Ahmed	41
F. M. Engineer	46	Saeed Ahmed	41
M. A. K. Pataudi	46	Majid Khan	37
V. M. H. Mankad	44	Fazal Mahmood	34
P. Roy	43	Sadiq Mohammad	34
G. R. Viswanath	43	Nasim-ul-Ghani	29
R. G. Nadkarni	41		

ICC ASSOCIATE MEMBERS' WORLD CUP COMPETITION 1979

The Associate Members' World Cup Competition, scheduled to take place in the Midlands prior to the Prudential World Cup in May/June 1979, will incorporate 15 member nations playing in three groups, each team playing the others in its group once on a league basis.

The leading team in all the groups and the best runner-up will contest the semi-finals and the finalists will immediately qualify to participate in the Prudential Cup Competition which follows.

On Thursday 21 June at Worcester, the finalists will play each other for the *ICC Trophy*, and the losing semi-finalists will play off for third place.

The three groups are constituted as follows:

Group I	Group II	Group III
East Africa	Denmark	Israel
Papua New Guinea	Fiji	USA
Argentina	Malaysia	Holland
Singapore	Canada	Gibraltar
Bermuda	Bangladesh	Sri Lanca

The dates fixed for group matches, to be played on leading club grounds in the Midlands, are 22 May, 24 May, 29 May, 31 May, 4 June – and 6 June for the two semi-finals, which will be drawn by lot.

TEST CAREER RECORDS
ENGLAND
BATTING AND FIELDING

	M	I	NO	Runs	HS	Avge	100	50	Ct	St
D. L. Amiss	50	88	10	3612	262*	46.30	11	11	24	—
G. G. Arnold	34	46	11	421	59	12.02	—	1	9	—
J. C. Balderstone	2	4	0	39	35	9.75	—	—	1	—
G. D. Barlow	3	5	1	17	7*	4.25	—	—	—	—
J. Birkenshaw	5	7	0	148	64	21.14	—	1	3	—
I. T. Botham	11	13	1	500	108	41.66	3	1	12	—
G. Boycott	74	128	17	5675	246*	51.12	16	32	22	—
J. M. Brearley	21	34	1	845	91	25.60	—	5	32	—
D. J. Brown	26	34	5	342	44*	11.79	—	—	7	—
G. A. Cope	3	3	0	40	22	13.33	—	—	1	—
M. H. Denness	28	45	3	1667	188	39.69	4	7	28	—
B. L. D'Oliveira	44	70	8	2484	158	40.06	5	15	29	—
P. H. Edmonds	13	16	4	195	50	16.25	—	1	19	—
J. H. Edrich	77	127	9	5138	310*	43.54	12	24	43	—
J. E. Emburey	1	1	0	2	2	2.00	—	—	2	—
K. W. R. Fletcher	52	85	11	2975	216	40.20	7	16	46	—
M. W. Gatting	2	3	0	11	6	3.66	—	—	3	—
N. Gifford	15	20	9	179	25*	16.27	—	—	8	—
G. A. Gooch	7	11	2	301	91*	33.44	—	3	5	—
D. I. Gower	6	8	0	438	111	54.75	1	3	—	—
J. H. Hampshire	8	16	1	403	107	26.86	1	2	9	—
F. C. Hayes	9	17	1	244	106*	15.25	1	—	7	—
M. Hendrick	16	17	5	64	15	5.33	—	—	19	—
K. Higgs	15	19	3	185	63	11.56	—	1	4	—
J. K. Lever	13	19	3	199	53	12.43	—	1	8	—
D. Lloyd	9	15	2	552	214*	42.46	1	—	11	—
G. Miller	14	17	2	398	98*	26.53	—	2	7	—
C. M. Old	40	57	6	722	65	14.15	—	2	22	—
P. I. Pocock	17	27	2	165	33	6.60	—	—	13	—
C. T. Radley	8	10	0	481	158	48.10	2	2	4	—
D. W. Randall	16	26	2	631	174	26.29	1	3	9	—
G. R. J. Roope	21	32	4	860	77	30.71	—	7	35	—
B. C. Rose	5	8	1	100	27	14.28	—	—	2	—
M. W. W. Selvey	3	5	3	15	5*	7.50	—	—	1	—
K. Shuttleworth	5	6	0	46	21	7.66	—	—	1	—
D. S. Steele	8	16	0	673	106	42.06	1	5	7	—
R. W. Taylor	13	14	1	202	45	15.53	—	—	36	3
R. W. Tolchard	4	7	2	129	67	25.80	—	1	5	—
D. L. Underwood	74	100	31	824	45*	11.94	—	—	39	—
P. Willey	2	4	0	115	45	28.75	—	—	—	—
R. G. D. Willis	41	56	31	328	24*	13.12	—	—	19	—
B. Wood	12	21	0	454	90	21.61	—	2	6	—
R. A. Woolmer	15	26	1	920	149	36.80	3	2	8	—

BOWLING

	Balls	Runs	Wkts	Avge	Best	5 wI	10 wM
G. G. Arnold	7650	3254	115	28.29	6–45	6	—
J. C. Balderstone	96	80	1	80.00	1–80	—	—
J. Birkenshaw	1017	469	13	36.07	5–57	1	—
I. T. Botham	2554	1059	64	16.54	8–34	8	1
G. Boycott	816	350	7	50.00	3–47	—	—
D. J. Brown	5098	2237	79	28.31	5–42	2	—
G. A. Cope	864	277	8	34.62	3–102	—	—
B. L. D'Oliveira	5706	1859	47	39.55	3–46	—	—
P. H. Edmonds	3013	901	43	20.95	7–66	2	—
J. H. Edrich	30	23	0	—	—	—	—
J. E. Emburey	175	40	2	20.00	2–39	—	—
K. W. R. Fletcher	249	173	1	173.00	1–48	—	—
M. W. Gatting	8	1	0	—	—	—	—
N. Gifford	3084	1026	33	31.09	5–55	1	—
G. A. Gooch	60	29	0	—	—	—	—
M. Hendrick	3136	1249	47	26.57	4–28	—	—
K. Higgs	4112	1473	71	20.74	6–91	2	—
J. K. Lever	2562	1058	44	24.04	7–46	2	1
D. Lloyd	24	17	0	—	—	—	—
G. Miller	1736	654	17	38.47	3–99	—	—
C. M. Old	7540	3510	125	28.08	7–50	4	—
P. I. Pocock	4482	2023	47	43.04	6–79	3	—
D. W. Randall	16	3	0	—	—	—	—
G. R. J. Roope	172	76	0	—	—	—	—
M. W. W. Selvey	492	343	6	57.16	4–41	—	—
K. Shuttleworth	1071	427	12	35.58	5–47	1	—
D. S. Steele	88	39	2	19.50	1–1	—	—
D. L. Underwood	18979	6600	265	24.90	8–51	16	6
P. Willey	24	15	0	—	—	—	—
R. G. D. Willis	7887	3653	151	24.19	7–78	10	—
B. Wood	98	50	0	—	—	—	—
R. A. Woolmer	546	299	4	74.75	1–8	—	—

AUSTRALIA

BATTING AND FIELDING

	M	I	NO	Runs	HS	Avge	100	50	Ct	St
I. W. Callen	1	2	2	26	22*	—	—	—	1	—
W. M. Clark	9	17	5	89	33	5.93	—	—	5	—
D. J. Colley	3	4	0	84	54	21.00	—	1	1	—
G. J. Cosier	16	28	1	845	168	31.29	2	3	12	—
W. M. Darling	4	8	0	164	65	20.50	—	2	1	—
G. Dymock	4	5	1	13	13	3.25	—	—	—	—
J. Dyson	3	6	0	101	53	16.83	—	1	—	—
W. J. Edwards	3	6	0	68	30	11.33	—	—	—	—
J. B. Gannon	3	5	4	3	3*	3.00	—	—	3	—
P. A. Hibbert	1	2	0	15	13	7.50	—	—	1	—
J. D. Higgs	4	7	4	10	4*	3.33	—	—	—	—
K. J. Hughes	3	5	0	65	28	13.00	—	—	2	—

	M	I	NO	Runs	HS	Avge	100	50	Ct	St
A. G. Hurst	2	3	1	42	26	21.00	—	—	1	—
R. J. Inverarity	6	11	1	174	56	17.40	—	1	4	—
T. J. Laughlin	2	3	0	80	35	26.66	—	—	1	—
A. L. Mann	4	8	0	189	105	23.62	1	—	2	—
A. D. Ogilvie	5	10	0	178	47	17.80	—	—	5	—
S. J. Rixon	10	19	3	341	54	21.31	—	2	31	4
C. S. Serjeant	12	23	1	522	124	23.72	1	2	13	—
R. B. Simpson	62	111	7	4869	311	46.81	10	27	110	—
J. R. Thomson	32	43	7	424	49	11.77	—	—	13	—
P. M. Toohey	8	15	0	705	122	47.00	1	6	2	—
A. Turner	14	27	1	768	136	29.53	1	3	15	—
G. M. Wood	6	12	0	521	126	43.41	1	4	7	—
A. J. Woodcock	1	1	0	27	27	27.00	—	—	1	—
G. N. Yallop	8	15	2	641	121	49.30	1	4	5	—
B. Yardley	6	11	2	254	74	28.22	—	1	5	—

BOWLING

	Balls	Runs	Wkts	Avge	Best	5 wI	10 wM
I. W. Callen	440	191	6	31.83	3–83	—	—
W. M. Clark	2489	1162	43	27.02	4–46	—	—
D. J. Colley	729	312	6	52.00	3–83	—	—
G. J. Cosier	803	306	5	61.20	2–26	—	—
G. Dymock	1352	452	14	32.28	5–58	1	—
J. B. Gannon	726	361	11	32.81	4–77	—	—
J. D. Higgs	896	384	15	25.60	4–91	—	—
A. G. Hurst	408	154	3	51.33	2–50	—	—
R. J. Inverarity	372	93	4	23.25	3–26	—	—
T. J. Laughlin	316	202	6	33.66	5–101	1	—
A. L. Mann	552	316	4	79.00	3–12	—	—
R. B. Simpson	6881	3001	71	42.26	5–57	2	—
J. R. Thomson	7158	3699	145	25.51	6–46	6	—
G. N. Yallop	18	8	0	—	—	—	—
B. Yardley	1447	573	19	30.15	4–35	—	—

WEST INDIES

BATTING AND FIELDING

	M	I	NO	Runs	HS	Avge	100	50	Ct	St
Imtiaz Ali	1	1	1	1	1*	—	—	—	—	—
Inshan Ali	12	18	2	172	25	10.75	—	—	7	—
R. A. Austin	2	2	0	22	20	11.00	—	—	2	—
S. F. A. Bacchus	2	4	0	42	21	10.50	—	—	3	—
L. Baichan	3	6	2	184	105*	46.00	1	—	2	—
G. S. Camacho	11	22	0	640	87	29.09	—	4	4	—
S. Clarke	1	2	1	11	6	11.00	—	—	—	—
C. E. H. Croft	7	10	8	60	23*	30.00	—	—	7	—
W. W. Daniel	5	5	2	29	11	9.66	—	—	2	—
T. M. Findlay	10	16	3	212	44*	16.30	—	—	19	2
M. L. C. Foster	14	24	5	580	125	30.52	1	1	3	—
J. Garner	7	10	1	97	43	10.77	—	—	6	—

							5 wI	10 wM
H. A. Gomes	5	9	0	276	115	30.66	2	—	1	—
A. T. Greenidge	2	4	0	142	69	35.50	—	2	2	—
C. G. Greenidge	19	36	2	1641	134	48.26	5	9	22	—
D. L. Haynes	2	3	0	182	66	60.66	—	3	1	—
V. A. Holder	34	51	9	603	42	14.35	—	—	15	—
M. A. Holding	13	20	5	213	55	11.21	—	1	3	—
R. R. Jumadeen	10	12	9	26	11*	8.66	—	—	4	—
A. I. Kallicharran	45	76	7	3331	158	48.27	10	17	35	—
C. L. King	7	7	1	211	63	35.16	—	2	3	—
C. H. Lloyd	65	113	8	4594	242*	43.75	11	22	43	—
D. A. Murray	3	6	0	67	21	11.16	—	—	6	3
D. L. Murray	51	80	8	1705	91	23.68	—	10	150	8
A. L. Padmore	2	2	1	8	8*	8.00	—	—	—	—
D. R. Parry	5	9	2	193	65	27.57	—	2	3	—
N. Phillip	3	6	1	120	46	24.00	—	—	2	—
I. V. A. Richards	28	47	2	2500	291	55.55	8	8	26	—
A. M. E. Roberts	27	36	5	229	35	7.38	—	—	5	—
L. G. Rowe	24	38	2	1706	302	47.38	6	5	13	—
J. N. Shepherd	5	8	0	77	32	9.62	—	—	4	—
I. T. Shillingford	4	7	0	218	120	31.14	1	—	1	—
S. Shivnarine	3	6	0	217	63	36.16	—	3	1	—
E. T. Willett	5	8	3	74	26	14.80	—	—	—	—
A. B. Williams	3	6	0	257	100	42.83	1	1	4	—

BOWLING

	Balls	Runs	Wkts	Avge	Best	5 wI	10 wM
Imtiaz Ali	204	89	2	44.50	2–37	—	—
Inshan Ali	3718	1621	34	47.47	5–59	1	—
R. A. Austin	6	5	0	—	—	—	—
G. S. Camacho	18	12	0	—	—	—	—
S. Clarke	294	141	6	23.50	3–58	—	—
C. E. H. Croft	1638	846	42	20.14	8–29	—	1
W. W. Daniel	788	381	15	25.40	4–53	—	—
M. L. C. Foster	1776	600	9	66.66	2–41	—	—
J. Garner	1690	883	38	23.23	4–48	—	—
H. A. Gomes	96	34	0	—	—	—	—
C. G. Greenidge	8	0	0	—	—	—	—
V. A. Holder	7877	3079	101	30.48	6–28	3	—
M. A. Holding	2910	1348	57	23.64	8–92	4	1
R. R. Jumadeen	2638	933	26	35.88	4–72	—	—
A. I. Kallicharran	151	73	1	73.00	1–7	—	—
C. L. King	276	113	2	56.50	1–30	—	—
C. H. Lloyd	1710	621	10	62.10	2–13	—	—
A. L. Padmore	474	135	1	135.00	1–36	—	—
D. R. Parry	748	360	12	30.00	5–15	—	—
N. Phillip	678	391	9	43.44	4–75	—	—
I. V. A. Richards	644	235	4	58.75	2–34	—	—
A. M. E. Roberts	6858	3298	134	24.61	7–54	9	2
L. G. Rowe	56	40	0	—	—	—	—
J. N. Shepherd	1445	479	19	25.21	5–104	1	—
S. Shivnarine	264	139	1	139.00	1–13	—	—
E. T. Willett	1326	482	11	43.81	3–33	—	—

NEW ZEALAND

BATTING AND FIELDING

	M	I	NO	Runs	HS	Avge	100	50	Ct	St
R. W. Anderson	9	18	0	423	92	23.50	—	3	1	—
S. L. Boock	6	11	4	24	8	3.42	—	—	3	—
B. P. Bracewell	3	6	1	4	4	0.80	—	—	1	—
M. G. Burgess	44	81	5	2426	119*	31.92	5	13	33	—
B. L. Cairns	11	20	4	279	52*	17.43	—	1	4	—
E. J. Chatfield	4	7	3	31	13*	7.75	—	—	—	—
R. O. Collinge	35	50	13	533	68*	14.40	—	2	10	—
J. V. Coney	4	7	0	123	45	17.57	—	—	6	—
B. E. Congdon	61	114	7	3448	176	32.22	7	19	44	—
B. A. Edgar	3	6	0	147	60	24.50	—	1	3	—
G. N. Edwards	5	10	0	244	55	24.40	—	3	7	—
D. R. Hadlee	26	42	5	530	56	14.32	—	1	8	—
R. J. Hadlee	23	42	4	729	87	19.18	—	2	13	—
G. P. Howarth	14	27	3	864	123	36.00	3	3	6	—
H. J. Howarth	30	42	18	291	61	12.12	—	1	33	—
W. K. Lees	9	18	1	452	152	26.58	1	—	15	7
J. F. M. Morrison	14	24	0	610	117	25.41	1	3	9	—
D. R. O'Sullivan	11	21	4	158	23*	9.29	—	—	2	—
J. M. Parker	28	49	2	1278	121	27.19	3	3	24	—
N. M. Parker	3	6	0	89	40	14.83	—	—	2	—
P. J. Petherick	6	11	4	34	13	4.85	—	—	4	—
A. D. G. Roberts	7	12	1	254	84*	23.09	—	1	4	—
M. J. F. Shrimpton	10	19	0	265	46	13.94	—	—	2	—
G. B. Troup	1	1	0	0	0	0.00	—	—	1	—
G. M. Turner	39	70	6	2920	259	45.62	7	14	40	—
G. E. Vivian	5	6	0	110	43	18.33	—	—	3	—
J. G. Wright	5	10	0	223	62	22.30	—	2	2	—

BOWLING

	Balls	Runs	Wkts	Avge	Best	5 wI	10 wM
S. L. Boock	1153	318	13	24.46	5–67	1	—
B. P. Bracewell	536	282	9	31.33	3–110	—	—
M. G. Burgess	498	212	6	35.33	3–23	—	—
B. L. Cairns	2400	909	20	45.45	5–55	1	—
E. J. Chatfield	1054	485	8	60.62	4–100	—	—
R. O. Collinge	7689	3393	116	29.25	6–63	3	—
J. V. Coney	16	13	0			—	—
B. E. Congdon	5620	2154	59	36.50	5–65	1	—
D. R. Hadlee	4883	2389	71	33.64	4–30	—	—
R. J. Hadlee	5434	2811	89	31.58	7–23	4	2
G. P. Howarth	240	109	2	54.50	1–13	—	—
H. J. Howarth	8833	3178	86	36.95	5–34	2	—
W. K. Lees	5	4	0			—	—
J. F. M. Morrison	24	9	0			—	—
D. R. O'Sullivan	2739	1291	18	67.72	5–148	1	—
J. M. Parker	40	24	1	24.00	1–24	—	—

P. J. Petherick	1305	687	16	42.93	3–90	—	—		
A. D. G. Roberts	440	182	4	45.50	1–12	—	—		
M. J. F. Shrimpton	257	158	5	31.60	1–35	—	—		
G. B. Troup	180	116	1	116.00	1–69	—	—		
G. M. Turner	12	5	0	—	—	—	—		
G. E. Vivian	198	107	1	107.00	1–14	—	—		

INDIA

BATTING AND FIELDING

	M	I	NO	Runs	HS	Avge	100	50	Ct	St
S. Abid Ali	29	53	3	1018	81	20.36	—	6	33	—
M. Amarnath	18	33	4	1183	100	36.96	1	8	20	—
S. Amarnath	7	13	0	403	124	31.00	1	2	4	—
B. S. Bedi	58	91	26	621	50*	9.55	—	1	24	—
B. S. Chandrasekhar	50	72	35	162	22	4.37	—	—	23	—
C. P. S. Chauhan	9	17	0	368	88	21.64	—	1	12	—
S. A. Durani	29	50	2	1202	104	25.04	1	7	14	—
A. D. Gaekwad	14	26	2	742	81*	30.91	—	4	5	—
S. M. Gavaskar	37	71	5	3226	220	48.87	13	14	35	—
K. D. Ghavri	11	19	3	333	64	20.81	—	1	8	—
S. Guha	4	7	2	17	6	3.40	—	—	2	—
Hanumant Singh	14	24	2	686	105	31.18	1	5	11	—
M. L. Jaisimha	39	71	4	2056	129	30.68	3	12	17	—
H. S. Kanitkar	2	4	0	111	65	27.75	—	1	—	—
S. M. H. Kirmani	20	32	4	795	88	28.39	—	5	35	15
P. Krishnamurthy	5	6	0	33	20	5.50	—	—	7	1
S. Madan Lal	16	30	6	428	55*	17.83	—	1	8	—
A. V. Mankad	22	42	3	991	97	25.41	—	6	12	—
S. S. Naik	3	6	0	141	77	23.50	—	1	—	—
R. D. Parkar	2	4	0	80	35	20.00	—	—	1	—
B. P. Patel	21	38	5	972	115*	29.45	1	5	17	—
E. A. S. Prasanna	47	81	18	720	37	11.42	—	—	18	—
A. Roy	4	7	0	91	48	13.00	—	—	—	—
R. Saxena	1	2	0	25	16	12.50	—	—	—	—
P. Sharma	5	10	0	187	54	18.70	—	1	1	—
E. D. Solkar	27	48	6	1068	102	25.42	1	6	53	—
D. B. Vengsarkar	11	20	1	472	78	24.84	—	1	11	—
S. Venkataraghavan	37	55	8	660	64	14.04	—	2	32	—
G. R. Viswanath	43	82	7	3154	139	42.05	5	21	33	—
Yajurvindra Singh	2	4	0	50	21	12.50	—	—	8	—

BOWLING

	Balls	Runs	Wkts	Avge	Best	5 wI	10 wM
S. Abid Ali	4164	1980	47	42.12	6–55	1	—
M. Amarnath	1803	726	17	42.70	4–63	—	—
B. S. Bedi	19135	6615	246	26.89	7–98	14	1
B. S. Chandrasekhar	14253	6270	222	28.24	8–79	15	2
S. A. Durani	6446	2657	75	35.42	6–73	3	1
A. D. Gaekwad	76	53	0	—	—	—	—
S. M. Gavaskar	172	72	0	—	—	—	—

214

K. D. Ghavri	1550	833	30	27.76	5–33	1	—
S. Guha	674	311	3	103.66	2–55	—	—
Hanumant Singh	66	51	0	—	—	—	—
M. L. Jaisimha	2091	829	9	92.11	2–54	—	—
S. Madan Lal	2457	977	29	33.68	5–72	2	—
A. V. Mankad	41	43	0	—	—	—	—
E. A. S. Prasanna	13867	5491	187	29.36	8–76	10	2
R. Saxena	12	11	0	—	—	—	—
P. Sharma	24	8	0	—	—	—	—
E. D. Solkar	2265	1070	18	59.44	3–28	—	—
D. B. Vengsarkar	5	7	0	—	—	—	—
S. Venkataraghavan	10301	3796	113	33.59	8–72	3	1
G. R. Viswanath	24	18	0	—	—	—	—
Yajurvindra Singh	6	2	0	—	—	—	—

PAKISTAN

BATTING AND FIELDING

	M	I	NO	Runs	HS	Avge	100	50	Ct	St
Abdul Qadir	3	3	0	36	21	12.00	—	—	2	—
Asif Iqbal	45	77	4	2748	175	37.64	8	10	29	—
Imran Khan	12	21	1	727	122	36.35	2	3	6	—
Haroon Rashid	15	26	2	503	59	20.95	—	1	8	—
Iqbal Qasim	11	16	5	34	8*	3.09	—	—	8	—
Javed Miandad	13	22	4	994	206	55.22	2	6	10	—
Liaquat Ali	5	7	3	28	12	7.00	—	—	1	—
Majid Khan	37	64	2	2651	167	42.75	5	13	47	—
Mohsin Khan	4	6	0	235	46	39.16	—	—	3	—
Mudassar Nazar	7	12	0	430	114	35.83	1	2	4	—
Mushtaq Mohammad	49	88	7	3283	201	40.53	10	17	33	—
Sadiq Mohammad	34	62	2	2330	166	38.83	5	10	24	—
Salim Altaf	20	31	12	276	53*	14.52	—	1	3	—
Sarfraz Nawaz	26	37	7	443	53	14.76	—	2	15	—
Shafiq Ahmed	4	7	1	82	27*	13.66	—	—	1	—
Shahid Israr	1	1	1	7	7*	—	—	—	2	—
Sikander Bakht	7	9	3	22	7*	3.66	—	—	1	—
Talat Ali	7	12	1	243	57	22.09	—	1	3	—
Wasim Bari	42	64	16	748	72	15.58	—	4	94	15
Wasim Raja	20	35	5	1096	117*	36.53	2	6	4	—
Zaheer Abbas	26	47	1	1583	274	34.41	3	6	18	—

BOWLING

	Balls	Runs	Wkts	Avge	Best	5 wI	10 wM
Abdul Qadir	1056	305	12	25.41	6–44	1	—
Asif Iqbal	3574	1401	50	8.02	5–48	2	—
Haroon Rashid	8	3	0	—	—	—	—
Imran Khan	8129	2043	62	32–98	6–63	4	1
Iqbal Qasim	2710	934	27	34.59	4–84	—	—
Javed Miandad	1162	510	15	34.00	3–74	—	—
Liaquat Ali	808	359	6	59.83	3–80	—	—
Majid Khan	2668	1066	24	44.41	4–45	—	—
Mohsin Khan	8	3	0	—	—	—	—
Mudassar Nazar	226	88	2	44.00	1–16	—	—
Mushtaq Mohammad	4063	1770	62	28.54	5–28	2	—

Sadiq Mohammad	170	78	0	—	—	— —
Salim Altaf	3827	1640	45	36.44	4–11	— —
Sarfraz Nawaz	6194	2625	82	32.01	6–89	2 —
Shafiq Ahmed	8	1	0	—	—	— —
Sikander Bakht	1346	641	18	35.61	4–132	— —
Talat Ali	20	7	0	—	—	— —
Wasim Bari	8	2	0	—	—	— —
Wasim Raja	1316	598	17	35.17	3–22	— —
Zaheer Abbas	20	2	0	—	—	— —

SCORING OF POINTS IN THE SCHWEPPES CHAMPION-SHIP

The scheme is as follows:

(a) For a win, 12 points, plus any points scored in the first innings,

(b) In a tie, each side to score 5 points, plus any points scored in the first innings.

(c) If the scores are equal in a drawn match, the side batting in the fourth innings to score 5 points, plus any points scored in the first innings.

(d) First innings points (awarded only for performances in the first 100 overs of each innings and retained whatever the result of the match).

    (i) A maximum of 4 batting points to be available as follows: 150 to 199 runs—1 point; 200 to 249 runs—2 points; 250 to 299 runs—3 points; 300 runs or over—4 points.

    (ii) A maximum of 4 bowling points to be available as follows; 3–4 wickets taken—1 point; 5–6 wickets taken —2 points; 7–8 wickets taken—3 points; 9–10 wickets taken—4 points.

(e) If play starts when less than eight hours playing time remains and a one innings match is played, no first innings points shall be scored. The side winning on the one innings to score 12 points.

(f) The side which has the highest aggregate of points gained at the end of the season shall be the Champion County. Should any sides in the Schweppes Championship Table be equal on points, the side with most wins will have priority.

Did overarm bowling begin with Right Guard?

Put it another way: would any self-respecting young Englishman raise his shirt-sleeved arm above his head in public unless he were wearing a reliable anti-perspirant? It would be enough to damn him in the eyes of the MCC for the rest of his career.

No, the pendants can quote 1835 and 1864 as the years when the underarm lob became the overarm bowl, but we beg to differ. We happen to know that Right Guard did not come on the scene until considerably later.

Gillette® RIGHT GUARD®
Anti-perspirant for dry comfort

PRINCIPAL FIXTURES 1979

Including play on Sunday

Saturday 21 April
*Lord's: MCC v Kent
Cambridge: Cambridge U v Essex

Wednesday 25 April
Cambridge: Cambridge U v Leics
Oxford: Oxford U v Glam

Saturday 28 April
Benson & Hedges Cup
Derby: Derbys v Hants
Cardiff: Glam v Worcs
Bristol: Gloucs v M Counties (S)
Trent Bridge: Notts v Middx
Oval: Surrey v Oxford U and
    Cambridge U
Eastbourne: Sussex v Northants
Edgbaston: Warwicks v Leics
Lincoln: M Counties (N) v Kent

Sunday 29 April
John Player League
Derby: Derbys v Hants
Cardiff: Glam v Worcs
Bristol: Gloucs v Lancs
Trent Bridge: Notts v Middx
The Oval: Surrey v Somerset
Hove: Sussex v Northants
Edgbaston: Warwicks v Essex
Middlesbrough: Yorks v Leics

Wednesday 2 May
Derby: Derbys v Leics
Chelmsford: Essex v Kent
Southampton: Hants v Glam
Lord's: Middx v Warwicks
Trent Bridge: Notts v Lancs
Hove: Sussex v Gloucs
Worcester: Worcs v Somerset
Middlesbrough: Yorks v Northants
Cambridge: Cambridge U v Surrey

Saturday 5 May
Benson & Hedges Cup
Southport: Lancs v Warwicks
Leicester: Leics v Derbys

Lord's: Middx v M Counties (N)
Northampton: Northants v Essex
Taunton: Somerset v Glam
Worcester: Worcs v Gloucs
Oxford: Oxford U and Cambridge
    U v Sussex

Sunday 6 May
John Player League
Chelmsford: Essex v Derbys
Maidstone: Kent v Warwicks
Leicester: Leics v Sussex
Lord's: Middx v Hants
Northampton: Northants v Glam
Worcester: Worcs v Gloucs

Monday 7 May
Benson & Hedges Cup
Bradford: Yorks v Notts

Wednesday 9 May
Swansea: Glam v Worcs
Bristol: Gloucs v Sussex
Old Trafford: Lancs v Surrey
Lord's: Middx v Essex
Taunton: Somerset v Northants
Edgbaston: Warwicks v Leics
Headingley: Yorks v Derbys
Cambridge: Cambridge U v Notts
Oxford: Oxford U v Hants

Saturday 12 May
Trent Bridge: Notts v Sri Lanka
Benson & Hedges Cup
Bristol: Gloucs v Somerset
Bournemouth: Hants v Warwicks
Canterbury: Kent v Middx
Leicester: Leics v Lancs
The Oval: Surrey v Essex
Jesmond (N-on-T): M Counties (N)
    v Yorks
High Wycombe: M Counties (S)
    v Northants
Cambridge: Oxford U and
    Cambridge U v Northants

218

Sunday 13 May

John Player League
Swansea: Glam v Sussex
Southampton: Hants v Essex
Old Trafford: Lancs v Leics
Trent Bridge: Notts v Yorks
Taunton: Somerset v Warwicks

Wednesday 16 May

Chesterfield: Derbys v Essex
Cardiff: Glam v Yorks
Lord's: Middx v Kent
Trent Bridge: Notts v Leics
Taunton: Somerset v Surrey
Hove: Sussex v Lancs
Edgbaston: Warwicks v Northants
Worcester: Worcs v Hants
Cambridge: Cambridge U v Gloucs

Saturday 19 May

Benson & Hedges Cup
Chelmsford: Essex v Oxford U and
    Cambridge U
Swansea: Glam v Gloucs
Old Trafford: Lancs v Hants
Trent Bridge: Notts v Minor
    Counties (N)
Taunton: Somerset v M Counties
    (S)
Hove: Sussex v Surrey
Edgbaston: Warwicks v Derbys
Headingley: Yorks v Kent

Sunday 20 May

John Player League
Bristol: Gloucs v Derbys
Old Trafford: Lancs v Northants
Lord's: Middx v Leics
Trent Bridge: Notts v Essex
Horsham: Sussex v Surrey
Worcester: Worcs v Somerset
Huddersfield: Yorks v Kent

Wednesday 23 May

Oxford: Oxford U v Gloucs
Edgbaston: Warwicks v Scotland
Benson & Hedges Cup
Chesterfield: Derbys v Lancs
Chelmsford: Essex v Sussex
Southampton: Hants v Leics
Canterbury: Kent v Notts
Lord's: Middx v Yorks
Northampton: Northants v Surrey

Worcester: Worcs v Somerset
Watford (Town Grd):
    M Counties (S) v Glam

Saturday 26 May

Derby: Derbys v Notts
Bristol: Gloucs v Somerset
Canterbury: Kent v Hants
Old Trafford: Lancs v Yorks
Lord's: Middx v Sussex
Northampton: Northants v Glam
The Oval: Surrey v Essex
Edgbaston: Warwicks v Worcs
Oxford: Oxford U v Free Foresters

Sunday 27 May

John Player League
Derby: Derbys v Notts
Bristol: Gloucs v Leics
Canterbury: Kent v Hants
Milton Keynes: Northants v Middx
The Oval: Surrey v Essex
Edgbaston: Warwicks v Worcs
Bradford: Yorks v Glam

Wednesday 30 May

Ilford: Essex v Glam
Old Trafford: Lancs v Gloucs
Leicester: Leics v Hants
The Oval: Surrey v Northants
Edgbaston: Warwicks v Somerset
Sheffield: Yorks v Notts
Oxford: Oxford U v MCC

Saturday 2 June

Ilford: Essex v Lancs
Leicester: Leics v Kent
Lord's: Middx v Gloucs
Trent Bridge: Notts v Glam
Taunton: Somerset v Hants
Hove: Sussex v Derbys
Worcester: Worcs v Northants
Bradford: Yorks v Surrey
Oxford: Oxford U v Warwicks

Sunday 3 June

John Player League
Ilford: Essex v Lancs
Leicester: Leics v Kent
Lord's: Middx v Gloucs
Trent Bridge: Notts v Glam
Glastonbury: Somerset v Hants

219

Hove: Sussex v Derbys
Worcester: Worcs v Northants
Hull: Yorks v Surrey

Wednesday 6 June
Benson & Hedges Cup
(quarter-finals)

Saturday 9 June
Derby: Derbys v Middx
Chelmsford: Essex v Leics
Swansea: Glam v Warwicks
Portsmouth: Hants v Northants
Canterbury: Kent v Sussex
The Oval: Surrey v Lancs
Worcester: Worcs v Gloucs
Cambridge: Cambridge U v Yorks
Oxford: Oxford U v Somerset
Prudential Cup
Lord's: Australia v England
Trent Bridge: New Zealand v
   Associate 'A'
Headingley: Pakistan v
   Associate 'B'
Edgbaston: West Indies v India

Sunday 10 June
John Player League
Chesterfield: Derbys v Middx
Swansea: Glam v Warwicks
Canterbury: Kent v Northants
Bristol: Somerset v Gloucs
The Oval: Surrey v Lancs

Wednesday 13 June
Dartford: Kent v Somerset
Lord's: Middx v Notts
Northampton: Northants v Derbys
Edgbaston: Warwicks v Essex
Worcester: Worcs v Lancs
Cambridge: Cambridge U v Sussex
Oxford: Oxford U v Leics
Prudential Cup
Trent Bridge: Australia v Pakistan
Old Trafford: England v
   Associate 'B'
Headingley: India v New Zealand
The Oval: West Indies v
   Associate 'A'

Saturday 16 June
*Chesterfield: Derbys v Lancs
Gloucester: Gloucs v Kent
Bournemouth: Hants v Notts
Leicester: Leics v Glam
Lord's: Middx v Surrey
Northampton: Northants v Yorks
Bath: Somerset v Essex
Hove: Sussex v Warwicks
Cambridge: Cambridge U v MCC
Oxford: Oxford U v Worcs
Prudential Cup
Edgbaston: Australia v
   Associate 'B'
Headingley: England v Pakistan
Old Trafford: India v Associate 'A'
Trent Bridge: West Indies v
   New Zealand

Sunday 17 June
John Player League
Gloucester: Gloucs v Kent
Southampton: Hants v Notts
Leicester: Leics v Glam
Lord's: Middx v Worcs
Northampton: Northants v Yorks
Bath: Somerset v Essex
Hove: Sussex v Warwicks

Wednesday 20 June
Old Trafford and The Oval:
Prudential Cup
semi-finals
Chelmsford: Essex v Derbys
Gloucester: Gloucs v Hants
Tunbridge Wells: Kent v Middx
Leicester: Leics v Sussex
Trent Bridge: Notts v Northants
Bath: Somerset v Glam
Edgbaston: Warwicks v Yorks
Cambridge: Cambridge U v Lancs
Oxford: Oxford U v Surrey

Saturday 23 June
Lord's Prudential Cup
final
Cardiff: Glam v Surrey
Tunbridge Wells: Kent v Essex
Old Trafford: Lancs v Middx
Leicester: Leics v Notts
Northampton: Northants v Gloucs
*Bath: Somerset v Cambridge U

220

Hove: Sussex v Hants
Worcester: Worcs v Yorks
Guildford: Derrick Robins' XI v
    Oxford U

Sunday 24 June
John Player League
Ebbw Vale: Glam v Surrey
Old Trafford: Lancs v Middx
Leicester: Leics v Notts
Tring: Northants v Gloucs
Nuneaton: Warwicks v Derbys
Worcester: Worcs v Yorks

Wednesday 27 June
Derby: Derbys v Sri Lanka
Northampton: Northants v India
    (Holt Products Trophy)
Taunton: Somerset v Worcs
The Oval: Surrey v Warwicks
Pagham: Sussex v Oxford U
Guildford: Derrick Robins' XI v
    Cambridge U
Gillette Cup 1st round
High Wycombe: Bucks v Suffolk
Durham City: Durham v Berks
Swansea: Glam v Kent
Bristol: Gloucs v Hants
Old Trafford: Lancs v Essex
Leicester: Leics v Devon

Saturday 30 June
Bristol: Gloucs v Glam
Canterbury: Kent v Sri Lanka
Southport: Lancs v Worcs
Lord's: MCC v India
Trent Bridge: Notts v Sussex
The Oval: Surrey v Leics
Harrogate: Yorks v Somerset
Portsmouth: Combined Services v
    Cambridge U

Sunday 1 July
John Player League
Long Eaton (Trent Coll): Derbys v
    Northants
Chelmsford: Essex v Kent
Bristol: Gloucs v Glam
Portsmouth: Hants v Leics
Old Trafford: Lancs v Worcs
Lord's: Middx v Warwicks
Trent Bridge: Notts v Sussex
Scarborough: Yorks v Somerset

Wednesday 4 July
Benson & Hedges Cup (semi-finals)
Southampton: Hants v India (Holt
    Products Trophy) (provided
    Hants are not in B&H Cup semi-
    finals)
Lord's: Oxford U v Cambridge U
    (if Middx drawn at home in B&H
    semi-final, University match will
    be played at Arundel)
Harrogate: Tilcon Trophy (three
    days): County not in B&H Cup
    semi-finals v Sri Lanka

Saturday 7 July
Chesterfield: Derbys v Yorks
Southend: Essex v Sussex
Swansea: Glam v Somerset
Southampton: Hants v Gloucs
Maidstone: Kent v Lancs
*Leicester: Leics v India
Northampton: Northants v
    Warwicks
Trent Bridge: Notts v Worcs
The Oval: Surrey v Middx
Dublin: Ireland v Sri Lanka

Sunday 8 July
John Player League
Southend: Essex v Sussex
Swansea: Glam v Somerset
Basingstoke: Hants v Gloucs
Maidstone: Kent v Lancs
The Oval: Surrey v Middx
Edgbaston: Warwicks v Notts

Wednesday 11 July
Southend: Essex v Notts
Cardiff: Glam v Gloucs
Basingstoke: Hants v Derbys
Maidstone: Kent v Leics
Lord's: Middx v Yorks
Northampton: Northants v Lancs
Taunton: Somerset v Warwicks
Hove: Sussex v Surrey
Worcester: Worcs v Sri Lanka

Thursday 12 July
EDGBASTON: ENGLAND v
    INDIA (first Cornhill Test
    match)

Saturday 14 July
Cardiff: Glam v Sri Lanka
Liverpool: Lancs v Derbys
Leicester: Leics v Somerset
Trent Bridge: Notts v Gloucs
The Oval : Surrey v Kent
Worcester: Worcs v Sussex
Bradford: Yorks v Hants

Sunday 15 July
John Player League
Maidstone: Kent v Surrey
Old Trafford: Lancs v Derbys
Leicester: Leics v Somerset
Luton: Northants v Essex
Trent Bridge: Notts v Gloucs
Worcester: Worcs v Sussex
Headingley: Yorks v Hants

Wednesday 18 July
Gillette Cup 2nd round
Chester-le-St or Reading: Durham
  or Berks v Yorks
Cardiff or Canterbury: Glam or
  Kent v Lancs or Essex
Leicester or Torquay: Leics or
  Devon v Worcs
Lord's: Middx v Gloucs or Hants
Northampton: Northants v Surrey
Taunton: Somerset v Derbys
Hove: Sussex v Bucks or Suffolk
Edgbaston: Warwicks v Notts
*County not in Gillette Cup v India
  (Holt Products Trophy)

Saturday 21 July
Lord's: Benson & Hedges Cup Final
Chesterfield: Derbys v Kent (29
  Aug if either county in B & H cup
  final)
Bristol: Gloucs v India (provided
  Gloucs not in B&H Cup final)
Edgbaston: Warwicks v Glam (15
  Aug if either county in B&H
  Cup final)

Sunday 22 July
John Player League
Chesterfield: Derbys v Kent
Colchester: Essex v Yorks
Portsmouth: Hants v Glam
Yeovil: Somerset v Northants

Byfleet: Surrey v Warwicks
Hastings: Sussex v Lancs
Worcester: Worcs v Notts

Wednesday 25 July
Derby: Derbys v Gloucs
Swansea: Glam v India (Holt
  Products Trophy)
Bournemouth: Hants v Essex
Old Trafford: Lancs v Warwicks
Leicester: Leics v Middx
Northampton: Northants v Kent
Worksop: Notts v Yorks
Guildford (provisional): Surrey v
  Worcs
Horsham: Sussex v Sri Lanka

Saturday 28 July
Colchester: Essex v Gloucs
Swansea: Glam v Lancs
Folkestone: Kent v Notts
Leicester: Leics v Worcs
Northampton: Northants v Sussex
*Taunton: Somerset v India (Holt
  Products Trophy)
The Oval: Surrey v Derbys
Nuneaton: Warwicks v Hants
Scarborough: Yorks v Middx
Dublin: Ireland v Scotland

Sunday 29 July
John Player League
Colchester: Essex v Gloucs
Cardiff: Glam v Lancs
Folkestone: Kent v Notts
Leicester: Leics v Worcs
The Oval: Surrey v Derbys
Edgbaston: Warwicks v Hants
Scarborough: Yorks v Middx

Wednesday 1 August
Burton-on-Trent: Derbys v
  Northants
Colchester: Essex v Middx
Bristol: Gloucs v Leics
Southampton: Hants v Somerset
Folkestone: Kent v Surrey
Eastbourne: Sussex v Glam
Worcester: Worcs v Notts
Sheffield: Yorks v Warwicks

Thursday 2 August
LORD'S: ENGLAND v INDIA
 (second Cornhill Test match)

Saturday 4 August
Chesterfield: Derbys v Warwicks
Cardiff: Glam v Hants
Old Trafford: Lancs v Somerset
Northampton: Northants v Middx
Trent Bridge: Notts v Somerset
Eastbourne: Sussex v Kent
Worcester: Worcs v Essex
Bradford: Yorks v Leics

Sunday 5 August
John Player Legaue
Chesterfield: Derbys v Yorks
Old Trafford: Lancs v Somerset
Northampton: Northants v
 Warwicks
Trent Bridge: Notts v Surrey
Eastbourne: Sussex v Kent
Worcester: Worcs v Hants

Wednesday 8 August
Gillette Cup (quarter-finals)

Saturday 11 August
*Chelmsford: Essex v India (Holt
 Products Trophy)
Cheltenham: Gloucs v Yorks
Portsmouth: Hants v Surrey
Canterbury: Kent v Worcs
Lord's: Middx v Glam
Wellingborough: Northants v
 Leics
Trent Bridge: Notts v Derbys
Weston-s-Mare: Somerset v Sussex
Edgbaston: Warwicks v Lancs

Sunday 12 August
John Player Legaue
Cheltenham: Gloucs v Yorks
Bournemouth: Hants v Surrey
Canterbury: Kent v Worcs
Lord's: Middx v Glam
Wellingborough: Northants v Leics
Weston-s-Mare: Somerset v Sussex
Edgbaston: Warwicks v Lancs

Wednesday 15 August
Cheltenham: Gloucs v Worcs
Portsmouth: Hants v Middx
Canterbury: Kent v Yorks
Leicester: Leics v Derbys
Weston-s-Mare: Somerset v Notts
The Oval: Surrey v Sussex
Edgbaston: Warwicks v Glam (if
 not played on 21 July)

Thursday 16 August
HEADINGLEY: ENGLAND v
INDIA (third Cornhill Test match)

Saturday 18 August
Derby: Derbys v Worcs
Cardiff: Glam v Leics
Cheltenham: Gloucs v Surrey
Old Trafford: Lancs v Hants
Lord's: Middx v Somerset
Northampton: Northants v Essex
Hove: Sussex v Yorks
Marchwiel, Wrexham: Wales v Ire-
 land

Sunday 19 August
John Player League
Derby: Derbys v Worcs
Cheltenham: Gloucs v Surrey
Old Trafford: Lancs v Hants
Leicester: Leics v Essex
Lord's: Middx v Somerset
Northampton: Northants v Notts
Hove: Sussex v Yorks

Wednesday 22 August
Gillette Cup (semi-finals)
Old Trafford: Lancs v India (Holt
 Products Trophy) (provided
 Lancs not in Gillette Cup s/f's)
Aberdeen: Scotland v MCC
Leicester or Worcester: Leics or
 Worcs v Ireland

Saturday 25 August
Chelmsford: Essex v Surrey
Swansea: Glam v Derbys
Bournemouth: Hants v Kent
Leicester: Leics v Northants
*Trent Bridge: Notts v India
 (Holt Products Trophy)
Taunton: Somerset v Gloucs

223

Hove: Sussex v Middx
Worcester: Worcs v Warwicks
Headingley: Yorks v Lancs

Sunday 26 August
John Player League
Chelmsford: Essex v Middx
Swansea: Glam v Derbys
Southampton: Hants v Sussex
Taunton: Somerset v Kent
The Oval: Surrey v Northants
Edgbaston: Warwicks v Leics
Bradford: Yorks v Lancs

Wednesday 29 August
Chesterfield: Derbys v Kent (if not
  played on 21 July)
Chelmsford: Essex v Northants
Bournemouth: Hants v Sussex
Lord's: Middx v Worcs
Edgbaston: Warwicks v Notts
Scarborough: Fenner Trophy KO
  competition (three days)

Thursday 30 August
THE OVAL: ENGLAND v
INDIA (fourth Cornhill Test match)

Saturday 1 September
Cardiff: Glam v Kent
Bristol: Gloucs v Warwicks
Blackpool: Lancs v Notts
Leicester: Leics v Essex
Taunton: Somerset v Derbys
Scarborough: T. N. Pearce's XI v
MCC.

Sunday 2 September
John Player League
Cardiff: Glam v Kent
Moreton-in-Marsh: Gloucs v
  Warwicks
Old Trafford: Lancs v Notts
Leicester: Leics v Surrey
Lord's: Middx v Sussex
Taunton: Somerset v Derbys
Worcester: Worcs v Essex

Wednesday 5 September
Bristol: Gloucs v Northants
Old Trafford: Lancs v Leics
Trent Bridge: Notts v Middx
The Oval: Surrey v Hants
Hove: Sussex v Somerset
Edgbaston: Warwicks v Kent
Worcester: Worcs v Glam
Scarborough: Yorks v Essex

Saturday 8 September
Lord's Gillette Cup final

Sunday 9 September
Derby: Derbys v Leics
Chelmsford: Essex v Glam
Bournemouth: Hants v Northants
Canterbury: Kent v Middx
Trent Bridge: Notts v Somerset
The Oval: Surrey v Worcs
Hove: Sussex v Gloucs
Edgbaston: Warwicks v Yorks